MW00810347

Buddhism and Whiteness

Philosophy of Race

Series Editor: George Yancy, Emory University

Editorial Board: Sybol Anderson, Barbara Applebaum, Alison Bailey, Chike Jeffers, Janine Jones, David Kim, Emily S. Lee, Zeus Leonardo, Falguni A. Sheth, Grant Silva

The Philosophy of Race book series publishes interdisciplinary projects that center upon the concept of race, a concept that continues to have very profound contemporary implications. Philosophers and other scholars, more generally, are strongly encouraged to submit book projects that seriously address race and the process of racialization as a deeply embodied, existential, political, social, and historical phenomenon. The series is open to examine monographs, edited collections, and revised dissertations that critically engage the concept of race from multiple perspectives: sociopolitical, feminist, existential, phenomenological, theological, and historical.

Titles in the Series

Buddhism and Whiteness, edited by George Yancy and Emily McRae
For Equals Only: Race, Equality, and the Equal Protection Clause,
    by Tina Fernandes Botts
Politics and Affect in Black Women's Fiction, by Kathy Glass
The Habits of Racism: A Phenomenology of Racism and Racialized Embodiment,
    by Helen Ngo
Philosophy and the Mixed Race Experience, edited by Tina Fernandes Botts
The Post-Racial Limits of Memorialization: Toward a Political Sense of Mourning,
    by Alfred Frankowski
White Self-Criticality beyond Anti-Racism: How Does It Feel to Be a White Problem?,
    edited by George Yancy

Buddhism and Whiteness

Critical Reflections

Edited by
George Yancy and Emily McRae

Foreword by
Jan Willis

Afterword by
Charles Johnson

LEXINGTON BOOKS
Lanham • Boulder • New York • London

Published by Lexington Books
An imprint of The Rowman & Littlefield Publishing Group, Inc.
4501 Forbes Boulevard, Suite 200, Lanham, Maryland 20706
www.rowman.com

6 Tinworth Street, London SE11 5AL, United Kingdom

British Library Cataloguing in Publication Information Available

Library of Congress Cataloging-in-Publication Data

Names: Yancy, George, editor. | McRae, Emily, 1981- editor.
Title: Buddhism and whiteness : critical reflections / edited by George Yancy
  and Emily McRae.
Description: Lanham : Lexington Books, [2019] | Series: Philosophy of race |
  Includes bibliographical references and index.
Identifiers: LCCN 2019006246 (print) | LCCN 2019010958 (ebook) |
  ISBN 9781498581035 (Electronic) | ISBN 9781498581028 (cloth : alk. paper)
Subjects: LCSH: Race relations—Religious aspects—Buddhism. | Racism—Religious
  aspects—Buddhism. | Whites—Race identity. | Race awareness.
Classification: LCC BQ4570.R3 (ebook) | LCC BQ4570.R3 B83 2019 (print) |
  DDC 294.3/376284—dc23
LC record available at https://lccn.loc.gov/2019006246

♾️™ The paper used in this publication meets the minimum requirements of American
National Standard for Information Sciences—Permanence of Paper for Printed Library
Materials, ANSI/NISO Z39.48-1992.

Printed in the United States of America

Contents

Foreword   vii
Jan Willis

Acknowledgments   xiii

Introduction   xv
Emily McRae and George Yancy

1   "We Interrupt Your Regularly Scheduled Programming to Bring
You This Very Important Public Service Announcement . . .": aka
Buddhism as Usual in the Academy   1
Sharon A. Suh

2   Undoing Whiteness in American Buddhist Modernism: Critical,
Collective, and Contextual Turns   21
Ann Gleig

3   White Delusion and Avidyā: A Buddhist Approach to
Understanding and Deconstructing White Ignorance   43
Emily McRae

4   Whiteness and the Construction of Buddhist Philosophy
in Meiji Japan   61
Leah Kalmanson

5   Racism and *Anatta*: Black Buddhists, Embodiment, and
Interpretations of Non-Self   79
Rima Vesely-Flad

6   "The Tranquil Meditator"   99
Laurie Cassidy

7 "Beyond Vietnam": Martin Luther King, Jr.,
       Thích Nhất Hạnh, and the Confluence of Black and
       Engaged Buddhism in the Vietnam War   119
       Carolyn M. Jones Medine

8 The Unbearable Will to Whiteness   143
       Jasmine Syedullah

9 Making Consciousness an Ethical Project: Moral
       Phenomenology in Buddhist Ethics and White Anti-Racism   161
       Jessica Locke

10 "bell hooks Made Me a Buddhist": Liberatory Cross-Cultural
       Learning—Or Is This Just Another Case of How
       White People Steal Everything?   181
       Carol J. Moeller

11 Excoriating the Demon of Whiteness from Within: Disrupting
       Whiteness through the Tantric Buddhist Practice of *Chöd* and
       Exploring Whiteness from Within the Tradition   207
       Lama Justin von Bujdoss

12 The Interdependence and Emptiness of Whiteness   229
       Bryce Huebner

13 Taking and Making Refuge in Racial [Whiteness]
       Awareness and Racial Justice Work   253
       Rhonda V. Magee

14 A Buddhist Phenomenology of the White Mind   277
       Joy Cecile Brennan

15 The White Feminism in Rita Gross's Critique of Gender
       Identities and Reconstruction of Buddhism   293
       Hsiao-Lan Hu

Afterword   309
Charles Johnson

Bibliography   315

Index   337

Contributor Notes   353

Foreword

Jan Willis

The chapters in this book represent some of the newest and most creative ways of conceptualizing race and racism and their possible Buddhist solutions. Their authors are young scholars and writers, all working at the intersections of race theory, philosophy of race, feminist and cultural studies, and Buddhist philosophy.

That there is only one race of human beings—*homo sapiens*—extant today should go without question; to hold otherwise is like holding the ancient and equally erroneous view that the world is flat. The sciences of biology and genetics have long since shattered the notion that there is more than a single race of human beings on earth.

Yet, racism still lives and thrives among us, though it is but an illusion, a mere social construct, a non-inherently existent and nonindependent phenomenon. (This notion, I believe, is what PBS intended to convey with the title of its 2005 documentary series, "Race: The Power of an Illusion.") In this so-called post-racial era of twenty-first-century America, we are supposed to know, and be, better.

But there is nothing "post" about the racism we see playing out every day in America and other regions of the world. Indeed, in America, the afterlife of the color-based slavery that existed here for centuries means that racism continues as a mighty, if "invisible," presence in social, political, economic, and other spheres today, granting advantages to one group (whites) while disadvantaging all others (blacks and other people of color). It continues to be the cause of much suffering and great harm—both physical and psychological—to those who are "disadvantaged" by it.

To speak of racism as being a systemic construct which, of course, it is, may actually give it too much weight, too much concreteness. (We point to signs saying "white" and "colored" above drinking fountains and say, "That's racism!" even though we know that they are just signs.) Perhaps it would be better to say that racism or white supremacy is like the water in which we all swim: some of us are aware of it, others do not notice it or are in denial of its existence. We are all fish swimming in white supremacy. Here I am reminded of two powerful lines in James Baldwin's "My Dungeon Shook: Letter to my Nephew": "But it is not permissible that the authors of devastation should also be innocent. *It is the innocence which constitutes the crime.*" This water in which we swim, this sea, must be recognized, acknowledged, understood, experienced, and called out. Only such seeing, such insight, can free us of it.

Those of us who study Buddhism are familiar with the notion that a non-inherently existent phenomenon or fiction—say, the "I"—is capable of wielding tremendous power in our lives. Indeed, according to Buddhism, it is our misunderstanding of the nature of reality that causes us to experience suffering: grasping onto the *conceit* of "I" (and its unspoken corollary, *I am* better *than others*), we think that the world should be as we want it to be.

All things are impermanent, however, and that means that our wish that *things be otherwise than they are* almost always leaves us frustrated, dissatisfied, and longing for some other state or condition or thing—hence our continual craving. This is Buddhism's key teaching: that erroneously grasping after and believing in a permanent, unchanging, inherently existent "I," separate from (and better than) others, sets us up for suffering. And, conversely: the wisdom that sees our error, that sees through the illusion of a permanent, independent, and separate "I," is the only wisdom that can and will free us from the suffering that we have caused for ourselves. In the *Dhammapada*, we are told in verses 153 and 154 that the Buddha, just as he was on the cusp of full enlightenment, declared the following two statements:

> I, who have been seeking the builder of this house (body), failing to attain Enlightenment which would enable me to find him, have wandered through innumerable births in *samsara*. To be born again and again is, indeed, suffering (*dukkha*)!
>
> Oh, house-builder! You are [now] seen, you shall build no house (for me) again. All your rafters are broken, your roof-tree is destroyed. My mind has reached the unconditioned, *Nibbana*; the end of craving has been attained.

The house-builder here is *aham-kara*, the "I-maker." As Buddhists, we are encouraged to find, see directly, and thereby completely destroy the illusory notion of the erroneously grasped-after "I" in order to wake up, put an end to craving, and reach freedom. Can we do the same for "racism"? For "whiteness"?

The chapters in this book seek to answer such urgent queries. Can we, through intensely investigating the erroneous constructs of racism and whiteness, confront their power to harm and their illusoriness, and free ourselves of their ignorance?

Of course, we must first *see* both constructs clearly. Then, we need to investigate what causes them. We must interrogate not only their origins, but their end. These steps are reminiscent of Buddhism's Four Noble Truths. We might say: there is racism, there is a cause, there is an end to it, and a path to that end.

Just as the Buddha saw that grasping at a nonexistent "I" was the cause of pain and suffering for the human condition generally, what if we could, after clearly perceiving racism's raison d'etre, be courageous enough to destroy it? I am again reminded of Baldwin. In his final challenge to white America as voiced in Raoul Peck's film, *I Am Not Your Negro*, he said, "I know who I am. But you have created this 'N . . .'. And it's up to you to figure out why you needed it."

All the chapters here are in one way or another concerned with the liberative prize of "seeing" itself and (at least implicitly) challenge us to *take action* once we have seen the truth. These endeavors, it seems to me, are distinctly Buddhist at their core.

Seeing, in Buddhism, is of paramount concern. In the Buddha's very First Discourse (*Dhamma-cakkapavattana-sutta*, "Setting in Motion the Wheel of the Law"), this formula is repeated again and again to characterize the Buddha's newly found wisdom: "It gives vision, insight, wisdom, leads to nibbana, enlightenment." Indeed, before he could deliver his first teachings to his first five followers, the Buddha had to instruct and transform them with the words *ehi passika*, or "Come and *see* (for yourself)." Seeing is believing in Buddhism and experiencing the truth is the only way to know it, thus replacing mere faith with conviction.

It is always worth recalling that "Buddha" itself is a title—not a name—for one who has "woken up." The man born Siddhārtha Gautama woke up while he was awake: he saw in a new and different way; he saw, finally, what was real and true. So, one repeatedly finds throughout these chapters the trope or meme of interrogating, of seeing correctly, and waking up from our ordinary "epistemologies of ignorance."

Thích Nhất Hạnh is said to have remarked, "Once one sees, one must act." Yes. But not everyone agrees. Some argue that Buddhist Dharma and activism do not belong together. They point to the Buddhist "two-truths theory" and proclaim that though difference prevails from the point of "relative truth," from the absolute point of view (their own, perchance?), no distinctions pertain. Thereby they ignore historical fact: namely, that the Buddha was quite the revolutionary activist himself.

In sixth-century BCE India, in spite of all the strict societal structures and social norms of Aryan society, the Buddha allowed followers from all castes, and even women (after some convincing), to join his new community. Such allowances were quite radical for their time. Clearly, his Dharma did not preclude actual activism and change. It did not exclude certain people with certain bodies from its community. Still, there are those today who argue that the Dharma and activism must be kept separate, that Buddhism focuses on individual, inner revolution, not outward activism or change.

Such a view would favor the titular model of Laurie Cassidy's provocative chapter, "The Tranquil Meditator." The essay explores "how American capitalism hijacks spiritual practices, such as Buddhist meditation, thereby subverting their liberative human potential." Moreover, Cassidy tells us, "I intentionally use the word hijack because it refers to how a vehicle for transport is seized and forced to a destination other than was originally intended." For Cassidy, American capitalism itself intends to subvert the possibility of change, and she employs a cultural and feminist lens to look closely at the virtual and structural venues of Buddhist propagation in America.

Carolyn M. Jones Medine's exploration of "the Confluence of Black and Engaged Buddhism in the Vietnam War" uses memoir and other literary and historical sources to shed light on precisely *why* Thích Nhất Hạnh and the Rev. Dr. Martin Luther King, Jr. became brothers in struggle.

Joy Cecile Brennan's full-throttled philosophical inquiry powerfully interrogates "A Buddhist Phenomenology of the White Mind" by deftly employing Yogācārin principles to show how the "epistemological ignorance of 'whiteness'" originates, and why it ought not be trusted. Her opening comments are powerful:

> It has been amply demonstrated that whiteness is a construct that is socially, emotionally, psychologically, and somatically reproduced in the class of people who thereby come to be known as—and to know ourselves as—white. The general question is then: what can Buddhist thought tell us about how this construct functions? And what therapy can Buddhist traditions of practice recommend as a method of stripping the power from this construct, of exposing it for what it is, of *de*-constructing it?
>
> More particularly, I should like to examine the social epistemology of ignorance that shapes the perceptions and conceptions of whites. Following Charles Mills' work on racialized epistemologies, this chapter looks at the epistemic asymmetry between whites and blacks, and the phenomenology of the white mind that manifests the white side of this asymmetry.

Bryce Huebner's chapter, "The Interdependence and Emptiness of Whiteness," likewise draws on Yogācāra philosophy but focuses primarily on Dharmakirti's work to describe how our minds categorize and label reality, and beings, on the basis of our own *vasanas* (previous karmic imprints).

It goes further to incorporate historical examples which highlight precisely how we Americans have "conjured whiteness into existence."

A number of the chapters here speak to the embodied experience of Blackness, in general, and within Buddhist sanghas in particular, bringing feminist and cultural studies' critiques to bear. Thus, Sharon A. Suh speaks of "Buddhist killjoys" and of the experiences of hypervisibility in her chapter, "'We Interrupt Your Regularly Scheduled Programming to Bring You This Very Important Public Service Announcement . . .': aka Buddhism as Usual in the Academy." And Rima Veseley-Flad's "Racism and *Anatta*: Black Buddhists, Embodiment, and Interpretations of Non-Self" discusses the memoirs of three African American women Buddhist teachers (Reverend angel Kyodo williams, Zenju Earthlyn Manuel, and myself) as she explores this embodied experience. Lastly, at least one of the chapters (Rhonda V. Magee's "Taking and Making Refuge in Racial [Whiteness] Awareness and Racial Justice Work") speaks explicitly about the need for social justice activism and how that might take ritual form.

My remarks here have focused on only a few of the many constructive ideas and philosophical strategies adopted in the fifteen thought-provoking chapters contained here. I hope that they have whetted your appetite to read further. I invite you now to take a calm and deep breath, wade into the individual pieces, and to see for yourself.

Acknowledgments

Yancy: I would like to thank Jana Hodges-Kluck, senior acquisitions editor at Lexington Books, whose vision for critically engaging books has been absolutely spot-on. Jana is a superb editor to work with, especially as she carefully walks authors through often unknown editorial territory. She is also just a sheer delight to work with. I would also like to thank Trevor F. Crowell at Lexington Books for his logistical assistance. Emily McRae, my coeditor, is thanked for her inspiration, her commitment, and passion for this project, and her significant philosophical work within the areas of emotions, Buddhist contemplative practices, and ethical practices vis-à-vis challenging and overcoming injustice. Emily, thanks so very much for your appreciation of my work within the areas of critical philosophy of race and critical whiteness studies. I am honored. It has been a wonderful experience working with you. In fact, it has been seamless. I am so thankful to work with you on such an unprecedented and significant book project. Your insights were indispensable for making this book what it is. I would also like to thank my friend Charles Johnson for writing his brilliant Afterword for this book. I'm not sure if there is a day that goes by where I don't hear from Chuck. I see this as a beautiful form of epistemic and ethical humility. He shares when unasked and does so with great abundance. I am so grateful for the instructional Dharma that he sends almost daily. I also thank the brilliant and self-giving scholar Jan Willis for writing such an engaging Foreword. Although we have never met, your spirit and writing are palpably present. Thank you. To the contributors, I send out a loud and joyous shout of thanks. This book is a cooperative project, a project of love and commitment to undoing the violence and injustice that kills both the body and the soul. Thanks for your time and your enthusiasm. This book would not have been possible were it not for your steadfastness, faith, and firm dedication and belief in the possibilities within the strength and beauty of Buddhist practices. Thanks for making this book a reality. As always, thanks to Susan for her assistance and incredible patience with me. To the Yancy boys, know that your father refuses to retreat despite the backlash. Know that there are multiple spiritual traditions that will provide you with wisdom and compassion. Let your heart be moved by the love offered within those traditions. Be mindful of what it means to dwell near and to love humanity. As you know, I am a *hopeful* Christian theist, and it is the hopeful part that sustains. Your father continues to seek the meaning of the divine, of the holy, of the spiritual. I do so with both suffering and joy, committed to the vision that there is so much more than we can know. Just days before your paternal grandfather left us, I asked him what he thought happens after death. He said, "It's too complex to know." Hopeful and humble, I remain.

McRae: My deepest thanks to my colleague and friend, George Yancy, whose work has been a profound source of philosophical and spiritual inspiration for me. George, it has been a pleasure and privilege to work with you on this project. Your vision was the motivation for beginning this volume and your expertise was critical in seeing it through to the end. Jan Willis and Chuck Johnson, too, deserve special thanks for their brilliant Foreword and Afterword (respectively) that serve as the perfect "bookends" that give shape to this volume. I would also like to thank Jana and Trevor at Lexington Press for their helpfulness in accommodating our needs and the enthusiasm they have shown for this project. We appreciate you! I thank my husband, Surya, for his support and conversation. And, finally, my deep gratitude to my daughter, Asha. You make me a better philosopher.

Introduction

Emily McRae and George Yancy

Emily McRae: My interest in this project began with two events. The first
was listening to a talk by George Yancy for my Philosophy Department's
colloquia series. Although I had read George's work before, I had never heard
him speak. His talk was a brilliant analysis of whiteness that performed the
dual function of explaining and exposing whiteness *and*, by doing so, desta-
bilizing, deconstructing, and—as he puts it—"un-suturing" whiteness for (at
least some of the) white members of the audience, including me. I was moved
and challenged. George advised white people to tarry in the uncomfortable
space of trying to understand what our claims to whiteness really amount to,
to resist the hasty conclusions of whiteness, and to notice when our whiteness
"ambushes" us.

This excellent advice immediately reminded me of the Buddhist concept
of equanimity, the ability to abide in an unpleasant (or pleasant) experience
without getting high-jacked by our knee-jerk reactions of hostility and ego-
preservation. Buddhist philosophy, I thought, may have something very useful to contribute to understanding contemporary racial injustice in the United
States. Charles Johnson's Buddhist-inspired response to the police brutality
and murder of Black men and boys in the United States ("Every 28 Hours")[1]
further strengthened my sense of the importance of Buddhist ethical and
philosophical perspectives for understanding racism and white supremacy.

Not long after this encounter, I went on a seven-day meditation retreat
with an esteemed Tibetan Dzogchen master. The pinnacle of this retreat was
receiving "pointing-out" instructions in which a qualified master "points
out" to the practitioner the nature of her own mind. This is considered a
rare and precious opportunity, and one that practitioners prepare for through
preliminary meditation practices. Ideally, the teacher points out the nature
of the disciple's mind in an intimate one-on-one encounter. This was not the

case in this retreat, however. There were over 100 people in attendance. Still, great effort was made to maintain the sacred and precious environment for the teaching by, for example, asking people to remain in their seats for the entirety of the teaching so as not to disturb the transmission of the instructions. We had also taken a vow of silence for several days.

I give this background in order to better contextualize what happened next. During these precious teachings, the Dzogchen master made a "joke" about white people having better karma than Black people, which explains their/ our white privilege. Some people laughed, some people seemed embarrassed. But one person left. She was one of (as I recall) two Black practitioners in the sangha of over 100 people, the vast majority of whom were white. That she left during the pointing-out instruction was significant and noticed by nearly everyone, including, it turned out, the master himself.

An emergency discussion session was quickly scheduled to talk about the incident (we all had to be temporarily "released" from our vow of silence). During this session various opinions were expressed: a few expressed disappointment with the teacher, but many others defended him by explaining that US racial politics are difficult to understand for people who are not from the United States (the teacher was Tibetan). Some pointed out that the teacher was not white, and implied that he therefore should not be implicated in pathologies of whiteness. Still others considered the incident to be an overreaction to a bad joke. My own contribution was to point out, in a shaky voice unused to speaking for several days, the whiteness of the sangha and to ask what mechanisms were in place to maintain such a white sangha. I was surprised to find that my fairly tepid and hardly insightful remarks were met with hostile defensiveness. The sangha was diverse, I was told, because there were (white) Americans, (white) Europeans, (white) Russians, (white) Argentinians. You get the point. This experience tempered my enthusiasm for Buddhism's potential to speak meaningfully in our (US) critical conversation about race and racism. How, I wondered, could a community that is so white—and so defensively white—possibly contribute to dismantling white supremacy?

Of course, not all US sanghas are so white. There are sanghas that are majority Asian-American, as well as a few that are actively committed to racial diversity and achieving racial justice, some of which are mentioned in the chapters that follow. Even in my own sangha some progress was made. The Tibetan teacher spoke privately with the Black practitioner who had left the teachings (it turned out that she did not leave the retreat altogether). After this private conversation, the teacher publically apologized to the sangha, an action that I had never seen a prominent Buddhist teacher do before. Still, clearly, much work needs to be done.

It was with these conflicting experiences in mind that I eagerly agreed to George's suggestion to coedit a volume on Buddhism and whiteness.

This volume is the first of its kind to offer a collection of philosophical analyses of whiteness, race, and racism using Buddhist conceptual frameworks. It operates with the assumption that we can learn from Buddhist philosophical traditions about the nature of race and racism, the mechanisms for racial injustice, and the potential for dismantling such injustice. At the same time, the chapters in this volume recognize, and criticize, the ways in which white supremacy (as well as capitalism and patriarchy) are operative in Western Buddhism and the academic study of Buddhism in the West.

The chapters in this volume are diverse, drawing not only from different Buddhist traditions and schools, but also employing different disciplinary methodologies. This, I think, is appropriate, since it underscores the fundamentally interdisciplinary nature of both Buddhist Philosophy and Critical Philosophy of Race. The topics covered in this volume include a Dharmakīrtīan analyses of the construct of whiteness; a Yogācāran account of white subjectivity; an inquiry into white avidyā (ignorance); several explorations into the intersections of white supremacy, capitalism, and patriarchy in Western cultural and academic discourse on Buddhism as well as within Buddhist sanghas; a description of the resonance and connections between the philosophies of Dr. King and Thich Nhat Hanh; a presentation of an embodied practice of liberation from whiteness; and a Tibetan chöd-inspired practice to uproot white supremacy, to name just a few. Although diverse along several axes, these chapters raise questions and arguments that speak to core philosophical issues, including the nature of cognition and subjectivity, the limits of knowledge and ignorance, and the ethical demands that arise from the fact of human and sentient suffering.

All of the chapters in this volume integrate two philosophical traditions—Critical Philosophy of Race and Buddhist Philosophy—that are rarely in dialogue, in academia or outside it. The volume is, I think, a testament to the fruitfulness of this integration. It is my hope that this volume will provide a source of inspiration for scholars and practitioners who seek to understand the benefits and dangers of Buddhist models of social justice.

George Yancy: Sharing stories about one's life, one's identity, is a constructive affair. After all, memories lapse, discourse can reveal and conceal, courage and embarrassment mediate what is or is not said, and the imagination fills lacuna. With that in mind, though, I have been "haunted"—from the moment that I can really recall when I became conscious of the world (or conscious of myself as being-in-the-world with any seriousness)—with a feeling of existential melancholy paradoxically linked to a wonderful feeling of existential joy and ecstasy. So, there was (and is) this sense of being awed by the fact that I am, that we are; the dread and the beauty are mixed together. By "haunted," I mean the sense of being frequented by a sense of overwhelming desire to know why I exist, why there is something rather than nothing. This can clearly be described as a profound sense of wonder, but, for me, it is linked, and has always been linked, to a sense of suffering; it is the weight of finding that one has awakened in medias res where there is no satisfying and epistemologically certain preamble and no sure end that makes sense with any certainty. Death makes no sense to me, even if it is a biological necessity. So, I carry the weight of this. It arises at different times with various affective intensities. There are times when my body literally shakes. But why begin here with a book titled, *Buddhism and Whiteness: Critical Reflections*?

My interest in Buddhism, and Eastern thought more generally, is linked to that existential and paradoxical sense of suffering and joy, of seeking a meaning to the whole that isn't at all obvious. At about twenty years old, I read obsessively, but didn't understand much of what I read. But I was driven. The suffering was too weighty. I read J. Krishnamurti, Aldous Huxley, Tarthang Tulku, Peter D. Ouspensky, Alan Watts, G. I. Gurdjieff, Khalil Gibran, Bhagwan Shree Rajneesh, and others. I bought and read parts of the *Bhagavad-Gita*, the *I Ching*, the *Upanishads*, and other religious texts. Of course, by this time, I was majoring in philosophy at the University of Pittsburgh, having committed myself to philosophy at seventeen years old, but my hunger for meaning wasn't driven simply by philosophical wonder, but by a deep hunger for *something more*, something spiritually transcendent. That hunger formed who I was. The hunger was encouraged when I was introduced, while an undergraduate, to prominent Hindu spiritual leader Swami Bhashyananda who, after answering a question that I raised, said to me, "You will someday become a very wise man." At nineteen years old, hearing that meant the world to me, confirmed what felt like my "destiny." This search or hunger for the transcendent is why, I'm sure, I've always had a penchant for Plato's theory of Forms.

Reading Krishnamurti, introduced to me by my father and his close friend, George Williams, made me soar and yet travel *inward*. They introduced me to his books, and later I bought his records and actually had the pleasure to meet him, and to shake his hand when I went to Ojai, California, to hear him speak. And while Krishnamurti didn't offer "the way," in fact was critical of any such discourse, I was enthralled by his emphasis upon mindfulness, having the capacity to possess a silent mind. Around this time, I became aware of Bhagwan Shree Rajneesh, who spoke of the practice and art of dying to the self, the ego. At the time I was unaware of the controversy surrounding him or his followers. Later, I was fascinated and transfixed by the transformative narrative of Siddhartha Gautama. The idea of remaining completely still despite the outward distractions is still incredibly fascinating to me. I even envisioned myself as a monk—quiet, enlightened, and enveloped in divine reality. As you can see, my conceptual understanding of all of this was being driven by various spiritual orientations, but I was seeking with a passion. Devotees within the Hare Krishna movement wanted me to join them. People of the Unification Church (founded by its controversial leader Sun Myung Moon) tried desperately to recruit me. I didn't join. *I was still seeking.* There were times when I thought that it wasn't philosophy with its analytic style that moved me, but something similar to mysticism, something that resulted in a profound and unutterable experience.

So, when I initially began to think about how Buddhism might speak critically to whiteness,[2] I'm pretty sure that it was the work of Krishnamurti that was in the back of my mind. While not a Buddhist practitioner, Krishnamurti offered a way of challenging what I had much later come to refer to as the opacity of whiteness, the ways in which white people fail or refuse to look at their own whiteness, or even the ways in which whiteness, structurally, obfuscates its own self-interrogation, burying itself deeper into the white psyche such that white people may not even possibly know the depths of their own racism. Buddhism offered (and offers) a language and a practice that suggests strong conceptual family resemblances to concepts that I later brought to bear on thinking about whiteness—for example, the concept of un-suturing, vigilance, ambush, tarrying, and kenosis or emptying. Each of these concepts resonant with Buddhist practices of mindfulness, of remaining still, watching, opening the self to the unknown, experiencing the pain and the horror of embedded and opaque forms of whiteness, and the process of emptying, letting go.

Of course, none of this has to do with navel gazing. As Krishnamurti says, "Meditation is not an escape from the world; it is not an isolating self-enclosing activity, but rather the comprehension of the world and its ways."[3] Given this understanding, meditation is not ahistorical or trapped within some ethereal domain of solipsistic self-enlightenment removed from the world. Within this concrete quotidian context, the removal of masks, giving thanks to moments when one is ambushed by one's whiteness, is about a certain quality of death. And if whiteness lives through a parasitic relationship to people of color, then whiteness (*not white people*) must atrophy—undergo a form of death of white narcissism, white hegemony, white colonial expansionism, white domination, white desire, white consumption, white privilege, white epistemic totalization, white illusions of safety and superiority. It is a form of atrophy or death in the name of love. As Mary E. Hobgood's writes, "For whites to construct an identity outside the racist construct, we would need to give up our socially constructed white selves and *embrace the rejected parts of our humanity* that require scapegoats."[4] The concept of scapegoating points to forms of poisonous white self-rejection, not accepting loving compassion. James Baldwin writes, "White people in this country will have quite enough to do in learning how to accept and love themselves and each other, and when they have achieved this—which will not be tomorrow and may very well be never—the Negro problem will no longer exist, for it will no longer be needed."[5]

There is a relationship between a lack of white self-loving compassion, which is not about being selfish, and white people's hatred of, disregard for, or alienation from people of color. There are forms of self-compassion that are not egocentric and that actually expand one's consciousness. If whiteness is a covered-over wound, then one must un-suture as an act of loving kindness and touch that wound. Indeed, mindfully, one must embrace that wound. Although he did not have in mind the interior structure of whiteness, through a beautiful and moving meditative practice and imaging that is applicable to my point here, Zen Buddhist Thich Nhat Hanh says, "Breathing in, I see myself as a 5-year-old child. Breathing out, I hold that 5-year-old child in me with tenderness. Breathing in, I see the 5-year-old child in me as fragile, vulnerable, easily wounded. Breathing out I feel the wound of that little child in me and use the energy of compassion to hold tenderly the wound of that child."[6] Think of this in terms of Baldwin's idea of white people "learning how to accept and love themselves." What is clear to me is that whiteness, as a site of brokenness, which reinforces itself through repetitive acts of distancing, stereotyping, hating, and alienating people of color, must be undone, shattered, through a mindful tarrying of its always already brokenness. And while there is so much more that Buddhism has to offer in terms of dismantling the poisonous reality of whiteness, which is precisely the motivation for this text, it is because of that powerful sense of mindfulness as a site of temporal disruption vis-à-vis the sedimented and habitual practices of whiteness that I eagerly asked my colleague and friend, Emily McRae, to join me in producing this unprecedented and collective meditation on whiteness.

NOTES

1. Charles Johnson, "Every 28 Hours: The Case of Trayvon Martin," https://tricycle.org/trikedaily/every-28-hours/ (July 18, 2013).

2. My philosophical work on whiteness is well known. As of this writing, I am but one of a few professional philosophers (and even fewer philosophers of color) who has published extensively on the topic. And while it is true that the historical sedimentation of whiteness, its structural and institutional existence, its lived and expressive embodiment, and its psychic opacity—indeed, its violent backlash—causes great harm, suffering, and death vis-à-vis people of color, my interest in Buddhism began with that initial sense of suffering, that sense of confronting a cosmos that appears not to have any meaning whatsoever.

3. J. Krishnamurti, *Meditation on Interior Change: The Only Revolution* (New York: Harper & Row, Publishers, Inc., 1970), 9.

4. Krishnamurti, *Meditation on Interior Change*, 9.

5. James Baldwin, *The Fire Next Time* (New York: Modern Library, 1962/1995), 21.

6. https://upliftconnect.com/power-of-compassion/ (assessed on December 18, 2018).

Chapter 1

"We Interrupt Your Regularly Scheduled Programming to Bring You This Very Important Public Service Announcement..."

aka Buddhism as Usual in the Academy

Sharon A. Suh

Are the eyes in the audience beginning to shift? Check. Are their eyes rolling? Check. Are those sideways glances and smirks I see? Check. And what about the sighing and the subsequent arms crossed over the body and the telltale signs that signify their exhaustion? Check.

Their white mostly male bodies shift as if to get out of harm's way and dodge the arrows of alleged racism in Buddhist Studies I shoot their way as if to say, "No, not me. I am not one of those unenlightened Orientalist scholars and why do they always have to make it about race?"

I remind myself to breathe in from my nose to my toes and ground the underside edges of my feet in the carpet so I can feel the floor. I drop into my body which has begun to tingle with anxiousness and nervousness, hold the sides of the podium with a seemingly casual grip, and say in the calmest voice I can muster, "As a Buddhist feminist killjoy, I take it as a win when the eyes begin to roll."

I already see a lot of eye rolling as I lay bare the white supremacist body aesthetics that shape many sanghas today. There, I said it—the it word— white supremacy at the American Academy of Religion, and I can sense the shift in the room that reminds me, "She [I] is [am]not one of us [them]. She [I] is [am]no serious scholar of Buddhism. She [I] speaks [speak] of [raced] bodies and we speak of intellectual things."

I then do what I often do when I speak of uncomfortable things, I scan the audience looking for my companions—those whom Buddhist Studies proper

1

renders interlopers, "amateurs," provocateurs, and problems. Those who actively return my gaze with a nod of the head as if to say, "Yes. Carry on." They are my fellow Buddhist killjoys.

In the sketch above, I illustrate my recent adoption and adaptation of the persona of the Buddhist killjoy, a term I borrow readily from Sara Ahmed's provocative term, the "feminist killjoy," to address the multiple instantiations of Buddhism and white privilege, supremacy, and fragility that co-conspire in the academy to uphold the happiness of the powerful, which cannot but rest on the presumption and reality that others be unhappy.[1] In this chapter, I find inspiration in Ahmed's feminist killjoy and bring to the concept and persona a particularly Buddhist inflection that draws from non-Western embodied contemplative practices and approaches meditation as a political and reparative strategy that attends to the lived realities and bodies of the "unhappy" whose flourishing is undercut in the service of the happiness of the property-holding (physical and intellectual) of white men.[2] The approach I take in this study is intentionally combinative in that it weaves together critical and creative methods to make "textual space for bodies to speak in multiple genres," including my own field notes from silent retreat, studies in trauma theory, somatic therapy, psychology, and critical race theory.[3]

The event recounted above also illustrates the need for a killjoy survival kit when pointing out the problem of power and privilege in the academy to those who have benefitted most from the institution itself.[4] In pointing out white supremacy and white male privilege in the creation and circulation of Buddhist knowledge, I had become the problem instead of the critic of the problem in which most of the audience had already been invested. I had set eyes rolling, I had said out loud what Buddhist Studies scholars and the guild itself refuses to hear—that Buddhism in America thrives on a culture of whiteness at the expense of and eclipse of people of color.[5]

In *Living a Feminist Life* (2017), Ahmed reminds us that explicitly addressing racism and sexism as a recipient of its historical legacy is to suddenly embody the very problem itself rather than being the bearer of unwanted news. For Ahmed, the feminist killjoy "begins as a sensationalist figure. It is as if the point of making her point is to cause trouble, to get in the way of the happiness of others, because of her own unhappiness."[6] The killjoy, in other words, is perceived to be the intentional creator of tension who causes a sensation rather than the one who draws attention to the preexisting problem. She is said to take the joy out of everything simply because she is unhappy and unwilling to go along and get along. Others in fact would prefer her to just get going. But rarely do her critics stop to consider what it is that compels her refusal to create, uphold, and go along; they hardly take a moment to examine the conditions of her unwillingness. A killjoy does not take it upon herself to generate the happiness of others if that happiness is a proxy for the inheritance of patriarchy, whiteness, as well as race, sexuality, and gender violence. The unwillingness to see one's own whiteness and, instead, to roll one's eyes, and to shift one's body to avoid acknowledging one's complicity is an ignoble silence that does not wish to be broken. I found and continue to derive much tonic and salve in Ahmed's feminist hero which I have come to adopt and adapt as a witness and foil to the whiteness that comprises much of the American Buddhist world of the academy and the *sangha*, a whiteness whose imprint is as indelible as it is invisible and therefore shocking when brought into stark relief by the Buddhist killjoy.

This invisible whiteness as the center and normative yardstick to measure nonwhites operates in many Buddhist *sanghas* and meditation centers where white privilege is shrouded in ignoble yet seemingly golden silence, a gilded refusal to speak up lest one breaches the oneness that emptiness and interdependence connote. The silence venerated in the space of retreat halls echoes the silent refusal of white supremacy to lay bare its privilege. After all, silence is golden. Whiteness and whites do not need to say anything, especially when their rolling eyes express it all. If good Buddhists refuse to speak the inconvenient truths of white supremacy out of fear of risking their coveted ultimate truth of oneness and their well-earned spots in the meditation hall, then it is the bad Buddhist or the Buddhist killjoy who gives lie to the rhetoric of the emptiness that many white Buddhists allude to when abdicating any responsibility to speak up and out about injustices.[7] These wise Buddhists might try to dismiss these complaints by invoking the Buddhist philosophical notion of Two Truths which goes something like this: "Buddhism adheres to the two truths theory after all—conventional truth and ultimate truth. Conventional truth means that gender, race, and sex are but conventions and heuristic designations, but, ultimately, they are not real. Through the lens of ultimate reality, these are but more illusions." This defensive application of ultimate reality to the lived experience of difference does little more than render the critique empty of significant weight. Earthlyn Zenju Manuel similarly asks us to consider how in "using such ancient teachings to promote favorable blindness, we end up turning away from the very types of lived experiences that motivated such teachings in the first place."[8] In this appeal to ultimate reality in response to the dissolution of their happiness by references to embodied difference, whiteness recenters itself through the language of emptiness. Such recourse to emptiness belies an equivalence drawn between whiteness and oneness that makes no room for the particulars of race, gender, and sexuality.[9] It is at this moment that the Buddhist killjoy's own eyes begin to roll.

I take the Buddhist killjoy to heart and build my own Buddhist killjoy survival kit that is inspired by Ahmed's "killjoy survival kit," a veritable tackle box that enables me to wrestle against the continual assaults to think well and feel good about oneself.[10] The survival kit also serves as a requisite companion assisting other minoritized bodies continually set with the task of navigating the labyrinth of racialized spaces within the academy and *sanghas*. In what follows, I highlight three out the eight items in Ahmed's survival kit that I employ with a Buddhist twist to address the collision and collusion of Buddhism and whiteness where it is nonwhite bodies that become the casualties—*time* (during retreat where we take and build refuge), *other killjoys* (other people of color with whom I take temporary and temporal refuge), and *bodies* (our corporeally specific bodies whose continual subjection to assaults from external forces have often left us hating our bodies, being unable to feel our bodies, or at best, ignoring bodily sensations).[11] Time, other killjoys, and bodies all come together to form what I consider my own sanctuary in time—the annual people of color (POC) silent retreat. I have taken refuge from the storm of white supremacy once a year for a week-long silent meditation retreat in the foothills of Northern California for the past few years, for as Ahmed reminds us:

> Time out from being a killjoy is necessary for a killjoy if she is to persist in being a killjoy. Being a killjoy is not all that you are, and if you are too consumed by her, she can drain too much energy and will. Come back to her; she will come back to you; you will, she will.[12]

Silent retreats provide time to rest, time to find refuge, to cultivate resilience, and to take temporary shelter from the catastrophic assault on the ability to think well of oneself. Meditative silence in community brings us literally to our senses and allows us to settle into bodies through meditation which itself is a radical act of embodiment and self-other embrace.

The refuge offered in the silent spaces through the POC retreat becomes the proximate cause for seeing ourselves in the fullness of our humanity despite the debilitating white gaze that has rendered us less than fully human. The noble silence observed on retreat makes us more sense(able) so that we learn to find safety in our bodies as we feel our feet on the ground and the panoply of sensations of our bodies as we practice in a safe container away from the white gaze and any other confrontational ones. The POC silent retreat allows us to explore felt-sensations in the body that draw us into the present moment and gives us a respite from the external world of whiteness that can keep us stuck in the past or guarding against an unknown future.

"WE INTERRUPT YOUR REGULARLY SCHEDULED PROGRAMMING TO BRING YOU THIS VERY IMPORTANT PUBLIC SERVICE ANNOUNCEMENT . . .": AKA BUSINESS AS USUAL IN THE ACADEMY

"We interrupt your regularly scheduled programming to bring you this very important public service announcement. . . ." Many of us grew up with this interruption, eyes glued to Saturday-morning cartoons, cereal bowl and spoon in hand. Or maybe it was the regular evening sitcom—an important announcement appears on the screen, the spectator watches with some concern, but maybe grows restless with the interruption of their televised fantasies, and then the programming we all expect and have invested in comes back on screen. I was reminded of these televised public service announcements while participating on a recent panel on power, privilege, and identity in American Buddhisms at the annual conference of the American Academy of Religion in 2017. The panel presenters included critical remarks on whiteness, class privilege, and sexual difference to a largely white audience of Buddhist Studies scholars who attended presumably to listen to some of the leading voices in Buddhism and difference. However, as the panel proceeded, it became readily apparent that the majority white audience was merely tolerating our scholarly interruptions (albeit with growing agitation) and that they could not wait to return to their regular programming of presentations analyzing Buddhist sutras or "real" scholarship. In other words, they wanted to change the channel on us and return to the disciplinary discussions they recognized—those that did not need to mention whiteness and that did not need to include much discussion of the simultaneity of identities that comprised much of the panel—Asian and Asian American Buddhist scholars, a queer white scholar from England, a white female scholar who studies whiteness and Buddhism, a black gay Buddhist lama, and myself—a second-generation Korean American cisgendered woman who studies Buddhism, gender, and race.

After the first few discussions of sexuality, the panel moved to the theme of race and that is when I began to sense in my bones that feathers were ruffled. Somehow, a presentation on sexuality was acceptable, but as soon as the term whiteness was uttered and whiteness in American Buddhism brought to the forefront, especially by an Asian American female body, there was a palpable shift in the room. I was not performing race in the ways the audience expected after all, for I began by troubling the whiteness in the room, the academy, and in *sangha* spaces. Our scholarly audience that was presumably here to listen to what we had to say about power and privilege began to fold arms over chests, shift in chairs, and the façade of exasperation and shut down ensued. They were not here for the purposes of genuine engagement and the egoless listening and epistemological humility that Charles Johnson offers as the foundations of Buddhism, but rather, out of a desire to gaze at difference with curiosity which soon turned into displeasure.[13] They were there to witness the temporary disruption of their regular programming (an uncritical study of Buddhism steeped in Orientalist flavoring and racial superiority of whiteness and white normativity) and to show their support—tolerance—for diversity so they could return to their regular programming and business as usual.

In my own presentation, I spoke about the importance of acknowledging the hypervisibility and hyperinvisibility of people of color in American *sanghas* and studies of Buddhism in the West and how solid scholarship should engage in the requisite of interrogating power and privilege which induced sighs that seemed to complain "oh, this again?" I addressed the investments in whiteness that the field of Buddhist Studies has made and the costs of marginalization, racism, and minoritization of their knowledge meted out on people of color in the academy and in American *sanghas*. While their body language spoke volumes, their mouths remained silent. In the follow up question and answer, not one white scholar wanted to engage my explicit critique of Buddhism and whiteness. The experience was like a pin dropping—a silent but potential threat. As I gazed out at the audience, I could only see people of color with smiles on their faces; I got vigorous shakes of the head, thumbs up, and wide vocal applause. It was as if the only people in the room listening were the other people of color; white scholars neither challenged me nor expressed congratulations. In my hypervisibility I became invisible again. I was a flash on the screen giving a public announcement about whiteness and white supremacy and in an instant the channel returned to business as usual.

I am not sure why I was surprised by how the panel and presentation transpired; after all, it follows a formulaic storyline. This seems to be the way that spectatorship works with whiteness—a white gaze falls upon the spectacle of a person of color who has entered the guild, listens for evidence of their right to be part of the guild, notes the person's failure to engage in "real scholarship," and quickly returns to the gaze upon itself. It was in the question and answer period that I reached for my Buddhist killjoy survival kit and quickly devised an expedient mean to shift the dynamics of the panel itself, for several white male scholars of the audience began to pose exceptionally long questions about subjects not related to our panel and proceeded to answer the questions themselves. In so doing, they recentered whiteness as once again all eyes were on them; they attempted to reestablish that their words were the product of serious scholarship and that our time in public was up.

A seemingly endless debate about largely unrelated issues ensued as several white scholars in the audience began to pose critiques in the form of questions they themselves had the answers for and, in so doing, they shifted the attention of the room onto themselves. We, the actual panelists, were now sitting in the back of the room as the white male scholars suddenly recentered themselves and reestablished whiteness as the prevailing norm. I quickly decided in that moment that I no longer wished to be on air in this strange exhibition of power and privilege. I suddenly reached out for another Buddhist killjoy, one whose support I needed for my survival kit. I turned to the Buddhist lama, looked him in the eye and said, "I think we should have a moment together." Shifting our gaze away from this curious spectacle of whiteness, our eyes locked and he said, "yes, let's have a kumbayah moment" as he picked up my hands. Although the gesture was spontaneous, I reached out to the lama as another Buddhist killjoy, knowing that the gesture "is about the experience of having others who recognize the dynamics because they too have been there, in that place, that difficult place."[14] In so doing, we became the refuge and a gem to each other and created sanctuary in the midst of whiteness. I sought out safety and the only way that I knew how in that moment was to turn to my fellow Buddhist killjoy whose work on Buddhism, sexuality, and race I had deeply admired. I wanted to make a lateral dialogical move because I knew that the programming had just returned to "normal" so I shifted the landscape. Rather than become a silent voyeur to the new mini-panel that developed as a few audience members took over the space, I reached out to my co-panelist as a refuge and a lifeline that Ahmed describes as "a fragile rope, worn and tattered from the harshness of weather, but it is enough, just enough, to bear your weight, to pull you out, to help you survive a shattering experience."[15] It was a moment of co-bearing witness to whiteness.

"TAKING REFUGE: THE POC SILENT RETREAT AS TEMPORARY SHELTER AND SANCTUARY IN TIME"

The benign and bemused white gaze fixes on my travel mate Zora (POC silent retreat attendee) and I at Sea-Tac airport—in the politics of race in white America, we are an unusual pairing—Zora, an African American woman wearing wooden mala beads wrapped around her wrist and index finger, and me, a Korean American woman laughing our way to the gate. We are unsettling the expected norms, for African Americans and Korean Americans do not get along—right? Zora released me from a bear hug with a loud shriek of joy, for it has been nearly a year since we sat together during the annual POC silent retreat in Northern California and here we are ready to do it all over again. We are conspicuous in our excitement, joy, and beads. We board our plane, manage to sit side by side, and Zora fills me in on the details of the past year in broad brush strokes. We land in San Francisco, summon an Uber, and make the ninety-minute drive through Marin County to the site of our silent retreat. Zora, the extrovert, regales me with story after story the entire ride as if to exhaust all of her words that she might want to say over the next week. I, the introvert, begin to sink into the silence of my own body as I peel away the layers of protective shell that I often wear in white America.

We make the familiar cross over the Golden Gate Bridge and wind our way through the gentle mountain slopes to the meditation center. I wonder what the year-round inhabitants of this little town must think of us as we drive past the predominantly white stores and realize that I had been holding my breath until we reached the welcome kiosk of the retreat center. The bodily sensation of tension suddenly loosens in my body as we enter through the gates of the center and see what I have always wanted to experience on an everyday basis—a sangha or Buddhist community made whole by the many bodies of color wandering around. Before the silent meditation retreat commences, we reacquaint with old retreatants from years prior and smile at the faces of our dharma leaders for the week. They are like celebrities because of what all of us have been looking for in the dharma—faces through which we can see ourselves. In the noble silence and in the safe container of practice that was likened to a petri dish where we could explore with kind curiosity what grew, little needed to be said. We all had racialized trauma etched into our derma and were here to explore what lay beneath that trauma to untangle the knots of our experiences living in a white world.

> This POC retreat is about embodiment and settling into our very bodies in the safety of the *sangha* while maintaining noble silence. One of the important things about being on retreat is to learn to feel your own body, its sensations, and become familiar with internal cuing and what makes us react to external phenomena. Rather than reacting unskillfully, we are learning to settle into our experience in the body and develop mindfulness that allows us to experience reality as it is, in its immediate and raw state rather than through add-ons and narrative overlays atop the experience.

The words of our meditation teacher settle into my ears as I feel my body loosen up and finally relax into the meditation cushion that will be what I have come to affectionately call my *bodhimanda* or seat of enlightenment. I am not on the silent retreat to experience the release of all attachments to myself and attain the ultimate *nirvana*. I am here to retreat, find time for refuge and restore my ability to think well of myself so that I can return to the world with a refreshed willingness to engage in eye-rolling pedagogies.[16] As an essential component of the killjoy survival kit, Ahmed reminds us "when you have willingly accepted the killjoy assignment, you are more than this assignment. Take breaks; do other things, with things. Time out might be required for time in."[17] I came to hone my mindfulness practice, one that brings the breath and body together to create stability and equanimity in skillful response to life's vicissitudes and challenges. By way of watching, observing, and investigating the body, feelings, thoughts, and cultivating the four *brahmaviharas* (Buddhist virtues) of *metta* (loving-kindness), *karuna* (compassion), *upekkha* (equanimity), and *mudita* (sympathetic joy at the happiness of others) we develop spiritual fortitude as well as strength and radical courage needed to heal and dismantle injustices without rage or violence but love, respect, and dignity. The noble silence I willingly practice with great relief over the next week dissolves the need to constantly react to the world around us, it teaches us to soften our gaze on others and ourselves, and gives us the required killjoy time to reinhabit our bodies and learn to listen to them from the inside out. Our meditation teacher reminds us that the POC silent retreat also helps us to "be where we are celebrated, not just tolerated."[18]

Ennobling silence, as our meditation guides refer to it, means that there is one less barrier between us, one less vehicle for dualistic interactions where I and ego become a dominant force. Our teachers, all people of color dharma teachers, support us during the difficult times of retreat and remind us that "it takes radical courage to sit, be aware, be mindful, and investigate our reality and our truth. We are able then to truly *see* ourselves through our *own* eyes and not how dominator culture chooses to see us and how we see ourselves." The People of Color silent retreat becomes a safe container to train our hearts and minds to navigate in a protected environment that can hold us with love, compassion, and care—temporarily free from the surveillance of the white gaze, it is experienced as a sanctuary in time.[19]

Throughout that week, we sit through several sessions of meditation which sometimes fly by and sometimes seem interminable, we engage in walking meditation, we eat with eyes cast down next to one another, we learn to detach ourselves from the storylines that we tell about ourselves as racialized bodies to find safe haven from the world of labels and the power of whiteness to unsettle our sense of self, and we meet ourselves anew. We are guided through loving-kindness meditations to liberate ourselves and others from the mental distortions that freeze us into bodies that others can exploit, ignore, or dispose; we are encouraged to treat ourselves as our own beloveds as we cocreate Martin Luther King Jr.'s networks of mutuality and the Buddha's teachings of interdependence that Charles Johnson draws together in *Taming the Ox*.[20] We become the proximate cause of our own temporary liberation. We become fellow Buddhist killjoys taking respite, making time, and settling into our bodies through a form of mindful self/other care—in other words, we bring and continue to replenish our killjoy survival kits. The occasion to sit together in a co-created sanctuary in time, a moment set aside where we could experience the sacredness of our lives while exploring opportunities within the body to experience resilience is what draws us back year after year.

Make no mistakes about it though, taking time out can rub one spiritually raw, for there is a deep vulnerability and softness that comes from living in whiteness and when we quiet the mind, we tap into felt sensations of our bodies that are marked by generations of trauma. The results can provoke staggeringly intense emotions and tears. "Our bodies often carry the stress, trauma, and burdens that filter in when we are not aware, for we all suffer and carry somatic stress and trauma wherever we go," one of our teachers shares. "Because we have neglected the body in order to survive and our bodies have been neglected and abused in the outside world, it behooves us to pay attention." The heart of mindfulness is a kind attention to the tremors of the mind but also an attunement to the deep sensations within the body. Through careful and deep listening cultivated by sitting and paying attention to our bodies in the safety of compassionate silence, we begin to explore and release the felt-sensations of embodied trauma. We explore *vedana* or feeling tones, we explore our mental distortions and how we are conditioned to think of ourselves through the inheritance of white supremacy, and we learn that behind these burdensome thoughts, there is an expansive awareness and a self behind the projections of, and our own reactions to, whiteness.

It is not uncommon for practitioners to meditate through tears of grief and relief, and where no one seeks to contain those tears. Instead, we acknowledge past hurts and sob ourselves clean as we work through the difficult emotions that well up inside us when it feels safe to have them. "We are in training to meet our lives with wisdom and compassion and we are being seasoned here, our hearts are made open and more tender on retreat," as another teacher reminds us. We were not there to escape reality, but rather to meet reality full on with tenderly seasoned hearts. It is this tenderheartedness that gives rise to deep compassion and resonance or what I call broken openheartedness—the capacity to hear the suffering of the world and respond precisely because I have a wounded tender heart that has been rendered open.[21]

Silent retreats incubate and grow nonjudgmental curiosity about our experiences; rather than transcending the body, we explore the layers of social sedimentation that has accrued atop and limited our mobility due to the weightiness of race. Writing about the importance of grounding and settling into the body, Zenju Earthlyn Manuel urges us not to transcend the body itself through meditation, for there is no need to transcend the body. In fact, there is no need to transcend it. "We need to transcend, instead, our belief that spirituality does not include the body."[22] Rather than letting go of our attachments to self, which can be harmful when one has not had a sense of the fullness of an authentic agency, meditation becomes the practice of reinhabiting the body and finding safety in the corporeal container of all of our prior experiences. The refusal to escape into an abstract bodily transcendence, into the rhetoric of oneness (itself another form of racialized violence and a bodily dismissal), shows how the people of color silent retreat is designed to embrace and hold the "affect alien," the one "not made happy by the right things," the one who refuses to let go of and ignore the body whose marking as different has been the cause of its abjectness.[23] Here, we practice meditation to develop a particular kind of sense-ability, the ability to feel sensations in the viscera, the ability to drop into the body, to occupy the fullness of its boundaries from the inside out rather than from the outside in. In so doing we rediscover trust in our own bodies and bring clarity to the unseen and frightening effects of racialized trauma that has left its imprint. If the labor of meditation is to reveal and uproot past conditioning, then the fruits of this work, the proof of the pudding, is found in meditation's ability to serve as a recuperative strategy where we begin to heal the body from the inside out. And we need a sanctuary in time and place. Manuel encourages us to intentionally seek out these sanctuaries.

> The sanctuaries help us to voice and heal the suffering we have endured because of the misinterpretations and misconceptions based on our particular embodiments. We share this in common because our bodies, with unacceptable differences that set them apart, are the very foundation of the personal and systematic oppression within our society. To enter a sanctuary of healing is the way of tenderness—a way to provide needed compassion, perhaps a tender response to those entering an unfamiliar spiritual path. Sanctuaries based on love, rather than hatred, of others cannot harm anyone.[24]

On the final day of my most recent POC retreat, Maya Angelou's poem of resilience, "Still I Rise," posted on the message board outside of the meditation catches my eye. I read her words as a call to which I began my own silent response and was reminded again of the need to have this gift of time in my Buddhist killjoy survival kit:

She calls: Still I rise.
I respond: In the depths of great sorrow, violence, and trauma, I *still* rise up.
She calls: Still I rise.
I respond: In stillness, I rise and emerge anew.
She calls: Still I rise.
I respond: And yet, the I still rises. *No* matter the depth of the practice, the I, the ego, the I-maker, arises.
She calls: Still I rise.
I respond: And yet, I still can rise and meet the world with dignity, mindfulness, and compassion.
She calls: Still I rise.
I respond: Still I rise to meet that which arises. Nevertheless, I keep on.

BODIES—CHOICE AS AN ESSENTIAL TOOL
IN MY BUDDHIST KILLJOY SURVIVAL KIT

When you are ready, feel free *to come to the front of your mat and* if it feels good, *root down on the edges of your feet.* Notice *if you can feel any sensation under your toes, maybe bringing your attention to the weight of the feet on the floor.* Maybe *you feel some tingling, some warmth, maybe some moisture. Just bringing a* gentle awareness *to whatever arises.* If you don't feel anything, that's okay too. Perhaps you might *scan other areas of the feet to explore sensation.* I invite you *now to close your eyes* if that feels okay, *or* you might try *softening the gaze onto the floor about a foot in front of your feet.* Maybe *you try keeping the eyes closed first and then shift to opening your eyes. Remember, we are not looking for anything in particular or trying to make a body shape of a special kind. We are just bringing* kind attention *to the body* without judgment or criticism.

Against the stark relief of whiteness, our bodies become simultaneously hyper-visible and hyper-invisible. Racialized bodies suffer from a kind of habituation to multiple forms of violence directed toward our bodies; thus, our bodies hold the imprints of the habits of whiteness which affect us deep beneath the layers of our derma. While working to "not adjust to an unjust world," our bodies bear witness to the burdens of this continual struggle.[25] As part of my own commitment to radical self-care and mindful embodiment for myself and others, I recently began training in trauma-informed yoga after completing my 200-hour Registered Yoga Teacher (RYT) certification. It may seem unusual for a Buddhist Studies professor to pay such close attention to the body and to be using such invitational language, for academia projects belief that we should be more like disembodied brains ruling with our razor-sharp intellect and speaking with great authority, but as a Buddhist killjoy, I recognize that our bodies have been in constant contact with the world of whiteness which, at the moment of contact, can bring about a sense of alienation or lack of attunement to its internal logic. As a result, many of us have felt constricted or limited in how we self-express in the wrong time and place and our ability to choose how, when, where, and why we move our bodies has been compromised. The compromise made by our bodies to accommodate whiteness by growing smaller, less threatening, less confrontational is also a survival tactic, one that has the further effect of also reinforcing the hegemony of whiteness which insists on an unequal distribution of power.[26] Our nonwhite bodies out of order are bodies put in line and often in front of the line of fire. Our bodies have been traumatized by white supremacy.

Ahmed's feminist killjoy develops a conscience that emerges from the experience of having "a body in touch with a world, a body that is not at ease in a world, a body that fidgets and moves around."[27] As a result of sensing that things are not quite "right" or that we do not want to make things "right" if it means that we are complicit in "white as right," the body accumulates the imprints of these multiple experiences, as if to become a vessel of accumulated misalignments which, trauma studies informs us, leave their imprints. In writing about the feminist killjoy out of which I fashion the Buddhist killjoy, Ahmed explains,

> Feminism can allow you to reinhabit not only your past but also your own body. You might over time, in becoming aware of how you have lessened your own space, give yourself permission to take up more space, to expand your own reach. It is not necessarily the case that we take up this permission by simply giving ourselves permission. It does take time, to reinhabit the body, to become less wary, to acquire confidence. Feminism involves a process of finding another way to live in your body.[28]

In other words, as trauma specialist Bessel van der Kolk famously noted, "the body keeps the score."[29] In keeping the score, our bodies suffer from chronic pain, autoimmune disease, high blood pressure, dissociation, depression—the list goes on. And, as Ahmed notes,

> The violence does things. You begin to expect it. You learn to inhabit your body differently through this expectation. When you sense the world out there as a danger, it is your relation to your own body that changes; you become more cautious, more timid, you might withdraw in anticipation that what happened before will happen again. It might be your own experiences that lead you here, to caution as withdrawal, but it might also be what you learned from others.[30]

Racialized violence seeps into the body through boundaries made porous by the constant vigilance of whiteness that wears away at the membrane of our protective capacities. This violence can make us strangers to our own bodies where we become desensitized by the routine of race, we become dissociated from sensations in the body, that might once have had the resilience to protect us. Our bodies become the beleaguered bag of past experiences that keep us in a constant state of disease and dis-ease.

> You begin to feel a pressure, this relentless assault on the senses; a body in touch with a world can become a body that fears the touch of the world. The world is experienced as sensory intrusion. It is too much. Not to be assaulted: maybe you might try to close yourself off, to withdraw from proximity, from proximity to a potential. Or perhaps you try to deal with this violence by numbing your own experiences, by learning not to be affected or to be less affected. Perhaps you try to forget what happened. You might be ashamed. You might stay silent. You

might not tell anyone, say anything, and burn with the sensation of a secret. It becomes another burden: that which is not revealed.[31]

The symptoms outlined above by Ahmed reflect textbook symptoms of trauma survivors whose traumatizing experiences are not only the result of singular catastrophic events but ones that can develop over time such as childhood abuse, sexual abuse, and racialized violence. Trauma survivors often react to triggers as if they were still stuck in the past event/events which range from individual experiences of interpersonal trauma or a large-scale event such as the conditions of combat. What draws these different iterations of trauma together is the deep betrayal of what is presumed to be ordinary and expected (such as a violation of trust between parent and child). The bodies of traumatized people are altered from these multi-form betrayals in that they are often stuck in fight or flight modes as the rational function of their brains may shut down during acute moments of stress. Either way, trauma leaves its imprint on the body and mind in ways that are not immediately recognized or processed as brain matter transforms and the physical components of the body are compromised.

Van der Kolk observed through his study of traumatized war veterans that trauma includes an initial event, "but is also the imprint left by that experience on mind, brain, and body. This imprint has ongoing consequences for how the human organism manages to survive in the present."[32] Traumatized people do not have a choice in deciding what happened to their bodies at the onset of trauma, but the effects of trauma bleed into our bodies, and our bodies habituate in both skillful and unskillful ways, often through hyper-arousal or hypo-arousal. Through trauma sensitive practices such as a trauma-informed yoga, survivors of everyday racial traumas can discharge excess energies that accumulate in their bodies and develop at moments of high stress. Embodied practices such as yoga are invaluable for addressing the energy stored in the body, "for the survivor's energy now becomes focused on suppressing inner chaos, at the expense of spontaneous involvement in their life. These attempts to maintain control over unbearable physiological reactions, can result in a whole range of physical symptoms, including fibromyalgia, chronic fatigue, and other autoimmune diseases."[33] Trauma survivors continually release stress hormones to protect themselves against real and perceived dangers shaped by the triggering event, of which racism is a primary ongoing one, and unless discharged through somatic practice, the trauma stored in the body will continue to wreak havoc on the mind-body complex. In other words, much like our minds are conditioned by the past, our bodies are habituated to be on high alert; this high state of bodily emergency has also had an exponentially higher impact on bodies of color. A trauma-informed yoga utilizes choice-based language that I highlighted above as an opportunity for practitioners to choose whether or not they wish to move their body in a particular way. Moreover, with what I refer to as trauma-informed mindfulness, the residual effects of racialized trauma and sexist violence can be healed over the long course of one's life so long as the survivor is given the choice to determine what happens to their body.

Inviting practitioners to explore the felt-sensations in their bodies and explore what it feels like to be rooted on the earth with the support of the ground that usually shifts as rugs are pulled from under us can be a tremendous resource in anchoring ourselves in the present. In my own teaching of mindfulness and yoga, I have found the work of David Emerson, founder of Trauma Sensitive Yoga (TSY), to be of immense benefit—the healing modality he created aims to bring traumatized people back into their bodies on their own time and by their own agency by focusing on interoception or the felt-sensations of the body.[34] For Emerson, somatic healing directly focuses on giving clients more opportunities to experience choice making in their lives. He notes, "the point is simply to have and notice the body experience as it is right now, to choose what to do with it once it is felt, and then to take action based on your choice."[35] In other words, knowing what we are feeling in our bodies becomes the initial stage in knowing why we feel something and that gives us the choice to decide what to do. Sensing a mis-attunement or a misalignment of our bodies in reaction to external forces, like the whiteness that Ahmed discusses, can be articulated and clarified in the body-mind complex through naming the experiences of interoception or felt-sensation. Central to this process of developing interoception is the development of trust in those experiences and sensations; thus, the Buddhist killjoy would become aware of the sensations in the body that arise when encountering foul play and trust that felt sense of when things have gone awry. Rather than gloss over these visceral sensations that emerge from contact with multiple injustices, we would do well to "attend to the bumps" as Ahmed advises.[36] The sense that something is amiss is indeed an unsettling event that if not appropriately addressed, may recede into the background of dismissal if not directed "toward a world that reproduces that violence by explaining it away."[37] Like Buddhist mindfulness practice, somatic healing therapies like TSY deliberately focus on bringing practitioners back into the present despite the continual threats of the past to break into the present.[38] If the body keeps the score and past traumas are rooted in our very viscera, then healing modalities such as Trauma Sensitive Yoga certainly fit as an adjunctive practice within the Buddhist killjoy's survival kit.

Our traumatic histories are written into our viscera, they shape our brains and change us physiologically; and yet, we often bury the story deep in our tissues. Yoga, as a form of mindful movement, connects mind to body through breath and the breath becomes an anchor that can keep us grounded in the midst of the racially charged vicissitudes of our lives. The practice has the potential to bring freedom to move the body and connect to that experience of dynamic stillness that comes from holding *asanas* or postures. Trauma Sensitive Yoga can be such a powerful resource because it removes the external authority of the teacher as the one in charge of how and what one should feel. As an adjunctive practice to therapy, Trauma Sensitive Yoga offers a somatic modality based in interoceptive experience rather than kinds of cognitive processes observed through meditation. As I have often heard from my meditation students, it is so difficult to stop the mind from racing and from the high speed of intrusive thoughts; thus, mindful meditation can sometimes lead to triggering traumatic responses. Emerson thus advocates for a body-centered healing focusing more on an experience of "what is happening right now in the body—what it feels like to exist in this body right now—and less about thoughts about trauma or thoughts about the past or the future. Ultimately, this treatment attempts to go directly to where trauma lives: in the body."[39]

The bodies and minds of people of color are continually under racist threat, which requires ever present awareness to guard against its internalization and recognition that the body's hyper-vigilance and hyper-arousal are rooted in previous trauma. For a Buddhist killjoy to survive and continue to make eyes roll, the body must be taken into account in order to be recuperative. Audre Lorde famously proclaimed that self-care was an act of political warfare and, in so doing, she expressed the deep recognition that self-care is also an act of self-love and agency—the very things that racialized trauma diminish. If traumatized people cannot feel parts of their body, or if they experience perpetual dissociation, then the mere acts of noticing sensation and making choices based on those sensations are simply profound.

The invitation to notice, feel, and be aware of bodily sensations *and* to make choices based on those sensations are foundational to Trauma Sensitive Yoga and share much of the Buddha's exhortation to note feelings and feeling tones or *vedana* (aversion, desire, and neutral) to loosen the bond to these feelings. In other words, through the notation of a sensation, we learn that sensation and self are neither permanent, nor enduring. The heart of the practice is in recognizing and acknowledging all bodily sensations with kind curiosity. Thus, in my Buddhist killjoy survival kit, I include somatic modalities and cognition-based practices in meditation to encourage deep attention and listening to the internal sensations of the body as a resource for trust, agency, and survival.

In mindfulness and yoga practice, the body as the locus of trauma also becomes the locus of freedom, but this freedom can only come from internal sources and not an external authority like a yoga teacher. If the body keeps the score, then certainly the ubiquity of violence particularly against bodies of color cannot help but leave its mark. Such violence cannot often be spoken about by the trauma survivor, thus trauma-informed practices can be particularly useful in healing racialized trauma to "allow the body to have experiences that deeply and viscerally contradict the helplessness, rage, or collapse that result from trauma."[40] In her chapter dedicated to the practice of love in *Writing Beyond Race: Living Theory and Practice*, bell hooks reminds us that "white supremacist aesthetics, especially as they pertain to body image, promote the cultivation of a diminished sense of self-worth."[41] In revealing what I carry in my own Buddhist killjoy survival kit, I therefore conclude this chapter with the hope that whatever merit comes from these practices will benefit and fortify us all.

NOTES

1. I would like to thank my friend and colleague, Ali Altaf Mian for his creative, generative, and insightful suggestions on an earlier draft of this chapter. His input was invaluable.

2. Commenting on an earlier draft of this chapter, Ali Altaf Mian wisely pointed the individual and communal pursuit of happiness or *Eudaimonia* as a goal of Western philosophical traditions that the Buddhist killjoy seeks to resist by recourse to alternative sources of embodied knowledge.

3. I owe a debt of gratitude again to Ali Altaf Mian for this wonderful turn of phrase. He has indeed become a co-killjoy for me.

4. Sara Ahmed, *Living a Feminist Life* (Durham, NC: Duke University Press, 2017).

5. See Joseph Cheah, *Race and Religion in American Buddhism: White Supremacy and Immigrant Adaptation* (New York: Oxford University Press, 2011).

6. Ahmed, *Living a Feminist Life*, 37.

7. See Ann Gleig's, "Queering Buddhism or Buddhist De-Queering? Reflecting on Differences Among Western LGBTQI Buddhists and the Limits of Liberal Convert Buddhism," *Theology & Sexuality* 18, no. 3 (2012): 198–214. In addition to Ahmed's killjoy, I embrace Roxane Gay's self-styled term "bad feminist" as a way to trouble the categories of our beloved inherited -isms such as feminism and Buddhism. See Roxane Gay, *Bad Feminist: Essays* (New York: Harper Collins, 2014).

8. Zenju Earthlyn Manuel, *The Way of Tenderness: Awakening Through Race, Gender, and Sexuality* (Somerville: Wisdom Publications, 2015), 27.

9. I would like to thank Ali Altaf Ahmed for highlighting this point in my own writing.

10. Ahmed, *Living a Feminist Life*, 235–249. Ahmed's survival kit includes the following items: books or companion texts, things, tools, time, life, permission notes, other killjoys, humor, feelings, and bodies. While I readily construct my own kit with

the same items, for the sake of this chapter, I will limit my study to those that have a readily recognizable connection to Buddhism—time, other killjoys, feelings, and bodies.

11. I use the term Buddhist killjoy as an abbreviation to the longer title of a Buddhist feminist killjoy with full acknowledgment of my unwavering commitment to the principles of the feminist killjoy and the interconnections between the two, or the simultaneity of different identities as Zenju Earthlyn Manuel suggests in *The Way of Tenderness*.

12. Ahmed, *Living a Feminist Life*, 242.

13. Charles Johnson, *Taming the Ox: Buddhist Stories and Reflections on Politics, Race, Culture, and Spiritual Practice* (Boston: Shambala Publications, 2014).

14. Ahmed, *Living a Feminist Life*, 244.

15. Ibid., 12.

16. Ibid., 38.

17. Ibid., 242.

18. Manuel, *The Way of Tenderness*.

19. Here I draw inspiration from Rabbi Abraham Joshua Heschel's description of the Sabbath as a "great cathedral" of time that brings about rest, renewal, and peace free from the tyranny of linear time. Abraham Joshua Heschel, *The Sabbath: Its Meaning for Modern Man* (New York: Farrar Straus and Young, 1951), 8. Rather than attaching oneself to the ordinary flow of horizontal flow time marked by the past, present, and future, the silent retreat also offers the opportunity to experience what Taitetsu Unno calls "timeless time" or the vertical and depth dimensions of time. Quoting Shinran, the founder of Jodo Shinshu Buddhism in Japan, Unno observes, "According to Shinran, religious awakening is the realization of timeless time in each moment of temporal activity." See Taitetsu Unno, *Shin Buddhism: Bits of Rubble Turn into Gold* (New York: Doubleday, 2002), 63.

20. Johnson, *Taming the Ox*.

21. I write about brokenopenheartedness, co-experience, and resonance born of having one's heart deeply broken Sharon A. Suh, "Women in Asian/Asian North American Religions: Whose Asian/North America? Whose Religion," *Journal of Feminist Studies in Religion* 31, no. 1 (Spring 2015): 137–142.

22. Manuel, *The Way of Tenderness*, 32.

23. Ahmed, *Living a Feminist Life*, 57.

24. Manuel, *The Way of Tenderness*, 61.

25. Ahmed, *Living a Feminist Life*, 84.

26. I am grateful to Ali Altaf Mian's insightful suggestions here to explicitly highlight the hegemony of whiteness that rests upon an unequal distribution of power between different bodies.

27. Ahmed, *Living a Feminist Life*, 22.

28. Ibid., 30.

29. Bessel van der Kolk, *The Body Keeps the Score: Brain, Mind, and Body in the Healing of Trauma* (New York: Penguin Books, 2014).

30. Ahmed, *Living a Feminist Life*, 24.

31. Ibid.

32. Van der Kolk, *The Body Keeps the Score*, 21.

33. Ibid., 53.

34. David Emerson, *Trauma Sensitive Yoga: Bringing the Body into Treatment* (New York: W. W. Norton & Company, 2015).

35. Emerson, *Trauma Sensitive Yoga*, 12.

36. Ahmed, *Living a Feminist Life*, 31.

37. Ibid.

38. Van der Kolk, *The Body Keeps the Score*, 21.

39. Emerson, *Trauma Sensitive Yoga*, 49.

40. Van der Kolk, *The Body Keeps the Score*, 3.

41. bell hooks, *Writing Beyond Race: Living Theory and Practice* (New York: Routledge, 2013), 193.

Chapter 2

Undoing Whiteness in American Buddhist Modernism

Critical, Collective, and Contextual Turns

Ann Gleig

Near the closing of a Buddhist Peace Fellowship workshop held at the New York Insight Meditation Center in November 2015, Katie Loncke and Dawn Haney, the co-facilitators, asked participants to invite the spiritual ancestors that influenced and inspired them into the room. Engaged Asian Buddhists such as Thích Nhất Hạnh and Sulak Sivaraksa, beloved Asian American and African American grandmothers, the Prophetic figures of Martin Luther King Jr and Cornel West, and Black and Latina feminist visionaries such as bell hooks, Octavia Butler, and Gloria Anzaldua entered the room bringing a palpable intimacy into the space with them. The exercise captured three distinctive features from the event: First, it reflected the significant range of racial, class, sexual, and gender diversity in the group; second, it highlighted the presence and strength of community underlying that diversity; and third, it explicitly identified and embraced the specific context that Buddhist teachings and practice were being put into dialogue with.

As well as capturing much of what was unique about the weekend, the closing "welcoming the ancestors" exercise also stood out to me as symbolic of significant shifts underway in North American "convert" Buddhist lineages. The first generation of convert practitioners made up of an overwhelmingly white and upper-middle-class demographic explicitly brought the discourses of psychotherapy and liberal feminism to their encounter with already modernized forms of Asian Buddhism. With communities such as the Buddhist Peace Fellowship a much more diverse demographic is bringing previously excluded, neglected, or entirely new conversation partners—such as critical race theory, intersectional feminism, and postcolonial thought—into the dialogue. One major part of this debate has been to illuminate how a more implicit and insidious discourse has also been unconsciously introduced into Buddhism by the first generation of American converts: whiteness.

In this chapter, I examine how whiteness has been reproduced within convert meditation-based Buddhism and the ways in which Buddhists of Color and their white allies have exposed and challenged it. The first section of the chapter will locate meditation-based convert communities as expressions of Buddhist modernism and consider the ways in which whiteness functioned in the construction of Buddhist modernism in Asia and has become amplified in its North American iterations. The following section will glance at some key attempts by Buddhists of Color, and their white allies, to expose and overcome such whiteness before turning to a detailed examination of the pioneering work of Zenju Earthlyn Manuel from the Soto Zen lineage and Larry Yang from the Insight Community to forge a Buddhist hermeneutics of multiculturalism and difference. In particular, I will highlight how Manuel and Yang expose how Buddhist philosophical concepts such as the Two Truths doctrine and *upaya* or skillful means have been interpreted through a modernist lens to maintain whiteness, and how they offer alternative readings of these doctrines to support a liberatory Buddhist racial awareness. In conclusion, I situate their work as reflecting critical, collective, and contextual turns in North American Buddhism that signify a wider shift from Buddhist modernism to Buddhism in a postmodern and postcolonial climate.

Before proceeding, however, some clarification on the concept of whiteness. As Eric Tranby and Douglas Hartman note, critical whiteness studies is an ever-expanding field but some of its key analytic insights include the recognition (1) that the Jim Crow era of white supremacy has been replaced by a subtler legitimation of structural dominance; (2) of the maintenance of white Anglo-American identity and culture as normative and dominant and; (3) of the "taken-for-grantedness" of white power and the hidden nature of white identity or what has been called "color-blindness."[1] I am particularly interested in how whiteness is maintained and reproduced through modern liberal values of individualism and universalism and how such principles intersect with and are amplified by religious commitments. A number of sociologists of religion, for example, have pointed to connections between Christian evangelicals and whiteness. Michael Emerson and Christian Smith, for instance, have documented how white Christian evangelicals' strict, uncompromising adherence to individualist, meritocratic, anti-structural ideals prevents effective responses to structural racism. They identify three lens through which evangelicals view reality—freewill individualism, relationalism, and anti-structuralism—showing how each reduces both the causes of and solutions to racism to individual responsibility or interpersonal actions.[2] Extending Emerson and Smith, Tranby and Hartman argue that evangelical values of individualism are shared by both American conservatives and liberals and are at the very core of white identity in the United States.[3] I am interested here in a parallel investigation of how Buddhist modernist discourse and practice—particularly the focus on individual meditation practice, the distinction between "essential" and "cultural" Buddhism, and the presentation of Dhamma as universal truth—have intersected with whiteness in a North American liberal individualist context.

BUDDHIST MODERNISM IN ASIA

North American meditation-based convert lineages are expressions of what has been alternatively identified as "Protestant Buddhism," "modern Buddhism," or "Buddhist modernism,"—a historically new and distinct form of Buddhism that resulted from the encounter between traditional Asian Buddhism and Western modernity under the conditions of colonialism. Scholars such as George Bond, Donald Swearer, Donald S. Lopez, and David McMahan have examined the modern reformation of Buddhism across South-East Asia in the late nineteenth and early twentieth centuries.[4] Simultaneously demonstrating accommodation and resistance to colonialism, the vision of Buddhism that emerged from these reforms selectively privileged aspects of Buddhism that were compatible with modern Western discourses, particularly science, and discarded elements that were incompatible. Common characteristics include, (1) a claim to return to the "original," "pure," and "authentic" teachings of the Buddha that have been distorted by cultural and institutional overlays; (2) a framing of Buddhism as a rational and empirical religion aligned with science; (3) a rejection of the traditional Theravadan separation of the mundane and supermundane levels and a blurring of the roles of the layperson and the monk; (4) a revival of meditation practice and a claim that Nibbana is an attainable goal in this lifetime for not only monastics but also the laity; and (5) an interest in social reform issues such as gender equality.

A number of scholars have critiqued and de-legitimated Buddhist modernism because of its colonial origins and departure from traditional forms of Asian Buddhism. Robert Sharf, for example, problematizes the modern emphasis on individual meditation experience, which he argues has resulted in a loss of connection with traditional Buddhist lineage, community, and ritual.[5] Donald S. Lopez's pointedly titled *The Scientific Buddha: His Short and Happy Life* suggests that it is time to retire the highly selective modernist vision of the Buddha as an early empiricist and its reduction of Buddhism to a scientific paradigm.[6] Joseph Cheah argues that racial hierarchies played a foundational role in the construction of Buddhist modernism and sees white supremacy at the heart of American Buddhist modernist communities such as the Vipassana movement, which have been founded upon their ethnocentric distinction between "essential" (i.e., modern Western) and "cultural" (i.e., traditional Asian) Buddhism.[7]

Given the colonial heritage and underpinnings of Buddhist modernism, it is tempting to dismiss it as an inherently white project. Such an approach, however, fails to acknowledge the agency of Asian Buddhists in the creation of Buddhist modernism, the subversive ways Buddhist modernism functioned against colonialism, and risks assimilating Asian Buddhists and Asian American Buddhists to whiteness. As McMahan notes, Asian Buddhists played a key role in fashioning Buddhist modernism and employed it to undermine Christian claims of superiority. He argues that Buddhist modernism is neither unambiguously "there" in classical Buddhist texts and lived traditions nor is it merely a fantasy of an educated white Western elite population. Rather this new form of Buddhism has been fashioned by modernizing Asian Buddhists and Westerners deeply engaged in creating a Buddhist response to the dominant problems and questions of modernity.[8] Similarly, Erik Braun has documented how the Theravada meditation revival began in Myanmar, formerly Burma, as a form of resistance to colonialism. Before the nineteenth century, Burmese monastics devoted their time to scholarship or devotional merit-making activities and interest in meditation practice was very rare. Between 1824 and 1885, however, Burma had come under control of the British and this occupation was seen as posing a great threat to the safety of the Dhamma. With the king no longer able to serve his traditional role as protector of the Dhamma, monastic Ledi Sayadaw (1846–1923) believed the responsibility fell to the Burmese Buddhist population. He popularized the study of Buddhist doctrine and made *vipassana* practice available to the laity in a way that was unprecedented in Buddhist history.[9] Natalie Quli has also cautioned that scholarly critiques of the inauthenticity of Buddhist modernism too often fetishize Asians as the carriers of the "traditional" and Westerners as the carriers of the "modern," thereby merely reinforcing and reproducing stereotypes of the passive Asian and the active Westerner.[10]

Given the above considerations, I differentiate between Buddhist modernism as a complex historical and cultural phenomenon, which has served both radical and assimilative ends for Asian Buddhists, and whiteness as a component of Buddhist modernism. As I will now discuss, this component became particularly prominent and problematic when Buddhist modernism took root in North America and its core characteristics—a distinction between essential and cultural Buddhist practice, an emphasis on the universal nature of Dharma, and a focus on individual meditation experience—were adopted and rearticulated in a white-dominant cultural context marked by an ongoing legacy of racial discrimination. Here I am indebted to Joseph Cheah's distinction between cultural and racial rearticulation, and his argument that there are numerous places of slippage between the two in Euro-American Buddhist modernism. Cheah adopts this distinction from Michael Omi and Howard Winant and extends their work to define "cultural rearticulation" as "a way of representing religious tradition from another's culture into ideas and practices that are familiar and meaningful to people of one's own culture."[11] Such a process is inevitable when religions travel across cultural contexts and examples from Buddhist history include the sinicization of Buddhism in China. By contrast, racial rearticulation is "the acquisition of the beliefs and practices of another's religious tradition and infusing them with new meanings derived from one's own culture in ways that preserve the prevailing system of racial hegemony."[12]

BUDDHIST MODERNISM IN NORTH AMERICA: MEDITATION-BASED CONVERT BUDDHISM

Scholars generally trace the beginnings of meditation-based convert lineages to the appearance of Theravada monk Anagarika Dharmapala (1864–1933) and Japanese Rinzai Zen Buddhist, Shaku Soen (1859–1919) at the World Parliament of Religion held in Chicago in 1893.[13] While there is certainly historical and thematic continuity between these early Asian Buddhist "missionaries" to the United States and contemporary convert meditation-based Buddhism, the latter have their more immediate origins in the cross-cultural flows and exchanges between Asia and North America in the 1960s. During this period, Asian Buddhist teachers came to the United States and founded major convert lineages such as Japanese Soto Zen teacher Shunryu Suzuki who established Tassajara, the first Zen training monastery outside of Japan, and the San Francisco Zen Center, one of the most influential Zen centers in the United States. Similarly, Americans traveled to Asia where they trained in Buddhism under Asian monastics and lay teachers before returning home to start their own centers. Joseph Goldstein, Jack Kornfield, Sharon Salzberg, and Jacqueline Schwartz-Mandell, for instance, cofounded the Insight Meditation Society (IMS) in May 1975 after spending several years practicing Theravadin Buddhism.

The first wave of academic scholarship on these communities was published around the turn of the millennium as the study of Buddhism in America emerged as a distinct subfield in the wider field of Buddhist Studies.[14] An early common distinction made in this research was between two forms of Buddhism in America: one associated with Asian American immigrants and their descendants and one associated with largely white Euro-American converts. The former was characterized as focused on communal, devotional, and merit-making activities within a larger cosmological context. "Immigrant" or "ethnic" Buddhists were seen as primarily concerned with cultural preservation and operating within a traditional soteriological and ethical Buddhist framework. In contrast, "convert" communities tended to downplay the ritual, devotional, and cosmological aspects of Buddhism and present it through a heavily psychologized lens. Cutting across the different denominational forms of Insight, Zen, and Tibetan Buddhism, these communities were characterized by a strong focus on meditation practice and Buddhist philosophy. They were highly individualistic with participants showing little interest in community building. Participants were overwhelmingly white, middle to upper-middle class, highly educated and tended to be politically liberal. Within these communities, there had been a democratization of power structures seen in both a move toward gender equality, with an increasing number of women in positions of authority, and the blurring of authority between monastic and lay populations. While scholars such as Wakoh Shannon Hickey have pointed out the deeply problematic racialized dimensions of the "two Buddhism" model, its description of white convert communities at the turn of the twenty-first century is a reliable one.[15]

POC CHALLENGES TO WHITENESS IN MEDITATION-BASED CONVERT BUDDHISM

In June 2000, a small group of Buddhist practitioners of color and their white allies compiled and distributed a booklet titled *Making the Invisible Visible: Healing Racism in Our Buddhist Communities* to the Buddhist Teachers in the West conference at Spirit Rock Meditation Center in June 2000. This compilation declared that for many years Euro-American middle-class sanghas had been resistant to the efforts of people of color to raise awareness of the reproduction of oppressive racial and socioeconomic within them. Interweaving personal experiences of racism with Buddhist teachings and critical race theory, this landmark collection offered a number of resources to combat racism ranging from institutional diversity trainings to addressing racism in Dharma talks.[16] *Making the Invisible Visible* is one of a number of attempts and initiatives by POC Buddhists over the last two and a half decades to overcome whiteness in American Buddhism. Much of this work is documented in *Awakening Together: The Spiritual Practice of Inclusivity and Community*, which is Insight teacher Larry Yang's invaluable autobiographical and multicultural history of diversity and inclusion work in the Insight network.[17]

One major area has been to raise awareness through forums and literature. Examples here include the 2004 *Dharma, Color, and Culture: New Voices in Western Buddhism*, edited by Hilda Gutiérrez Baldoquín, a lineage holder in the Soto Zen tradition, which was the first collection to bring together the voices of Western Buddhist practitioners of color, and *BuddhaDharma*'s 2011 forum "Why is American Buddhism So White?" and their 2016 summer issue on "Free the Dharma: Race, Power, and White Privilege in American Buddhism."[18] A second area is the emergence of people of color (POC) specific retreats and sitting groups. One example is that in August 2002, Spirit Rock hosted the first-ever African American Dharma Retreat and Conference, and they have held POC specific retreats almost annually since 1999.[19] A third area is the emergence of POC teachers who are actively promoting diversity, inclusion, and racial justice initiatives. Pioneers include Tibetan Buddhists Jan Willis and Lama Rangdrol, Insight teachers Marlene Jones and Ralph Steele, and Zen teachers Zenju Earthlyn Manuel and Mushim Patricia Ikeda as well as GEN X teachers such as Rev. Angel Kyodo Williams, Lama Rod Owens, and Kaira Jewel Lingo. Closely related is the development of communities with specific attention to issues of multiculturalism and racism: at the forefront of these is the East Bay Meditation Center in Oakland, CA, and New York Insight, with Flowering Lotus Meditation and Retreat Center in Mississippi, the Brooklyn Zen Center, and Insight Meditation Community of Washington also active.

A fifth area is the adoption of diversity and inclusion plans and staff and teacher diversity and anti-racist trainings by Buddhist centers such as Insight Meditation Society and the San Francisco Zen Center. A sixth is non-sectarian Buddhist organizations that have taken up racial justice work as a major concern. The Buddhist Peace Fellowship has a long history in racial justice initiatives and more recently the North American Buddhist Alliance has adopted "Buddhists for Racial Justice" as one of its primary initiatives. A seventh area is the development of Buddhist trainings and practices to combat racism. One example of this is African American Insight teacher Ruth King's training, "Mindful of Race: A Stimulus for Social Healing and Leadership," which combines mindfulness practice with diversity awareness training. Another is the white awake training run at New York Insight, which explores whiteness and racism in the context of Buddhist teachings and practices. Finally, one of the most radical recent initiatives has come in the Insight community in which the efforts of Yang and Gina Sharpe, cofounder of New York Insight, have resulted in significant changes in the Insight leadership and teacher training demographics.[20] In the next section of this chapter, I focus on the work of two of the most influential figures in the above landscape—Yang and Zenju Earthlyn Manuel from the Soto Zen lineage—who have revealed the exclusionary operations of whiteness in North American Buddhist modernism and created alternative Buddhist hermeneutics and communities liberated from such whiteness.

LARRY YANG: DHARMA
AS CULTURE AND COMMUNITY

Larry Yang is a cofounder of the East Bay Meditation Center in Oakland, California, which has been at the forefront of racial justice work in the Insight network, the founding teacher of the Insight Community of the Desert in Palm Springs, and a member of the Spirit Rock Teachers Council.[21] Yang identifies as an Asian American gay male and has been a pioneer of multicultural awareness and diversity and inclusion initiatives in the Insight community. For instance, he has engineered and implemented significant shifts in the demographics of two Insight spiritual leadership and teacher training programs: the Community Dharma Leadership (CDL) program, which trains long-term practitioners to begin and lead Insight groups in their local communities with a focus on underserved communities, and the more advanced Dharma Teacher Training Program, which empowers graduates to teach intensive residential retreats.[22] Here, I will focus more specifically on his presentation of Buddhist thought and practice through the lens of what he calls a "multicultural hermeneutics of Buddha, Dharma, and Sangha," identifying the ways in which his framing of the Dharma as both culture and community interrogates the entwinement of whiteness with the core Buddhist modernist principles of universalism, the essential/cultural dichotomy, and individualism.[23]

At the foundation of Yang's approach is the understanding that Buddhism has always been shaped by and taught through specific cultural contexts. As he puts it, "The Buddha's expression about Freedom and Awakening has always been about culture, about diversity, and about the infinite variations in human experience with all the 10,000 joys and 10,000 sorrows of this life."[24] Yang establishes and validates the inherent cultural aspects of Buddhism through recourse to the historical trajectory of Buddhism as well as canonical sources. He traces the growth of Buddhism across Asia, noting the multiple ways in which the tradition shaped and was shaped by local cultural contexts, and reads the emergence of the major Buddhist schools of Theravada, Mahāyāna, and Vajrayana as being as much about cultural transformation as new scriptural interpretations and developments.[25] He invokes canonical legitimacy through reference to a vinaya passage in the Pali Canon in which the Buddha encounters two Brahmin monastics who are complaining that others are corrupting the Dharma by putting it into their own languages and insist rather that the teachings should be preserved in classical dialect. The Buddha rebukes these monastics, however, and replies, "Monastics, the word of the Buddha is not to be rendered into classical metre. Whoever does so commits an offence of wrongdoing. I allow the words of the Buddha to be learnt in one's own language." Pointing out that in oral cultures language is determinative of culture, Yang argues that the Buddha was, in effect, saying that it was misguided to teach the Dharma in only one cultural form and encouraging an expression of the teachings in ways that reflect the diversity of cultures and languages.[26]

Having established culture as a core historical and canonical component of the Dharma, Yang turns to a critical analysis of the "dominant culture" of mainstream Euro-American meditation-based convert Buddhism. He correctly observes that the first generations of Euro-American practitioners did not join or reproduce the Asian American forms of Buddhism available in North America, but rather created their own culturally congruent centers and communities. This is understandable, Yang states, because culture functions as a doorway into the teachings and allows them to become relevant to a specific community.[27] Moreover, for Yang, culture is not only a helpful but also a necessary part of "awakening." As he explains,

> One view is that when our spiritual practice grows sufficiently deep, our awareness and spiritual development will transcend the influence of culture. I have seen this idea expressed specifically in regard to practice of the Buddha's teachings and even in the context of secular mindfulness practice. Some might disagree, but I believe that if Dharma practice is meant to be comprehensive—that is, to leave nothing outside of its scope—then culture is not to be transcended or left behind. In fact, culture is something to be integrated into the very fabric of our spiritual practice, including the diverse facets of our behaviors and identities.[28]

The problem with dominant convert culture is not, therefore, that it is culturally situated but rather that it has a "cultural unconsciousness," heavily marked by white privilege, racism, and homophobia. Much of this is due to the overwhelming demographic whiteness of meditation-based convert communities. Yang notes, for instance, that out of over three hundred trained Insight teachers, only eleven self-identify as POC. Further, Yang has amassed numerous personal testimonies from POC practitioners and teachers who have experienced racial discrimination and injury while on retreat or in meditation group settings. In reflecting on his own first retreat experience, for example, he shares,

> All I could focus on was that I was the only person of color out of about a hundred people—and how awkward, lonely, and even unsafe I felt. Of course, my experience was partially due to my own psychological conditioning at the time (itself socially influenced), but it was also due to the external conditions of how the teachings, teachers, community, and organization had manifested.[29]

A dominant feature of the cultural unconsciousness is to be unaware of its own cultural particularity, which results in a slippage between white experience and "universal" experience. As Yang notes, "Those who belong to the dominant or mainstream culture are usually most unconscious to their own cultural experience." Due to such an unawareness, white members of the dominant sanghas are unable to recognize the ways in which their presentations of the Dharma reflect their own specific experience and exclude the different experiences of minority groups. Hence, Yang continues, "our stories are overlooked, instructions are not made relevant to us, or the dominant cultural interpretation of the Dharma is assumed to be the only interpretation possible."[30]

Another consequence of the inability of dominant sanghas to recognize their cultural particularity—in this case, their whiteness—is to critique groups that explicitly embrace cultural difference. Yang details the significant amount of pushback POC affinity groups have received from the dominant sangha who claim that such groups discriminate against white people and are at odds with the foundational teachings of Buddhism. For example, at the 2013 International Vipassana Teacher Conference, held at Spirit Rock, one teacher had asked, "When can we end the proliferation of special interest retreats like LGBTQI and POC and return to the unity of One Sangha?"[31] For Yang, such a question is misguided as it fails to recognize that white Euro-American sanghas have never been racially unified or places of safety and belonging for POC and LGBTQI practitioners. This teacher, in effect, has made the same slippage between whiteness and "One Sangha" as dominant sangha members do between white and universal experience. Further, for Yang, not only does this reflect a failure to acknowledge the whiteness of dominant Insight culture, it is also a misunderstanding of the Buddhist Two Truths doctrine, which affirms the reality of both relative difference and absolute unity rather than assimilating the former to the latter. Here, Yang quotes from Soto Zen Buddhist teacher Shunryu Suzuki's classic text *Zen Mind, Beginner's Mind* on the importance of both levels of reality: "Sometimes people put a stress on oneness, but this is not our understanding. We do not emphasize any point in particular, even oneness. Oneness is valuable, but variety is also wonderful. Ignoring variety, people emphasize the one absolute existence, but this is a one-sided understanding."[32]

Yang adopts the Two Truths doctrine as a way to ontologically legitimate the pragmatic need of sanghas to balance the universality of the Dharma with the particulars of cultural experience.[33] One way such a balance can be achieved is by bringing a contextual sensitivity to Buddhist practices and not following a "universal" "one-size-fits all" approach. Yang frames this as an expression of "skillful cultural means," and gives an example of how the Buddhist practice might have different impacts on vulnerable populations due to their social and cultural history of marginalization. As he explains,

An example of skillful cultural means within the context of mainstream Western Buddhist practice is the experience of silence. The container of meditative silence has become a highly-respected format, treasured and revered. It is called "noble silence." Unquestionably, the nobility of silence is not only beautiful but allows us to explore our lives beyond the chatter both external and internal. However, if we honor the sense of a larger sangha, the practice of silence should not occur without a broader awareness that for some communities, and in some cultural contexts, silence can become repressive, especially when one is new to this form of spiritual practice. It does not take much for people who have been continually discriminated against or who have been injured repeatedly to feel that the silence itself is oppressive.[34]

As before, Yang is quick to point out that such a contextual sensitivity not only has precedents in canonical Buddhism (with the Mahāyāna concept of *upaya*) but is also consistent with Euro-American renderings of the Dharma, which discarded those practices that were not culturally compatible with it:

In Western iterations of Theravadan practice, few practitioners, much less teachers, practice devotionally. Bowing is not taught as a practice of mindfulness in many Western centers, even though it is a highly-prized form of practice in Asia. Not unlike the queer communities' association of silence as repression, for highly individualistic Westerners, bowing can feel like submission or capitulation. The lived cultural experience is dissonant from the original intent of the practice.[35]

Yang's illumination of the cultural components of dominant American Buddhist sanghas includes a critique of their individualism. Congruent with scholarship on American meditation-based Buddhism, Yang observes that the Insight community has not placed as much emphasis on sangha or community as practitioners from traditional Buddhist countries. He attributes this to the American cultural values of "rugged individualism, the socio-literary narrative of raising oneself by one's own bootstraps, and the psychological ideal of healthy individuation in the process of human psychological development."[36] Yang shares that it was only during his experience of monastic practice in Thailand that he came to understand the importance of community as practice: "It was during that time that I first encountered the deep and direct experience of community and relationship along a collective spiritual path." He felt a deep sense of belonging that he had not experienced in fifteen years of practicing within the lay Insight network and was deeply impacted by the reciprocity and interdependence between Thai monastic and lay communities.

Reflecting on the difference between his experience in North America and Asia, Yang suggests that the Insight community has placed too much emphasis on individual meditation practice and has neglected the third jewel of sangha or community. As a corrective, he brings together canonical and lived Asian Buddhist understandings of sangha with the Western concept of the "beloved community," which originated with the American philosopher Josiah Royce and was expanded on by Martin Luther King, Jr. Quoting from the Samyutta Nikaya and Dr. King's famous reference to the "inescapable network of mutuality," Yang suggests that underlying and interlinking both concepts is a deep acknowledgment and appreciation of ontological and social interdependence. While sangha originally referred to the community of ordained monastics, it "has since come to mean more broadly the assembly of communities who will provide a healthy foundation on which the Buddha's teaching can be sustained far into our future."[37] Yang draws on the life of the Buddha, as well as contemporary Thai Buddhist monastics such as Ajahn Chah, to emphasize the importance of community as a practice.

> The Buddha was always precise in his guidance and he elevated community as one of the three most important aspects of our spiritual life in the teachings of the Three Refuges. He did not do this just to pay obligatory lip service to the collective aspect of our spiritual journey. He was inviting us to explore, as deeply as meditation itself, what it means to awaken together in community. He was inviting us to explore community as a practice of meditation or cultivation.[38]

As evident in the title of his recent text, *Awakening Together: The Spiritual Practice of Inclusivity and Community*, Yang frames the practice of community as indicating a shift in focus from individual to collective liberation. As he explains, "This path is not just about our own personal awakening, enlightenment or freedom. The path is not just about personal salvation. It is about our collective journey and transformation toward a shared experience of wisdom and tenderness."[39] One key hermeneutical strategy that Yang employs in his move from the individual to the collective is an interpretation of the *Satipatthana* sutta, arguably the foundational sutta of the Insight community. Yang refers to Bhikkhu Analayo's commentary in which he discusses the refrain on internal and external mindfulness within the sutta, noting that the presence of the latter has been put aside in modern translations. After considering different interpretations, he concludes that external mindfulness means being mindful of other people and discusses several ways to practice this.[40] Following Analayo, Yang notes that the Insight community has exclusively focused on mindfulness in the internal realm of the individual meditator: "The portion of the *Satipatthana* Sutta with which most Westerners are usually most familiar is the part on internal mindfulness, which is most often the primary focus of silent practice in both retreat and in daily life."[41] However, as Analayo has pointed out, the Buddha taught a second component: external or relational mindfulness practice, which Yang explicates "would include being aware of our impact on other individuals, groups, or communities."[42]

Summing up, Yang's hermeneutics of Dharma as culture and community can be read as a potent emic critical-constructivist revisioning of the modernist foundations of the Insight community: it critiques the ways in which whiteness has become entangled with the core Buddhist modernist components of universalism and individualism and offers a constructive alternative model based in other key hermeneutical sources from the Pali Canon and the lived experiences of marginalized communities such as POC and LGBTQI populations.

ZENJU EARTHLYN MANUEL: DHARMA AS EMBODIED DIFFERENCE

Zenju Earthlyn Manuel is the first African American to receive Dharma transmission in Suzuki Roshi's Soto Zen Buddhist lineage, in the seventy-one years of the institution's existence, and is the lead teacher at Still Breathing Sangha in Oakland, California.[43] Manuel is an artist and prolific author who has written five books, including the groundbreaking *The Way of Tenderness: Awakening Through Race, Sexuality, and Gender* (2015), as well as contributing a number of articles on the intersections of Buddhism and race including a chapter for the seminal anthology *Dharma, Color, and Culture: New Voices in Western Buddhism*.[44] A distinctive feature of Manuel's approach is her application of Buddhist and spiritual teachings to the lived experience of racial, gender, and sexual difference. She has pioneered a Buddhist hermeneutics in which embodied difference is placed at the very core of awakening and the hierarchical distinction between "spiritual awakening" and "social identity" is replaced by an integrated model of liberation, which affirms and intimately connects both levels of reality. Here, I will focus my attention on the ways in which Manuel's embodied awakening illuminates and undoes the entwinement of Buddhist modernist hermeneutics of the absolute and the universal with the discourse of whiteness. Her work, in short, shows how Buddhist soteriology has been (mis)used to maintain and reproduce whiteness in North American sanghas, and how a more complete understanding of awakening disrupts and undoes that process.

At the foundation of Manuel's Buddhist hermeneutics is the Two Truths doctrine: absolute truth (*paramartha-satya*), which refers to the ontological ultimate nature of reality, and relative truth (*samvrtti-satya*), which refers to conventional daily existence. Manuel shares that when she first heard the teachings on Two Truths, she found it deeply liberatory as it reconciled different aspects of her identity and experience. As she explains,

> When I was taught Buddha's Two Truths, I heard the choir sing hallelujah. There are two basic truths in regards to the nature of life—the relative and the absolute. These teachings are vast, but briefly, the relative is that which you can sense about life—what you see, taste, smell, etc. While the absolute nature of life goes beyond those senses, seeing into the true nature that we cannot touch or see. So, the tension between the two is inherent in our existence. We can find ourselves holding to the relative and not the absolute or vice versa. When I can be African or descended from Africans and be awakened to life, be Buddha within my darkness, the tension dissolves. With Buddha's teachings of the Two Truths, I returned to that expansive way of seeing myself before I was told that I could not go to a particular place because I was black. I returned to that original moment when I was born free from the hatred placed on darkness and on dark things and dark people.[45]

While Manuel experienced an immediate sense of personal liberation through the Two Truths doctrine, she soon observed that it and other related foundation Buddhist teachings such as *anatta* (no-self) and nonduality were being (mis)represented and (mis)interpreted in majority white American Zen sanghas as ways not to embrace and integrate the lived experience of difference that constitutes relative reality, but rather to attempt to erase and bypass it. She points to numerous examples of how these teachings have been reductively translated to assert a basic sameness or universality among humans and to dismiss differences in identity as illusory and not of significance. As Manuel correctly points out, however, such an interpretative lens fails to recognize that in an ongoing historical, cultural context that is marked and marred by racial discrimination and violence the category and lived experience of identity is not the same for white people and for people of color. For the latter group, the dismissal of identity conveyed by the unskillful presentation of these teachings can evoke the traumatic social and political erasure and exclusion of their communities. As Manuel shares from her own experience as an African American female:

> Some suggested that if I "just dropped the labels" I would "be liberated." Some said, "We are delusional; there is no self." Others said, "We are attached to some idea of ourselves." If I could "just let go of being this and that, my life would be freed from pain." I thought for a time that perhaps I was holding on to my identity too tightly. Perhaps, I thought, if I "empty" my mind the pain in my heart will dissolve. What I found is that flat, simplified, and diluted ideas could not shake me from my pain. I needed to bring the validity of my unique, individual, and collective background to the practice of Dharma. "I am not invisible!" I wanted to shout.[46]

As well as causing significant emotional, social, and political harm for Buddhists of Color, Manuel suggests that the dismissal of identity also forms a barrier to spiritual awakening because it is only through the relative that the absolute can be fully realized. By the "relative," Manuel means the lived experience of the body as both a physical and social entity that is marked by differences of race, gender, and sexuality. She references African American philosopher George Yancy's understanding of the body as socially constituted within a particular lived historical context, and notes that as a lived embodied experience and not a mere "label," identity cannot be casually sidestepped or bypassed. As she explains, "Our identities cannot be ignored for the sake of spiritual transcendence. We are not capable of being 'unembodied' selves."[47]

The dismissal of identity is a one-dimensional and reductive understating of the Two Truths doctrine and other related Buddhist concepts and practices. As Manuel explains, "Universal Truths fall empty against such human conditions. To simply say 'We are not our bodies' is to flatten and eliminate all of the nuance that appears in teachings like the Satipatthana sutta which teaches mindfulness of the body."[48] A one-sided emphasis on the absolute produces a "disembodied" and "transcendental" form of awakening that is removed from the particularities of the world. Rather than attempt such a misguided (and impossible) transcendence, the point of practice is to realize the inseparability of relative and absolute. Manuel presents an alternative path of embodied awakening through the twin concepts or what she posits as "two interrelated states of being," of "multiplicity-in-oneness" and "Body as Nature." Multiplicity in Oneness is an awareness that oneness includes difference and that "the sameness of being one does not erase difference." She supports her articulation with Zen quotes about multiplicity in oneness.[49] "Body as nature," indicates an awareness that the body itself is an inherited form of nature. Manuel identifies how the American Zen over-emphasis on the absolute and universal has colluded and collided with whiteness to erase the relative and the particular. In recovering lived embodied experience as the necessary site of awakening, she valorizes difference as a gateway to the Dharma rather than obstacles to be erased, and illuminates the inseparability of relative and absolute dimensions of ultimate reality.

As with Yang, the theme of community and the collective is deeply embedded within Manuel's approach. She links whiteness with individuality and POC with a collective orientation: "White people can only relate to things in an individual way rather than a collective point of view. . . . People of color mostly, and I can speak for black people, think of things more from the collective point of view because we have been collectively injured."[50] She shares how this collective history opened up a distinct experience of *dukkha* for her during her Soka Gakkai chanting practice:

After about two years of chanting with this pain, I realized that the suffering I felt was part of a much broader suffering in the world. It was not mine but a suffering that existed before my birth. I recognized that I felt separate from the rest of the world, that I did not belong, and that I was not an acceptable part of the dominant culture because I was so different from the majority in terms of my appearance. The world had structured itself around appearance. The way in which I was perceived and treated depended on a structure of race, sexuality, gender, and class. The perverse power of these structures made my embodiment unacceptable to others and myself. As a result, I was paralyzed by feelings of isolation in my younger days.[51]

Manuel calls on Buddhists to recognize the multiple levels that the collective dimension of reality plays out in practice. To begin with, Buddhists must recognize that *dukkha* does not just refer to individual personal suffering but also to the collective suffering endured by vulnerable and oppressed minority populations. Similarly, Buddhist analyses of the poisons or impurities that afflict mind or consciousness must be extended to include how the collective mental state of dominance and oppression invade and structure social environments.[52] Further, Buddhists must realize that individual liberation is not sufficient to overcome such collective *dukkha* and afflictions, rather liberation must occur on a collective or societal level. As Manuel puts it, "Our collective liberation requires that society, which is a collective body, must reconcile the harm within and without. It must say, 'Ah, we have willingly hurt ourselves and other people. We have covered up our mess for so long.' Society must learn to see. A society that does not examine itself is an unenlightened one."[53]

Another way the collective is affirmed is through Manuel's emphasis on the importance of the sangha. She identifies a general individualism within American Zen and affirms the important support, guidance, and mirroring that sangha members bring to each other. As she explains, "Many have said to me that they do not need Sangha. My response has been, 'Then where will you go when you begin to experience liberation? Who will know the journey you have taken and your vow to be awake?'"[54] She also, however, shares how painful and unsafe white-dominant sanghas can be for practitioners of color and asserts the necessity and power of POC sanghas, which she calls "cultural sanctuaries" and "places of healing."[55] Like Yang, Manuel points out that the Dharma has always been shaped by the cultures in which it is adopted and "When Buddhism first came out of Asia, it was shaped by white men of European descent who were taught by Asian men."[56]

Congruent with her recovery and honoring of the reality of relative difference, Manuel emphasizes the importance of allowing difference in sanghas and not merely reproducing whiteness:

I feel it is crucial to support other kinds of Buddhist communities that will be created by folks from different cultures. Instead of re-shaping what has already been
done, allow for something new to be constructed and not worry about whether it
is too far from the root or not. We have already gone a long ways from Buddha's
days. If new relations look and sound different, existing western Buddhist communities must be willing to open to that difference rather than saying, "This is
how we do it." If not, what is different will disappear and what is left is the same.
And perhaps keeping a particular sameness is the intention. If so, then that must
be acknowledged and the quest for diversity set aside. I say this knowing there are
many who will not want to or not be able to honestly assimilate into the current
western Buddhist communities and therefore the practice must take shape again
and again for the people, the time, and the place.[57]

While Manuel has a history in social justice work, including a stint as
the director of the Buddhist Peace Fellowship, she does not understand her
approach as being reducible to political action. In fact, she shared that one of
the main reasons she wrote *The Way of Tenderness* was because white Buddhists tend to see race, sexuality, and gender as political and not belonging in
the spiritual realm. She noted that the compartmentalization of these dimensions of reality was further reinforced when Buddhist organizations invited
outside experts to present diversity and inclusion trainings. For Manuel, it is
essential to see that such work is not separate from, or even a compliment
to Buddhism, rather it is an inherent and integral part of awakening itself.[58]
However, Manuel is more ambivalent about the specific label of "Buddhism,"
identifying her approach rather as the "way of tenderness," which precedes
Buddhism.[59] Just as she situates the way of tenderness as exceeding the institutional and doctrinal boundaries of Buddhism, so Manuel herself comfortably
resides across multiple spiritual and religious traditions. She grew up in the
Church of Christ, an African American evangelical community, and joined
the African tradition of Yoruba with a transplanted tribe from Dahomey as
an adult as well as practicing for fifteen years in Soka Gakkai before coming to Zen. Manuel describes herself as a "practitioner of Earth practices,"
and an "intuitive" and is passionate about recovering indigenous aspects of
Buddhism that have been ignored and discarded through its modernization
process. She sees Buddhism as "an earth practice that was taken away from
the earth," and calls attention to the role of divination and Shamanism in
Asian Buddhist traditions such as Shingon and Tibetan Buddhism—lineages
that have been ignored by many modern Buddhists.[60]
In short, Manuel's work is a sophisticated emic challenge to the harmful ways in which a Buddhist modernist hermeneutical privileging of the
absolute over the relative plays out in the racialized cultural context of
North America. Whereas Buddhist teachings of "absolute oneness" and

"universalism" might be revolutionary in Asian cultural contexts marked by rigid social hierarchies—such as the caste system in India—in North America, as she shows, these discourses effectively function to reproduce and reinforce dominant cultural hierarchies by enabling whiteness to flourish under the guise of a false universalism or superficial "oneness." Further, Manuel's recovery of indigenous aspects of Asian Buddhism also resists the Protestant Buddhist privileging of canon and textual analysis, which itself has been complicit in maintaining harmful distinctions between "authentic" and "cultural" Buddhism.[61]

AFTER BUDDHIST MODERNISM: CRITICAL, COLLECTIVE, AND CONTEXTUAL TURNS

What does the work of teachers such as Yang and Manuel signify in terms of the wider status of Buddhist modernism? In my recent research on American meditation-based convert communities, I identify three emerging sensibilities or turns: critical, contextual, and collective. The critical turn refers to a growing acknowledgment among participants of certain limitations within their communities such as a lack of racial and socioeconomic diversity and the problematic ways in which Western ethnocentrism has discarded selective, certain aspects of the expansive range of traditional Asian Buddhist practices such as devotional and communal elements. The contextual turn refers to the fact that practitioners are increasingly aware of how the specific social and cultural contexts in which Buddhist practice occurs shapes and limits it, particularly in regard to issues of power and privilege. The collective turn refers to multiple challenges to the individualism of meditation-based convert Buddhism ranging from efforts to build more inclusive sanghas to the application of Buddhist principles and practices to the collective *dukkha* caused by systems of oppression such as racism and capitalism. As should be evident, the work of Yang and Manuel amply demonstrates all three turns.[62]

These three emerging sensibilities put pressure on the modernist foundations of American Buddhism: the critical reveals its ethnocentrism, the collective challenges its individualism, and the contextual undermines its false universalism. In earlier work on the East Bay Meditation Sangha, I argued that its emphasis on difference, intersectionality, and collectivity interrogated key components of Buddhist modernism and displayed characteristics more associated with the postmodern and postcolonial than the modern.[63] I come to a similar conclusion here seeing the work of Yang and Manuel, and the wider field of racial justice work in which they are situated, as indicative of a growing postcolonial sensibility that attempts to decolonize Buddhist modernism from some of the more problematic aspects of its colonialist heritage, which have become amplified due to its recontextualization in a dominant white cultural context.

A glimpse of what can emerge from the undoing of whiteness in American Buddhist modernism was offered at an historic retreat on "The Courage to Live: The Practice of Forgiveness" that took place at Spirit Rock Meditation Center in California, which is one of the two main Insight centers in North America, between December 3 and 10, 2017.[64] This was the first general retreat at Spirit Rock to be led by an all people-of-color teaching team: Yang, Noliwe Alexander, Devin Berry, Konda Mason, and Amana Brembry Johnson, and thirty-two out of the seventy-eight attendees were POC. Yang was keen to point out, however, that it was not just the demographics of the teaching body that marked the retreat as unique, but also the fact that "the combined skills of the teaching team taught from their own lived diverse experiences gave everyone permission from any community to be completely present for all of who they were and what they were experiencing." He observed "a palpable sense of safety that was felt by all communities, not just communities of color, but also white practitioners," noting that there was "zero blow-back or expressed resistance from dominant cultures communities."[65]

My interviews with nine of the retreatants—four teachers and five participants who identified across a range of racial, class, gender, and sexual signifiers—echoed Yang's sentiments. All nine discussed how "powerful," "moving," and "precious" it was to hear the teachings being expressed across a diversity of lived experiences and the "profound impact" of practicing together across demographic lines. All of the POC interviewees talked of the "relief" and "joy" in being able to bring their whole selves to the retreat, without fear of misunderstanding or injury, and the safety engendered by the teaching body. For instance, Indigo, a Chinese American queer female, shared, "This is how every retreat can be. We can have that type of balance in the sangha. Where POC can totally inhabit their entire selves." A sense of belonging and connection was experienced in different but related ways by white participants. For example, David, a heterosexual white man, declared, "To look around the room and see such a diverse mix, it was the most home, I have ever felt in a retreat." Reflecting on the retreat as a teacher, Amanda explained, "the most important thing was to bring diverse communities together so the sangha can be exposed to and understand difference. This cannot happen in white majority or all POC sanghas."[66] As these remarks should indicate, the undoing of whiteness in American meditation-based Buddhism has the potential to forge truly connected and inclusive sanghas based in a postmodern and postcolonial embrace of difference rather than a modern "universal" erasure of difference.

NOTES

1. Eric Tranby and Douglas Hartman, "Critical Whiteness Theories and the Evangelical 'Race Problem': Extending Emerson and Smith's *Divided by Faith*," *Journal for the Social Scientific Study of Religion* 47, no. 3 (2008): 341–359, 346–347.

2. Michael Emerson and Christian Smith, *Divided by Faith: Evangelical Religion and the Problem of Race in America* (New York: Oxford University Press, 2000).

3. Tranby and Hartman, "Critical Whiteness Theories and the Evangelical 'Race Problem,'" 345–346.

4. George Bond, *The Buddhist Revival in Sri Lanka: Religious Tradition, Reinterpretation and Response* (Columbia: University of South Carolina Press, 1988). Donald Swearer, *The Buddhist World of South-East Asia* (Albany: State University of New York Press, 1995). Donald S. Lopez Jr., *A Modern Buddhist Bible: Essential Readings from East and West* (Boston: Beacon, 2002). David L. McMahan, *The Making of Buddhist Modernism* (Oxford: Oxford University Press, 2008).

5. Robert Sharf, "Experience," in *Critical Terms for Religious Studies*, ed. Mark C. Taylor (Chicago: University of Chicago Press, 1998), 94–116; and Robert Sharf, "Losing Our Religion," *Tricycle* (Summer 2007).

6. Donald S. Lopez Jr., *The Scientific Buddha: His Short and Happy Life* (New Haven, CT: Yale University Press, 2012).

7. Joseph Cheah, *Race and Religion in American Buddhism* (New York: Oxford University Press, 2011), 1–5.

8. McMahan, *The Making of Buddhist Modernism*, 4–5.

9. Erik Braun, *The Birth of Insight* (Chicago: University of Chicago Press, 2013).

10. Natalie Quli, "Western Self, Asian Other: Modernity, Authenticity, and Nostalgia for 'Tradition' in Buddhist Studies," *Journal of Buddhist Ethics* 16 (2009): 1–38, 18.

11. Cheah, *Race and Religion*, 60. See also, Michael Omni and Howard Winant, *Racial Formation in the United States: From the 1960s to the 1990s,* 2nd ed. (New York: Routledge, 1994), 163 n. 8, 195 n. 11.

12. Cheah, *Race and Religion*, 59–60.

13. Anagarika Dharmapala, "The World's Debt to Buddhism," in *Asian Religions in America: A Documentary History*, eds. Thomas A. Tweed and Stephen Prothero (Oxford: Oxford University Press, 1998), 133–137.

14. Influential books include Charles S. Prebish, *Luminous Passage: The Practice and Study of Buddhism in America* (Oakland, CA: University of California Press, 1999), Richard Hughes Seager, *Buddhism in America* (New York: Columbia University Press, 1999), and James William Coleman, *The New Buddhism: The Western Transformation of an Ancient Religion* (New York: Oxford University Press, 2002).

15. Wakoh Shannon Hickey, "Two Buddhisms, Three Buddhisms, and Racism," in *Buddhism Beyond Borders: New Perspectives on Buddhism in the United States*, eds. Scott A. Mitchell and Natalie E. F. Quli (Albany: State University of New York Press, 2015), 44–46.

16. Sheridan Adams, Mushim Patricia Ikeda, Jeff Kitzes, Margarita Loinaz, Choyin Rangdrol, Jessica Tan, and Larry Yang, eds., *Making the Invisible Visible:*

Healing Racism in Our Buddhist Communities, 3rd ed. (2000), https://www.dharma.org/wp-content/uploads/2018/07/making-the-invisible-visible.pdf.

17. Larry Yang, *Awakening Together: The Spiritual Practice of Inclusivity and Community* (Boston: Shambhala Publications, 2017). See, Appendix Four, "The History of Diversity-Related Events in the Western Insight Meditation Community," 237–240.

18. Hilda Gutiérrez Baldoquín, ed., *Dharma, Color, and Culture: New Voices in Western Buddhism* (Berkeley: Parallax Press, 2004). "Why Is American Buddhism So White?" *Lion's Roar*, November 10, 2011, https://www.lionsroar.com/forum-why-is-american-buddhism-so-white/ (accessed March 29, 2017). "Free the Dharma: Race, Power and White Privilege in American Buddhism," *BuddhaDharma: The Practitioner's Quarterly* (Summer 2016).

19. For details on some of these, see Jaweed Kaleem, "Buddhist 'People of Color Sanghas,' Diversity Efforts Address Conflicts About Race Among Meditators," *Huff-Post*, November 18, 2012, https://www.huffingtonpost.com/2012/11/18/buddhism-race-mediators-people-of-color-sangha_n_2144559.html.

20. For details on these teacher training changes, see Chapter 5 in Ann Gleig, *American Dharma: Buddhism Beyond Modernity* (New Haven: Yale University Press, 2019).

21. Larry Yang, http://00597e6.netsolhost.com/larryyang/.

22. Gleig, *American Dharma*.

23. Larry Yang, "Buddha is Culture," *Huffpost Religion*, September 19, 2012, https://www.huffingtonpost.com/larry-yang/buddha-culture_b_1192398.html, Larry Yang, "Dharma is Culture," *Huffpost Religion*, June 27, 2012, https://www.huffingtonpost.com/larry-yang/Dharma-culture_b_1599969.html, and Larry Yang, "Sangha is Culture," *Huffpost Religion*, July 10, 2012, https://www.huffingtonpost.com/larry-yang/sangha-culture_b_1600095.html (accessed September 5, 2015).

24. Yang, "Buddha is Culture."

25. Yang, *Awakening Together*, 51–73.

26. Ibid., 53–54.

27. Ibid., 66–67.

28. Ibid., 45.

29. Ibid., 83.

30. Ibid., 56.

31. Ibid., 63.

32. Ibid., 65.

33. Ibid., 93.

34. Ibid., 90.

35. Ibid., 90.

36. Ibid., 45.

37. Ibid., 63.

38. Ibid., 48, 166.

39. Ibid., 130.

40. Bhikkhu Analayo, *Satipatthana: The Direct Path to Realization* (Birmingham: Windhorse Publications, 2004).

41. Yang, *Awakening Together*, 120.

42. Ibid., 119.

43. Mention here should also be made of Merle Kodo Boyd who was the first African American female to receive Dharma transmission in the White Plum Asanga lineage, and currently the lead teacher at Lincroft Zen Sangha in New Jersey. See Emma Varvaloucas, "Okay As It Is, Okay As You Are: An Interview with Merle Kodo Boyd," *Tricycle*, Fall 2013, https://tricycle.org/magazine/okay-it-okay-you-are/.

44. For biographical information and a list of her publications, see her website, http://zenju.org.

45. "Difference and Harmony: An Interview with Zenju Earthlyn Manuel," *Tricycle*, November 8, 2011, https://tricycle.org/trikedaily/difference-and-harmony-interview-zenju-earthlyn-manuel/.

46. Zenju Earthlyn Manuel, *The Way of Tenderness: Awakening Through Race, Sexuality and Gender* (Somerville: Wisdom, 2015).

47. Ibid., 41.

48. Ibid., 107.

49. Ibid., 54–62.

50. Zenju Earthlyn Manuel, interview with author, June 11, 2015.

51. Manuel, *The Way of Tenderness*, 4.

52. Ibid., 88.

53. Ibid., 81.

54. Tricycle, "Difference and Harmony."

55. Manuel, *The Way of Tenderness*, 56.

56. Ibid., 70.

57. Tricycle, "Difference and Harmony."

58. Manuel, interview with author.

59. Manuel, *The Way of Tenderness*, 28–29, 124.

60. Tricycle, "Difference and Harmony."

61. See Natalie Quli, "Western Self, Asian Other," for a reflection on the costs to lived Asian and Western Buddhist communities that the textual bias in Western Buddhist scholarship has.

62. Gleig, *American Dharma*, Chapter 9. See also Ann Gleig, "The Shifting Landscape of Buddhism in America," *BuddhaDharma*, https://www.lionsroar.com/the-shifting-landscape-of-buddhism-in-america/.

63. Ann Gleig, "Dharma Diversity and Deep Inclusivity at the East Bay Meditation Center: From Buddhist Modernism to Buddhist Postmodernism?" *Contemporary Buddhism: An Interdisciplinary Journal* 15 (2014): 312–331.

64. The Courage to Live: The Practice of Forgiveness Retreat, Spirit Rock Meditation Center, December 3–10, 2017.

65. Larry Yang, personal correspondence with author, December 11, 2017.

66. I interviewed nine participants, four teachers and five retreatants, between December 11 and 20, 2017 and interviews lasted between 45 and 60 minutes. The sample size was too small and selective to come to definitive conclusions, but there was a strong consensus across the board on the themes highlighted above.

Chapter 3

White Delusion and Avidyā

A Buddhist Approach to Understanding and Deconstructing White Ignorance

Emily McRae

I begin with an example of my own white delusion. I can use this example because, in this case at least, I was lucky enough to have someone explain my white delusion to me. This is lucky because it is the nature of delusion to not see itself for what it is. For many years I thought that my husband, who is Black, was (from my point of view) inexplicably concerned with his appearance. This concern was hard to explain since he is not vain or materialistic, or particularly vigilant about fashion trends. But when we go out together to an event, he is the one who manages the question of whether we look good enough (is a tie required? A dress? Is this shirt wrinkled?). I am ashamed to admit that it did not occur to me (for years, and not until he explained it to me) that this psychological burden of managing appearance was related to his racial identity. As a (white) feminist, I was used to thinking about the burden of managing physical appearance as being primarily gendered: women have to put in all the effort and men can coast by on basic hygiene. With this framework in mind, it was bewildering to me that my male partner, at least in some contexts, seemed to care about appearance more than I did.

My husband is a physician, which is a field that has very few Black men (and is actually losing Black men).[1] He has no Black male colleagues and never has. Although he is always well dressed, he has, more than once, been accused of lacking professionalism in his attire or "attitude" by white and Asian colleagues. As a Black man in a white professional setting, he *has* to manage his appearance. Because he explained all of this to me, I can see now that his concern about his appearance was not vanity or superficiality, nor was it motivated by a desire to conform to social conventions or a desire to control my appearance, as I sometimes suspected in my more cynical moments. It was, and is, a reasonable response to an impossible situation: being a Black male professional in a white profession. My confusion and bewilderment by this fairly obvious fact is a display of my white delusion.

I offer this story not only as an example of everyday white delusion, but also to set the tone of this chapter: From both the Buddhist and critical race theoretical perspectives that I draw on here, ignorance (delusion) is not someone else's problem. There is a moral, and epistemic, imperative to confront our own ignorance, to dismantle the false beliefs and misunderstandings that inform our everyday sense of reality. In this chapter, I use the Buddhist concept of avidyā (ignorance, confusion, delusion) to analyze the causes, mechanisms, and possible correctives for white delusion. In Buddhist contexts, avidyā refers not only to a lack of knowledge but also (and primarily) to an active misapprehension of reality, a warped projection onto reality that reinforces our own dysfunction and vice. Ignorance is rarely innocent; it is not an isolated phenomenon of just-not-happening-to-know-something. It is maintained and reinforced through personal and social habits, including practices of personal and collective false projection, strategic ignoring, and convenient "forgetting." This view of avidyā has striking similarities to philosophical analyses of white ignorance, such as Charles Mills's, which understand white ignorance not in terms of a passive lack of knowledge but as an active refusal by whites to confront basic facts about our social world.[2]

I argue that Buddhist analyses of avidyā may help us understand the mechanisms of white ignorance and the practices for deconstructing it. On the Buddhist view, the mechanisms for maintaining avidyā include obsession with self and clinging to fixed narratives about the self (in the case of white delusion, "I'm not racist" or "I've earned and deserve everything I have") and the refusal to take seriously cause and effect (such as a failure to historicize racism, the failure to understand broad, systemic effects of racism, and the inability to apply abstract knowledge of racism to specific cases). In my own case of white delusion, I was guilty of both kinds of mistakes: I was clinging to a narrative that obscured reality—that it was only women who bore the burden of managing physical appearance in our society—and I failed to apply my knowledge of how racism works in the abstract to the specifics of my partner's life.

Buddhist conceptions of ignorance or delusion may also help to locate possible correctives for white ignorance. Because avidyā is not simply a lack of knowledge, it cannot be completely remedied by exposure to facts and analyses of those facts. To be receptive to such knowledge in the first place, to remember and apply it, we must overcome our own dysfunctional emotional patterns that sustain our confusion. So, on a Buddhist ethical view, white people cannot combat white ignorance simply with knowledge about racism (which is already widely available) but rather white people need to do the personal and emotional work of deconstructing our own whiteness, as it arises in our own lives, to uproot our white ignorance. This is uncomfortable and ugly (but necessary) work that will require white people to correct for major moral blind spots by developing the moral skill of equanimity (or "tarrying," as George Yancy has argued).[3]

WHITE IGNORANCE

In Western philosophical traditions, epistemologies of ignorance—the "examination of the complex phenomena of ignorance, which has as its aim identifying different forms of ignorance, examining how they are produced and sustained, and what role they play in knowledge practices"[4]—have largely been ignored. (This is not true in the Buddhist tradition, as we will see in the next section). Ignorance is often assumed to be a passive phenomenon, a lack or absence of knowledge. This implies that ignorance is fairly straightforward to correct: we simply fill in the gap in our knowledge, we account for our epistemological oversight.

For a number of reasons, such a model of ignorance cannot account for white ignorance, the racial ignorance of whites within a white supremacist society. First, this model of ignorance inherits from classical epistemology a focus on *individual* cognition. But white ignorance, as Charles Mills has argued, is a kind of "structural, group-based, miscognition."[5] Of course, it is the individual white person who exhibits white ignorance. But this ignorance is based on and explained by one's group membership as a white person living in a white supremacist society, such as the United States. That white ignorance is social and systematic is important, since it helps us to understand many of the mechanisms by which it is maintained, namely the collective endeavors of white society, such as the management of collective memory, official or state-sponsored histories, media representations, and so forth.

Although white Americans inherit and are socialized in the context of white ignorance, this does not mean that white ignorance should be understood as passive, or blameless, since it is actively maintained at both the collective and individual levels. This is the second reason why white ignorance is not well explained as a simple lack of knowledge. Mills argues that ignorance, including white ignorance, "covers both false belief and the absence of true belief."[6] White ignorance—and related group-based miscognitions, such as male ignorance and American ignorance—trades mainly in actively maintained miscognition, including false beliefs ("The United States in a meritocracy"), misinformation ("9/11 was the deadliest attack to ever be perpetrated on American soil"), faulty histories (of happy slaves and benevolent slave owners), and illogical social theories (such as nineteenth-century theories of manifest destiny). These are not absences of knowledge but are cases of mis-knowledge, actively created and maintained.

The final reason that white ignorance should not be thought of as (merely) a lack of knowledge is that this ignorance, unlike a mere absence of knowledge, requires effort—sometimes prodigious—to maintain itself. The mis-cognitions that characterize white ignorance fly in the face of reason and, in many cases, easily accessible evidence and so, to maintain them, one must carefully insulate oneself from such evidence or critical thinking: one must *try* to be (or remain) ignorant. This requires effort. As Elizabeth Spelman has argued, white ignorance is "an appalling achievement" that requires "grotesquely prodigious effort" to maintain itself.[7] Such is not true of mere absences of knowledge. That I do not know that the capital of Vermont is Montpelier—that I am ignorant of this fact—typically does not require any effort on my part, nor does it take much effort to correct.

White ignorance, however, can only be maintained through considerable effort and the application of epistemic (mis)strategies. One such strategy is the careful management of collective memory.[8] To use an example from my home state of New Mexico: public schools in Santa Fe participate in what is called the "Fiestas de Santa Fe" that honor the Spanish reoccupation of Santa Fe after the Pueblo Revolt of 1680. During this "celebration," students are visited by the "Fiesta Court," which includes "people portraying Don Diego de Vargas and his soldiers and Catholic missionaries."[9] This reoccupation is the subject of an annual (since 1911) reenactment—the "Entrada"—in the city's main plaza. The (re)conquering of Santa Fe by the Spanish is portrayed as "bloodless," and even as a symbol of the peaceful unification of the Pueblo peoples and the settlers. Pueblo protesters have long challenged this white-washed history and the celebration of an event that led to the oppression of indigenous people, and, recently, with some success: 2017 was the first year that Santa Fe students could opt out of Fiesta activities. But the Fiestas de Santa Fe is not an isolated event. It is one small part of a larger state narrative about the "peaceful" coexistence of Pueblo, Spanish, and Anglo peoples that seeks to justify or, at least, defang European colonialism. The official seal of the University of New Mexico, for example, is a conquistador with a sword and an Anglo frontiersman with a rifle.[10] These are complex examples, as they involve not simply "whites" and "non-whites," but at least three distinct groups: Spanish, Pueblo, and Anglo peoples. But, at the very least, these examples show the complex ways that racialized ignorance is actively maintained through the collective management of memory and how the use of holidays, educational curricula, visual culture, and historical narratives all work to perpetuate racial ignorance.

There are also more individual, psychological forces that maintain white ignorance. James Baldwin once claimed that "White America remains unable to believe that Black America's grievances are real; they are unable to believe this because they cannot face what this fact says about themselves and their country; and the effect of this massive and hostile incomprehension is to increase the danger in which all black people live here, especially the young."[11] White ignorance must be maintained because to expose it would be to expose one's own racial ugliness and moral culpability in systems of racial oppression. If the United States is not a meritocracy but a white supremacist society predicated upon racial discrimination and racial oppression, then this means that I, as a white person, cannot have faith that my accomplishments are due to my efforts or natural talents. I would have to face up to the fact I, my family, and my ancestors have been the recipients of years of compounded race-based privilege, and that that privilege has been at the expense of people of color in the United States. Owning up to white ignorance means accepting that our "founding fathers" are not idols to be revered but men with deep moral faults. It would mean understanding the American political system not as "the world's greatest democracy," but as a system consistently threatened and undermined by projects of race-based disenfranchisement. Insofar as these are ugly truths for many white Americans, they are ignored, and strategies of ignorance are in place to continually hide them from collective and personal awareness.

AVIDYĀ IN BUDDHIST PHILOSOPHY

Epistemologies of ignorance are of central importance in Buddhist philosophy, especially Buddhist ethics, and much philosophical effort is given to ethical and epistemological analyses of ignorance. According to all forms of Buddhism, ignorance—or avidyā—is at the root of human suffering, violence, and vice. The project of liberation is, essentially, liberation from avidyā. For these reasons, understanding what avidyā is, how it manifests, the mechanisms for creating and maintaining it, and the spiritual technologies to eliminate it are of central concern to Buddhist philosophers.

In Sanskrit, avidyā is a negation ("a") of vidyā (knowledge). For this reason, avidyā has often been translated as ignorance, the lack of knowledge. In his survey of Indian Buddhist conceptions of avidyā, Bimal Matilal argues that such an English translation is, at best, misleading for two main reasons, one grammatical and the other philosophical. The grammatical reason is that, although the negation "a" can mean "lack" or "absence," it can also mean, among other things, "that which is not X," "that which is in opposition to X," or "that which is similar, but not equivalent to X." In the case of avidyā, these different grammatical interpretations lead to substantial philosophical differences: (1) avidyā could be "lack of knowledge," (2) that which is "not knowledge," (3) that which is "the opposite of knowledge," or (4) that which is "mistaken for knowledge."[12]

In the context of Buddhist philosophy, the first two possible understandings of avidyā are ruled out: avidyā cannot mean simply that which is not knowledge or the lack of knowledge (which is why both Matilal and Wayman argue against "ignorance" as a suitable translation of avidyā). In the *Abhidharmakośa*, the fourth-century Buddhist philosopher Vasubhandu asks, "What is avidyā?" His answer:

> The non-vidyā (knowledge), that which is not vidyā. Impossible; for the eye is also non-vidyā. It is an absence of vidyā, "ignorance." This is also impossible, for an absence is not a thing and avidyā must be a thing, since it is a cause. Thus, Avidyā is a separate entity (dharma), the opposite of vidyā or knowledge, like a non-friend, the untrue, etc. The non-friend (amitra) is the opposite of friend, not a non-friend, that is, anyone other than a friend, not the absence of the friend . . . . Thus avidyā is the opposite of vidyā.[13]

Here Vasubhandu is arguing that defining avidyā as simply "non-knowledge" will not do, since there are many things that are not knowledge—such as the eye—but that does not mean that they are avidyā. Moreover, understanding avidyā as the lack or absence of knowledge is "impossible" in the context of Buddhist philosophy. This is because avidyā is causally efficacious; it is one of the root causes of suffering. And a non-entity, according to Vasubhandu, cannot be a cause. For this reason, Vasubhandu claims that we should understand avidyā as that which is opposed to knowledge. (Alex Wayman argued, along these lines, that we should translate avidyā as "unwisdom."[14]) It is important to note that, philosophically, understanding avidyā as "that which is opposed to knowledge" includes the other grammatical interpretation of avidyā as "that which is mistaken for knowledge," since false views that are mistaken for knowledge are in opposition to knowledge.

Analyses of avidyā are prioritized because avidyā is claimed by all Buddhist schools to be a foundational cause of suffering, which is why it is important to Vasubhandu that avidyā has causal efficacy. The link between avidyā and suffering is also important for moral psychological reasons: it explains our experience of suffering in the world and the psychological mechanisms of that suffering. Along with desire and hatred, avidyā is one of the three root "poisons" (and the most foundational of the three) that cause suffering. The basic idea is that our experiences of suffering—from minor dissatisfaction to abject misery—can be explained by our habit of projecting false views and assumptions and taking them to be real or accurate. For Buddhist philosophers, this is true on a mundane level: If I am upset because I was passed over for a promotion, this suffering is due to craving the promotion, aversion to being passed over, both of which are based on false ideas about the nature of reality (that getting overlooked never happens, that promotions are to be valued over other things, etc.). But it is also true on a deeper level. The suffering I experience in my life, it is claimed, is caused by a more fundamental delusion: that I am an independent, essential self, metaphysically distinct from other independent, essential selves. But we do not exist in this way, Buddhists argue; we are simply a collection of ever-changing parts, which are dependent on changing conditions, and are themselves empty of any inherent existence. Not recognizing this is avidyā. Because avidyā causes us to expect and desire things to be other than they are, it sets us up for suffering.

Since it is the fundamental cause of suffering, the elimination of avidyā is central to the Buddhist project of liberation, that is, the cessation of suffering. But the elimination of avidyā cannot simply be about attaining knowledge. This would be true if we understood avidyā as a lack of knowledge; then the antidote would simply be getting more knowledge.[15] But since avidyā is better understood as that which stands in opposition to knowledge, as Vasubhandu argues, the elimination of avidyā demands that we actively dismantle these *mis*understandings of the world and replace them with accurate understandings that we have reached through sound philosophical analysis and correct interpretation of experience.

AVIDYĀ AND WHITE IGNORANCE

There are some obvious differences between avidyā and white ignorance. Avidyā affects all non-liberated beings (that is, all beings who suffer), white ignorance does not affect everyone (although, as Mills notes, it is not strictly limited to white people). The elimination of avidyā constitutes a complete cessation from suffering, or at least that is what is claimed; the elimination of white ignorance constitutes the cessation of, at most, racial injustice, and even then, probably not all of it.

But there are some substantial points of conceptual overlap between avidyā and white ignorance that can motivate integrating Buddhist and critical race analyses. First, both avidyā and white ignorance are normative (broadly moral) concepts of ignorance. Avidyā has moral significance due to its direct link to human (and sentient) suffering. Moreover, the reason that we care about avidyā is for liberatory ends.[16] White ignorance is also a moral ignorance. Mills argues that white ignorance is "not merely ignorance of facts with moral implications but moral non-knowings, incorrect judgments about the rights and wrongs of moral situations themselves."[17] And we want to eliminate white ignorance because we want to eliminate the racial injustice and suffering that is caused by it.

Second, due to their normative orientations, both avidyā and white ignorance are intended to pick out certain kinds of morally and soteriologically
important delusions; neither concept is concerned with all forms of not-
knowing. Matilal argues that, even though "in a general context, avidyā may
stand for false beliefs or a false belief-system which we all grow up with in
the worldly environment," in the Buddhist context, "it obtains a specialized
meaning" because "not all false beliefs are technically called avidyā in Buddhism."[18] The reason that not all false beliefs count as avidyā is because not
all false beliefs are implicated in human and sentient suffering and bondage. In
most circumstances, the fact that I do not know how many pebbles there are in
my yard, or that I assume there are more than there are, does not constitute a
cause of my (or others') suffering. Similarly, the domain of white ignorance is
limited: it is not about all the things white people do not know, but what white
people do not know *qua* white people in a white supremacy. That a white person does not know the distance between the Earth and Saturn does not count
as the relevant form of white ignorance, since this not-knowing is not due to
being a white person in a white supremacist society and it is not a moral non-
knowing. That a white person believes "that the academy is a meritocracy, that
modernity begins in Europe and then spread outward, and that global poverty
is disconnected from Western wealth" would count as white ignorance since
the miscognitions are due to being a white person and, because they obscure
the realities of racial injustice, it is a moral non-knowing.[19]

The third point of similarity is that Buddhist accounts of avidyā and critical
race accounts of white ignorance both emphasize the active dimensions of
ignorance. Both insist that the ignorance in question is not a passive absence
but an active delusion that is maintained through effort. It is an "active
production" that is maintained for personal, social, political, and economic
reasons.[20] Because both avidyā and white ignorance are active projections of
falsity, I will translate avidyā as delusion and change "white ignorance" to
"white delusion." I think that the term white delusion is in line with many
of the descriptions found in critical race theory/critical philosophy of race.
Mills, who tends to use "white ignorance," nevertheless sometimes describes
it as an "invented delusional world, a racial fantasyland, a consensual hallucination."[21] In the remainder of this chapter, I will examine how Buddhist
analyses of delusion (avidyā) help to further understand the causes and conditions of white delusion, and the possibility of eliminating it.

WAYS OUT OF WHITE DELUSION?

Buddhist ethics presents several ways of addressing and eliminating the
delusions that cause suffering. I will focus on two antidotes to delusion: the
contemplation of causation and the cultivation of equanimity.

As may be clear by this point, knowledge, on its own, is not sufficient for liberation from suffering on the Buddhist view. It may seem strange, since a philosophical system that claims ignorance to be the fundamental source of suffering seems required to also say that knowledge is the fundamental source of liberation from that suffering. But, clearly, knowledge by itself does not always liberate us from suffering, a fact that David Burton has referred to as a "conundrum" of Buddhist philosophy.[22] After all, we may already know that everything is impermanent, and it is not too difficult to understand the arguments for no-Self or even emptiness (we teach them in college classrooms). But this knowledge alone clearly does not liberate us from suffering, at least not completely. (If it did, philosophy departments would be much happier places than they usually are!) But if we understand avidyā as delusion, rather than ignorance, the claim that knowledge cannot alone liberate us from suffering is less perplexing. Delusion cannot be eliminated just by exposure to, or even acceptance of, the facts. For example, I (irrationally) experience driving as very dangerous; every intersection, every turn and stop light seem to me to be an opportunity for disaster. I know that this perception is false; driving is risky but not that risky. I know that people much less attentive than me drive successfully and without anxiety. This knowledge is helpful, but it has not uprooted my delusion of danger and, for that reason, has not eliminated my anxiety. To uproot this or any other delusion, knowledge needs to be integrated in the right ways, remembered and applied at the right times, and, perhaps most importantly, must be supported by and harmonize with emotions, desires, and perception.

REFLECTING ON CAUSATION AS AN ANTIDOTE TO DELUSION

One way to integrate our knowledge so that it is efficacious in our lives is through practices of repeated contemplation and reflection. In Buddhist philosophy, one of the most common antidotes to delusion is the frequent contemplation of cause and effect.[23] Although no one would deny cause and effect—and it is not a difficult concept to grasp or assent to—we often fail to properly recognize, remember, and make logical use of certain causal relationships. We fail both to recognize and remember how our current mental, emotional, and physical state is the effect of various causes and how it is itself the cause of future states. For example, we fail to understand, or remember, how our habit of comparing ourselves to others contributes to our suffering. Or we may refuse to appreciate how our habit of prioritizing ourselves over others will lead to loneliness and unhappiness. We maintain the delusion that we can continue to prioritize ourselves over others and compare ourselves with others and that this will lead to our happiness. But this delusion fails to understand fundamental cause and effect relationships between our attitudes about others and our own happiness.

It is not reflection on any case of cause and effect, or cause and effect in general, that will uproot delusion on the Buddhist view. Rather, specific causal links are selected as proper objects of contemplation because of their relevance to understanding and overcoming human suffering. These specific causal links, the twelve links of dependent origination, are designed to show how our delusion predictably leads to our own suffering. The twelve links connect basic delusion (avidyā) to the structure of our psychology and embodiment, showing how delusion conditions sensation, perception, and other mental phenomena. (That delusion could condition perception will not be surprising to scholars of race and bias, as studies show that whites are more likely to "see" a weapon in the hand of a Black man than a white man.[24]) These sensations and perceptions create craving and grasping that lead to suffering. In the contemplation of the twelve links, then, delusion is featured at two distinct levels: delusion is a causal link in the chain, *and* it is by contemplating this causal chain that delusion is claimed to be eliminated.

It is not enough to learn these twelve links once, or to even memorize them, since they can be conveniently forgotten, especially in times when we need them the most, such as during powerful emotional experiences or when we are distracted. These causal links should be contemplated frequently and sincerely, over a lifetime. This frequent reflection forces us to do something we are not usually inclined, or well-positioned, to do: consider how our delusions may be conditioning our perceptions, desires, aversions, and judgments. The hope is that we can create a habit of thinking that fully recognizes the causal relationship between our delusional assumptions and our (and others') suffering and, by doing so, we begin to deconstruct and eventually eliminate our delusion.

There is, I think, deep insight in the claim that delusion is maintained through a failure or refusal to recognize certain cause and effect relationships. We could accurately characterize white delusion as a failure or refusal to recognize certain racially significant causal relationships. In a recent study by sociologist Jennifer Mueller, 105 college students were asked to write analyses of their family's intergenerational wealth transmission using concepts they had been taught in class, such as the racial wealth gap, historically discriminatory asset-building policies, and racial disparities across different kinds of capital.[25] That is, students were asked to write an explicitly *racial* history of their family's wealth transmission. In her analysis of their responses, Mueller identified four "epistemic maneuvers" of white racial delusion. The first, evasion, is when a student completely fails to make race-based understandings of her data. Students who used this maneuver would present their data but avoid using any terms relating to race or racism.[26] This was striking, especially considering that the assignment (which was graded) explicitly required a race-based analysis.

The second epistemic maneuver is "willful colorblindness," which "introduced alternative factors to neutralize evidence of white privilege."[27] For example, one student, who in her paper had acknowledged the benefits her white family received from discriminatory housing policies, ultimately rejected the claim that white privilege contributed to her family's wealth because her family were immigrants who did not know English. She used an alternative factor—lack of English proficiency—to neutralize the evidence of white privilege. Tautological ignorance, the third epistemic maneuver, "produces racially conscious logic, but embeds morally laden assumptions of whites' sincere, passive ignorance."[28] Students who used this maneuver would admit their family's race-based privilege but insist that their family members and ancestors could not have possibly known the moral implications of the policies from which they benefited. The final epistemic maneuver is mystification, which produces "racially conscious logic, but embed(s) doubt and mystery about logically related solutions."[29] After producing cogent racial analyses, students who used this maneuver would then claim that they did not know what to do about racism, that it was too embedded in society to change, and doubted that there were any practical solutions whatsoever.

These epistemic maneuvers show a deep unwillingness on the part of whites to recognize and take seriously the causal connections between their own (and their families') privilege (as assessed in terms of wealth in Mueller's study) and the racial injustice suffered by people of color. Mueller's analysis shows some of the common places in which logical reasoning about causation can break down: we can refuse to acknowledge any causal connection at all (evasion) or we can acknowledge some causal connections but fail to continue, by either refusing to apply what we know (willful colorblindness), applying what we know but refusing to acknowledge the implications of it (tautological colorblindness), or applying what we know and recognizing its implications but failing to admit our own agency in altering the causal chain in the future (mystification).

The epistemic maneuvers that maintain white ignorance are cognitive errors, often surprisingly obvious ones. In this sense, they are similar in kind to the errors that Buddhist ethicists are keen to point out: my refusal to acknowledge that my habit of prioritizing myself over others contributes to my suffering is, at least in part, a cognitive error; it is failure to fully apply consistent reasoning to my situation. Similarly, white delusion, as Mueller's study illustrates, is a deep cognitive error, a failure to be fully rational and to apply knowledge in a consistent, logical way. So, although it is not the case that white delusion (or general delusion, for that matter) can be eradicated by simple exposure to knowledge, Mueller's analysis suggests that interventions in critical reasoning about the *specific causal relationships* between white privilege and racial injustice could be helpful in addressing white delusion. To borrow from Buddhist philosophers, such reasoning about specific causal relations must be sincerely and repeatedly practiced in order to be remembered and applied in the right way at the right time. This is because the cognitive errors that are characteristic of white delusion are not so much failures to know something—recall that many of Mueller's students were able to present all sorts of relevant facts and theories about racial injustice—but about failures to make the right (that is, logical) connections, to apply knowledge in an appropriate way, and to make rational predictions about the future based on that knowledge.

CULTIVATING EQUANIMITY

Even though white delusion is characterized by serious cognitive errors and faulty logic, it is not sufficient to describe it only as a problem in reasoning, since this obscures the large role that emotional habits, desires, and aversions play in maintaining this delusion. Recall Baldwin's description of white delusion as not simply incomprehension, but *hostile* incomprehension.[30] Indeed, these emotional habits, such as hostility, white fear and white fragility, can explain *why* white people fail to be rational about issues regarding race.[31] Because of our (white people's) emotional dysfunction, we cannot face the facts of our racial reality.

Buddhist moral psychology is a particularly helpful resource for understanding the moral deficiency of being emotionally unable to face reality. Along with more high-profile moral qualities, such as love and compassion, Buddhist ethicists also prioritize equanimity, the freedom from self-centered craving and aversion, which, on this view, are the main psychological mechanisms that keep us from facing reality. Craving, the sense of "I want" and "I must have," and aversion, the sense of "I don't want" and "I can't possibly tolerate," are fundamental constituents of a variety of dysfunctional mental and emotional states. According to Buddhist moral psychology, most of us simply react to events on the basis of craving and aversion: we try to obtain the things we think we want and to avoid those we do not want. The person with equanimity does not react in this way. By having freedom from her cravings and aversions, she is able to live her life with greater agency since she has the freedom to choose more virtuous ways of engaging with others. Her actions are not determined by her immediate feelings of what she needs and what she cannot tolerate. For this reason, she is able to act instead of react.

The fourteenth-century Tibetan philosopher Longchenpa claims that equanimity is an antidote to delusion.[32] This is especially clear in the case of white delusion. White delusion is a deep failure of whites to reason well or even think clearly about issues involving race. But this failure is (or is due to) a *refusal* to engage, which itself is due to an emotional immaturity that is characteristic of whiteness. There are predictable sets of cravings and aversions that are part of white psychology within the context of white supremacy. These cravings and aversions have been well theorized in terms of racial stereotypes, raced-based implicit bias, and the phenomenology of whiteness. For example, George Yancy's famous example of the white woman's hostility toward a Black man in an elevator highlights a predictable set of aversion narratives that arise in the context of white womanhood: "I'm not safe," "He'll attack me," "He's dangerous," "I'm vulnerable," "I've got to get out of here," etc.[33] Without equanimity, one simply reacts on the basis of these deep and, often, visceral aversions, for instance by clutching one's purse, averting one's eyes, moving as far away as possible, and so forth. This reaction not only maintains one's racial delusion—that Black men are intrinsically dangerous—but it also has moral consequences since it results in racially hostile actions that impact, in this case, Black men.

The person with equanimity, however, has the ability to act in better ways, to not simply react on the basis of her deluded aversion narratives. Although it may be the case that a person with perfected equanimity would simply lack such cravings and aversions, it is not necessary that cravings and aversions never arise. For my purposes here, the important thing is that the person cultivating equanimity does not take her cravings and aversions so seriously; she does not take them as the unquestioned reality on which she bases her thoughts and actions. This allows the person with equanimity to break the otherwise predictable causal chain between "I feel fear" to "I fear you" to "You are dangerous" to hostile action against you, however subtle. Equanimity is the ability to notice that I feel fear in this situation without automatically believing that this situation is indeed dangerous or that any defensive or hostile action is justified. In fact, as I have argued elsewhere, someone with equanimity is more likely to engage in loving and compassionate ways because she has the freedom to do so.[34] Without at least some degree of equanimity, we lack the ability to engage lovingly in aversive situations.

In Buddhist ethics, one *trains* in equanimity; it is too important as a moral skill to be left up to chance or natural tendencies. In general, we cultivate equanimity through practices that encourage us to not take as fact what our initial cravings and aversions seem to be telling us. For example, simply sitting in meditation can be a lesson in equanimity, since most of us, especially beginners, feel all sorts of cravings and aversions, such as "This is boring" or "I hate this" (aversion) and "I want this to end" or "I want to get up" (craving), that we learn to not take seriously. This is good practice for situations when the stakes are higher: if we have enough (daily, regular) practice in not automatically believing that when we feel something is hateful it actually is, eventually we will be able to apply this to more morally meaningful settings. Through meditation, I develop a new habit with regard to how I relate to my craving and aversion, a habit that, hopefully, will extend beyond the meditation seat.

There are other equanimity practices that are more explicitly moral. Many Tibetan Buddhist equanimity practices are focused on developing some freedom with regard to craving and aversion in the context of human relationships. We train in overcoming "us vs. them" (or "friend vs. enemy") mental habits, by forcing ourselves to consider ways in which our "friends" may hurt us and "enemies" may help us.[35] It is difficult to consider these ugly or nonintuitive possibilities, but, when we do, it becomes clear that there is truth to the claim that our loved ones, at least in certain situations, may be the ones that harm us the most and that people who we cannot stand, our "enemies," can actually help us in profound ways. For example, loved ones—out of their love for us—may shelter us from harsh realities that, in the end, stunts our moral and emotional growth. And our enemies do sometimes encourage our moral and emotional growth if only because they provide the opportunity to develop virtue. As the eighth-century Buddhist moral philosopher Śāntideva famously remarked, "a person in need who turns up at a suitable time is not a hindrance to generosity" but rather a necessary condition for the virtue of generosity.[36]

In the context of race relations, the Buddhist advice to seriously challenge our assumptions about "friends" and "enemies" seems especially apt, at least for white people. White people may, for example, feel "comfortable" around other white people and "uncomfortable" around people of color and use this as an excuse not to engage with or listen to non-white people. An equanimity practice could help in this situation since such a practice would habituate one to challenge the associations between "I feel comfortable" and "This is good for me" on the one hand, and "I feel uncomfortable" and "This is bad for me" on the other. Whiteness may *feel* comfortable for many white people, but whiteness is bad for white people (and everyone else). Having one's moral faults and delusions reinforced by people with the same faults and delusions is not helpful; having one's faults and delusions exposed by people who do not share them and can see them for what they are is helpful, though, of course, often painful. Yancy calls his appeal to white Americans to confront their/our own racism a "love letter" and a "gift" to white people.[37] Buddhist philosophers, I think, would have to agree.

In general, developing equanimity in the context of whiteness is difficult because it requires us to face our racist cravings and aversions, to recognize them for what they are and not react on the basis of them. In this way, equanimity, perhaps especially in the context of whiteness, is more about not-doing than doing; it is about learning how to *refrain* from reactive urges by getting some perspective on our cravings and aversions. This means that white people who cultivate equanimity as an antidote to white delusion will have to tackle their own racism by recognizing it and coming to understand its scope and force in one's own moral psychology without immediately trying to "fix" it, since this urge to fix our racism (or hide from it) is itself another craving to be observed rather than immediately acted on. White craving for moral purity should itself be held at a distance. Equanimity, then, has the potential for increasing self-knowledge for white people—understanding our own whiteness—since it is what allows one to remain in the space of the discomfort of recognizing one's own racism. George Yancy has argued that white people need to "to tarry, to linger, in the ways in which you perpetuate a racist society, the ways in which you are racist."[38] Equanimity is the underlying moral skill that allows one to tarry, rather than react on the basis of racist cravings and aversions or try to hide from them, which is another kind of reactive habit. This may sound like a small thing—simply refraining from acting on craving and aversion and waiting—but it could, literally, be a matter of life or death. As Yancy notes, had George Zimmerman had the equanimity necessary to tarry, Trayvon Martin would probably still be alive.[39]

CONCLUSION

Mills claims that white delusion "is best thought of as a cognitive tendency—an inclination, a doxastic disposition—which is not insuperable."[40] Like avidyā, it is tenacious, but we are not stuck with it. White people can be more or less delusional, and we can become more deluded or less deluded over the course of our lives depending on our choices and habits. As Yancy has noted, the ability to recognize white racism and white delusion is not, in principle, impossible for white people. People of color can "communicate the shared experiences, conceptual frameworks, and background assumptions to [whites] if they are open to instruction and willing to take the time to listen."[41] I do not pretend to have offered ways to liberate white people from our white delusion, but I hope, with the help of Buddhist analyses of avidyā, that I have begun to locate some possible ways out of white delusion. Whether we who are afflicted by white delusion take these ways out is up to us.

NOTES

1. Alicia Gallegos, "AAMC Report Shows Decline of Black Males in Medicine," *AAMC News*, September 27, 2016, https://news.aamc.org/diversity/article/decline-black-males-medicine/.

2. Charles Mills, "White Ignorance," in *Race and Epistemologies of Ignorance*, eds. Shannon Sullivan and Nancy Tuana (Albany, NY: SUNY Press, 2007), 11–38, 16.

3. George Yancy, "Dear White America," *New York Times*, December 24, 2015, https://opinionator.blogs.nytimes.com/2015/12/24/dear-white-america/.

4. Sharon Sullivan and Nancy Tuana, "Introduction," in *Race and Epistemologies of Ignorance*, eds. Shannon Sullivan and Nancy Tuana (Albany, NY: SUNY Press, 2007), 1–10, 1.

5. Charles Mills, *Black Rights/White Wrongs: A Critique of Racial Liberalism* (New York: Oxford University Press, 2017), 49.

6. Mills, "White Ignorance," 6.

7. Elizabeth Spelman, "Managing Ignorance," in *Race and Epistemologies of Ignorance*, eds. Shannon Sullivan and Nancy Tuana (Albany, NY: SUNY Press, 2007), 119–134, 120.

8. Mills, "White Ignorance," 28.

9. Santa Fe New Mexican, "Santa Fe Public Schools Gives Students Option of Skipping Fiesta," *Santa Fe New Mexican*, August 30, 2017, http://www.santafene wmexican.com/news/education/santa-fe-public-schools-gives-students-option-of-skipping-fiesta/article_6d01e403-77bd-5db8-abbf-c48b5ae8a46a.html.

10. UNM Newsroom, "University Seal Remains the Same," *UNM Newsroom*, November 15, 2016, https://news.unm.edu/news/university-seal-remains-the-same.

11. James Baldwin, *The Price of the Ticket: Collected Non Fiction, 1948–1985* (New York: St. Martin's Press, 1985), 536.

12. Bimal Matilal, "Ignorance or Misconception? A Note on Avidyā in Buddhism," in *Buddhist Studies in Honor of Walpola Rahula*, ed. Somaratna Balasoorriya (London: Roundwood Press, 1980), 154–164.

13. Vasubhandu, *Abhidharmakośabhāṣyam* (vol. II), trans. Louis de La Vallée Poussin (French) and Leo M. Pruden (Asian Humanities Press, 1991), 419–420.

14. Alex Wayman, "The Meaning of Unwisdom (Avidyā)," *Philosophy East and West* 7, no. 1 (1957): 21–25.

15. See also David Burton, "Knowledge and Liberation: Philosophical Reflections on a Buddhist Conundrum," *Philosophy East and West* 52, no. 3 (2002): 326–345.

16. As Matilal noted, "If we can call nirvāṇa salvation, then avidyā becomes essentially a soteriological concept. It stands for the opposite of that ultimate knowledge or insight which brings about the goal of nirvāṇa, final freedom from suffering." Matilal, "Ignorance or Misconception?" 162.

17. Mills, "White Ignorance," 22.

18. Matilal, "Ignorance or Misconception?" 162.

19. Linda Alcoff, "Epistemologies of Ignorance: Three Types," in *Race and Epistemologies of Ignorance*, eds. Shannon Sullivan and Nancy Tuana (Albany, NY: SUNY Press, 2007), 39–58, 49.

20. Sharon Sullivan, *Race and Epistemologies of Ignorance*, eds. Shannon Sullivan and Nancy Tuana (Albany, NY: SUNY Press, 2007), 153–172, 154.

21. Charles Mills, *The Racial Contract* (Ithaca: Cornell University Press, 1997), 18.

22. Burton, "Knowledge and Liberation."

23. For example, see Gampopa, *The Jewel Ornament of Liberation: The Wish-fulfilling Gem of the Noble Teachings*, trans. Khenpo Konchog Gyaltsen Rinpoche (Boston: Snow Lion, 1998), 225–228.

24. Brian Keith Payne, "Prejudice and Perception: The Role of Automatic and Controlled Processes in Misperceiving a Weapon," *Journal of Personality and Social Psychology* 81, no. 2 (2001): 181–192.

25. Jennifer Mueller, "Producing Colorblindness: Everyday Mechanisms of White Ignorance," *Social Problems* 64, no. 2 (2017): 219–238.

26. Ibid., 225–227.

27. Ibid., 225, 227–229.

28. Ibid., 225, 229–231.

29. Ibid., 225, 231–233.

30. Baldwin, *The Price of the Ticket*, 536.

31. Robin DiAngelo, "White Fragility," *The International Journal of Critical Pedagogy* 3, no. 3 (2011): 54–70.

32. Longchenpa, *Finding Rest in the Nature of the Mind: Trilogy of Rest*, trans. Padmakara Translation Group (Boulder, CO: Shambhala Publications, 2017), 82.

33. See George Yancy, *Black Bodies, White Gazes: The Continuing Significance of Race* (Lanham, MD: Rowman & Littlefield, 2008), Chapter 1.

34. Emily McRae, "Equanimity in Relationship: Responding to Moral Ugliness," in *A Mirror is for Reflection: Understanding Buddhist Ethics*, ed. Jake Davis (New York: Oxford University Press, 2017), 336–351.

35. See, for example, Patrul Rinpoche, *Words of My Perfect Teacher* (Lanham, MD: Altamira Press, 1994), 196–198.

36. Śāntideva, *The Bodhicaryāvatāra*, trans. Kate Crosby and Andrew Skilton (New York: Oxford University Press, 1998), 59.

37. Yancy, "Dear White America."

38. Ibid.

39. George Yancy, "Interpretive Profiles on Charles Johnson's Reflections on Trayvon Martin: A Dialogue between George Yancy, E. Ethelbert Miller, and Charles Johnson," *Western Journal of Black Studies* 38, no. 1 (2014): 1–12, 7.

40. Mills, "White Ignorance," 23.

41. Yancy, *Black Bodies, White Gazes*.

Chapter 4

Whiteness and the Construction of Buddhist Philosophy in Meiji Japan

Leah Kalmanson

Is philosophy "white"? Peter K. J. Park has argued that the disciplinary identity of philosophy, as we understand it today, was indelibly marked by the emerging pseudo-science of race in eighteenth- and nineteenth-century Europe. Whereas histories of philosophy once posited a variety of possible origins (Egypt, India, or Mesopotamia, for example), the eighteenth century saw the rise of a clear preference for naming the Athenians as the unique originators of philosophy, along with the development of a racial classification system that for the first time allowed the Greeks to be called "white." Indeed, the architects of contemporary philosophical historiography, Immanuel Kant and G. W. F. Hegel, both famously promoted the idea that philosophy is the special province of white people. At least Kant and Hegel, then, would affirm that philosophy is and must be white.

When the Japanese first encountered the word "philosophy" in the Meiji period (1868–1912), this post-Kantian, racialized version of the discipline was already firmly entrenched in Western academies and academic discourses. The Meiji period is also when the Japanese first became aware of their rank according to European theories of race, which placed "yellow" somewhere below "white" and above "black." In what follows, I look at how certain Japanese scholars resisted this racial hierarchy by deploying characteristically "white" categories, such as philosophy, in ways that aimed to subvert the Eurocentric worldview. One casualty of this subversive move, however, was the intentional parsing of Buddhism into its "philosophical," "religious," and "superstitious" aspects. As the scholar Jason Ānanda Joseph-son-Storm[1] has discussed at length (2006, 2012), all three terms—*tetusgaku* 哲学 (philosophy), *shūkyō* 宗教 (religion), and *meishin* 迷信 (superstition)— were coined around the same time as translations of Western concepts. The resulting construction of "Buddhist philosophy" both inside and outside of

Japan has influenced the reception of Buddhism in America in academic as well as practitioner contexts.[2] The present study (1) examines the historical conditions surrounding the operation of whiteness as a hidden norm in the formation of academic Buddhist philosophy during the Meiji period and (2) foregrounds those aspects of the dharma that do not register readily on the model of Buddhist philosophy that this time period produced.

PHILOSOPHY AND WHITENESS

Park's recent work on racism and philosophy is particularly relevant when considering the reception of "philosophy" in the Meiji period.[3] As Park asks, "Was Kant a racial thinker? According to [Robert] Bernasconi, he was one of the founding theorists of race. Was Kant a racist? A first-time reader of 'Observations on the Feeling of the Beautiful and the Sublime' may well be shocked and disturbed by Kant's racial stereotypes and racist remarks."[4] Park elaborates that these statements include Kant's conviction that no African person has ever made any artistic or scientific achievements, and that black skin color is proof of stupidity. According to the theories of racial essentialism that inform Kant's anthropology, the relative achievements of the different races reflect their respective abilities and limitations: "Kant taught that the Hindu race did not develop philosophy because they did not have that capacity. In his anthropology lectures, Kant explicitly attributes this lack *not* to the form of government or customs of the Asians, but to their descent (*Abstammung*). Montesquieu had famously argued that the form of government or customs of a people determined its character. Kant taught his students that it was the other way around. It is race that determines the form of government and the customs."[5] In other words, for Kant, "white" Europeans are the only people who developed philosophy, whereas "black," "yellow," and "red" people did not, because of their inherent characteristics as members of different races.

Moreover, as Park's work makes clear, philosophers today should not assume that Kant was simply a victim of his time, that is, that he absorbed a racist worldview from prevailing currents. To the contrary, theories of race were hotly debated, being divided among a range of positions, some quite egalitarian. From out of this spectrum, Kant chose to advance a contentious theory of racial essentialism, promoted by three specific figures: the historians Christoph Meiners and Wilhelm Gottfried Tenneman, and the physiologist Friedrich Tiedemann. The core thesis of Park's book is that Kant's contentious view on racial essentialism undergirds his work on the history of philosophy—it informs Kant's arguments for the exclusion of African and Asian sources from the canon and his insistence that philosophy flowered spontaneously among the Greeks with no influence from the non-Greek-speaking world. Again, as Park makes clear, Kant was here advancing what we might call a fringe view, which was not representative of the diversity of opinions on philosophy's history available to Kant at that time.

For example, many histories, both before and after Kant, did not posit the Greeks as the originators of philosophy, but instead contextualized the influence of the Athenians in a variety of other ways. By my count, Park reviews over twenty histories of philosophy written between the 1500s and 1800s, which either attribute the origins of philosophy to a non-Greek source (such as Egypt or India), or which survey multiple philosophical traditions originating in different areas, including (to name just a few) Persia, Ethiopia, China, and, in one case, Canada (by which the author meant the indigenous peoples of the Americas).[6] As Park says, "That philosophy was exclusively of Greek origin was an opinion held by only three published historians of philosophy in the eighteenth century"[7]—namely, the same Meiners, Tiedemann, and Tenneman whose theories so influenced Kant's anthropology. So, Park's research allows us to make the claim, fairly confidently, that the Greeks enjoy the status they have today largely because they were appropriated in the late 1700s into the racist narrative of world-historical development promoted by a small subset of scholars at the time. This fringe view went on to influence the Kantian School, and then Hegel, and from there to assume a dominant position within academia. Today, philosophy departments worldwide are the inheritors of a historical narrative and a textual canon shaped by the dubious racial theories of Kant and Hegel.

THE AMBIGUOUS CLAIMS OF "WHITENESS" IN JAPAN

Kant's whitewashed story of philosophy reached Japan in the Meiji period, around the same time that the Japanese first became aware of their "inferior rank" according to European racial theories.[8] European narratives at the time identified "whiteness" with a number of related, but sometimes conflicting, markers of so-called civilization, such as philosophy, science, and religion, which were all seen as the unique achievements of whites. Selectively deploying these markers to classify other cultures allowed for multiple avenues toward the same end, that is, the delegitimization of nonwhite peoples. Although the Japanese did not at first have the full picture regarding race, religion, and European imperialism, they had long been aware that European merchants and missionaries opened the gateway to military takeover, a pattern they had observed as colonial powers spread throughout Asia and the Pacific. As Josephson-Storm recounts, the scholar Miura Baien wrote in 1784:

I have heard that when the Westerners want to take a country, they consider the use of arms to be simplistic. When they want to take a country, they first use gold, silver, grain and silk . . . they use tricks to confuse the senses of the people and finally employing the doctrine of the Lord of Heaven and the three worlds [i.e., the afterlife] they move the hearts of the people. . . . Seeing that they have drawn the people to their own will, they complete the job simply by bringing in an army which under such conditions cannot fail to succeed in one stroke.[9]

In Miura's assessment, religion is simply a ploy designed to render people more susceptible to military overthrow. Although Europeans at the time might not have taken such a cynical view of this process, nonetheless they did indeed invoke religion to justify colonization, or to cast colonial takeover as a civilizing and evangelizing mission. In other words, because religion functions as a marker of (white) civilization, the accusation of lacking religion is one strategy for delegitimizing nonwhite people and classifying them as candidates for colonization.

That said, as Josephson-Storm has demonstrated, "religion" travels across cultures not alone but as a part of a larger conceptual apparatus. In his essay "The Superstition, Secularism, and Religion Trinary" (2017),[10] he argues against a simplistic opposition between religion and the secular. Rather, the under-theorized category of "superstition" serves to police the boundaries of both religion "proper" and the assumed rational character of secular, scientific inquiry. Looking back at his 2006 essay on Buddhist scholar Inoue Enryō (1858–1919), "When Buddhism Became a 'Religion,'" we see the same normative operation of "superstition" in Inoue's parsing of Buddhism into its religious and philosophical aspects. This gives us perspective on how different and sometimes competing markers of white civilization can be selectively deployed as the context demands. Inoue's work, in particular, foregrounds one such point of tension: Is "religion" aligned with reason or with superstition? When deployed as an excuse for colonization, the rational and universal aspects of religion are emphasized. From this perspective, true religion (i.e., Christianity), as opposed to the superstitions of "paganism," is a friend to science, progress, and other Enlightenment values. However, as the fraught history of the Enlightenment in Europe shows, Christianity itself was often cast as the superstitious element in contrast to the rationality of science, philosophy, and secular humanism. For example, this accounts for Hegel's claim, in *Lectures on the History of Philosophy*, that what "we call Eastern Philosophy is more properly the religious mode of thought. . . ."[11] Here, following the general trajectory of whiteness and philosophy initiated by Kant, for Hegel the religious mode of thought (even Christian religious thought) takes second place in relation to the "pure reason" of philosophy. Hence, thanks to the flexible deployment of these civilizational markers, even if some nonwhite people can be said to have religion "proper," they can nonetheless still be delegitimized for lacking philosophy.

Japanese scholars and officials responded in a variety of ways to the combined threats of European military power and the dangerously ambiguous conceptual apparatus of Josephson-Storm's "superstition, secularism, and religion trinary." Some were eager to dismiss Buddhism as backward and to counter colonial powers through Japan's own military and technological prowess. Others, like Inoue, sought to demonstrate the status of Buddhism as a major world religion.[12] In many ways, Inoue's work manages to beat Christianity at its own game, as it were—elevating Buddhism as *the* paradigmatic case of a rational, science-friendly, and humanistic religion. To contextualize Inoue's work and its implications for Buddhist philosophy, we look next at the reception and translation of the terms "religion" and "philosophy" in the Meiji period.

"RELIGION" IN JAPANESE DISCOURSE

In the European context, the word "religion" derives from a Latin root (*religio*), whose precise meaning is unclear; although, as Josephson-Storm says, "Regardless of its origins, in pre-Christian Roman usage, *religio* generally referred to a prohibition or an obligation."[13] By the fifteenth century, *religio* was used in Catholicism to refer to "the performance of ritual obligations, especially . . . to describe a state of life bound by monastic vows"; and, accordingly, "the noun 'the religious' referred to monks and nuns."[14] Strictly speaking, these terms are specific to European intellectual history; or, as Robert Ford Campany says, "Discourse about religions is rooted in Western language communities and in the history of Western cultures . . . . To speak of 'religions' is to demarcate things in ways that are not inevitable or immutable but, rather, are contingent on the shape of Western history, thought, and institutions. Other cultures may, and do, lack closely equivalent demarcations."[15] By the eighteenth and nineteenth centuries, European scholars had developed a specific way to "demarcate things" with a hierarchical schema that tended to include Christianity as the one true religion, Judaism and Islam as "almost Christian, or at least would-be Christians,"[16] and a multitude of "idolators" or "heathens" who did not possess true religion at all.

Prior to colonial contact, the Japanese demarcated things differently. As was evident when Japanese scholars first encountered European cultures and traditions, the Japanese language had no precise equivalents for terms such as "philosophy," "religion," or "science." In other words, these were not the generic categories by which the Japanese would attempt to understand and classify foreign traditions. To the contrary, Japanese discourses were shaped by at least three major categories, including the Chinese "scholarly lineage" (Ch. *rujia* 儒家), the South Asian *dharma* ("teachings") of Śakyamuni Buddha, and, later, the Tokugawa-period "ancient studies" (*kogaku* 古学) or "national learning" (*kokugaku* 国学) movements. China's scholarly lineage or "Ruism" (commonly called "Confucianism"[17]) is a diverse tradition that encompasses studies of ethics, politics, and statecraft; empirical investigations of the natural world (especially astronomy); training in music, poetry, and gymnastics; the maintenance of official court rites and ceremonies; and institutions of family and civic ancestor worship. The *buddha-dharma* (*buppō* 佛法), in comparison, is concerned with existential questions and the conditions of future rebirths; it is associated with monasticism, on the one hand, and lay practices for generating merit, on the other. Like Ruism, the dharma comprises diverse schools of thought marked by, at times, radical disagreements over how to interpret and practice basic Buddhist principles.

When the Japanese first encountered Jesuit priests in the mid-1500s, they classified Christianity as a deviant form of dharma and promptly banned it.[18] Some level of this ban remained in place until the Perry Expedition's forceful opening of the Japanese economy to international trade in the mid-1800s, when Japan was compelled to sign a number of treaties with American and European governments, all of which included clauses requiring Japan to acknowledge "freedom of religion." As Josephson says,

> When Japanese translators first encountered the English word "religion" in the international trade treatises of the late 1850s, they were perplexed and had difficulty finding the proper corresponding term in Japanese. There was no indigenous word that referred to something as broad as "religion" nor a systematic way to distinguish between "religions" as members of a larger generic category. Instead, words such as *shū* 宗, *kyō* 教, *ha* 派 or *shūmon* 宗門 were used interchangeably to designate Christianity, divisions within Buddhism, distinctions between Daoism and Confucianism, and different strands of intellectual thought (such as different schools of painting or mathematics) . . . . Ultimately, some translators chose to render "religion" as "sect law" (*shūhō* 宗法) while others settled on "sect doctrine" (*shūshi* 宗旨). Regardless, both terms were already situated in their own system of meaning, referring generally to a preexisting sub-categorization of Buddhist schools.[19]

The word that eventually sticks, and which we use today, is *shūkyō* (宗教); like the other words Josephson cites above, it has a notably Buddhist flavor. Specifically, *shūkyō* was an obscure compound from Chinese sources that referred to doctrinal differences between Buddhist sects. This is perhaps a small victory in the colonial context in which these translations were taking place, because the Buddhist-flavored terminology does not fully capitulate to foreign categories; that is, the use of *shūkyō* retains the impression that Christianity, and religion at large, can be categorized in Buddhist terms. Or, as Josephson says: "This representation reverses contemporary English usage of the term 'religion,' rendering it not universal, but instead a specific interpretation of the Buddhist dharma (*buppō* 仏法) or Buddhist way (*butsudō* 仏道). Put differently, 'religion' was Buddhism (or a subset of Buddhism)."[20]

At this point, however, I suggest that this way of conceiving of the relation between "religion" and "Buddhist dharma" is not a clear-cut reversal of contemporary usage.[21] In other words, there is a sense in which the usage of dharma, like religion, is universal. If we can speak about *dharmakāya* as reality itself, or if we can say that all things have buddha-nature, then we can certainly use dharma as a generic category that applies cross-culturally. This universalizing trajectory of the dharma is precisely what allows for Inoue's subversion of Eurocentric discourses in the Meiji period.

INOUE AND THE CONSTRUCTION
OF BUDDHIST PHILOSOPHY

By the time Inoue was researching and writing about Buddhism in Japan, the terms *shūkyō* 宗教 (religion), *tetsugaku* 哲学 (philosophy) and *meishin* 迷信 (superstition) were all recent entries in the Japanese lexicon coined in the process of translating an influx of Western materials in the Meiji period. Just as *shūkyō* has Buddhist connotations, the term *tetsugaku* "echoes older Confucian words such as *tetsujin* or sage."[22] That said, Nishi Amane, who coined the term *tetsugaku* in 1874, was clear that his intention was to translate the name of a Western discipline that had no precise analogue in either Chinese or Japanese traditions.[23] He defines philosophy according to Western accounts influential in his time, describing it as the love of wisdom, a discourse on first principles, and the unitary foundation underlying the various sciences.[24]

In Inoue's hands, *tetsugaku* takes on further Kantian associations. In his 1886 work *An Evening of Philosophical Conversation*, he imagines a group of travelers on a boat discussing the meaning of philosophy: "This *tetsugaku* is a new kind of discipline that has come from the West, but just what sort of discipline is it?" Inoue answers, "There are . . . several disciplines that have to do with matters of the mind: psychology, logic, ethics, and pure *tetsugaku*. People are more or less familiar with psychology, logic, and so forth, but when it comes to pure *tetsugaku* people haven't the slightest idea of what it is. In short, pure *tetsugaku*, as the study of the pure principles of *tetsugaku*, must be called the study that inquires into the axioms of the truth and the foundation of the disciplines."[25]

Here Inoue's notion of "pure *tetsugaku*" (*junsei tetsugaku* 純正哲学) recalls Kantian terms "pure philosophy" (*reine Philosophie*) and pure reason (*reinen Vernunft*),[26] but let us consider the implications of being "pure" (*rein*) in Kant's work. As Park discusses, Kant was highly critical of various histories of philosophy that related anecdotes of philosophers' lives or that paid any attention whatsoever to cultural or historical context. In that sense, the "history" of philosophy is unlike other histories, in that it needs no empirical grounding in the actual record of events. Or, as Kant says, the history of philosophy is "so special a kind that nothing of what is recounted therein could happen without knowing beforehand what should have happened and therefore also what can happen."[27] In other words, philosophy is premised on a collection of a priori truths, and so the actual unfolding of the development of the discipline over time is of no consequence. To borrow Inoue's words, the history of philosophy is "the study of the pure principles of *tetsugaku*."

But, Kant's motive in rejecting earlier histories of philosophy is not simply in the service of promoting his particular understanding of truth—it is also in the service of promoting his racial essentialism. As already noted, Kant believed that only the people of the white race, thanks to their inherent "superior" racial characteristics, were capable of thinking at the level of a priori truth and pure reason. Therefore, histories of philosophy that spilled ink on the philosophies of non-Western cultures were problematic, according to Kant, not just because they strayed from a priori reasoning, but because they gave the mistaken impression that nonwhite people have philosophy in the first place. In other words, the "purity" of reason serves both a philosophical and a racial agenda.

Can we neatly sever Kant's philosophical project from the racial essentialism that informed it? That is a question for another essay. I only note here that Inoue certainly did not intend to promote a racialized notion of *tetsugaku* when he adopted the Kantian language of "pure philosophy." Nonetheless, in Meiji Japan, we find purity as a marker of whiteness operating far outside its indigenous European context, helping Inoue to parse Buddhism into its superstitious, religious, and philosophical aspects. In this, we see Inoue disregard any definition of Buddhism informed by empirical evidence of what Buddhists actually do and say, defining true Buddhism instead in terms of the pure experience of the "absolute" (*zettai* 絶対).

Seeking to defend Buddhism against those who would dismiss it as mere superstition, Inoue traveled the country documenting regional Japanese beliefs about ghosts, monsters, and other supernatural entities. His ultimate aim was the eradication of these so-called superstitious practices from Buddhism to whittle the tradition down to what he saw as its fundamental core. Josephson-Storm describes Inoue's late work *Superstition and Religion* (*Meishin to shūkyō*) as the application of a "metaphorical structure in which 'superstitions' are stripped away from Buddhism. Layer by layer, rituals, prayers, and invisible beings are lost until most of what is recognizably Buddhist has vanished. It is only here that 'religion' is encountered and defined largely as a remainder—that which is not superstition."[28] This remainder— the experience of the "absolute"—is not *irrational* but *trans-rational*, in that it transcends human reason.[29]

On the one hand, Inoue associates this idea of the "absolute" with the existing concept of Buddhist "thusness" (Sk. *tathātā*, Jp. *shin'nyo*真如); on the other, his understanding of *zettai* reflects the whitewashed version of philosophy he inherited from Western discourses. As Josephson-Storm says,

> Inoue attributes the absolute to Western philosophy, referring to the Hegelian absolute, although parallels with Kant's thing-in-itself are also made. As Inoue states explicitly, both Buddhism and nineteenth-century philosophy have the same goal: to approach the absolute. He agrees that they do this differently, and he thinks that Buddhism is better at it than other religions such as Christianity, but by and large the focus for both religion and philosophy is nothing more than the absolute.[30]

Here we see the subversion of Eurocentrism driving Inoue's work on Buddhism. In his reformulation of the relations between religion, philosophy, and superstition, both Western philosophies and Western religions are found to be lacking. Christianity, it turns out, is not philosophical enough—it fails to apprehend the true nature of reality as expressed in Buddhist thusness. Western philosophy, however, is *too* philosophical—that is, it is constrained by the arid, lifeless, and ultimately trivial exercise of pure reason, and therefore it fails to achieve direct experience of the trans-rational absolute. In contrast to both, Japanese Buddhism stands out as the ideal combination of philosophy and religion, and "the ideal Buddhist is like [Inoue], a Buddhist philosopher contemplating the limits of knowledge."[31]

WHITENESS AND BUDDHIST PHILOSOPHY TODAY

Josephson-Storm refers to this as Inoue's "pared-down Buddhism," commenting, "It should be apparent that Inoue has radically re-conceptualized Buddhism."[32] Yet this would not necessarily be apparent to many Americans, including both American Buddhist practitioners and philosophers, who have inherited precisely the "pared-down Buddhism" that Inoue helped to promote. Inoue's emphasis on the pure, direct experience of "suchness" reappears in the work of D. T. Suzuki, for example, whose writings introduced many Americans to Zen. T. Griffith Foulk asserts, "Westerners interested in

Zen . . . are often attracted to the 'practices' of seated meditation (zazen), manual labor, and doctrinal study but uncomfortable with the 'rituals' of offerings, prayers, and prostrations made before images on altars."[33] These latter activities speak to Buddhism's rich and robust engagement with unseen forces, including Buddhas and bodhisattvas living in heavenly realms; the spirits of ancestors reborn in non-earthly places; and the circulation of merit (*kudoku* 功徳), which connects the human and nonhuman realms in a bustling karmic economy. Regarding the tendency to downplay these aspects of Buddhism in American Zen, Foulk observes, "The underlying assumption is that 'merit' is a magical, superstitious, or at best symbolic kind of thing that no rational, scientifically-minded person could take seriously as actually existing."[34] Inoue would surely agree.

However, this takes our discussion into complicated terrain. On the one hand, I do not wish to say that countering the "whiteness" of Buddhism somehow means a return to "magic." That would only affirm, through a backhanded compliment, that rational thought *is* the province of white people, whereas nonwhite people specialize in mysticism, magic, and myth. On the other hand, I do wish to suggest that we recover a sense of dharma, and dharma-philosophy, that is not fractured according to the philosophy-religion-superstition paradigm that Inoue imposed on it and that continues to be influential.

For example, Inoue's ideas exerted a strong influence on Nishida Kitarō, whose presence looms large in Japanese Buddhist philosophy to this day. Indeed, Nishida attributes his early interest in philosophy to his reading of Inoue's *An Evening of Philosophical Conversation*,[35] and aspects of Nishida's notion of "pure experience" (*junsui keiken* 純粋経験) can be traced back in part to Inoue's work.[36] Moreover, if we turn to a survey of contemporary English-language Japanese Buddhist philosophy, we see many topics that would likely be acceptable to Inoue: (1) writings on Zen (especially the twelfth-century monk Dōgen), with attention to meditative practices and the trans-rational paradoxes of Zen language and logic; (2) writings on the Kyoto School's synthesis of Buddhist thought and Western philosophy; and (3) Zen-influenced works in aesthetics dealing primarily with varieties of direct experience (e.g., of impermanence, of the present moment, and so forth).

This is not to say that such topics are not highly philosophical and worthy of our continued investigation—my own academic work is largely focused on Zen, Dōgen, the Kyoto School, and Japanese aesthetics. This is also not to say that Inoue's "pared-down" Buddhist discourse on direct experience of the absolute does not capture an important aspect of the dharma. It is to say, however, that we who work in areas shaped by Inoue's legacy (and I count myself here) must be critically mindful of the operation of whiteness as a hidden norm in the time period when certain foundations for future academic

Japanese Buddhist philosophy were being laid down. From our current vantage point, we are better able to assess the ways in which the pared-down philosophy that Inoue inherited from Western discourses was constrained by the racist worldviews of Kant and Hegel—not only in its narrow focus on the operation of pure reason but in its intentional exclusion of African and Asian sources, as Park's work so clearly shows. Indeed, in the wake of Park's book, I think that *all* philosophers, not just Buddhist philosophers, must wrestle with the racist legacy that continues to inform our canon, our disciplinary methodologies, and our departmental structures and curricula. But that is also a topic for another essay.[37]

Here, I would like to conclude by foregrounding those aspects of dharma-philosophy that do not register as readily on Inoue's paradigm of trans-rational direct experience. Japanese Buddhism, as a living tradition, remains actively engaged with the "rituals, prayers, and invisible beings"[38] that Inoue sought to exclude. As Joseph-Storm says, "Despite the strenuous anti-super-stition climate of Meiji Japan, many people continued to believe in monsters, they continued to have a need for faith healing, and they continued to go to Buddhist priests for the performance of magical rituals. Thus, the result of Inoue's efforts was an increasing dissonance between Buddhism as a 'philo-sophical religion' and Buddhism as a lived practice."[39] Japanese Buddhist philosophy today, with the benefit of hindsight, can reassess this exclusion of the full range of Buddhist thought from philosophy "proper." What results is not a naïve return to superstition but rather, as I suggest below, renewed attention to historical and cultural context, engagement on issues of social justice, and an expanded understanding of Buddhist liberation in the context of the "scholar-practitioner."

A DHARMA-PHILOSOPHY OF LIBERATION

I have argued elsewhere that the relative popularity of Zen in the West, as compared to Pure Land Buddhism (the largest sect in Japan), is no doubt attributable to the same unease with "magical, superstitious, or at best symbolic kind[s] of things" that Foulk mentions above.[40] In line with this point, the dissonance that Joseph-Storm describes between Buddhism as a constructed subject of scholarship and Buddhism as a lived religion has also helped to elevate Zen as "philosophy" above the more "religious" Pure Land schools.[41] In Pure Land practice, adherents open themselves up to the "other-power" (*tariki* 他力) of Amida Buddha's radical compassion through sincere trust (*shinjin* 信心). This "other-power" facilitates rebirth in the Pure Land, a "buddha field" established by Amida where practitioners can continue their journey toward becoming bodhisattvas. Ultimately, these enlightened practitioners will return to the human world to fulfill the bodhisattva's vow of freeing all sentient beings from suffering.

Although Pure Land thought is too often considered the less philosophical cousin of Zen, its radical, liberatory message speaks to us from outside the confines of "pared-down" philosophy. As Melissa Anne-Marie Curley has argued, Pure Land Buddhist philosophy has been aligned with progressive politics, precisely because of, not in spite of, the supernatural power of Amida. As she says, "practices oriented toward the Pure Land both relied upon and generated an understanding of space as heterogeneous: within this world, there come to be multiple sites in which Amida's Western Paradise is established, sometimes entirely and sometimes partially, sometimes permanently and sometimes contingently. I suggest that these sites are best understood as 'supernatural.'"[42] The supernatural force of the Pure Land heightens its potential to subvert accepted orders of power, whether this is the karmic order that governs death and rebirth or the social order that governs the human world: "by reorganizing the elements of the phenomenal world in the shape of the otherworldly Pure Land, they make present the moment of cathexis in which Amida grasps the practitioner and carries him or her to the Pure Land. . . . As sites of cathexis, they destabilize the real world, interrupting the real social order."[43] In other words, it is precisely Amida's supernatural reach into the everyday world that, as Curley says, interrupts the "real social order." This is why, she concludes, several early Japanese leftists found inspiration in the Pure Land not only as an image for socialist utopia but as a program for enacting that utopia in the present.

James Mark Shields makes a similar observation about the Japanese Marxist and Pure Land priest Takagi Kenmyō: "Takagi envisioned social change arising from a process of individual transformation, based on a reformulation of the traditional Shin Buddhist concept of *shinjin*—usually translated as 'faith' but with the nuance of 'opening oneself up' to the saving grace of Other-power."[44] Similar to Curley, Shields notes that Takagi takes the existence of the Pure Land seriously: "it would seem clear that Takagi believes in the Pure Land as an actual realm (as opposed to simply a metaphor, existential condition, or ideal of a future society). . . . In other words, Takagi's Pure Land acts not only as a heavenly model and guide for those of us remaining in the fallen world; it is also a place where beings are able to act on their fundamental reorientation towards compassion by engaging with this world of suffering."[45]

With this in mind, we can better appreciate Jennifer Leath's Womanist reading of Pure Land philosophy in "Canada and Pure Land, a New Field and Buddha-Land: Womanists and Buddhists Reading Together." She begins by citing Alice Walker's declaration that a Womanist is "Traditionally capable, as in: 'Mama, I'm walking to Canada and I'm taking you and a bunch of other slaves with me.' Reply: 'It wouldn't be the first time.'"[46] Leath comments,

"This is important because it underscores the three-dimensional nature of Womanism: (1) it is rooted in convictions (i.e., faith), not least of which is a commitment to liberation;[47] (2) it is confirmed through praxis (i.e., *walking* to Canada—and *taking* others); and (3) it is something about which one may write (i.e., scholarship)."[48] She goes on to describe how both Womanist and Pure Land thought converge on the importance of "orthopraxy" that "revives traditional models of collective scholarship, honoring the gifts of community orientation characteristic of both Womanism and Buddhism. Such methodology deeply affects the culture of scholarship, . . . engendering an ethic of sharing and mutual edification."[49] For both Womanists and Pure Land philosophy, "liberation is an essentially dynamic objective"[50] of engaged scholarship geared toward the enactment of a better world.

Leath's comments on Womanist-Buddhist discourse remind us that philosophy may be liberatory while still constituting an important site of *scholarship*. I am cognizant here of Hegel's claim, mentioned earlier, that non-Western traditions give us "religious thinking" but not philosophy—indeed, it is still common in academic philosophy today to hear the assertion that Asian traditions are not adequately philosophical because they lack argumentation.[51] As a result, Asian traditions are too often taken as the objects of scholarly inquiry but are not seen as conducting their own scholarship, or as offering their own scholarly methodologies that others might consider adopting. A liberatory dharma-philosophy takes the opposite approach—rather than view Buddhist ideas as the objects of philosophical study (leaving "philosophy" as a marker of whiteness unchallenged), dharma-philosophy takes Buddhist scholarly methodologies as principles of orthopraxy. Leath's Womanist-Buddhist dialogue helps us imagine a dharma-philosophy that addresses suffering, the causes of suffering, and the path to liberation from suffering for the sake of all sentient beings.

CONCLUSION: BUDDHIST ORTHOPRAXY IN THE TEMPLE OF PHILOSOPHY

This critical study of whiteness in the construction of Buddhist philosophy in Meiji Japan has largely been aimed at airing out some of the dubious racial theories from philosophy's not-too-distant past still lurking around in academia today. Here, at the end, I have only gestured toward a few aspects of dharma-philosophy that do not fit so well on Inoue's model of Buddhism as the encounter with the trans-rational absolute.

However, I would like to point out, in closing, that Inoue himself was an ordained priest in a Pure Land sect (the Ōtani branch of Shin Buddhism), and moreover he was deeply concerned with orthopraxy. Indeed, he is well-known for building an elaborate "temple of philosophy" park (*tetsugakudō kōen* 哲学堂公園), still located in Tokyo today. His plans for the park surrounding the temple reflect his own elaborate, visceral mapping of philosophy. As he says,

> In the right wing is a garden designed in the shape of the sinograph character for *matter*, and in the left another in the shape of the sinograph for *mind*. These express materialism and idealism respectively . . . . *At the bottom of the hill, on the left wing (of idealism)*: the Station of Consciousness, the Path of Intuition, the Road of Knowledge, the Barrier of Logic, the Pass of Dogma, the Cliff of Psychology, the Spring of A Priori, the Bridge of Concepts, the Pool of Ethics, the Island of Reason, the Pond in the Shape of the Sinograph for "Mind," the Resting Place of Subjectivity.[52]

Inside the temple itself, philosophers could gather to participate in liberatory philosophical ceremonies. Such ceremonies involved venerating the four sages—Buddha, Confucius, Socrates, and Kant[53]—and chanting "*namu-zettai-mugenson*," or, "I entrust myself to the absolute infinite."[54] This of course recalls the well-known Pure Land practice of enacting one's trust in Amida Buddha by chanting "*namu-Amida-butsu*."

How can Inoue's efforts at de-ritualizing Buddhism to remove the so-called superstitious elements be reconciled with his elaborate schemes for introducing various rites and ceremonies into the practice of philosophy? In short, fully in line with liberatory Buddhist orthopraxy, Inoue believed that the absolute cannot merely be contemplated intellectually but must be enacted viscerally. For philosophers today—not just Buddhist philosophers, but for all of us who are seeking anti-racist strategies to remake our current institutions, curricula, pedagogies, and methodologies—enacting dharma-philosophy cannot remain a topic of theoretical speculation. Much like the grounds of Inoue's philosophy temple park, which remakes a slice of Tokyo into the instantiation of "pure *tetsugaku*," we must seek creative solutions to the institutionalized racism in contemporary academic departments. Certainly Inoue's structural interventions in academic philosophy, through his detailed designs for spaces and practices, are an under-appreciated aspect of his legacy. In his temple of philosophy we can see that, despite the hidden operations of whiteness that marked the influx of Western ideas in Meiji Japan, dharma-philosophy readily exceeds the constraints of any "pared-down" academic discipline.

NOTES

1. His 2006 and 2012 works cited here were published under the name Jason Ānanda Josephson, but I refer to him throughout this chapter by his current hyphenated name Josephson-Storm. In the notes and bibliography, I cite his name as it appears in the individual published works.

2. Another major factor in this transmission, which I will not be able to focus on in this chapter, concerns the history of colonialism in India and the impact of Indian Buddhist philosophy in the Western academy. See, for example, Richard King, *Orientalism and Religion: Postcolonial Theory, India, and "the Mystic East"* (London: Routledge, 1999).

3. An earlier version of this summary of Park's book appears in Leah Kalmanson, "Decolonizing the Department: Peter K. J. Park and the Profession of Philosophy," *Journal of World Philosophies* (Winter 2017): 60–65.

4. Peter K. Y. Park, *Africa, Asia, and the History of Philosophy: Racism in the Formation of the Philosophical Canon* (Albany, NY: SUNY Press, 2013), 93.

5. Ibid., 94.

6. Ibid., especially 70–77.

7. Ibid., 8.

8. In fact, throughout the Meiji, efforts were made to downplay or outright distort the racial hierarchies of European theories to group the Japanese with whites. See Yasuko Takezawa, "Translating and Transforming 'Race': Early Meiji Period Textbooks," *Japanese Studies* 35, no. 1 (2015): 5–21. There, Takezawa states, "Early Meiji period textbooks generally do not make clear the relative civilizational level of Japanese people. . . . This can be clearly found in textbook passages that group the Mongolian race and Japanese people with the Caucasian race—distorted interpretations markedly different from the various theories of European racial studies" (14). However, Takezawa goes on to explain, "This discrepancy in the understandings of race and civilization between Japan and the West reached its culmination when Japan's Racial Equality Proposal, which attempted to address legal racism against Japanese immigrants on the west coast of the United States, was rejected by the United States and its allies at the 1919 Paris Peace Conference. The great disappointment made Japan finally recognize that the dream of joining the ranks of Europe and America—asserted as a possibility in some textbooks—was unattainable" (18).

9. Qtd. in Jason Ānanda Josephson, *The Invention of Religion in Japan* (Chicago: University of Chicago Press, 2012), 54.

10. Jason Ānanda Josephson-Storm, "The Superstition, Secularism, and Religion Trinary: Or Re-Theorizing Secularism," *Method and Theory in the Study of Religion* (2017): 1–20.

11. Georg Wilhelm Freidrich Hegel, *Lectures on the History of Philosophy* (vol. 1), trans. E. S. Haldane (London: Kegan Paul, Trench, Trübner and Co., 1892), 117.

12. Jason Ānanda Josephson, "When Buddhism Became a 'Religion': Religion and Superstition in the Writings of Inoue Enryō," *Japanese Journal of Religious Studies* 33, no. 1 (2006): 143–168, 151.

13. Josephson, *The Invention of Religion in Japan*, 17.

14. Ibid., 16.

15. Robert Ford Campany, "On the Very Idea of Religions (in the Modern West and in Early Medieval China)," *History of Religions* 42, no. 4 (2003): 287–319, 289.

16. Tomoko Masuzawa, *The Invention of World Religions: Or How European Universalism Was Preserved in the Language of Pluralism* (Chicago: Chicago University Press, 2005), 49.

17. I prefer the alternate translation English term "Ruism," which better reflects the original Chinese.

18. Josephson, *The Invention of Religion in Japan*, 24–28.

19. Josephson, "When Buddhism Became a 'Religion,'" 144.

20. Ibid.

21. For a fuller discussion of this claim, see Leah Kalmanson, "Dharma and Dao: Key Terms in the Comparative Philosophy of Religion," in *Ineffability: An Exercise in Comparative Philosophy of Religion*, ed. Tim Knepper and Leah Kalmanson (London: Springer, 2017). An earlier version of this discussion of religion in Japanese discourses appears in that essay.

22. James W. Heisig, Thomas P. Kasulis, and John C. Maraldo, eds., *Japanese Philosophy: A Sourcebook* (Honolulu: University of Hawai'i Press, 2011), 555. John C. Maraldo, シ゛ョン・マラルト゛. "Nihon no kindai shoki ni okeru seiyō tetsugaku no sesshu" 日本の近代初期における西洋哲学の摂取 [The reception of Western philosophy in early modern Japan], trans. (from the English) Shirai Masato 白井雅人, *International Inoue Enryo Research* 2 (2014): 200–216.

23. Heisig et al., *Japanese Philosophy*, 556.

24. Ibid., 556–558.

25. Qtd. in ibid., 561.

26. Maraldo, "Nihon no kindai shoki ni okeru seiyō tetsugaku no sesshu," 213.

27. Qtd. in Park, *Africa, Asia, and the History of Philosophy*, 23.

28. Josephson, "When Buddhism Became a 'Religion,'" 152.

29. Ibid., 160.

30. Ibid., 159.

31. Ibid., 162.

32. Ibid., 161.

33. Griffith T. Foulk, "Ritual in Japanese Zen Buddhism," in *Zen Ritual*, ed. Steven Heine (Oxford: Oxford University Press, 2007), 21–82, 23.

34. Ibid., 64.

35. Shirai Masato, 白井雅人. "Inoue Enryō 'tetsugaku issekiwa' to Nishida Kitarō" 井上円了『哲学一夕話』と西田幾多郎 [Inoue Enryō's *Evening of Philosophical Conversation* and Nishida Kitarō], *Kokusai tetsugaku kenkyū* 国際哲学研究 1 (2012): 101–108, 101.

36. Shimizu Takashi, "Aim of the Idea of Pure Experience: William James, Nishida Kitaro and Inoue Enryo," *Annual Report of the Inoue Enryo Center* 24 (2016): 55–71, 62–63.

37. For more on these issues, see Kalmanson, "Decolonizing the Department."

38. Josephson, "When Buddhism Became a 'Religion,'" 152.

39. Ibid., 162.

40. See Leah Kalmanson, "Pure Land Ecology: Taking the Supernatural Seriously in Environmental Philosophy," in *Japanese Environmental Philosophy*, eds. J. Baird Callicott and James McRae (Oxford: Oxford University Press, 2017).

41. Although, as we will discuss in the conclusion, Inoue himself was a Pure Land, not a Zen, Buddhist.

42. Melissa Anne-Marie Curley, *Pure Land/Real World: Modern Buddhists, Japanese Leftists, and the Utopian Imagination* (Honolulu: University of Hawai'i Press, 2017), 18.

43. Ibid., 23.

44. James Mark Shields, "Zen and the Art of Treason: Radical Buddhism in Meiji Era (1868–1912) Japan," *Politics, Religion, and Ideology* 15, no. 2 (2014): 1–19, 8.

45. Ibid., 9–10.

46. Jennifer Leath, "Canada and Pure Land, a New Field and Buddha-Land: Womanists and Buddhists Reading Together," *Buddhist–Christian Studies* 32 (2012): 57–65, 57.

47. It is worth noting that the notion of conviction as "commitment to liberation" is an appropriate gloss on *shinjin*. For example, Musashi Tachikawa criticizes the claim that Pure Land practices are the passive or submissive inactivity of the self before the other-power of Amida. Rather, he says, "entrusting to the other" is a dynamic attitude of active resoluteness. See Musashi Tachikawa, "Mandala Contemplation and Pure Land Practice: A Comparative Study," in *Toward a Contemporary Understanding of Pure Land Buddhism: Creating a Shin Buddhist Theology in a Religiously Plural World*, ed. Dennis Hirota (Albany, NY: SUNY, 2000), 101–126, 112.

48. Leath, "Canada and Pure Land," 57–58.

49. Ibid., 61–62.

50. Ibid., 61.

51. Consider the vitriolic online discussions that appeared in the wake of Jay L. Garfield's and Bryan W. Van Norden's op-ed, "If Philosophy Won't Diversify, Let's Call It What It Really Is," *New York Times*, May 11, 2016, https://www.nytimes.com/2016/05/11/opinion/if-philosophy-wont-diversify-lets-call-it-what-it-really-is.html, as well as the debates that ensued on various philosophy blogs, such as the discussions at *The Daily Nous* (http://dailynous.com/2016/05/11/philosophical-diversity-in-u-s-philosophy-departments/ and http://dailynous.com/2016/05/13/when-someone-suggests-expanding-the-canon/).

52. Enryō Inoue, "The Temple of Philosophy," trans. Gerard Clinton Godart, in *Japanese Philosophy*, 629–630.

53. For a discussion of the philosophy temple and ceremonies, see Michael Burtscher, "Facing 'the West' on Philosophical Grounds: A View from the Pavilion of Subjectivity on Meiji Japan," *Comparative Studies of South Asian, Africa, and the Middle East* 26, no. 3 (2006).

54. Enryō Inoue, "Addressing the Divine," trans. Gerard Clinton Godart, in *Japanese Philosophy*, 630.

Chapter 5

Racism and *Anatta*

Black Buddhists, Embodiment, and Interpretations of Non-Self

Rima Vesely-Flad

BLACK BUDDHISTS' EXPERIENCES OF RACISM

Racism induces suffering.

The personal accounts of Black Buddhist teachers and long-term practitioners detail wrenching accounts of racially driven hatred and brutality, insensitive microaggressions, and self-loathing that results from these experiences. Numerous memoirs—ranging from Rev. Angel Kyodo Williams's *Being Black*[1] to Jan Willis's *Dreaming Me*,[2] and more recently, Zenju Earthlyn Manuel's *The Way of Tenderness*[3]—offer cogent narratives on systemic racism, painful interpersonal interactions, and the practice of the dharma as a way forward.

These personal reflections on Black embodiment propel forward an important conversation within Buddhist communities in the United States. Immigrant Buddhist communities are sometimes inaccessible to English-speaking Black Buddhists, due to cultural and linguistic barriers. "American" Buddhist communities attract white, middle-class spiritual seekers. In homogenous *sangha* settings, dharma practitioners of African descent generally find themselves keenly aware of racially charged dynamics and the cultural dominance of whiteness.

One of the foremost critics of whiteness in American Buddhist *sanghas*, Rev. Angel Kyodo Williams, reflects on the isolation experienced by dharma practitioners of African descent. She recounts one marginalizing experience at the Shambhala Center in New York City, and speculates that her experience is in fact widespread.

I went to Shambhala New York and I just could not bear it. There's whiteness as a racial construct, there's whiteness as we talk about white folks. I come from New York, where whiteness shows up in such different ways. It wasn't the sort of massive thing that I felt was overwhelming. There are Jewish and Irish and Italian. My dad was a fireman and his dad was a fireman, so [we had] lots of contact with Irish and Italian folks in the fire department, and Polish people, so my range of white-skinned people was quite vast. And Shambhala New York was a kind of form, a particular strain of upper-middle-class whiteness that had a feeling of being oppressive, where people turned around and looked at you, and I had a strong feeling that I was not welcome.[4]

The dominant whiteness Williams experienced at Shambhala New York is but one example of the cultural exclusivity expressed in homogenous Buddhist *sanghas*. In Williams's later book *Radical Dharma*, coauthored with Lama Rod Owens and Dr. Jasmine Syedullah, she describes attending a retreat of fifty people, in which forty-seven were white. Williams states,

One woman looked at me and asked, "Do you know that they're going to have a *Martin Luther King* Day retreat here?" She put great emphasis on "Martin Luther King." The color of my skin was both something to be called out and yet something to be utterly undealt with. . . . The real question remains: How can we address the barriers for people like me when the predominant culture cannot acknowledge its privilege? We are born into a particular body, and this can be a great source of pain, depending on how society views the identity [associated with it]. And yet, communities in power pretend the difference, and the pain, is not there, which causes the individuals in that skin to question our value.[5]

Seeing skin color—but pretending not to—in white dharma spaces spurs Williams to assert the critical practice of paying attention to the historical and contemporary forms of racialized suffering.

Asian teachers who have faced discrimination acknowledge the particular form of suffering that results from social practices, rather than suffering that is solely driven by the mind. Thus there is among Eastern practitioners and Black Buddhists a common language about suffering due to exclusion. Jan Willis, author of *Dreaming Me*, traveled to India in her college years and encountered Tibetan monks who had been exiled. In seeing parallels between their expulsion and US racial exclusion, she gained an ability to deal with an internal suffering that was wrought, in part, by her experience of racism in the United States. When she met her first teacher, a Tibetan monk, Willis wrote,

I should have told him the truth when he'd first asked; should have blurted out that I suffered; that I was often frustrated and angry; that slavery and its legacy of racism had taken their tolls on me; that I had come seeking help in coping with feelings of inadequacy, unworthiness, and shame. I should have told him that I felt a certain kinship with the Tibetans because they, too, had suffered a great historical trauma and yet seemed able to cope very well and, indeed, even to be quite joyful.[6]

The suffering of Black people, Willis concluded, could not *only* be over-come with marches and activism; she was deeply aware of the resentment and anguish that resided in her heart. The way forward for her was in meditation practice: sitting with painful feelings and, over the course of time, befriend-ing them. Silent practice under the guidance of a skilled teacher was a means to heal the mind. Yet, Willis was keenly aware of the racism of the South, of becoming peaceful and *still* experiencing the anger triggered by white people who exhibited racism.

As a child, I had been shown off because I was smart; but when Lama Yeshe showed me off it was a loving way of healing a long list of old wounds: my mother calling me evil, the white superintendents' amazement at a black child's intelligence, the sense of the dire mistake I'd committed by solving my sister's math problem, the humiliation I'd later suffered because I couldn't spell, going to college amid Klan threats, and the bogus idea that universities were lowering their standards in order to let in black students.[7]

Willis describes particular forms of suffering that are both interpersonal and systemic. Her memoir anticipates the reflections of Manuel, whose 2015 meditations in *The Way of Tenderness* preceded her 2018 essays in *Sanctu-ary*. Manuel's stories of childhood exclusion convey the psychological dam-age wrought due to particular experiences of racism:

When I got home [from school], I asked my mother why I wasn't chosen [for a program], and watched her eyes drop. That night, I cried in my bed until it finally became clear to me. I wasn't white. I had moved from the black school where my identity was closely tied to our culture. My innocence vanished, and I learned that for some, love is conditioned. Once a talkative child, I grew quiet in the struggle to regain my balance. I felt a keen sense of loss, living in a world that favored white people.[8]

Through rituals and concentration practices, Manuel deconstructed the derogatory social messages that shaped her earliest cognitive experiences. She was able to recognize that the hatred directed at her was part of a larger, oppressive social consciousness. Rejection was not a response to her personal deficiencies, but rather, the ways in which she was constructed within the white myopic and cognitive dysfunction of systemic white supremacy.

I am a survivor of the same hatred my parents experienced. The body I inhabit has experienced nearly every category of hatred that exists within this society, directed toward the various unacceptable differences that characterize its appearance. Perhaps it is a result of these experiences that I have paid fierce attention to liberation. And perhaps it is due to the intensity of my suffering, combined with the enchantment that I always felt to be so near, that I want to share the way that has unfurled itself before me, on which I now walk in wellness.[9]

The "wellness" Manuel actively pursued is a commitment that Williams, Owens, and Syedullah articulate in *Radical Dharma*. Williams explains *Radical Dharma* as an elaboration of a "third space that emerges when radically inhabiting the two: the inner *and* outer paths toward liberation."[10] The authors argue that the whiteness of and racism within mainstream Buddhist communities and organizations in the United States "amplifies" rather than "deconstructs" systems of suffering, thus perpetuating racialized social divisions.

For Black Buddhist teachers and practitioners, the dharma itself teaches the origins of suffering and the end to suffering, and is thus enduringly relevant to Black people who face violence and microaggressions in the US context. The Black Lives Matter movement surfaced insidious targeting and exploitation of Black people at the hands of police officers and state officials. Systemic oppression is a pervasive force that causes relentless suffering against Black people.

Furthermore, the emergence of the Black Lives Matter movement has spurred dharma practitioners to acknowledge violent, systemic racism, particularly against economically marginalized communities as well as queer persons of color. *Radical Dharma*, speaking directly to white dharma practitioners, asserts,

> The police force is the state institution carrying out a specific mandate . . .
> That mandate is to control Black bodies . . .
> Your compliance maintains the system.
> You are policed, too.
> . . .
> Once you are aware of how you are being policed, you can begin the process of self-liberating, from the position of realizing the mutuality of our liberation rather than suffering under the delusion that you are doing something for me. There is an intimacy in that realization. And because dharma is ultimately about accepting what is, it can undermine the need for control that keeps you invested in the policing of my body, thus freeing yours.[11]

Williams, Owens, and Syedullah, then, recognize the spectrum of racism, from interpersonal interactions to systemic brutality. They furthermore see the relevance of the dharma for recognizing the different meanings constructed for bodies, according to skin color. Embodied Blackness brings suffering, because Blackness is laden with socially constructed negative connotations. For these authors of *Radical Dharma*, the practice of silence, clarity, and ease is life-giving among the deadly conditions that confront Black people.

The internalization of hatred due to skin color is a particular form of suffering. It can be healed by dharma practice—yet the isolation experienced in predominantly white *sanghas*, along with microaggressions and an inability to relate to cultural perspectives, creates a divide that must be acknowledged.

Thus, it is critical, these writers argue, that Buddhist *sanghas* acknowledge the social conditions of Blackness and the unique perspectives of Black Buddhist practitioners. Black people have undergone a particular form of suffering that is often perpetuated in predominantly white Buddhist communities. Suffering is expanded, rather than alleviated, in white *sanghas* that fail to do the work of acknowledging racism in the community and broader society.

Owens states that in a racialized social reality, there is not the possibility of Black people "being at home in whiteness," for it "goes hand-in-glove with the presumption that everything whiteness does must be best, right, noble, beautiful, moral, and productive."[12] Owens further writes: "The problem with becoming myself was that, no matter how nice I had learned to be, no matter how smart or accommodating, sitting with myself meant I was becoming more myself, more Black."[13]

> Dharma practice called my attention to the deepest of my investments in white supremacy and made me feel, without sugar coats, without apology or redemption, how deeply destructive it is to live in the afterlife of slavery as the unembodied trauma of the white experience.[14]

In short, it is not possible for Black people to encounter the naked truths that arise during sitting practice *and* to assimilate into white communities that perpetuate suffering through unacknowledged racism. Thus *Radical Dharma* is a critique of white supremacy and correspondingly, a challenge to predominantly white *sanghas*. For Black practitioners, the social meanings of the Black body must be acknowledged, reconstructed, and embraced. This process is deeply internal and solitary, and overtly external and communal. These Black teachers and practitioners emphasize the primacy of the *body*: a material body composed of flesh and blood that is socially constructed in degrading ways. For Black people, these social constructs lead to enduring psychological and often physical suffering. Buddhist practitioners—white as well as Black—must reckon with the forces of racism that emphasize the body and have led to rejection, misery, and self-hatred.

The Three Markers of Existence: Non-Self, Suffering, and Impermanence

Buddhist practitioners of African descent encounter the teachings of *Anatta*—non-self—through a dual lens: they hold in tension the recognition of relative social reality—and thus socially constructed bodies—alongside the ultimate experience of non-self. In Buddhist doctrine, the teaching of non-self is one of the three markers of existence, alongside *Dukkha* (suffering) and *Anicca* (impermanence). Scholars argue that understanding the three markers of existence must start with an understanding of *Dukkha* that is derived from the hallmark of the Buddha's teaching: the Four Noble Truths.

The First Noble Truth is that Life is Suffering. Theravada monk and scholar Ven. Bikkhu Bodhi writes that suffering is not simply due to pain, but also, that the notion of suffering extends to the reality of impermanence. Everything that arises passes away. The doctrine of impermanence character-izes all substances, including the notion of the self.[15]

The doctrine of non-self asserts that, unlike in the predominantly Western worldview—in which a personal self is identified and articulated—there is not a permanent, underlying substance that is identified as a personal self. Rather, each person is composed of five *khandas* (Sanskrit: *skandhas*), that are constantly in flux, in relation to environment, context, and interpersonal interactions. The five *khandas*, sometimes translated as "aggregates," are form, feeling, perception, fabrications, and consciousness. Form refers to physical phenomena. Feeling refers to pleasure, pain, and neutral sensations. Perception refers to the process of mentally labeling and identifying objects. Fabrication refers to active processes in the mind, including attention and evaluation. Consciousness refers to awareness of the five senses: seeing, hearing, smelling, tasting, and perceiving.[16]

The Buddha argued that the five *khandas* constantly shift and lack inherent stability; that is, they are impermanent. What is understood as the "self," then, is a collection of constantly changing *khandas*. There is no experience of self outside of the *khandas*, so therefore there is no permanent self. Yet, as Black Buddhists have argued, this doctrine must not be interpreted as negating self-dignity and human rights. Rather, the doctrine of non-self must be articulated with nuance and sensitivity in a racialized social context that arises from a history of degrading Black bodies, denying Black personhood, and refusing human rights to any person with Black blood.[17] The doctrine of non-self must take into account the lived experiences of Black people, while also acknowl-edging the depth of suffering due to desire and mental constructs, and the radical freedom inherent in practices of stillness, silence, and liberating one-self from the beliefs of how we should relate to our bodies.[18]

NON-SELF AND THE BLACK BODY

Black Buddhists speak of the importance of bringing lived experience, including suffering due to racism, to the cushion. Indeed, for many, it is imperative that they could claim their social identity as Black persons and transform what had often been degraded into an experience of self-love. Rhonda Magee, a law professor who practices in the Zen and Shambhala traditions, notes that lived experiences are present on the cushion, and thus it is important to remember one's lineage while embracing non-self and silence.[19]

Lovingkindness practices toward the self, alongside personal interpretations of the Four Noble Truths and the Eightfold Noble Path, guide many Black Buddhist practitioners who have suffered generational trauma and racist degradation in our contemporary moment. Valerie Mason-John, also known as Vimalasara, an African-Canadian teacher in the Nichiren tradition, speaks of the importance of the Four Noble Truths for people of African descent in particular. The First Noble Truth is that suffering is a universal experience. Mason-John states, "We of African descent know what suffering is. It's in our DNA."[20] The Second Noble Truth states that suffering is a result of ignorant craving. For many Black Buddhists, the interpretations of the causes of suffering are greatly expanded into teachings of white myopia, the desire to exist in delusion, and the collective ego of the dominant white culture. The Third Noble Truth is that there is a path to end suffering. The very promise of liberation is enticing for people of African descent. The Fourth Noble Truth describes the path of liberation, known as the Noble Eightfold Path. In this path, "Right Concentration," which leads to settling the mind, is a particularly compelling practice.

Manuel writes in *The Way of Tenderness*:

> Only in the deep silence of meditation did I begin to disbelieve that I was born only to suffer. Eventually after many years of sitting meditation, I recognized the root of my self-hatred, both external and internal, as a personal and collective denial or denigration of the body I inhabited.[21]

Her reflections are echoed by Owens's reflections on silence: "silence became the medium in which I was reborn into a sense of happiness and contentment. But overall, it ushered me into a period of thriving and flourishing in my life."[22]

In meditation, practitioners cultivate their ability to confront the suffering wrought by their mental constructs rather than avoid pain. They seek to heal the damage wrought by racism and to rearticulate profound teachings that are rooted in concentration practices. In-depth interviews with Black Buddhist teachers and practitioners illuminate a progression in the process of acknowledging one's racial identity and embracing teachings of non-self. The progression begins with claiming and rearticulating Blackness as part of the social self, and in so doing, embracing African ancestry. For many, the next step is entering into an experience of silence that facilitates a recognition of the truth of non-self. Finally, Black Buddhist teachers and long-term practitioners integrate embodiment with the psychologically liberating practice of silence. The ten Black Buddhist teachers and long-term practitioners interviewed for this chapter emphasized four primary themes in their articulation of embodiment and *Anatta*: (1) Being visible in social spaces; (2) Claiming African ancestral lineages; (3) Embracing the two truths of relative and absolute existence; and (4) Liberating the self and the community.

Visibility

The Black Lives Matter movement thrust the brutal actions by police officers against Black bodies into the national spotlight. Trayvon Martin, a seventeen-year-old Black youth, was killed by a white neighborhood volunteer. Social media platforms facilitated international expressions of outrage at the 2013 acquittal of the volunteer, George Zimmerman. One year later, Michael Brown, an eighteen-year-old Black youth, was murdered by white police officer Darren Wilson. The assassination of these Black youths, along with the murders of Renisha McBride, Aiyana Stanley-Jones, Rosann Miller, Alesia Thomas, Mya Hall, Eric Garner, Tamir Rice, Freddie Gray, Philando Castile, Alton Sterling, Terence Crutcher, and Keith Lamont Scott, among others, propelled Black Buddhist teachers and long-term practitioners to articulate the dharma in new ways. Whereas early reflections had emphasized individual stories, Black Buddhist teachers and long-term practitioners recognize the pivotal moment prompted by the outrage of Black grassroots activists, as well as those working with incarcerated Black youth and with white people in predominantly white Buddhist *sanghas*. Thus, Black teachers and long-term practitioners have sought to address rage, burnout, divisions in activist communities, and white ignorance and microaggressions. If Buddhist teachings assert that existence is marked by suffering, impermanence, and non-self, how does a Black practitioner heal the trauma that results from racism, and in so doing, claim the value of Blackness and the importance of honoring the Black body?

Jylani Ma'at, a long-term practitioner in the Vipassana tradition and the mother of two Black teenagers, spent many months going into juvenile jails to meditate with youth. For Ma'at, the present-day brutality against Black people spurred the need for activism rooted in contemplative practices.

> There's no distant past. It's happening right now. We are witnessing hangings, lynchings, head decapitation, and burnings. This is very reminiscent of a not so distant past. And this to me really challenges my practice, because this is not a turn the cheek kind of thing. This is not a sit on the mat and cross your legs kind of thing. This is a get up and do something kind of thing with compassion for those who obviously are mentally ill, but still holding them fully accountable.

And I don't believe that any path that I would be on, any religion that I would participate in, any faith or anything would direct me to be complicit. . . . I said, "There have to be tangible consequences. Operating solely in a spiritual mode on an earthly plane is not aligning with my spirit." And the concept of suffering is not intended to only include people of color, namely black and brown and indigenous peoples of America. Joy, safety, and freedom are entitlements for everybody. And to me that is what a full practice is. When you feel free to fully be in it and to be able to fully address your concerns, your fear, your anger, all of that. I don't think that there's any practice that says you can't be angry and you can't be mad. It's how you respond to things, but that's a human experience. And so what is it that you are asking me to do? Like who do you want me to be? And if you are asking me to withdraw and be a void of certainness and indelible in my spirit, then you don't really want me to show up. And then you are rendering me invisible almost.[23]

The experience of being rendered invisible in mainstream society, as well as in predominantly white *sanghas*, has led Black Buddhist teachers to emphasize a progression in how the teachings are articulated: the construct of the Black body must be acknowledged before the teachings of impermanence and non-self can be understood.

It has been critical for Black embodied activists and professionals to encounter Buddhist teachings that explicitly recognize the trauma that is distinct within Black communities. Unique Holland, a Zen practitioner in the Bay Area, speaks of multiple challenges that arise from confronting racism as well as wearing masks in a professional environment.

Over the years, I lost track as there were multiple masks that I put on . . . I got to a point where I just really felt like I lost who was underneath all of that. It's just a feeling that this is what's required of me to gain entrance to the space, this professional space, this academic space or whatever. And it got to a point where that just caused way more suffering than I could imagine. And I'm so grateful for East Bay Meditation Center. And so here was a place that was actually saying supposedly yeah, I know we're really calling folks in. We got space for POC; we got the space for queer folks. We're integrating this into our practice together and it felt really good. It felt like home. And so that's where I felt like my practice started to get to sync in as more than just an intellectual exercise. And then I came across Zenju's work and someone who was willing to step in and explicitly saying you know what, I'm talking to and I'm working towards black liberation. I'm talking to black women. This is the dharma again.[24]

Holland acknowledges the difficulty of hearing teachings on non-self in the early stages of her meditation practice. It was important to be seen and affirmed in her social identity as she committed to the difficulty of encountering painful feelings and mental constructs. Holland is among other practitioners who sought to interpret their embodied life experiences through their own lenses, without having their experiences filtered through the interpretation of the dominant culture. This practice of hearing, seeing, and interpreting one's own mind on the meditation cushion helps Black practitioners to deconstruct and understand teachings of non-self in a racialized social world.

Responding to people of African descent in the meditation hall is an important practice for Vipassana teacher JoAnna Hardy, who acknowledges that her own personal journey as a mixed-race person serves as a vehicle for welcoming people of color to the dharma. Hardy states, "If there are any brown faces in the room, if even one, I just want to make sure that we are seen. It's sort of a calling and making visible, of all of the people that might not feel seen in the room. It's important to me to do that every time I teach."[25]

Practicing with Ancestors

For many Black Buddhist practitioners, the practice of envisioning ancestors of African descent while sitting in predominantly white meditation centers allows them to enter into psychological ease. Devin Berry, a Vipassana teacher, reflects that he can be in large meditation halls in which he is one of two black practitioners "because I bring all of my people with me."

> I see it as an honoring of my ancestors, bearing witness to all that they went through just to survive. They survived so that I could be able to do anything that I want. That allows me to be in the room. And so, I bring that to my practice. I bring that to my teaching and I bring my flavor to it. I bring our ancestral flavor to that and I want to marry those things of this eastern religion with now this Western psychology and my Mississippi sharecroppers on my mother's side and then Kansas City educated middle class folks on the other side, I bring all of that. If I can't bring that full identity, I don't want it . . . having to put a mask on, having to perform.[26]

The desire to create a bridge between African ancestry and dharma practice emerged as a prominent theme in the reflections of Black Buddhists, who spoke of practicing the concepts of non-self *in order to see themselves as full selves*. Practicing concepts of no-self allows the trauma of racialized existence to drop away, so that Black practitioners need not constantly relate to their own lives through whiteness. In short, they can recognize the depths of their own lives outside of an external white gaze. Because there is historical and contemporary stigmatism attached to dark bodies, Vipassana teacher JoAnna Hardy says, dharma teachings have to be interpreted specifically for people of color. For Hardy, spiritual practices that honor ancestors and heal trauma can be a first step; she embraced the dharma after early forays into African traditions.

The path of first embracing African lineage prior to embracing dharma teachings is a prominent theme in Manuel's *Sanctuary*. She writes of a twenty-one-day Zen Buddhist ceremony that she conducted in her home, during which she placed three Haitian Vodoun deities on her alters. These Haitian figures corresponded to three figures in Zen: the gatekeepers, protectors, and bodhisattvas.

> As I lit a candle at each altar, I called forth the Haitian spirits with their chants along with hymns to the Zen deities, and I touched a distinct and ancient place inside me. I could feel my blood ancestors, who had been forced from their homes and taken up Christianity, still having the need to invoke their own lineage and deities. I felt myself touching *home* saying Legba Atibon, Ayizan Velèkètè, and Erzulie Jan Petro, invoking at the same time Avalokiteshrava, and Bodhidharma. As I invoked the name of Shakyamuni Buddha as a great teacher, I invoked the sky by blowing an eagle whistle. Incorporating Vodoun deities into the Zen ceremony created a familiarity I found deeply resonant with home and therefore my heart.[27]

Manuel's use of the term "familiarity" illuminates understanding of why Black Buddhists seek to honor ancestors, particularly at the beginning of starting a dharma practice. Honoring ancestors is a way of acknowledging that Black people come from somewhere, geographically and spiritually, even as they embrace teachings that emphasize formlessness, non-self, and silence. This can be an important practice especially in light of the utter geographical dislocation that occurred during the Transatlantic slave trade and the complete rupture of African ancestors who were enslaved and taken from their families, languages, and traditions. Enslavement resulted in a primary relationship to one's owner and "social death" in one's broader existence.[28] Furthermore, the slave owner possessed absolute authority to brand, rape, exploit, and sell the isolated Black people whose social status was now in relation only to the owner. For Black Buddhist practitioners, then, to embrace—indeed, *reclaim*—African ancestry and traditions in the commitment to healing one's psyche is a practice that allows the mind to heal generational trauma as the mind recalls racialized suffering. Over time, dharma practice facilitates remembering and reinterpreting painful experiences without reliving them. The entry into silence fosters a practice of emptying the mind of rejection, degrading narratives, and defensiveness; whiteness ceases to be the sole facilitating landscape against which Black experience is measured.[29]

The experience of silence is deeply liberating. Hardy notes that even as she engaged with ancestral practices in early years of cultivating spiritual rituals, and even as she intentionally speaks to people of color during dharma talks as a present-day dharma teacher, "when I'm on a cushion alone now, race doesn't come into my practice."[30]

Yet the experience of non-self must begin with recognition of the social self: the experience of people, tradition, and community and the suffering wrought by living in a degrading social context.

Relative and Absolute Reality

Lama Rod Owens, a Black Buddhist teacher in the Kagyu school of Tibetan Buddhism, emphasizes the importance of relating to oneself through one's own eyes, rather than through the lenses inflicted by the outside world. Enlightenment in Buddhism, he states, is not extinguishing the self, "it is recognition of the self." He asserts that we need ego—the self—to relate to one another. At the same time, he argues, "the ultimate truth is non-self."

> In order for me to earn my experience of the ultimate I have to actually earn the experience of the relative. So I have to come really close and really solid into what my experience of having a self is. Because once I get really curious about this idea of self and I begin to understand how to actually undo the self, and undo my fixation on the self, I think the self is so deeply, deeply entwined in a very way of being in the world and I have to actually understand the mechanisms of the self in order to transcend the self. So I can start speaking in very general non-self terms, but actually that's going to be the root of increasing my suffering, of increasing my suffering on the relative, because I just don't understand the self enough in order to move through it or to transcend it yet. But that's always the ultimate always on the horizon. So I can talk about the self, but I also know at the same time there's no self. This is the tricky part of integrating justice and dharma. Both of these ideas have to be held together. The relative and the ultimate. You can't skip around to either or. You have to be right with both of those always at the same time, and then that actually begins to help us move more towards the ultimate.[31]

Owens's analysis of the teachings on non-self incorporates two extremes: being something and being nothing. He refers to his analysis as "sitting in the middle." He can be Black and queer, and can absorb the traumatizing blows inflicted in a social world in which Blackness and queerness are marginalized and degraded precisely because he practices a meditative stability in which he accesses an inner spaciousness, a nothingness.

> I think it's the teachings of the heart sutra. Those have been quite important to me. It's just then how do we actually begin to hold the space for messing in something at the same time. . . . So that's what I'm trying to work with. I am something, but I'm nothing, but in the relative I am something. So if I don't

embrace that and understand that then I won't know how to let it go and I need to. I can be both at the same time. I can be something and nothing.[32]

A worldview that balances the tensions between embodied identity and non-self furthermore allows Black Buddhists to function in the world in a psychologically healthy way. They can be "within the world but not of it," according to Bushi Yamato Damashii, a Buddhist monk and lead resident teacher of Daishin Zen Buddhist Temple in North Carolina. "Outside of myself there is only opinion. Inside of myself there is only me. If I bring outside opinion in, then I corrupt me. So the practice of existing in the world, I have pauses within the world but am not of it."[33]

Williams similarly speaks of an internal groundedness while operating in a hostile, racialized social context. Choosing Blackness and embracing queerness—choosing "complex locations"—from a place of mental stability allows Black Buddhists to reintegrate multiple social identities alongside an experience of non-self. In short, the ability to claim multiple and dynamic social identities means that Black Buddhists can, in turn, recognize the reality of the ultimate non-self.

The psychological stability in seeing one's own social conditioning, as well as others' social conditioning allows Black Buddhist teachers and long-term practitioners to clearly see a broad pattern of how people often relate to each other out of ignorance. Vipassana teacher Spring Washam simply states that other peoples' interpretations of her embodiment "don't get in." The conventional ways of operating in the social world, and all of the social inter-pretations of Blackness, operate as one "great truth." Yet, Washam realizes, there is a "universal level"—that of "mystical" non-self—in which human beings are but moving particles in a vast universe. There is a basic truth of impermanence. Human understandings of the conventional self are limited. People miss broader and deeper dimensions of understanding if the only real-ity that they consider is that of the conventional self.

Liberation

All ten long-term practitioners and teachers emphasize the profound practice of entering into silence. Indeed, liberation of the dark-skinned body is insepa-rable from the life-changing experience of entering into silence. In this way, embracing silence is distinguished from *being silenced.*

In *Sanctuary*, Manuel describes an early self-retreat, prior to learning instructions in meditation practice, in which she was instructed not to read or write.

> The silence I experienced was just that, silence. Not a word. Thoughts rose and fell like waves in the ocean. I turned inward and the doors of my heaven were

opened. I needed only to walk in. I became intensely interested in living from a place of silence and intimacy, a place I begin to call a spiritual life. I had allowed silence to be spiritual medicine rather than the coping skill I learned as a child who wanted to be invisible in her dark skin. The swami's guidance of silence was an immeasurable gift.[34]

Ultimately, for Manuel, Berry, and other Black Buddhist practitioners, silent meditation practice and dharma teachings on non-self are about liberation. For Berry, dharma practice is an opportunity to write his "own liberation narrative" that incorporates the Four Noble Truths, the Noble Eightfold Path, Baptist preaching, Martin Luther King, Jr., Malcolm X, and, ultimately, stillness. At a point, in deep meditation, social identity falls away and the mind is still. The clarity that arises from such stillness allows Berry to deeply embrace, with more depth, his social identity as a Black man, along with multitudinous Black ancestors. Like other interviewees, he no longer sees himself as trapped by the perceptions of those who internalize the dominant white culture. Rather, he is able to see the flaws and failings, as well as the brutal consequences, of that culture.

Rev. angel Kyodo williams similarly speaks of liberation as a psychological state. "There's a real powerfully felt experience in confrontation—in the midst of confrontation, like, choosing liberation or choosing pride in one's Blackness and the association that comes with that, like, being in camaraderie with other people choosing just centered Blackness. And that's healing powerful unto itself."[35]

Williams acknowledges the difficulty of choosing Blackness in a white supremacist culture. She states,

> We all find some point at which we betrayed ourselves around race. We wanted to be white, we wanted to belong. We wanted to, like, not look at that Black person that's coming in that's, like, going to make us look more Black. But we all had those types of moments. And then white people have their broken moments, right, in which they were wounded by the confrontation with race. And honoring [those moments] and reintegrating and forgiving oneself, because we see that we're operating inside of a larger system, it's redemption, right? And so, we have this redeeming experience that is not only the path to liberation, but it's a path to liberation that is inherently liberatory because we are able to include others in it. And we're able to include complex locations, right? I think that ideology creates an in and an out. And the lived embodied experience that comes out of applied mindfulness or radical dharma creates something different.[36]

Psychological liberation is the essential step to the process of "getting free." Half of the Black Buddhist teachers and practitioners interviewed for this chapter spoke of psychological liberation as essential, in that Black people no longer need to engage the degradations manifested by white supremacy. These practitioners engage in Black Lives Matter activism, cultivate people-of-color spaces, and reach into communities that disproportionately suffer from systemic violence. But they start from an inner stability that filters out degrading interpretations of Blackness (and queerness). Lama Rod Owens states,

> I think of how we talk about liberation, we are not just liberating ourselves socially and institutionally, we are also liberating ourselves from these beliefs around how we should relate to our bodies. I want more of that. I want more politics around self-care. I want more politics around self-love and that's the piece that we are not doing in Black Lives Matter.[37]

The language of love arises repeatedly in interviews with Black Buddhist practitioners. Owens speaks of "an ethic of love."[38] Ma'at articulates "breathing in peace and exhaling love."

> The deepest thing in spirit is to really access a sense of deep love for yourself, because without that you are not even hearing anything, you are not even alive enough to practice anything, to embrace anything. There's no space for it. You know, it's just the foundation, that is the container for which I hold everything.[39]

Ma'at acknowledges that the love is complicated, that hatred and fear coexist with a deep sense of inner stability and refuge. She continues,

> what I'm doing for myself physically, spiritually, emotionally, somatically is like being fully aware of like, "Okay, this is where I want to go with it and I want my body to be the vessel of that change so that whatever I do, whatever my response is, is coming out better, but processed." Like fully aware that I am processing it. So when I'm saying breathe in love, that's with patience and acceptance, and forgiveness. And exhale peace . . . and that's, you know, to me that's an extreme lovingkindness practice.[40]

Metta (lovingkindness) practice, with concentration and clear seeing as a foundation, allows practitioners to process feelings of hatred and fear and at the same time, embrace those to whom they feel aversion. In finding the "meditative stability" about which Owens spoke, Williams states that thoughts about ourselves are inherited from family, society, upbringing, region, and embodiment. And yet, she says, non-self is something different than the way in which people respond to the self.

> I'm something different than the way in which people respond. I have to enter and function in the world inside of that response as well, but I'm really clear

that it's not me. So, if people are disrespectful or dismissive of this embodiment of a brown woman in this time and place, my fundamental truth of who I am is not disturbed by that.[41]

Long-term practitioner Unique Holland, who has studied with Manuel as well as Washam, stated,

> When I'm committed to working towards the liberation of others and social justice, I recognize very clearly that I really cannot be effective in that work unless I'm really working on my own liberation. And I have to see myself to do that, right. And I need teachers who can see me to do that.

Studying with seasoned teachers, and going on long retreats, is essential for being able to see oneself clearly, and, perhaps paradoxically, let go of the construct of the self. Owens writes, "In the end, my healing has been learning to see myself and to celebrate myself. It is interrogating the stories about how I do not matter and choosing to let go of those narratives and engage in the necessary and revolutionary work, self-love, and liberation."[42] The practice has the power to heal the heart/mind. It is fundamentally inclusive, in that all genders and sexual identities are embraced.

CONCLUSION

The suffering induced by racism compels Black Buddhists to interpret teachings on non-self in nuanced ways. Many practitioners spoke of the importance of bringing lived experience—including suffering due to racism—to the cushion. These practitioners spoke of the trauma endured by African ancestors and a need to honor the cultural heritages within African traditions, as well as to remember the agony of being dislocated from families, land, traditions, and languages. The Black Buddhist teachers and practitioners interviewed for this study are keenly aware that they stand on the shoulders of those who have paved a path to social and institutional access; they are also deeply in touch with the anguish that they themselves feel. Black Buddhist practitioners feel the weight of oppression in predominantly white *sanghas* as well as the larger social environment. They note that white practitioners will notice dark skin color without acknowledging their own discomfort and myopia. The hegemonic whiteness of American Buddhism can feel alienating and isolating; whiteness perpetuates suffering in an environment that is, paradoxically, actively focused on alleviating suffering. As Black people become liberated, it is critical that white practitioners who possess privileged bodies—within white hegemonic contexts that privilege them—be compelled to interrogate their assumptions, their social power, and their tendency to individualize suffering.

As white people "do their work," it is important that Black people be visible and affirmed in predominantly white spaces: in *sanghas*, workplaces, and in a society that aggressively polices people of color. In addition to promoting the value of Blackness, it is important to promote queer identity: to embrace the intersection of race, gender, and sexuality. For many Black Buddhist teachers, finding a spiritual home in which queer identity is welcomed is as paramount as finding a *sangha* that grapples with race, racism, and privilege.

In short, promoting Blackness and queerness allows for a social ease in a broader culture that suffers from white myopia, microaggressions, and systemic injustices. The ability to be honest about the origins of suffering facilitates exhaling, taking off masks, and cultivating of authentic presence. Practitioners feel that they are showing up for their own lives, in their entirety; that they can embrace Black identity and also let it dissolve; and that race does not have to be the central facilitating aspect of their relationships with themselves. They can be whole people who possess dark skin, and at the same time, they do not have to focus entirely on their embodiment, even as skin color mediates their experience in predominantly white social spaces, including *sanghas*.

In being able to take off masks and establish an authentic presence, Black Buddhist practitioners see themselves as being able to embrace two truths: conventional and mystical; relative and absolute. They can be "in the world, but not of it." They acknowledge the importance of embodiment, but in the practice of silence, can also transcend the messages and norms that are relied upon in the social world. This is often a progression: Black practitioners grapple with their social identity while sitting on the cushion. Over time, the mind settles and a state of non-thinking is accessible. As Black practitioners access a psychological state of emptiness, not thinking, they can eventually hold together two ways of being: a self in the social world, and a non-self in a state of impermanence and constant change.

The ability to reach this internal state is psychologically liberating. The Black Buddhists who participated in this study assert that psychological liberation is a precursor for social liberation: Black people must be able to acknowledge, transcend, and transform the degrading constructs of Blackness in order to achieve political freedom. Sitting with racially induced suffering is essential for seeing the depth of it, allowing these messages to loosen their grip on the mind, and deconstructing the damage that has been wrought. Meditation practice facilitates liberation.

The foundation of liberation is self-love. Herein, Black practitioners come full circle: they start with the self—damaged, degraded, suffering—and eventually transcend that self. In the state of non-self, they dissolve the outdated ideas that have perpetuated suffering. As they strive to hold the self and non-self in tension, they evoke an energy of love toward all beings, including themselves. Sitting with one's internalized messages of degradation, rather than rejecting oneself, is a process of self-love. Challenging white supremacy and whiteness, in *sanghas* and broader US society, is self-love. In these parallel contemplative and activist practices, Black Buddhist teachers and long-term practitioners are liberated.

NOTES

1. angel Kyodo williams, *Being Black: Zen and the Art of Living with Fearlessness and Grace* (New York: Viking Compass, 2000).

2. Jan Willis, *Dreaming Me: An African American Woman's Spiritual Journey* (New York: Riverhead Books, 2001).

3. Zenju Earthlyn Manuel, *The Way of Tenderness: Awakening through Race, Sexuality, and Gender* (Somerville, MA: Wisdom Publications, 2015). Throughout this chapter, I will refer to her as Zenju Roshi.

4. Rev. angel Kyodo williams, Interview with Auburn Media, June 16, 2016, 8: 56.

5. Rev. angel Kyodo williams and Lama Rod Owens, with Jasmine Syedullah, *Radical Dharma: Talking Race, Love, and Liberation* (Berkeley, CA: North Atlantic Books, 2016), 118–119.

6. Willis, *Dreaming Me*, 149.

7. Ibid., 300.

8. Zenju Earthlyn Manuel, *Sanctuary: A Meditation on Home, Homelessness, and Belonging* (Somerville, MA: Wisdom Publications, 2018), 22.

9. Manuel, *The Way of Tenderness*, 10.

10. Williams, Owens, and Syedullah, *Radical Dharma*, xxii.

11. Ibid., xxvi–xxvii.

12. Ibid., 18.

13. Ibid.

14. Ibid.

15. Ven Bhikkhu Bodhi, "What Are the Four Noble Truths?" *Tricycle*, https://tricycle.org/magazine/impermanence-and-four-noble-truths/.

16. Consciousness refers to the basic awareness that makes sensory experience possible. Buddhist teachings illuminate subjective reality which is subject to change and dissolution. See Thích Nhất Hạnh, *Old Path White Clouds: Walking in the Footsteps of the Buddha* (Berkeley, CA: Parallax Press, 1991), 436. Nhất Hạnh explains, "All dharmas are contained in the eighteen realms: the six sense organs, the six sense objects, and the six sense consciousnesses. The six sense organs . . . are eye-consciousness, ear-consciousness, nose-consciousness, tongue-consciousness, body-consciousness, and mind-consciousness. The six sense objects are form, sound, smell, taste, touch, and objects of mind. The six sense consciousnesses are seeing, hearing,

smelling, tasting, and perceiving. There are no dharmas apart from the eighteen realms. All eighteen realms are subject to birth and death, to change and dissolution."

17. For example, consider the "one drop rule" in which Blackness refers to any person with one drop of sub-Saharan Black blood. See Christine B. Hickman, "The Devil and the One Drop Rule: Racial Categories, African Americans, and the U.S. Census," *Michigan Law Review* 95, no. 5 (1997): 1161–1265.

18. Interview with Owens, July 2017.

19. Interview with Rhonda Magee, June 2017.

20. Interview with Valerie Mason-John, also known as Vimalasara, July 2017.

21. Manuel, *The Way of Tenderness*, 23–24.

22. Ibid., 13.

23. Interview with Jylani Ma'at, June 2017.

24. Interview with Unique Holland, June 2017.

25. Interview with JoAnna, June 2017.

26. Interview with Devin Berry, June 2017.

27. Manuel, *Sanctuary*, 10.

28. Orlando Patterson, *Slavery and Social Death: A Comparative Analysis* (Cambridge, MA: Harvard University Press, 2018).

29. For an explanation of whiteness as landscape, see Willie Jennings, *The Christian Imagination: Theology and the Origins of Race* (New Haven, CT: Yale University Press, 2011).

30. Interview with JoAnna Hardy, June 2017.

31. Interview with Lama Rod Owens, September 2017.

32. Ibid.

33. Interview with Bushi Yamato Damashii, July 2017.

34. Manuel, *Sanctuary*, 85.

35. Interview with Rev. angel Kyodo williams, April 2017.

36. Ibid.

37. Interview with Owens, July 2017.

38. Ibid.

39. Interview with Jylani Ma'at, June 2017.

40. Ibid.

41. Interview with Rev. angel Kyodo williams, April 2017.

42. Owens, Radical Dharma, 72.

Chapter 6

"The Tranquil Meditator"[1]

Laurie Cassidy

"You just want white people to feel peaceful!"

This observation has haunted me. After giving a talk on confronting white-ness in the United States through contemplative practice, an African American man in the audience stood up and said to me, "Black men are being murdered by the police! What difference will any of this make for them? You just want white people to feel peaceful!"[2] Since hearing this indictment I have wondered how the spiritual practices of white people can be accountable to Anti-Black violence.[3] According to the US Department of Health and Human Services, eighteen million Americans meditate.[4] In this seeming cultural embrace of meditation by Americans, how do spiritual practices break open the "white fragility" that keeps us ignorant and obdurate to the systems of white supremacy within which we live and that we (re)produce?[5]

My argument interrogates how American capitalism hijacks spiritual practices, such as Buddhist meditation, and thereby subverts their liberative human potential. I intentionally use the word hijack because it refers to how a vehicle for transport is seized and forced to a destination other than was origi-nally intended. This seizure commandeers a vehicle away from its intended purposes. Using this metaphor, American capitalism subverts spiritual prac-tices away from their intended purpose, which is the transformation of human consciousness. This subversion is to reinforce individualism,

> and this in turn has the effect of not only turning the attention of those seeking deepened spirituality away from issues of justice, but of also leaving the efforts for justice to those who have abandoned concern with spirituality, seeing it as having nothing to offer in the work for structural change.[6]

This commandeering by capitalism subverts spiritual practices to maintain our white racial frame and worldview—and, moreover, the political, cultural, and economic social status quo.[7]

My chapter explores this corruptive power play in three turns. First, I begin by exploring the conundrum of white people engaging in spiritual practice in the context of the United States: white ignorance. To engage in practices intended to bring awareness poses a basic epistemological problem for white people. To be white, we agree,

> to an officially sanctioned reality (that) is divergent from actual reality . . . one has an agreement to misinterpret the world. One has to learn to see the world wrongly, but with the assurance that this set of mistaken perceptions will be validated by white epistemic authority, whether religious or secular.[8]

Being born white we sign onto the racial contract, "producing the ironic outcome that whites will in general be unable to understand the world they themselves have made."[9] How do practices of awakening and awareness enable white people to understand the world in which we live?

Second, I explore the connection between spiritual practice and power. As Michel Foucault has taught us, "power and knowledge directly imply one another . . . there is no power relation without the correlative constitution of a field of knowledge, nor any knowledge that does not presuppose and constitute at the same time power relations."[10] Drawing upon the work of Grace Jantzen, I illustrate how power determines the very language use regarding spiritual practices. Jantzen's work raises questions about the philosophical context for the concepts of rationality and personhood that determine our conversations in America. Her work raises the question, "Who benefits from our language about spiritual practice?"

Finally, I explore the workings of power and how such workings are demonstrated through representations of Buddhist meditation within contemporary popular culture. My analysis demonstrates how Scott Mitchell's notion of "The Tranquil Meditator" reproduces the depoliticizing of spiritual practice.[11] Mitchell reveals that "The Tranquil Meditator" is used in advertising and film to question or to promote individual well-being, health, and quality of life. "In this way meditation becomes . . . safe for cultural consumption, nothing more harmless than a trip to a spa or vacation. And it is almost always something done in isolation, apart from one's family or community."[12] Exploring the cultural representations of Buddhism is one way to understand who benefits from our language about spiritual practice.

To be clear—to interrogate how we (mis)represent Buddhism within American popular culture *is not a critique of Buddhism*. In the United States, this process of representation is at the service of maintaining white supremacy, *by any means necessary*. Ironically, the very notion of self as autonomous and individualized is an illusion and is the cause of suffering described by the Buddha. My study of meditation's representation verifies "the Buddhist diagnosis of our condition . . . that we are all practicing a 'religion of the self'—namely devotion to ourselves."[13]

I am one of the eighteen million Americans who practice mediation. My purpose in this exploration is to invite those of us who are white to critically reflect upon how spiritual practices enable us to deconstruct the white racial frame and resist the individualism that reinforces it. As Robin DiAngelo explains,

> the ideology of Individualism is one of the primary barriers to well-meaning (and other) white people understanding racism: As long as I don't see myself as *personally engaged* in acts of racism, I am exempt from it. Individualism is so entrenched that it is virtually immovable without sustained effort.[14]

An assumption embedded within my work is that the sustained effort to interrupt and dismantle individualism is the work of love.[15] Whether we are Buddhist, Christian, Hindu, Jewish, spiritual and not religious, or identify as secular practitioners, how does our meditation enable us to explore our socialization living in a white supremacist society? What I am suggesting is likened to what Fredric Jameson calls "cartographic" proficiency, "this form of skilled dissidence . . . requires the skill of knowing how to chart or map social and cultural territories in consciousness and imagination."[16] To dismantle this white worldview it is necessary to "engage in a conscious dialogue/interaction among the self, the community, and the society within a global culture."[17] Is this mapping enough? No! This mapping is one small step in awakening us to the reality of living in America, "whether we like it or not . . . we are bound together forever. We are all part of each other."[18]

A CONUNDRUM

I do not want white people to just feel peaceful in the face of anti-black violence; rather, I would ask: how do spiritual practices perpetuate a "racialized selective sympathy and indifference" to this horror?[19]

Let's explore the purpose and end of spiritual practice in order to reflect upon this question.

> Once you change your philosophy, you change your thought pattern. Once you change your thought pattern, you change your attitude. Once you change your attitude, it changes your behavior pattern. And then you go into some action.[20]

These words from Malcolm X may seem an unlikely source in a chapter on spiritual practices in America, but he is calling for the cultivation of critical consciousness, a consciousness "that attains the truth of one's situation."[21] Understanding the truth of our situation is also the aim of Buddhist meditation practice. As Dharma teacher Gil Fronsdal explains,

> But the function of meditation in Buddhism is not simply to become calm or peaceful in some kind of conventional way. Rather, it is to use the level of calm, or peace, or well-being that come from meditation, as a springboard for developing greater insight or greater understanding of our life.[22]

How do we awaken to our situation and understand our life as white Americans? How do spiritual practices create the possibility of such understanding? Malcolm X taught in order for people to awaken to the suffering caused by white supremacy, and the Buddha taught for people to awaken to the truth of suffering as a fundamental element of human existence. In both cases there was an assumption that there are practices that can bring suffering to an end. How in a white supremacist society can meditation practice be an authentic catalyst for critical consciousness?[23] This question is not only theoretically and philosophically provocative but by drawing upon the vision of Malcolm X these questions take on political and historical importance. This question demands that we address how spiritual and religious practices make us more able to awaken to what it means to live in America, a nation built upon race.[24] America is like a house whose foundation is built on the system of white supremacy. Awakening to this systemic reality involves understanding and taking responsibility for how this systemic reality is legitimized and rationalized by processes of socialization.[25]

> The centuries-old white racial frame is a gestalt, a composite of elements and subframes fused into a whole. Countering it in white adults and children is difficult because it is so fundamental to the social, material, and ideological construction of U.S. society. This white frame severely limits what most white people believe, feel, say and do in regard to racial matters.[26]

I draw upon Malcolm X because he sets a context for exploring how we judge "developing greater insight or understanding of our life." He makes us investigate whether our growth in consciousness is a quality that engages historical reality—or transcends it.[27] Malcolm X's voice is a beacon that can be deployed to explore what it may look like for our understanding of reality as integrally related to our contending with the American history that we want to ignore. He encourages us to critically deal with the internalized system of white supremacy we are taught to deny, and to question any religion or spiritual practice that—implicitly or explicitly—"justifies" dominance and subordination. To listen and learn from Malcolm X in our inquiry into the function of religious practices in the United States is a way for us "to recognize ourselves and each other in our stories, our memories, our hopes; to grapple with our collective and intersection pasts" in America.[28]

Being born white we sign onto the racial contract, "producing the ironic outcome that whites will in general be unable to understand the world they themselves have made."[29] This poses a problem for how white people awaken to the truth of our existence. This ignorance is not simply a gap in knowledge, but is actively (re)produced to maintain multiple and interlocking systems of supremacy. White people are socialized into epistemologies of ignorance, which are fundamental to our functioning within white supremacy.[30] This ignorance is particularly seditious for those of us who do not identify ourselves as racist.[31] As Linda Martín Alcoff explains, "not only are whites inculcated in some pernicious epistemic practices, but will have less motivation or ability than others would have to either detect their errors or correct them."[32]

To untangle the contradictory and complex connection between spiritual practice and systems of white supremacy in America is a lifetime of work for persons and communities.[33] In the limited space of this chapter, I explore how our contemporary discourse about spiritual practices, particularly about meditation, is always also about power. To explore representations of Buddhist meditation we need to explore the philosophical foundation that condition these representations. To understand how this power operates in collective conversations about spiritual practice in America is one way we can be actively involved in "developing greater insight or understanding of our life."

To explore the dynamic relationship between spiritual practice and power I draw on the groundbreaking scholarship of Grace Jantzen.[34] A feminist philosopher of religion, Jantzen documents that privatizing spirituality is a political process through which hegemony enables a "transcendence" of historical reality. "The net result . . . is the reinforcement of the social status quo, as intellectual and religious energy is poured into an exploration of private religiosity rather than into social and political action for change."[35] This "turn toward the subject" is the result of Kant's understanding of rationality, which is still determining language about mysticism and spirituality.

Jantzen's analysis is also case-in-point for modernity's grasp on the discourse of mysticism. In revealing the impact of Kant's rationality on our conversations about mysticism, unfortunately her gender analysis is colorblind.[36] However, I draw upon Jantzen because of her fierce determination to deconstruct the modern philosophical hold on understanding and defining mysticism. In retelling the modern approach to mysticism she neglects to see how Kant not only determines our current approach to rationality, but also personhood.[37] As Charles Mills argues, we must expose the racism of the liberal theorists, such as Kant, who have been and are foundational to the

ideology of white supremacy in America.[38] Without overlooking this limita-
tion I will critically engage Jantzen's research because she enables us to interrogate the modern philosophical underpinnings of how we talk about spiritual
practice in America, and she makes an opening for us to see who is excluded.

TURN TOWARD THE SUBJECT

> To the extent that prayer and meditation and books on spirituality actually help
> people to cope with the distresses of life that arise out of unjust social condi-
> tions, without challenging those conditions themselves, to that extent they act as
> a sedative which distracts attention from the need to dismantle the structures that
> perpetuate the misery. If books and practices of spirituality help people to calm
> jangled nerves and release anxieties and renew courage to re-enter the world
> as it is, then whatever the good intentions of the authors and practitioners (and
> these are usually not in doubt) what is actually happening is that the structures
> of injustice are being reinforced. The social and political policies that make for
> starving children, battered women and the evils of rising fascism are still being
> unchallenged as people learn through prayer to find tranquility to live with cor-
> rupt political and social structures instead of channeling their distress and anger
> and anxiety into energy for constructive change.[39]

This extended quotation from Jantzen clearly describes the problem she seeks
to contest in her volume *Power, Gender and Christian Mysticism*. She reveals
the practical implications of defining mysticism and spirituality to be "a subjective psychological state" devoid of social and political context.[40] Mysticism that is assumed to be an individual, interior, psychological state defaults
to practices of self-soothing, even functioning as a sedative that does not
create the possibility for engaging in social change. Her incisive critique of
privatized spirituality goes so far as to deem them reinforcing social injustice.
Drawing on Foucault, Jantzen's feminist analyses deconstructs the current
understanding of mysticism. She also historically documents how power has
determined the social construction of mysticism in the history of Christianity.
    My purpose for drawing upon Jantzen's work on Christian mysticism in
this chapter on representations of Buddhism in popular culture is because
she demonstrates how power is always at work in defining what constitutes
as spiritual practice. Extending her logic to discourse about spiritual practice
in the United States suggests that any depoliticizing or decontextualizing of
Buddhist spiritual practice is a contemporary example of an ongoing and
repeated historical struggle. As Jantzen explains, she does not want to show
a development in the notion of mysticism, "rather to uncover the power
struggles which were inherent in the emergence of particular concepts."[41]
Jantzen's scholarship provides a larger philosophical and political frame of

reference for the operations of power we see in the contemporary representations of Buddhist meditation in America. She confronts us with how the
Enlightenment continues to inform our thinking, and situates contemporary
conversations about mysticism amid the grasp of modernity and coloniality.
As Jeremy Carrette notes, Jantzen introduces the question, "Who benefits
from such thinking?" and this question is critical to how we define spiritual
practices in America.

Jantzen explains that contemporary Anglo-American [male?] philosophers
of religion have paid a great deal of attention to the concept of mysticism,
while feminist scholars have been focused upon spirituality.[42] This distinction
underscores a problem in how feminist theorists have understood the critical
connection of mysticism and power. "There has been virtually no attention
paid to the way in which the delimiting of mysticism through the centuries
was crucial to maintaining male hierarchical control in church and society."[43]
For Jantzen, understanding the "technologies of patriarchy" in the past is
critical to "the question of what power relations *current* social constructions
might contain, and who benefits from them."[44]

Jantzen offers an extensive review of white, male philosophers and scholars of mysticism who share the assumption of mysticism "to be a subjective
psychological state."[45] Whether contemporary authors acknowledge this or
not, Jantzen explains that this shared understanding is rooted in the work of
Fredrich Schleiermacher and William James. James characterized mystical
experience as having four essential elements: "ineffability, noetic quality,
transiency, and passivity."[46] Jantzen notes that even when problematizing this
approach and critiquing William James, scholars continue to adhere to this
notion of mysticism. After she provides a genealogy of philosophical commentary on mysticism she writes, "What is striking is that although the evaluation of mysticism among the writers . . . range from complete dismissal and
contempt to enthusiastic endorsement, there is virtual agreement that what
they are talking about is an intense psychological state."[47]

This knot of philosophical discourse binds the exploration of mysticism to
the long shadow of Kant.

> Kant's understanding of rationality and his theory of knowledge stands at the
> summit of what can be termed the enlightenment project. In his view, human
> knowledge can never extend to knowledge of things as they are in themselves;
> the best we can hope for is accurate knowledge of things as they appear to us.[48]

Jantzen's characterization of this discourse about mysticism as situated
squarely within modernity is indicting for many reasons. Two issues are
important to the purpose of this chapter. First, as she carefully documents,
Kant's questions are not those of Christian mystics such as Teresa of Avila or

Julian of Norwich. The preoccupation with the individualized idea of mysticism has arched back on Christian mystics and they "have been domesticated for a privatized spirituality."[49] For Jantzen this privatization of spirituality is at the service of maintaining patriarchal gender roles. She explains that privatized spirituality is,

> Open to women as well as men; but it plays directly into the hands of modern bourgeois political and gender assumptions. It keeps God [and women] safely out of politics and the public realm; it allows mysticism to flourish as a secret inner life, while those who nurture such a life can generally be counted on to prop up rather than challenge the status quo of their work places, their gender roles, and the political systems by which they are governed, since their anxieties and angers will be allayed in the privacy of their own hearts' search for peace and tranquility.[50]

Second, Jantzen enables us to confront how this discourse on mysticism and spirituality continue to be held hostage to modernity. By omitting any analysis of race in her deconstruction she reveals how this discourse goes unmarked as "white." To name the whiteness of this discourse would mean facing the deforming impact of white supremacy on the construction of Anglo-American philosophy, and the consciousness of the philosophers who create it. As Bryan Massingale has argued, such acknowledgment would be to face "being (de)formed by the systemic distortion of Western racism, [which] did not and could not have regarded persons of African descent as numbered among the 'subjects' to whom they should 'turn.'"[51]

Kant's notion of rationality not only reinscribes gender oppression, but his notion of personhood also undergirds the very notion of race.[52] As Emmanuel Eze explains, "The black person, for example, can accordingly be denied full humanity since full and 'true' humanity accrues only to the white European. For Immanuel Kant European humanity is *the* humanity par excellence."[53] In the context of the Americas this is a critical question because our colonization is the horrific underside of modernity. Peruvian sociologist Anibal Quijano has argued that a key enactment of coloniality functions through the defining of knowledge and subjectivity.[54] Jantzen's exploration of who counts as a mystic allows her only to explore this question through the lens of European Christianity.[55] Returning to Jantzen's question, "Who benefits from such thinking?"

WHO IS THE SUBJECT?

> Can you not flick the shit out of your fingernail these days and not have it hit one of those damn White Buddhists right in the lotus? . . . Nothing beats the calm, self-actualization of the Buddhist Thing. . . . Welcome to Lamapalooza.[56]

Justin Chin's sarcastic observation offers a humorous yet pointed portrayal of the proliferation of "white" and "calm" images of Buddhists in the lotus position, which are ubiquitous in American popular culture. Building upon Jantzen's analysis I will explore the image of the "Tranquil Meditator" as a key representation of spiritual practice in America and interrogate how intersecting dynamics of power can be read in the images of the Tranquil Meditator.[57] Moving forward with Jantzen's analysis I will inquire into how the Tranquil Meditator represents the white-neoliberal technology of the self.

Buddhist scholar Scott Mitchell introduces the notion of the "Tranquil Meditator" and describes the image as most always female (and read, "white") sitting in the lotus position, "commonly associated with the images of the Buddha at the moment of his enlightenment."[58] Mitchell explains that this image is found most often in advertising.

> Such advertisements work by making the explicit connection between calm, relaxed, centeredness, and the practice of seated meditation. Herein, the Tranquil Meditator is set apart from the world, apart from the demands of work or home or family. She meditates alone, and she meditates for the specific purpose of relaxation. Whereas iconographically, there may be a connection between her posture and that of a meditating Buddha figure . . . it is also clear that what she is striving for is not some sort of Buddhist enlightenment but more of a mundane sort of relaxation.[59]

TIME magazine offers us one such image of the white-female-"Tranquil Meditator." In 2003 *TIME* featured "The Science of Meditation" with the cover image of a young, white, female, with blonde hair, sitting in the lotus position with her eyes closed. She sits alone and barefoot on the parched earth of what looks like a desert landscape. She is clad in a sheer white slip like dress. The magazine cover states, "New Age mumbo jumbo? Not for millions of Americans who meditate for health and well-being. Here's how it works." At the bottom of the page it identifies this seated woman as the actress Heather Graham who it states, "has been practicing transcendental meditation since 1991."[60] A similar cover of *TIME* was published in 2014. This edition was entitled "The Mindfulness Revolution: The science of finding focus in a stressed-out, multi-tasking culture." The image is of a young, white, female, with blonde hair, standing and she is pictured from her chest up. This young white woman has her face slightly upturned with a faint smile and her eyes closed and clothed in a light-colored tank top. She is also alone and is pictured against a non-descript light blue background.[61]

Buddhologist Sharon Suh offers a contrasting picture of women engaging in Buddhist practices. She writes, "What I see in real life when I visit Buddhist temples . . . I see women chanting, prostrating, and burning incense while they socialize and the kids run around."[62] Suh's description is thought

provoking because she puts into stark contrast the language of representation
in the magazine cover and the communal and embodied practice of women
in a Buddhist temple. Suh's description verifies the observation that Buddhism has become a popular brand, which "has moved from the temple to
the market."[63]

This move from the temple to the market offers clues about what construction of the self is being (re)produced in this representation of the Tranquil
Meditator. Commenting on *TIME* magazine's covers, Joanna Piacenza offers
a scathing race, class, and gender analysis of the two images. Her insightful
critique centers around her claim that the two images are being used to sell a
number of different things. Piacenza claims that the images cohere with the
ideology in American culture that women are the ones who need to engage in
self-improvement. "To calm their culturally-assigned hysteria, if you will."
Moreover, she states that the physical appearance of these female images do
not represent women in America. "Does this continue our cultural ideology
that thin, white, blonde women are the beauty elites? Yes." Her observations
on the racialized portrait of the "Tranquil Meditator" conflate race and class
in a fascinating way,

> my tip-toe into the racial issues of this cover involve the bougie-ness of modern
> Buddhism. Meditation retreats are expensive and, as many social media-ers
> point out, mostly white. Because only affluent white people would be crazy
> enough to leave their cushy life, shell out $10,000, *temporarily* take retreat in an
> "impoverished" country, and meditate on another person's "suffering."[64]

Piacenza is offering a very clear account of what Foucault would define as
the normative gaze of society.[65] The image on the magazine cover suggests
the normative idea of a white self, which is approved by the white supremacist culture; meditation acts as a technology to realize and manage this individual, autonomous, and white self, and therefore be seen and approved.[66]
António Carvalho's critical observations support my analysis of the racialized
power dynamics of this white-female-Tranquil Meditator by using the lens of
Foucault. Carvalho notes that the subject of this representation is framed by
words such as "well-being, happiness and quality of life." For Carvalho, these
images of "well-being" and "happiness" refer to pernicious characteristics of
the neoliberal self, which is at the heart of capitalism in present-day America.
From this view, mindfulness meditation acts as a technology of the self by
which individuals act on themselves to fit into this contemporary capitalist
way of life. Carvalho contends that the self of this Tranquil Meditator is doc-
ile and adjusted to the norms of the neoliberal capitalist system. For a number
of commentators, the spiritual practice of mindfulness in this representation
is a new "opiate of the masses."[67]

Foucault's notion of governmentality is key to understanding how one could see mindfulness meditation to be an opiate of the masses. For Foucault, "Governmentality refers to the point of contact between technologies of domination and technologies of the self, to examine the operations of power/ knowledge within neoliberal capitalist societies."[68] As Foucault argues that since the Enlightenment power does not necessarily operate through overt acts of domination but through how the subject is defined and rationality ordered.[69] Through Foucault's lens, mindfulness becomes a technology of the self, whereby the individual can become a neoliberal subject. Slavoj Žižek states that meditation is the most effective technology of the self in a neoliberal economic system.

> The "Western Buddhist" meditative stance is arguably the most efficient way for us to fully participate in the capitalist economy while retaining the appearance of sanity. If Max Weber were alive today, he would definitely write a second, supplementary volume to his *Protestant Ethics*, entitled *The Taoist Ethic and the Spirit of Global Capitalism*.[70]

> Is not the "us" that Žižek alludes to, us—white people? The gaze of the dominant neo-liberal culture is on the white subject, a self who is calm, self-regulating and insulated (psychically, geographically, and socially) from the pain, suffering and violence of our racialized and gendered economic system. As Joe Feagin aptly points out, "Strikingly, colonialism, capitalism, modernity and global exploitation have a common genealogy."[71]

THIS IS NOT A CONCLUSION

> Racism is a systemic, societal, institutional, omnipresent, and epistemologically embedded phenomenon that pervades every vestige of our reality. For most whites, however, racism is like murder; the concept exists, but someone has to commit it in order for it to happen. This limited view of such a multilayered syndrome cultivates the sinister nature of racism and in fact, perpetuates racist phenomena rather than eradicates them.[72]

This definition of racism has a grotesque irony. If it is true that most of us who are white understand the term "racism" like the term "murder"—concepts that describe individual behavior—then how do we make sense of the murder of black people occurring day after day in our society? "But all our phrasing . . . serves to obscure that racism is a visceral experience, that it dislodges brains, blocks airways, rips muscle, extracts organs, cracks bones, breaks teeth."[73]

As I finish this chapter, news coverage gives the grim report of Stephon Clark's murder. Clark, a twenty-two-year-old black man was shot dead by

Sacramento police in a barrage of bullets in his grandmother's back yard. Clark is described as a loving father of two children, whose "independent autopsy affirms that Stephon was not a threat to the police and was slain in another senseless police killing."[74] Our spiritual practices seem impervious to the fact that black people cannot breathe (Eric Garner), "can't eat skittles or wear a hoodie (Trayvon Martin), can't play loud music, can't play as a child in a park (Tamar Rice), can't seek help after an accident (Renisha McBride), can't walk to a store with a friend (Rekia Boyd), can't move to a new city and start a new job (Sandra Bland)."[75] As Ta-Nehisi Coates has explained, even to live by middle-class standards does not shield African Americans from lethal violence.[76] The limited space of my chapter cannot adequately name the growing number of human beings, who, because of having black skin, are victims of anti-black violence in America. As Alex Mikulich states, "The cruel perversity of the U.S. empire we inhabit renders the daily violent premature death of black life as forgettable, inevitable, and banal."[77]

As white people how do we respond to the indictment, opening this chapter, that we meditate "just to feel peaceful?" We cannot deny this indictment when eighteen million of us meditate but our society is growing in hatred and violence. This brief deconstruction of representations of spiritual practices in America offers a sobering picture of the way in which these practices are being made part of the technologies of the white-neoliberal self, which is critical to globalized capitalism. Tibetan Buddhist teacher and scholar Judith Simmer-Brown diagnoses this subversion of spiritual practice as "spiritual materialism."[78] Drawing upon the work of her teacher Chögyam Trungpa Rinpoche, Simmer-Brown contends that the commodification of all things Buddhist is just an expression of a multi-leveled problem. "Unchallenged, materialism will co-opt our physical lives, our communities and our very practice."[79] For Simmer-Brown, the psychological dimension of spiritual materialism is in evading any discomfort, confusion or the pain of being wrong.

> Psychological materialism interprets whatever is threatening or irritating as an enemy. Then, we control the threat by creating an ideology or religion in which we are victorious, or correct, or righteous; we never directly experience the fear and confusion that could arise from facing a genuine threat.[80]

Simmer-Brown contends that consumerism is seducing Buddhism to promote individual ego, which I would say is the protection and reproduction of the white self. For example, a tempting white strategy of evasion of dealing with the agony of lethal anti-black violence is to hide behind our good intentions, in other words to say, "Oh my God I never intend any of this! This is not *my* intention when I meditate." But this evasion itself reveals the white frame, which "presumes that a desire that resides in my head can effectively ward off the society in which I am embedded."[81]

It is also tempting to believe that we just need to state more clearly the intended purposes of these spiritual practices; as if we say it louder we can break through the hegemony of this technology of the self. Research by Shankar Vedantam contradicts this belief. We can teach meditation as a practice to awaken consciousness of interdependence, but if the representations in society picture a peaceful "Tranquil Meditator" the latter will win out. Vedantam argues that we rely too much on conscious and rational formation when our unconscious messages in cultural representations are a much more powerful influence. Vedantum offers the example of teaching racial tolerance in public education, "there are many hundreds of implicit messages of racial bias that children absorb through culture—whether it's television, books or the attitudes of the adults and kids around them. . . . And it's these hidden associations that essentially determine what happens in the unconscious minds of these children."[82]

As the African American man challenged me, "Black men are being murdered by the police! What difference will any of this make for them?" Spiritual practices of white people must be accountable to this question. This accountability does not infer that spiritual practices will give us answers to fixing anti-black violence or to make us more "enlightened" than other white people, these two positions reinforce the construction of the white self. It may be that spiritual practices enable us to question how we are socialized to resist feeling uncomfortable, guilty, or confused by this man's question. Simmer-Brown explains that rather than avoid this confusion and pain our spiritual practice can enable us to face "our racing minds, our churning emotions, and constant plots."[83] Our ability to be with our own complicated, complicit, and painful experience of our white selves is not a way to recenter the conversation on ourselves, but rather one dimension of being capable of deeply listening to people of color and learning how to take responsibility for our shared reality. As Shannon Sullivan describes, "White people can find ways to live in their own skins *and* help bring about more racial justice in the world."[84]

NOTES

1. My title is drawn from Scott Mitchell, "The Tranquil Meditator: Representing Buddhism and Buddhists in U.S. Popular Media," *Religion Compass* 8, no. 3 (2014): 81–89. I appreciate Sharon Suh's sage advice in suggesting Mitchell's research.

2. I am very grateful to the gentleman who offered these comments; his frustration and anger with my presentation and his candid feedback were a real act of love. I want to thank Paul Pearson, PhD for inviting me to give the 2017 Merton Lecture,

"Merton's Prophetic Wisdom and the Dis-Ease of Whiteness" at the International Merton Center at Bellarmine University in Louisville, Kentucky.

3. "Why introduce this new term? Although the discourse of white supremacy illuminates the role that power plays in racial injustice, it falsely portrays racialized evil as an injustice that falls upon all peoples of color equally and in the same way. In truth, however, only black people endure and struggle against the afterlife of slavery." Please see the astute and penetrating analysis by Katie Grimes, "*Black Exceptionalism*: Anti Black Supremacy in the Aftermath of Slavery," in *Anti-Blackness and Christian Ethics*, eds. Vincent Lloyd and Andrew Prevot (Maryknoll: Orbis Press, 2017), 41. I see in Grimes's analysis a call for white people to understand the different but intersecting histories in the United States, which can be obfuscated by generalizing terms such as white supremacy. Though in this chapter I attempt to respond specifically to anti-black violence, white people must deal with native peoples who live in the aftermath of genocide (which is not present in her analysis) and other specific forms of violence specific communities of color.

4. This statistic is considered a "conservative" number, and is cited in a 2012 survey by the National Health Interview Survey, https://nccih.nih.gov/research/stat istics/NHIS/2012 (accessed March 27, 2018).

5. Robin DiAngelo has created the term "white fragility," which she defines as, "The result of white racial socialization. A state in which even a minimum amount of racial stress becomes intolerable, triggering a range of defensive moves. These moves include the outward display of emotions such as anger, fear and guilt, and behaviors such as argumentation, silence and leaving the stress-inducing situation. These behaviors in turn, function to reinstate white racial comfort and status quo." *What Does it Mean to be White? Developing White Racial Literacy* (New York: Peter Lang, 2016), 355–356.

6. Grace M. Jantzen, *Power, Gender, and Christian Mysticism* (New York: Cambridge University Press, 1995), 21.

7. Joe Feagin, *The White Racial Frame: Centuries of Racial Framing and Counter-Framing* (New York: Routledge, 2013).

8. Charles Mills, *The Racial Contract* (Ithaca, NY: Cornell University Press, 1997), 73, quoted in Barbara Applebaum, *Being White, Being Good: White Complicity, White Moral Responsibility and Social Justice Pedagogy* (Lanham, Maryland: Lexington Books, 2010), 37. Italics in the text.

9. Mills, *The Racial Contract*, 18.

10. Michel Foucault, *Discipline and Punishment: The Birth of the Prison* (New York: Penguin, 1977), 27.

11. Mitchell, "The Tranquil Meditator."

12. Ibid., 86.

13. Jeremy Carrette and Richard King, *Selling Spirituality: The Silent Takeover of Religion* (New York: Routledge, 2005), 101.

14. DiAngelo, *What Does it Mean to be White?* 195.

15. "Love does not begin and end the way we seem to think it does. Love is a battle. Love is a growing up." James Baldwin, *The Price of a Ticket: Collected Nonfiction, 1948–1985* (New York: St. Martin Press, 1985), 234.

16. Chela Sandoval, *Theory Out of Bounds: Methodology of the Oppressed* (Minneapolis: University of Minnesota Press, 2000), 28–29.

17. Emilie Townes, *Womanist Ethics and the Cultural Production of Evil* (New York: Palgrave, 2006), 5.

18. Baldwin, *The Price of a Ticket*, 234.

19. See Bryan Massingale, "The Systemic Erasure of the Black/Dark-Skinned Body in Catholic Ethics," in *Catholic Theological Ethics Past, Present, and Future: The Trento Conference*, ed. James Keenan (Maryknoll, NY: Orbis Books, 2011), 119. This term is defined as "the unconscious failure to extend to a minority the same recognition of humanity, and hence the same sympathy and care, given as a matter of course to one's own group." Charles R. Lawrence III, "The Id, the Ego, and Equal Protection: Reckoning with Unconscious Racism," *Stanford Law Review* 39 (1987): 317–388, n. 135.

20. Malcolm X, "The Ballot or the Bullet," Speech, April 3, 1964, quoted in Bryan Massingale, "*Vox Victimarum Vox Dei*: Malcolm X as Neglected 'Classic' for Catholic Theological Reflection," *Catholic Theological Society of America Proceedings* 65 (2010): 72.

21. Ibid.

22. "Four Noble Truths," transcribed from a talk by Gil Fronsdal, January 1, 2005, http://www.insightmeditationcenter.org/books-articles/articles/four-noble-truths/ (accessed March 7, 2018). Gil Fronsdal, PhD is a Buddhist scholar, Dharma teacher, and ordained Zen priest who has been practicing Sōtō Zen and Vipassanā since 1975.

23. I will use the term White Supremacy throughout this chapter because this is the system that legitimizes the economic system of the United States and is built into all the institutions of America. See the very helpful summary at SOA Watch, http://soaw.org/index.php?option=com_content&view=article&id=482verything.

24. The rising tide of White Nationalism in the United States and Europe is the context of this chapter. See Vegas Tenold, *Everything You Love Will Burn: Inside the Rebirth of White Nationalism in America* (New York: Nation Books, 2018). Also Adam Nossiter, "'Let Them Call You Racists': Bannon's Pep Talk to National Front," *New York Times*, March 10, 2018, https://www.nytimes.com/2018/03/10/world/europe/steve-bannon-france-national-front.html?module=WatchingPortal&region=c-column-middle-span-region&pgType=Homepage&action=click&mediaId=thumb_square&state=standard&contentPlacement=11&version=internal&contentCollection=www.nytimes.com&contentId=https%3A%2F%2Fwww.nytimes.com%2F2018%2F03%2F10%2Fworld%2Feurope%2Fsteve-bannon-france-national-front.html&eventName=Watching-article-click (accessed March 11, 2018).

25. Feagin, *The White Racial Frame*, x. This metaphor of America as a house built on race is Feagin's, and he explains that this metaphor is critical to understanding that white supremacy is not an "add on" to the structure of our country but the very foundation. This framing of the house is not only a systemic reality, but is also our worldview.

26. Ibid., 204.

27. See Christena Cleveland, "So Much of the Privileged Life is About Transcendence," *On Being*, July 7, 2017, https://onbeing.org/blog/christena-cleveland-so-

much-of-the-privileged-life-is-about-transcendence/ (accessed March 12, 2018). I am very grateful to Martin Byrne, CFC for introducing me to Cleveland's insightful work.

28. Shawn Copeland, "Memory, Emancipation, and Hope: Political Theology in the 'Land of the Free,'" *The Santa Clara Lectures* 4 (November 9, 1997): 6.

29. Mills, *The Racial Contract*, 18.

30. I use the plural here because as Sullivan and Tuana elaborate being socialized into the ignorance of whiteness takes many forms. Building upon the work of Charles Mills, Linda Martín Alcoff explains that " we clearly need to address the class, ethnicity, and gender heterogeneity among whites, and to think through the relationship between the objective interests of colonialism generally and the objective interests of whites as a group." See Alcoff's essay, "Epistemologies of Ignorance: Three Types," in *Race and Epistemologies of Ignorance*, eds. Shannon Sullivan and Nancy Tuana (Albany: SUNY Press, 2007), 50. See also Matthias Gross and Linsey McGoey, eds., *Routledge International Handbook of Ignorance Studies* (New York: Routledge, 2015).

31. Robin DiAngelo clearly and brilliantly deconstructs the way (we who do not identify as racist) have been collectively socialized to deny our socialization into White Supremacy. See *What Does it Mean to Be White?* 194–214.

32. Alcoff, "Epistemologies of Ignorance," 50.

33. One such collective inspired by Buddhism is White Awake, whose mission is to combat white supremacy "by focusing on educational and spiritual practices to facilitate white people's engagement in the creation of a just and sustainable society" (https://whiteawake.org/).

34. Please see Elaine L. Graham, ed., *Grace Jantzen: Redeeming the Present* (Burlington, VT: Ashgate, 2009).

35. Jantzen, *Power, Gender, and Christian Mysticism*, 21.

36. Jantzen's work addresses coloniality and draws upon the intersectional analysis of Patricia Hill Collins in Grace M. Jantzen, *Becoming Divine: Toward a Feminist Philosophy of Religion* (Bloomington: University of Indiana, 1999).

37. Charles W. Mills, "Kant and Race, Redux," *Graduate Faculty Philosophy Journal* 35 (2014): 125–157.

38. George Yancy and Charles Mills, "Lost in Rawlsland," *New York Times*, November 16, 2014, https://opinionator.blogs.nytimes.com/2014/11/16/lost-in-raw lsland/ (accessed March 22, 2018).

39. Jantzen, *Power, Gender and Christian Mysticism*, 20. I am deeply indebted to Jantzen for her scholarship and commitment for feminist modes of teaching. As Jeremy Carrette describes in an essay after Jantzen's untimely death in 2006, "In her research, Jantzen tried to think outside the academic model of combat and battle. Many students will know her seminar model of building ideas together rather than competing and destroying positions. This did not, however, reduce her own intellectual rigour and sharp demands on research students, not least by challenging others to explore the social and political relevance of their thinking with her question: 'Who benefits from such thinking?'" "Grace Jantzen: A Feminist Voice Expanding the Philosophy of Religion," *The Guardian*, May 10, 2006, https://www.theguardian.com/news/2006/may/11/guardianobituaries.gender (accessed March 14, 2018).

40. Jantzen, *Power, Gender and Christian Mysticism*, 5.

41. Ibid., 14.

42. A sample of key texts in feminist spirituality include Judith Plaskow and Carol Christ, eds., *Weaving the Visions: New Patterns in Feminist Spirituality* (New York: Harper and Row, 1989); Charlene Sprentak, ed., *The Politics of Women's Spirituality: Essays on the Rise of Spiritual Power within the Feminist Movement* (New York: Doubleday, 1982); Kathleen Fischer, *Women at the Well: Feminist Perspectives on Spiritual Direction* (New York: Paulist, 1988); Joann Wolski Conn, *Women's Spirituality: Resources for Christian Development* (Mahwah, NJ: Paulist Press, 1986).

43. Jantzen, *Power, Gender and Christian Mysticism*, 3. For recent work on the feminist theory and mysticism, see Amy Hollywood, *Acute Melancholia and Other Essays: Mysticism, History and the Study of Religion* (New York: Columbia University Press, 2016).

44. Jantzen, *Power, Gender and Christian Mysticism*, 25. Italics the author's.

45. Jantzen, *Power, Gender and Christian Mysticism*, 5. Jantzen documents a long list of scholars who hold this understanding of mysticism. For example, Nelson Pike, *Mystic Union: An Essay in the Phenomenology of Mysticism* (Ithaca, NY: Cornell University Press, 1992); Albrect Ritschl, *Theologie und Metaphysik* (Bonn: Marcus, 1887); John Hicks, *An Interpretation of Religion: Human Responses to the Transcendent* (New York: Macmillan, 1989); Richard Swinburne, *The Existence of God* (Oxford: Clarendon Press, 1979).

46. Jantzen, *Power, Gender and Christian Mysticism*, 7. See William James, *The Varieties of Religious Experience: The Gifford Lectures 1901–1902* (Glasgow: Collins, 1960).

47. Ibid., 6.

48. Ibid., 7.

49. Ibid., 19.

50. Ibid., 346.

51. See Massingale, "The Systemic Erasure," 119.

52. See Emmanuel Eze, "The Color of Reason: The Idea of 'Race' in Kant's Anthropology," in *Postcolonial African Philosophy: A Critical Reader* (Cambridge, MA: Blackwell, 1997), 103–104; Emmanuel Eze, *Race and the Enlightenment: A Reader* (Cambridge, MA: Blackwell, 1997); Robert Bernasconi, "Who Invented the Concept of Race? Kant's Role in the Enlightenment Construction of Race," in *Race* (Malden, MA: Blackwell, 2001), 11–36; Robert Bernasconi, "Kant as an Unfamiliar Source of Racism," in *Philosophers on Race: Critical Essays*, eds. Julie K. Ward and Tommy L. Lott (Malden, MA: Blackwell, 2002), 145–166.

53. See Eze, "The Color of Reason," 217.

54. Walter Mignolo, "Introduction: Coloniality of Power and De-colonial Thinking," in *Globalization and the Decolonial Option*, eds. Walter D. Mignolo and Arturo Escobar (New York: Routledge, 2010), 3.

55. Please see Maria Lugones, "The Coloniality of Gender," in *Globalization and the Decolonial Option*, 367–390.

56. Justin Chin, "Attack of the White Buddhists," in *Mongrel: Essays, Diatribes, and Pranks* (New York: St. Martin's, 1999), 113, 115.

57. See Stuart Hall, ed., *Representation: Cultural Representations and Signifying Practices* (Thousand Oaks, CA: SAGE Publications, 2007).

58. Mitchell, "The Tranquil Meditator," 84.

59. Ibid.

60. *TIME*, August 4, 2003 (162, no. 5), http://content.time.com/time/covers/0,16 641,20030804,00.html (accessed March 29, 2018).

61. *TIME*, February 3, 2014 (183, no. 4), http://content.time.com/time/covers/0,16 641,20140203,00.html (accessed March 29, 2018).

62. Sharon A. Suh, *Silver Screen Buddha: Buddhism in Asia and Western Film* (New York: Bloomsbury, 2015), 5.

63. Jørn Borup, "Branding Buddha-Mediatized and Commodified Buddhism as Cultural Narrative," *Journal of Global Buddhism* 17 (2016): 41.

64. Joanna Piacenza, "*TIME*'s Beautiful, White, Blonde 'Mindfulness Revolution,'" *HuffPost*, January 29, 2014, https://www.huffingtonpost.com/joanna-piacenza/time-mindfulness-revolution_b_4687696.html (accessed March 29, 2014).

65. C. Pierce Salguero contends that one way of looking at these covers is to see them as a translation of a foreign practice into an American context, which he sees as part of the ongoing history of Buddhism. However, he argues, "The *TIME* cover is an easy target for criticism because it utilizes the extreme domesticating end of the spectrum. In so doing it becomes a caricature of itself and lays bare its ideological commitments." Unfortunately he does not name any of those ideological commitments. Salguero underestimates this representation of Buddhism as not really about Buddhism, but about the ideologies he fails to name. "Translating Meditation in Popular American Media," *Patheos*, March 2, 2014, http://www.patheos.com/blogs/americanbuddhist/2014/03/translating-meditation-in-popular-american-media.html (accessed March 30, 2018).

66. Phil Arthington, "Mindfulness: A Critical Perspective," *Community Psychology in Global Perspective* 2, no. 1 (2016): 92.

67. Antonio Carvalho, "Assembling Mindfulness: Technologies of the Self, Neurons and Neoliberal Subjectivities," Paper presented at sixth STS Italia Conference/Sociotechnical Enviornments Trento, November 24–26, 2016, https://www.research gate.net/publication/320934809_Assembling_Mindfulness_Technologies_of_the_ Self_Neurons_and_Neoliberal_Subjectivities (accessed March 30, 2018). See also Nikolas Rose and Joelle M. Abi-Rached, *Neuro: The New Brain Sciences and the Management of the Mind* (Princeton: Princeton University Press, 2013); William Davies, *The Happiness Industry: How the Government and Big Business Sold Us Wellbeing* (London: Verso, 2015); G. Dawson and L. Trunbull, "Is Mindfulness the New Opiate of the Masses? Critical Reflections from a Buddhist Perspective," *Psychotherapy in Australia* 12, no. 4 (2006): 60–64.

68. Arthington, "Mindfulness."

69. Ibid.

70. Carvalho quotes Slavoj Žižek. Carvalho, "Assembling Mindfulness," 298. For a critique of Žižek's perspective on Buddhism, see Justin Whitaker, "Better than Zizek: A Critique of Contemporary Spirituality (and Many Buddhists) Worth Investigating," *Patheos*, February 14, 2013, http://www.patheos.com/blogs/americanbud

dhist/2013/02/better-than-zizek-a-critique-of-contemporary-spirituality-and-many
-buddhists-worth-investigating.html (accessed March 30, 2018).

71. Feagin, *The White Racial Frame*, 24.

72. This statement is by Omawale Akintude and quoted in DiAngelo, *What Does it Mean to be White?* 194.

73. From Ta-Nehisi Coates, *Between the World and Me*, quotation cited from Robin DiAngelo, *White Fragility: Why it's so Hard for White People to Talk about Racism* (Boston: Beacon Press, 2018), 89.

74. Frances Robles and Jose A. Del Real, "Stephon Clark Was Shot 8 Times Primarily in His Back, Family-Ordered Autopsy Finds," *The New York Times*, March 30, 2018, https://www.nytimes.com/2018/03/30/us/stephon-clark-independent-autopsy.html accessed July 16, 2018.

75. Please see Alex Mikulich,'s forthcoming essay, "Becoming Authentically Catholic and Truly Black: On the Condition of the Possibility of a Just Peace Approach to Anti-Black Violence," in *Becoming Nonviolent Peacemakers: A Virtue Ethic for Catholic Social Teaching and U.S. Policy*, ed. Eli S. McCarthy (Washington, DC: Georgetown University Press, 2018).

76. Ta-Nehisi Coates, *We Were Eight Years in Power* (New York: One World, 2017), 196.

77. Mikulich, "Becoming Authentically Catholic and Truly Black."

78. See Chögyam Trungpa Rinpoche, *Cutting Through Spiritual Materialism* (Boulder, CO: Shambhala Books, 1973).

79. Judith Simmer-Brown, "The Crisis of Consumerism," in *Mindfulness in the Market Place: Compassionate Responses to Consumerism*, ed. Allan Hunt Badiner (Berkeley, CA: Parallax Press, 2002), 5.

80. Ibid.

81. DiAngelo, *What Does it Mean to be White?* 199.

82. "How the Hidden Brain does the Thinking for Us," *Morning Edition Transcript*, National Public Radio, January 25, 2010, http://www.npr.org/templates/story/story.php?storyId=122864641 (accessed May 27, 2012). For more on this idea of the unconscious, but very active images that condition perception and judgment, see Shankar Vedantam, *The Hidden Brain: How Our Unconscious Minds Elect Presidents, Control Markets, Wage Wars and Save Our Lives* (New York: Spiegel and Grau, 2010).

83. Simmer-Brown, "The Crisis of Consumerism," 6.

84. Shannon Sullivan, *Good White People: The Problem with Middle-Class White Anti-Racism* (Albany: State University of New York Press, 2014), 151.

Chapter 7

"Beyond Vietnam"

Martin Luther King, Jr., Thích Nhất Hạnh, and the Confluence of Black and Engaged Buddhism in the Vietnam War

Carolyn M. Jones Medine

In *Meeting Faith: The Forest Journals of a Black Buddhist Nun*, Faith Adiele recounts one of her earliest memories: that of the Vietnam War, which for her resurrects scenes of fire.[1] She was a toddler, watching the self-immolation of Thích Quảng Đức:

> My mother cradles me in the hallway, preventing me from seeing the rest of the story: the flickering black-and-white monk becomes a charred skeleton. . . .
> I go to bed early. This is one of my earliest images, this charred monk, and the Napalm Girl, running down the road, skin dripping off her body in sizzling strips. . . . I have nightmares about Southeast Asia for years.[2]

Jan Willis, in *Dreaming Me*, also connects her practice of Buddhism to the Vietnam War. When she was a student at Cornell, she watched "as Buddhist monks and nuns set fire to themselves, with prayers for peace on their lips."[3] Willis wonders, "how those peace-loving people could continue to endure the constant terrors of air and chemical warfare . . . and still hold on to loving-kindness and peace." Willis marched in Birmingham, but, she says, she found it hard not to be angry; indeed, she felt, on leaving Cornell that "as a thinking black person in this country, I was left with no choice but to join the [Black Panther] party."[4] She continues, "Because of the war and the way Vietnamese Buddhists were dealing with it, my interests gradually turned to Buddhism."[5]

For Adiele and Willis, and others in my generation, images of Vietnam, of jungles and napalm, of body bags, and of burning monks, and, though we were not always aware of the politics, of the "Buddhist Crisis" precipitated by Ngo Dinh Diem, the Roman Catholic leader of Vietnam who persecuted its Buddhist majority, shaped our global imaginations.[6]

The Vietnam War stands as a watershed event in the American consciousness, with its inconclusive ending. It was not a war but a conflict. It also marked America's first experience of a fully integrated military, "[transferring] the effects of black power, the impact of the Civil Rights struggle and 'the resurgence of black sub-cultural style, expressed through dress, language and gesture'" to the war zone. It was, as Michael Mandelbaum writes, "the first [war] to be televised," in a time when Americans, engaging a new technology, had their televisions on much of the day.[7] The images, largely unedited, planted themselves in the American mind.[8]

Mary S. Mander, in *Pen and Sword: American War Correspondents, 1898–1975*, argues that the Vietnam War was the first postmodern war.[9] It was undeclared war, and the emergence of minoritized voices and youth protest surrounded it: it, along with other issues, generated a critique of the modern self and the nation state. In some ways, its undeclared status became a model for future wars, fought, as Dale Andrade, puts it, as "a counterinsurgency campaign," rather than a war.[10] Anti-war protests, both American and Buddhist, intersected with the Civil Rights Movement and aligned, in the persons of Dr. Martin Luther King, Jr. and Thích Nhất Hạnh, generating a new chapter in American, and, for us, African American Buddhist practice, creating a postcolonial, anti-racist, Engaged Buddhism.

Buddhism, in its second wave, arrived in the United States in the 1950s, with Tibetan Buddhism in New Jersey, and in the 1960s with the arrival of Shunryu Suzuki and Zen and the *vipassana* or "insight meditation" tradition. Even in this second wave, following the first wave's introduction of Buddhism to America in the mid-nineteenth century by scholars and immigrants, Buddhist adherents, both immigrant and convert, remained small—about thirty million or about 1 percent of the population.[11] The Vietnam War, as a postcolonial war, I will argue here, marked a third wave, in the prominence of Thích Nhất Hạnh, one of the developers of Engaged Buddhism, which intersected with Civil Rights in its methods. Dr. Martin Luther King, Jr., in his relationship with Thích Nhất Hạnh, brought Buddhism into the African American consciousness. For African Americans, as Faith Adiele and Jan Willis suggest, the Vietnamese were revealed as another oppressed minority, and "black soldiers began to identify with the enemy: they saw the Vietnamese as, like themselves, victims of white colonial racist aggression."[12]

To examine Vietnam and African American Buddhism, I, first, discuss the African American presence in the Vietnam conflict and how Vietnam emerged as a different kind of war for its generation. Second, I turn to Dr. Martin Luther King, Jr.'s Riverside Church speech, "Beyond Vietnam: A Time to Break Silence" (1967) and his relationship with Thích Nhất Hạnh, whom he nominated for a Nobel Peace Prize. Third, I turn to Ralph Steele's memoir and his journey from Vietnam into Buddhist practice and, particularly, his place in African American Buddhist thought after the war.

THE AFRICAN AMERICAN PRESENCE IN THE VIETNAM WAR

The Vietnam War was the longest war in American history. Whether it was a noble endeavor and whether the United States lost or withdrew continue to be debated.[13] It was a war that we watched on television, bringing images of death and destruction, as well as images of protest, into our living rooms nightly. It was a loss, in social terms, for emerging programs for the poor. Dr. Martin Luther King, Jr. recognized early that financing "guns and butter" at the same time was not possible. It was also the last American conflict for which there was a draft.[14]

Charles C. Moskos, Jr., in "The American Combat Soldier in Vietnam," argues that group coherency was formed, not in allegiance to patriotic symbols as in World War II, but in the extremity of the physical conditions under which the Vietnam solider fought[15] and the troop rotation system, which was different from previous wars. It was one "under which a solider served a twelve-month tour of duty," whether in the rear echelons or in combat.[16] Soldiers went into the Vietnam War individually and left it in the same way, each having his own "private terminal date,"[17] so there was little group or unit participation, and returning soldiers, who were often reviled, faced anti-war protesters alone. In addition, new arrivals with less experience faced "more actual combat" than those ending their twelve-month tour—men, who, knowing they were going home, became reluctant to engage in combat.[18]

Moskos points to race as a factor in the Vietnam conflict. Black soldiers, he argues, "would find they owed higher fealty to each other than to the United States Army" and, though the armed forces demonstrated a higher degree of racial integration than the rest of American society, the "Vietnam period was characterized by polarization between the races" brought about by discrimination, real and perceived, and the development of race consciousness, as well as the anti-war counter-culture.[19] Herman Graham III, in *The Brothers' Vietnam War*, argues that, for African Americans, a global consciousness emerged: "Radical African Americans began to see themselves as citizens of the Third World because their rights as citizens in the United States had been continually violated."[20]

Graham evaluates the position of African American and other minoritized persons, showing us that the Vietnam-era military "was composed of large numbers of working-class whites, southern whites, African Americans, and

Latinos."[21] College deferment was only possible for the 5 percent of African Americans in college during the war. While 31 percent of eligible whites were drafted, 64 percent of eligible black men were conscripted, and African Americans died in disproportionate numbers—for example, 21 percent of casualties in 1966 were African American.[22]

Graham argues that the "ideology" the American military was selling African Americans in Vietnam was "manhood," which included "generous benefits, marketable skills, and the opportunity for personal growth in a homosocial world" in which African Americans were having difficulty finding employment.[23] Young soldiers were adolescent males "seeking definitions of masculinity" and seeing the warrior role as the epitome of the masculine.[24] Graham argues that many American GIs experienced this patriarchal power—but at a great cost of dehumanizing the Vietnamese. "'Right away,' one soldier remembers, 'they told us not to call them Vietnamese. Call everybody gooks, dinks,'"[25] and the Vietnamese were thought of as animals. This racial prejudice was one element building military group loyalty.

Loyalty and masculinity were played out in violence. Claude Anshin Thomas, like Ralph Steele, whose memoir we will discuss later, was a helicopter door gunner. Thomas describes the chaos that was the life of a Vietnam soldier, as he describes a mission:

> We destroyed everything. The killing was complete madness. There was nothing there that was not the enemy. We killed everything that moved. . . . Without any feeling, without any thought. Simply out of this madness. We destroyed buildings, trees, wagons, baskets everything. All that remained when we were finished were dead bodies.[26]

In addition, American soldiers mutilated the bodies of dead Vietnamese, collecting ears, teeth, and fingers as trophies; castrated dead Vietnamese soldiers; and tortured prisoners. These young men—Graham asks us to remember that they were eighteen or nineteen, and may never have had sex before—raped women prisoners individually and in gang rapes.[27] There was also widespread use of drugs, including marijuana, heroin, amphetamines, and alcohol.[28]

Though interracial battlefield friendships formed, neither those nor the relative equality translated when men returned home. As Arnold R. Isaacs writes, like World War II veterans,

> African American soldiers returning from Vietnam could not escape the raw racial nerves and the social and economic problems affecting black society in general. And, even more than white veterans, they could not escape painful doubts about just what their service meant: had they gone to Vietnam as part of

assuming full citizenship in a society that aspired, at least, to true racial democracy? Or had they gone as expendable cannon fodder for a government and society that still denied basic justice to black citizens at home?[29]

Graham tells us that two outcomes of the war were sympathy, among some African American soldiers, for the Vietnamese, and the American encounter with Buddhism. Black soldiers recognized the irony that they were fighting for a democracy that they did not experience, and some came to identify with the Montagnards, "a mountain-dwelling ethnic group of dark-skinned Asians" marginalized in Vietnam. One solider remarked, "The Montagnards are the black men of Vietnam."[30] Graham argues that many men did not want to participate either in sexual violence or commercial sex and sought "more permanent, non-exploitative relationships with Asian women."[31] One solider, Bruce Humphrey, in his relationship with My Lee, "gained a more sophisticated understanding of Vietnamese culture and Buddhism."[32]

The elements that Dr. King would address in his "Beyond Vietnam" speech, therefore, were present in the African American GIs' experience: racial inequality, violence, and dehumanization affecting both sides. Addressing these had been King's project, but the Vietnam War heightened his work. His friendship with Thích Nhất Hạnh became a significant factor in his understanding of Vietnam, and I would argue, began to shape his thought, even as he shaped Thích Nhất Hạnh's.

MARTIN LUTHER KING, JR., *BEYOND VIETNAM*

Dr. King's "Beyond Vietnam" speech was not greeted warmly. The *New York Times* argued that, in his speech, King made a "too facile connection" between the Vietnam War and the "slowing down of the war against poverty." The *Times* wrote that his speech was confusing the issues, in that it fused "two public problems that are distinct and separate. By drawing them together, Dr. King has done a disservice to both": "to divert the energies of the civil rights movement to the Vietnam issue is both wasteful and self-defeating."[33] The *Washington Post* called the speech "A Tragedy," and argued that King "has diminished his usefulness to his cause, to his country, and to his people."[34] The *Chicago Tribune* agreed, writing "The unctuous Rev. Martin Luther King, Jr. has been something of a hindrance to the civil rights movement since he was awarded the Nobel Peace prize," addressing the world in "Olympian tones," rather than offering practical responses.[35] The more popular *Reader's Digest* and *Life* magazine also criticized King.

In many ways, King was being criticized for his call for a more engaged Christianity, one that emerged from his interactions with Thích Nhất Hạnh.[36] Gandhi's teachings had influenced both men. Thích Nhất Hạnh writes,

> The turn to action on the part of the monks and nuns was based in their Buddhist training, but was also partially influenced by both Gandhi and the American non-violent civil rights protests.[37]

King's relationship with Thích Nhất Hạnh began in the context of King's "Northern campaign," which was much less successful than that in the American south, and in Christianity's interest in Vietnam. As the Vietnam War dragged on, an interfaith delegation from the World Council of Churches traveled to Vietnam in 1965. King's nonviolence "architect," Methodist pastor James Lawson, was the only African American delegate. He "opened many doors" to King's work.[38] One contact he made was with Thích Nhất Hạnh, who had studied and spoken in the United States, who wrote a letter to King about the self-immolation of monks in Vietnam, titled "Vietnam: Lotus in a Sea of Fire: In Search of the Enemy of Man."[39]

Nhất Hạnh recognized that self-immolation is difficult for Western Christians to understand. He argues that the action was not suicide or even protest, but an action "aimed only at alarming, at moving the hearts of the oppressors,"[40] language that King's nonviolent movement had used itself. The important act, he argues, is not to take one's own life, but to burn, to suffer, and to die for the sake of one's own people: "The monk believes he is practicing the doctrine of highest compassion by sacrificing himself in order to call the attention of, and to seek help from, the people of the world."[41] The "enemy of man" is not the oppressor himself, but "intolerance, fanaticism, dictatorship, cupidity, hatred, and discrimination: which lie in the heart of human beings." Nhất Hạnh aligns these actions with King's work in Alabama, arguing that they both are fighting "not man himself," but "intolerance, hatred, and discrimination."[42] He calls on King not to remain silent.

Pacifist leader A. J. Muste arranged a meeting between the two in Chicago a year later, 1966. Thích Nhất Hạnh, urged to do so by the international Buddhist community, was in America for a "tour of witness against war," during which he met many religious leaders, including Rabbi Abraham Heschel, Father David Berrigan, and Thomas Merton.[43] King and Thích Nhất Hạnh met and held a press conference in Chicago in 1966. Thích Nhất Hạnh remembers,

> When I met Martin Luther King, Jr. in Chicago in 1966, we spoke about Sangha building. We met and had tea together before going to a press conference. In that press conference, Dr. King came out against the Vietnam War. I told the press

that his activities for civil rights and human rights went along perfectly with our effort in Vietnam to stop the killing and bring peace to the land, and that we should support each other.[44]

Andrew Young remembers the impact Nhất Hạnh had on King: "I remember the spiritual inspiration of Thích Nhất Hạnh on Martin. . . . His spiritual presence was something that [Martin] talked about afterward. . . . [It was] clearly Thích Nhất Hạnh's visit to Martin . . . that changed King's views on speaking about Vietnam."[45] King nominated Nhất Hạnh for the Nobel Peace Prize in 1967, calling him a "gentle Buddhist monk" whom he was privileged to call his friend and argued that awarding him the Peace Prize would "reawaken men to the teaching of beauty and love found in peace. It would help to revive hopes for a new order of justice and harmony."[46]

> He is a holy man, for he is humble and devout. He is a scholar of immense intellectual capacity. . . . Thích Nhất Hạnh offers a way out of this nightmare [Vietnam], a solution acceptable to rational leaders. His ideas for peace, if applied, would build a monument to ecumenism, to world brotherhood, to humanity.

King's meetings with Thích Nhất Hạnh led to his coming out publicly against the Vietnam War in his April 4, 1967 speech, "Beyond Vietnam: A Time to Break Silence" at Riverside Church in New York City. Riverside was founded as an interdenominational and multi-ethnic church and its pulpit has been the site of many important social justice sermons.[47]

King's speech, addressed to "Clergy and Laymen Concerned about Vietnam,"[48] was nearly an hour long. It was a manifesto, declaring that peace and civil rights mix and that King saw that his path "from Dexter Avenue Baptist Church" as leading to his receipt of the Nobel Peace Prize, and to allegiance with the peace movement.

King outlined seven reasons that he was against the war. The first and second included the recognition that the war in Vietnam was oppressing the poor further: it had taken away funds from nascent poverty programs, and the poor were "sending their sons and their brothers and their husbands to fight and to die in extraordinarily high proportions, relative to the rest of the population."[49] The poor in America had been sent to kill the poor in Vietnam, and this, for King, is a "cruel manipulation."[50]

Third, King, given the opposition he faced in his Northern campaign, had come to see that he could not ask anyone to be nonviolent when America was "the greatest purveyor of violence in the world today," being seen by Vietnam as "strange liberators"[51] who destroy family and village, land and crops, and the Buddhist church.[52] Here, I think King aligns the Vietnamese with African slavery, for which one rationalization was the saving of souls and which destroyed African families. King, fourth, recognizing that it is America's soul that is in peril, aligns peace with civil rights, which set out "To save the soul of America" being poisoned by this war.[53]

Fifth, his winning of the Nobel Prize for Peace in 1964 broadens King's vocational call to include the "making of peace" as, he argues in his sixth point, not just an American but as "a son of the living God."[54] His call is to create brotherhood and to preach the truth that God "is deeply concerned especially for his suffering and helpless and outcast children."[55]

King articulates his seventh point in Buddhist language, talking about compassion. In a cursory search of King's speeches compiled in *A Testament of Hope: The Essential Writings and Speeches*, I found that King uses the term compassion only four times between 1958 and 1965.[56] His "Beyond Vietnam" speech uses the term compassion five times, and he uses it in later books, including his *Where Do We Go from Here: Chaos or Community?* (1967) and *The Trumpet of Conscience* (1967). We sense, in the prevalence of the term in his work from 1965 on, the content and impact of his conversations with Thích Nhất Hạnh. He feels that he must "speak for the weak, for the voiceless, for victims of our nation, and for those it calls enemy, for no document from human hands can make these humans any less our brothers" and "raise the questions they cannot raise."[57] King enters, I think, the postcolonial, aligning Civil Rights, not just with peace, but also with worldwide postcolonial struggles for freedom and justice: "All over the globe men are revolting against old systems of exploitation and oppression and out of the wombs of a frail world new systems of justice and equality are being born."[58]

Most strikingly, King speaks of compassion and of suffering. He says,

> Here is the true meaning and value of compassion and nonviolence when it helps us to see the enemy's point of view, to hear his questions, to know his assessment of ourselves. For from his view we may indeed see the basic weaknesses of our own condition . . . and profit from the wisdom of the brothers who are called the opposition.[59]

He stands, he says, as a brother to "the suffering poor of Vietnam" and to the suffering poor fighting the war, both of whom are being made into "things" for the war machine. King, in a Christian way, calls for new values that challenge systemic violence.[60] In the "fierce urgency of the now," King argues, only love in a worldwide fellowship can make peace. King sees this as a "Hindu-Moslem-Christian-Jewish-Buddhist" common belief, binding all into a Beloved Community.[61]

Charles R. Johnson is the African American Zen Buddhist practitioner who has most clearly articulated King's connection to Engaged Buddhism. In his essays, Johnson articulates the continuity and connection between his own Buddhist practice and the Civil Rights Movement, highlighting King's alignment with Buddhism. Johnson argues that King is "the most prominent moral philosopher in the second half of the twentieth century, teaching an ethic that is part social gospel, part Personalism (the belief that God is infinite and personal), and part Gandhian *satyagraha*."[62] King articulated "as a Christian much of what a Buddhist would see as the Bodhisattva vow."[63] King set out, for Johnson, three "transcendently profound theses": First, that "nonviolence—in words and actions—must be understood not merely as a strategy for protest, but as a Way, a daily praxis people must strive to translate into each and every one of their deeds" extending "non-injury (ahimsa) to everything that exists."[64] Second:

> he urged us to practice agape, the ability to unconditionally love something not for what it currently is (for at a particular moment it might be quite unlovable, like segregationist George Wallace in the early sixties) but instead for what it could become, a teleological love that recognizes everything as process, not product, and sees beneath the surface to a thing's potential for positive change— the kind of love every mother has for her (at times) wayward child.[65]

Third, one of King's important questions, for Johnson, is "How do we acknowledge 'dependent origination' [*pratityasamutpada*] and create the beloved community?"[66] King's practice of nonviolence, centered on *ahimsa* and *agape*, Johnson writes.

> [King] understood integration and interdependence to be the life's blood of our being, proclaiming, "It really boils down to this: that all life is interrelated. We are all caught in an inescapable network of mutuality, tied in a single garment of destiny. Whatever affects one directly, affects all indirectly." In effect, King understood that our lives are already tissued, ontologically, with the presence of others in a we-relation, the recognition of which moves us to feel a profound indebtedness to our fellow men and women, predecessors and ancestors.[67]

Recognizing, in his anti-poverty campaign, that we are linked by capitalism and that capitalism depends on the victimization and "thingafication," of the other,[68] King called for reform of capitalism, and for the ongoing fight, as Mrs. King put it, for "the ideals of social and economic justice in a world of impermanence."[69] For Johnson the recognition of inter-being characterizes King's beloved community, which, for Johnson, as it is for Thích Nhất Hạnh, is another name for the Sangha, the site of the practice of the "We-relation."[70]

We saw that the press could not see the connection between peace and nonviolence, and neither could both classical and 1960s protest movements. Simon Hall, in *Peace and Freedom*, writes that, though many civil rights groups, like SNCC, CORE (the Congress of Racial Equality), and the SCLC,

King's Southern Christian Leadership Conference, opposed the war early on, others, like the NAACP, which feared that shifting the focus from civil rights to the war would undermine the former, did not.[71] The anti-war movement, Hall argues, was overwhelmingly white and college-based and had different reasons than African Americans for opposing the war.[72] As Brian Daugherity writes, in his review of Hall's book, black opposition to the war came for different reasons: Blacks linked the war with white colonialism and racism, because of the racially imbalanced draft system, and Black Power organizations feared being coopted by the white peace movement.[73] This alignment with the oppressed figured into the turn to Engaged Buddhism.

THÍCH NHẤT HẠNH, ENGAGED BUDDHISM, AND CIVIL RIGHTS

It was D. T. Suzuki who was a primary influence on American Buddhism from the Victorian era until the 1960s, creating a modernist Zen. Modernism can be dated from about 1850, answering the rebellion against nineteenth-century Victorian and Edwardian absolutism and reevaluation of values of the early twentieth century, particularly after World War II.[74] It also introduced new forms and styles that broke from the past. Suzuki's Zen is one element of American modernism. Thích Nhất Hạnh's Buddhism picks up this rejection of the past, but also influences a Buddhism that incorporates, in an American way, immigrant cultures and their styles and cultural understandings.

Thích Nhất Hạnh is the key figure after Suzuki, and has been a great influence on postmodern and postcolonial American Buddhism.[75] Suzuki, the heir of Buddhism as it was presented at the World Parliament of Religions, represented an attempt to make Buddhism "relevant" to the nineteenth century, styling it as "rational."[76] Suzuki's way of thinking changed over his ninety years, as Moriya Tomoe argues: though Suzuki's thought, first, was grounded in social thought, it moved "toward a more abstract but crystalized non-political 'spirituality.'"[77] This move also affected—or infected—American Buddhism from the 1940s to the 1960s. Dharmachāri Nāgapriya, tracing Suzuki's thought, suggests that he essentializes Zen for a Western audience, and doing so, takes it out of its historical and social context, intellectualizing it and ignoring spiritual practices.[78] As Pamela Winfield writes, this Buddhism's entrance into America had some unintended consequences. For example, writers, like Jack Kerouac, wanted individual Buddhist "awakening without the discipline of practice," and, Winfield argues, "New Age DIY self-helpers have also paradoxically mistaken Buddhism for a kind of self-indulgent narcissism, despite its teachings of selflessness and compassion."[79]

Engaged Buddhism, of which Thích Nhất Hạnh is one of the earliest thinkers, as we have shown, intersected with the Vietnam War, the Civil Rights Movement, and the rise of post-colonialism. Thích Nhất Hạnh, though now one who popularizes Buddhism, presented a very different figure. Like the Dalai Lama, Thích Nhất Hạnh was, then, an exile and a thinker from a postcolonial situation, a position that intersected with African American Buddhism in critical ways. Here, we utilize Ralph Steele's memoir, *Tending the Fire: Through War and The Path of Meditation* (2014) to demonstrate these intersections.

RALPH STEELE: TENDING THE FIRE

Ralph Steele was born on St. Pawleys Island in South Carolina into a Gullah community, descended from slaves brought to Charleston, SC in the 1500s.[80] He was a Theravada forest monk in Thailand and Myanmar, taking robes in 1999, though he took off his robes to support his son, Clarence, who was in prison and his partner Sabine, who had cancer. He wanted to make sure that both of them had his full support, particularly his son as he transitioned from prison back to ordinary life. He also wanted to support the black Buddhist community.[81] He writes that war veterans and oppressed peoples have a form of post-traumatic stress disorder. As a Vietnam War veteran and an African American, he faces both. The metaphor Steele uses for Buddhist skillful means is "tending the fire," recognizing that he can "either learn to tend the fire or let it burn [him] up,"[82] taking us back to the burning Buddhist monks who tended the fire in a radical way in their self-immolations. He emphasizes meditation as the path to healing, and he particularly works with veterans, as does Claude Anshin Thomas.

The unique and independent Gullah community from which Steele comes[83] influences how he adapts Buddhist practice to African American life. Steele writes that his sense of the world came from his grandmother, Sister Mary, who taught him, though he did not have this vocabulary, mindfulness and compassion:

> My sense of how the world works was formed by Sister Mary, and what I learned from her fit very naturally into my later spiritual development. I never had to face spiritual contradictions, and I believe it's because she prepared me for everything, from Vietnam to Insight Meditation.[84]

Steele's stepfather was in the military, and he lived in Japan as a young man and studied martial arts. Unlike many Americans, Steele volunteered for Vietnam. Steele tells us that, facing the chaos of Vietnam, he was careful not to "make any mistakes," and the mindfulness that his grandmother had taught him helped: "I tried to pay attention to my intentions. I didn't want to end up in a body bag."[85] Like Claude Anshin Thomas, he was a helicopter gunner, and he suffered from both post-traumatic stress disorder and physical pain, including a resurgence of the asthma he had as a child, reactivated by contact with Agent Orange.

Race was a factor in Vietnam, Steele tells us, but because the soldiers were in it together, their ways of seeing each other, for all but the most deeply racist, changed.[86] These changes did not make home, however, any different. Returning to the United States, Steele and Claude Anshin Thomas write, was a return to systemic and structural racism and disdain and outright violence from anti-war protesters.[87] To face this, Steele, like Thomas, self-medicated, which included drug use. Buddhism, for Steele, became a counter-structure to the racist structure of American society, calling for "structure, rehabilitation, something totally different . . . my practice of Buddhism became a pivotal part of my rehabilitation."[88]

Steele's path crossed that of many practicing African American Buddhists. A key encounter for him was with Jan Willis at the University of California, Santa Cruz. Willis was like Steele, a southerner who had experienced violence from the Ku Klux Klan. Willis studied yoga in India and, there, met her teacher, Lama Thubten Yeshe. Willis offered Steele "book after book" that opened his intelligence and consciousness, and, when she left to finish her dissertation, Steele studied with Lama Yeshe.[89] He also heard His Holiness, The Dalai Lama speak, and he was "attached to his presence."[90] What Steele noticed about both men was their naturalness.[91]

Steele's quest for naturalness, an authentically African American practice, meant that, like many African American Buddhists, he adapted practices. For example, as a monk, he never wore a robe, because it reminded him of wearing a uniform.[92] He, as a disabled veteran with back injuries, also had to adapt his form of seated meditation to be able to sit. He also helps us to see that Buddhism itself is being adapted. He practiced "American Vipassana in the Theravada tradition," with the numerous Jewish teachers who had brought and cultivated that tradition in America. Those teachers found, Steele writes, "that it was impossible to teach it in the format given in Asian monasteries. The Dharma had to be translated in an American way. They didn't change the Dharma, they changed the format and presentation for a different culture."[93] As Thích Nhất Hạnh put it, "The forms of Buddhism must change so that the essence of Buddhism remains unchanged."[94]

Despite the increased involvement of ethnic Americans in Buddhism, African Americans struggled to find a place in Buddhist practice. Steele coordinated and worked in retreats with Stephen Levine and Ram Dass. "I was often the bell-ringer," he tells us, and "I'll never forget one morning I rang the bell and heard a person say, 'Lord, you sent a nigger to wake me up!'"[95] He recognized that even Americans on a Buddhist retreat have difficulty with race and diversity.[96]

Often, as Steele found himself as the one of two practitioners of color at a retreat, he recognized that the teachers in these "conscious communities" were missing the "the real suffering that exists in" and that divides American culture: racism. To do anti-racist work, Steel argues, calls for mixing practice with engagement, "working like the Equal Opportunity Commission that helped people of color get into college during the 1970s."[97] This insight led to the formation of the Inter-Racial Buddhist Council and launched People of Color retreats. Jack Kornfield, who supported these segregated retreats, saw them as a step to an integrated American Buddhism, but "it seems to have been a naïve thought," he admits.[98] White practitioners expressed resistance, one saying, "I am a practitioner in this community, and I've been coming here for a long time. If people of color start coming here, I don't think I will be able to continue practicing here."[99]

In the face of this kind of racism, people of color organized their first retreat in 1992 at Spirit Rock Meditation Center in California, though it was not a residential retreat. As the retreat began, a dark-skinned monk entered the room to "authorize" this meeting. He was the Venerable Bhante Suhita Dharma (Venerable Thích An Đức), the first African American Buddhist monk.[100] Bhante, like many African American Buddhists, was steeped in many traditions: he had entered the Trappist community in his native Texas at age fourteen; he was ordained in the Theravada, Mahāyāna, and Vajaryana traditions; and, he also held a position in the Orthodox Christian Church. Bhante, Steele writes, "offered the invocation, and we chanted along. Afterward, he greeted us, and then walked out into the abyss from which he had come,"[101] true to the spirit of a man about whom an interviewer noted, "There isn't a lot of self there."[102]

African American Buddhists come together, as the Spirit Rock retreat shows, crossing boundaries of Buddhist schools. Steele has worked with numerous African American Buddhists from a variety of traditions—including Jan Willis, of the Tibetan Buddhist tradition, Gaylon Ferguson, of the Shambhala International Buddhist Community,[103] Angel Kyodo Williams, Zen Buddhist priest,[104] and Joseph Jarman, jazz musician and Shinshu Buddhist priest.[105] Steele also shows us that African spiritual practice infuses African American Buddhism. At a Spirit Rock retreat, one teacher brought in five-gallon buckets that were used as drums that invoked the ancestors. Alice Walker commented, "Well, you just can't take that music out of us; we do need that."[106] Steele recognized that Walker was saying "if the teaching and practice of the Dharma are going to take root with all people of color in America . . . it has to change its form of presentation and encompass all cultural forms of presentation."[107] It must be forged in the fire of real human life and suffering.

CONCLUSION: THE FIRE

The presence, at Spirit Rock, of Alice Walker, who links her practice to the Civil Rights Movement, and the sign of Steele's "deep bow" to Thích Nhất Hạnh for his support of People of Color retreats[108] illustrate the intersectional nature of African American Buddhism, the Civil Rights Movement, and the Vietnam War. The postcolonial, the disenfranchised and the poor, who turned to Buddhism, needed a larger tool kit for addressing racism and classism in America and so adapted a "world religion" to address their particular, "local" realities. King already had acknowledged the importance of Gandhi, calling him "the guiding light of our technique of nonviolent social change."[109] Thích Nhất Hạnh added two more insights for King, those of compassion and of inter-being, which King called the Beloved Community, a world woven together "in a single garment of destiny,"[110] motivated by a desire for freedom. King recognized that, in that global interdependence, whatever "affects one nation directly in the world, indirectly affects all." Nhất Hạnh carries on King's work, as he said in a retreat for the U.S. Congress in 2011: "Unfortunately, Martin did not have a chance to continue his sangha, his community building. . . . I continue the work of Dr. King."[111]

In retrospect, Vietnam, sadly, seems like a preview of wars and a world to come. Alice Slater, in January 2018, cited King's Riverside speech to inform activists from around the world gathering to discuss the American military presence in eighty countries around the globe.[112] Racism persists, and seems to flourish. And, African American Buddhists still struggle against the segregating impact of racism, often remaining, as Ralph Steele writes "in the closet" because they do not feel "part of the great white sangha."[113] In a letter to twenty-five American Buddhists, Steele warned, "Our sangha will end up being like the Christian Church—there will be a white Buddhist sangha, a black Buddhist sangha, an Hispanic Buddhist sangha—if we don't begin to do something about bringing Buddhism into the whole of an *American sangha*."[114]

The metaphor of painful but purifying fire sits at the intersection of African American Buddhism, the Vietnam War, and Civil Rights. The fire consumes, as it consumed immolating monks and Agent Orange victims, lynching victims and burning crosses. The fire of anger was present in urban outbreaks of rage, King warned. Rage seems to burn hotly in the human heart: we, too, are the source of its destructive power. Transforming this fire, this individual and social suffering, into healing warmth means tending it, as Ralph Steele tells us and as Thích Nhất Hạnh shows us in a poem he wrote after the bombing of Ben Tre that he holds his face in his hands to protect and nourish himself and his soul. This is a way of tending the fire without entering into anger.[115]

Without tending, through practice, the fire will flare up and destroy in continued racism, in separation, and in the criticisms that black Buddhists face, as Tuere Sala puts it, that they are "going against Buddhism"[116] in its imagined pure "essence."

This is not a time for purity. African American Buddhism is now addressing multiple destructive intersections in American and world culture. Venerable Thích Nhất Hạnh, now over ninety, continues to work for justice. In 2014, he accepted an invitation from Pope Francis to visit the Vatican to support a global initiative to end slavery. #BlackLivesMatter, Dylann Roof's murders of nine members of the Emmanuel African Methodist Episcopal Church in Charleston, and numerous police shootings like that in Ferguson have re-energized the discussion of Engaged Buddhism in America. Buddhists for Racial Justice, for example, have called on white Buddhists to "engage in the healing of racism as an essential part of our journey of awakening," and on Practitioners of Color Buddhists to witness to the "full spectrum of the Global Majority," the diversity and complexity of Buddhism in America and the world.[117]

Even though the scope is wide and seemingly unconquerable, nonviolence is achieved only through mindfulness, which King and Nhất Hạnh knew had to permeate every facet of daily life, not just fiery public protests. Nhất Hạnh wrote *The Miracle of Being Awake: A Manual on Meditation* for nonviolent practitioners: "Meditation is not evasion; it is a serene encounter with reality. The person who practises [*sic*] mindfulness should be as awake as the driver of a car."[118] Mindfulness is "the miracle by which we master and restore ourselves,"[119] exercised in all we do: walking, standing, and lying down; working, washing our hands, and sweeping the floor—"wherever [we] are."[120] Nhất Hạnh, says that, if those practicing peace are mindful in all ways, they will begin to see each other, building community across time and space.[121] In a similar way, Dr. King required all those volunteering for the nonviolent movement to sign a "Commitment Card," pledging to follow "ten commandments." These included meditating daily on the teachings and life of Jesus, walking and talking in the manner of love; and, striving to be in good spiritual and bodily health, among others.[122]

I end with the *Manual* and the Commitment Card to say that, though both King and Nhất Hạnh acted courageously in a particular, charged historical moment, for both, true peace is made over the long haul, through mindfulness practice[123] in relation to all we encounter and in all we do—in giving ourselves to Fire to undergo the reshaping that can change the world.[124]

NOTES

1. Faith Adiele, *Meeting Faith: The Forest Journals of a Black Buddhist Nun* (New York: W. W. Norton & Company, 2004), 17.

2. Ibid., 196.

3. Jan Willis, *Dreaming Me: Black, Baptist and Buddhist: One Woman's Spiritual Journey* (New York: Wisdom Publications, 2008), 91.

4. Ibid., 139. Willis decided not to join because of the position of women in the Party (see 142 ff.). Instead, she went to Nepal.

5. Ibid., 91.

6. See "The Buddhist Crisis," *The Vietnam War*, February 15, 2014, https://thevietnamwar.info/buddhist-crisis/.

7. Michael Mandelbaum, "Vietnam: The Television War," *Daedalus* 111, no. 4 (1982): 157–169, 157, 159.

8. Ibid., 160.

9. Mary S. Mander, *Pen and Sword: American War Correspondents, 1898–1975* (Champaign: University of Illinois Press, 2010), 30. Indeed, the conflict was concomitant with the student protests in France in 1968, which Jean-François Lyotard sites as the beginning of postmodernism. Mander writes that the war was postmodern because popular culture had pervaded the military and the press in such a way that altered what each would do in carrying out its duties, because mass media played an important role in how reporters understood themselves; and because the military, "like other institutions, was operating in an economy that since 1952 had been dominated by information and services" (4) and the war marked a transition from the manufacturing sector to that of information services (149). She adds that postmodern warfare does not have winners and losers but only "benchmarks" (15). America did not have to fear invasion, she argues, and was furthering its "socioeconomic vision." Vietnam, having no fronts and engaged largely as a guerrilla war, was a "laboratory" for "designing postmodern armed forces . . . a new kind of military" (20).

10. Dale Andrade, "Westmoreland Was Right: Learning The Wrong Lessons From the Vietnam War," *Small Wars and Insurgencies* 19, no. 2 (2008): 145–181.

11. See Kenneth Tanaka, "Dramatic Growth of American Buddhism: An Overview," *Dharma World*, July–September 2011, https://rk-world.org/dharmaworld/dw_2011julyseptdramaticgrowth.aspx.

12. Brendon Gallagher, "The Vietnam War and the Civil Rights Movement," *ARNet*, February 20, 2014, http://www.americansc.org.uk/Online/Vietnam_Civil_Rights.htm.

13. The Vietnam War cast a long shadow. We see this in the conflict over those who avoided service and in the backlash against veterans of the conflict. John Kerry became a target when he, after serving honorably, made a statement before the Senate Foreign Relations Committee in April 1971. He said that veterans in Detroit:

> told stories that at times they had personally raped, cut off ears, cut off heads, taped wires from portable telephones to human genitals and turned up the power, cut off limbs, blown up bodies, randomly shot at civilians, razed villages in fashion reminiscent of Ghengis Khan, shot cattle and dogs for fun, poisoned food stocks, and generally ravaged

the countryside of South Vietnam in addition to the normal ravage of war and the normal and very particular ravaging which is done by the applied bombing power of this country (http://historynewsnetwork.org/article/3631).

Speaking out about atrocities, which happen in every war, led to Kerry's shaming in the Swift Boat Veteran controversy during Kerry's run for president. Those who supported the Vietnam War sought to rehabilitate it, seeing anti-war protestors like Kerry as the cause of America's loss. In "Why the Vietnam War Still Matters," Jackson Lears writes,

> Since the rise of Ronald Reagan, right-wing journalists and intellectuals have successfully sold us a fictional explanation for American defeat in Vietnam. It is a variant of the "stab in the back" story concocted by German nationalists after their defeat in World War I. The American mission in Vietnam, from the post-Reagan view, was a "noble cause" done in by cowardly campus radicals and their allies in the "liberal media," whose combined pressure on politicians forced the military to fight "with one hand tied behind its back." During the last twenty-five years, this rightist fairy tale has seeped into our popular culture—in the regularly scheduled rants of talk-radio and cable-television hosts, in films from *Rambo* to *Forrest Gump*, and in the rhetoric of politicians in both parties. By the 1990s, even liberals were too cowed by this bizarre account of the Vietnam era to recall what actually happened (*In These Times*, October 22, 2004, http://inthesetimes.com/article/1421).

Evidence of atrocities have emerged, however, and have been more or less substantiated. See, for example, the *New York Times* article by John Kifner, "Report on Brutal Vietnam Campaign Stirs Memories," December 28, 2003, on a series of stories in the *Toledo Blade*: http://www.nytimes.com/2003/12/28/us/report-on-brutal-vietnam-campaign-stirs-memories.html.

14. Martin Luther King, Jr. quoted in Alan Rohn, "How Did the Vietnam War Affect America?" April 7, 2016, http://thevietnamwar.info/how-vietnam-war-affect-america/.

15. Charles C. Moskos, Jr. "The American Combat Solider in Vietnam," *Journal of Social Issues* 31, no. 4 (1975): 28.

16. Ibid., 30.

17. Ibid., 37.

18. Ibid., 31.

19. Ibid., 33–34.

20. Herman Graham III, *The Brothers' Vietnam War: Black Power, Manhood, and the Military Experience* (Gainesville: University Press of Florida, 2003), 27.

21. Ibid., 30.

22. Ibid., 17.

23. Ibid., 15.

24. Ibid., 30.

25. Ibid., 42.

26. Claude Anshin Thomas, *At Hell's Gate: A Soldier's Journey from War to Peace* (Boston: Shambhala Press, 2004), 20.

27. Ibid., 57–59.

28. Ibid., 62, 63.

29. Arnold R. Isaacs, *Vietnam Shadows: The War, Its Ghosts, and Its Legacy* (Baltimore: Johns Hopkins University Press, 2000), 18.

30. Graham, *The Brothers' Vietnam War*, 116.

31. Ibid., 59.

32. Ibid., 148, fn. 55.

33. "Editorial," *New York Times*, April 7, 1967, https://www.walterlippmann.com/docs1083.html.

34. Quoted in "Beyond Vietnam," The Martin Luther King, Jr. Research and Education Institute, https://kinginstitute.stanford.edu/encyclopedia/beyond-vietnam.

35. "Guest Editorial: Martin Luther King Crosses the Line," *Chicago Tribune*, April 8, 1967, cited in Prachi Gupta, "MLK Honored As An Icon, But 48 Year Ago the Media Attacked Him," *Animal New York*, January 19, 2015, http://animalnewyork.com/.

36. Nguyễn Xuân Bảo, Nhất Hạnh was born in the city of Quảng Ngãi in Central Vietnam in 1926.

37. Quoted in Judy D. Whipps, "Touched by Suffering: American Pragmatism and Engaged Buddhism," in *American Buddhism as a Way of Life*, eds. Gary Storhoff and John Whalen-Bridge (New York: SUNY, 2010), 106.

38. Taylor Branch, *At Canaan's Edge: America in the King Years 1965–68* (New York: Simon and Schuster, 2006), 263. See also http://www.umc.org/how-we-serve/james-lawson-reflections-on-life-nonviolence-civil-rights-mlk.

39. Thích Nhất Hạnh, "Vietnam: Lotus in a Sea of Fire: In Search of the Enemy of Man," The Ethics of Suicide Digital Archive, https://ethicsofsuicide.lib.utah.edu/selections/thich-nhat-hahn/. The letter is also available at the African American Involvement in the Vietnam War, http://www.aavw.org/special_features/letters_thich_abstract02.html.

40. Ibid.

41. Ibid.

42. Ibid.

43. Branch, *At Canaan's Edge*, 470. See also "When Giants Meet," *The Thích Nhất Hạnh Foundation*, January 11, 2017, http://thichnhathanhfoundation.org/blog/2017/8/9/when-giants-meet.

44. Thích Nhất Hạnh, *Good Citizens: Creating Enlightened Society* (Berkeley: Parallax Press, 2008), 120. The two men met one more time in Geneva, Switzerland "just a few months before his assassination at a peace conference . . . called Pacem in Terris, peace on earth" (121). The conference was named after Pope John XXIII's encyclical and was sponsored by the Center for the Study of Democratic Institutions in June 1967. Nhất Hạnh described their delight in seeing each other:

> Dr. King was staying on the eleventh floor; I was on the fourth floor. He invited me up for breakfast. On my way, I was detained by the press, so I arrived late. He had kept the breakfast warm for me and had waited for me. I greeted him, "Dr. King, Dr. King!."
>
> "Dr. Hanh, Dr. Hanh!" he replied. (Thích Nhất Hạnh, "Dr. Martin Luther King, Jr., Bodhisattva," http://www.earthspiritcenter.org/blog/author/Thich-Nhat-Hanh#, as reported in An Nghiem and Peggy Rowe, "What Happens When Two Giants Meet?" *Mindfulness Bell* 72 (Summer 2016), http://www.mindfulnessbell.org/news-updates/when-giants-meet).

He was moved that Dr. King kept their breakfast warm and waited for him to arrive before eating. At this meeting, Thay told Dr. King, "Martin, you know something? In Vietnam they call you a bodhisattva, an enlightened being trying to awaken other living beings and help them go in the direction of compassion and understanding" (3). Later, Thay said he was glad he had a chance to say this to Dr. King, because less than a year afterward, on April 4, 1968, Dr. King was assassinated in Memphis.

45. Christopher S. Queen, *Engaged Buddhism in the West* (New York: Wisdom Publications, 2000), 43.

46. Dr. Martin Luther King, Jr., "Nomination of Thích Nhất Hạnh for the Nobel Piece Prize," January 25, 1967, http://www.hartford-hwp.com/archives/45a/025.html.

47. The Riverside Church in the City of New York (https://www.trcnyc.org/history/). The church, in honor of Dr. King's "Beyond Vietnam" speech, has launched a "Beyond the Dream: Living King's Legacy" year for 2018 to "call us towards a more just and peaceful society" (http://www.beyondthedream50.org/). The website continues,

> The pulpit has welcomed speakers from far and near: The Rev. Dr. Martin Luther King, Jr., preached his famous anti-Vietnam War sermon, "Beyond Vietnam," from this pulpit. Nelson Mandela addressed the nation during an interfaith celebration welcoming him to America. Marian Wright-Edelman of the Children's Defense Fund spoke about the need to provide quality healthcare to all children; and the well-known Dr. Tony Campolo delivered a sermon concerning affluence in America.

48. Martin Luther King, Jr., "Beyond Vietnam: A Time to Break Silence," American Rhetoric: Online Speech Bank, http://www.americanrhetoric.com/speeches/mlkatimetobreaksilence.htm.

> King made a second speech at Riverside, "Why I Am Opposed to the War in Vietnam," on April 30, 1967. In that speech, he recognizes that the world praised him for being nonviolent against, for example, Bull Connor, but would "curse and damn him" for saying, "Be non-violent toward little brown Vietnamese children" (http://www.lib.berkeley.edu/MRC/pacificaviet/riversidetranscript.html).

49. Ibid.
50. Ibid.
51. Ibid.
52. Ibid.
53. Ibid.
54. Ibid.
55. Ibid.
56. Martin Luther King, *A Testament of Hope: The Essential Writings and Speeches of Martin Luther King, Jr.*, ed. James M. Washington (New York: HarperCollins, 1991). The term "compassion" occurs on pp. 93, 123, 181, 190, 233, 235, 237, 241, 243, 494, 602, and 630. The term is used once in 1958 ("Who Speaks for the South?" 92), once in 1963 ("The Ethical Demand for Integration,"123), twice in 1965 ("Negroes Are Not Moving Too Fast," 181, and "Civil Right No. 1: The Right to Vote," 190). The "Beyond Vietnam" speech contains five references: pp. 233, 235, 237, 241, and 243.

57. King, "Beyond Vietnam."

58. Ibid.

59. Ibid.

60. Ibid.

61. Ibid.

62. Charles R. Johnson, "The King We Need: Martin Luther King, Jr., Moral Philosopher," *Lion's Roar*, January 15, 2018, https://www.lionsroar.com/the-king-we-need-charles-r-johnson-on-the-legacy-of-dr-martin-luther-king-jr/.

63. Ibid.

64. Ibid.

65. Ibid.

66. Charles Johnson, *Taming the Ox: Buddhist Stories and Reflections on Politics, Race, Culture, and Spiritual Practice* (Boston: Shambhala Publications, 2014), 44–45.

67. Johnson, "The King We Need."

68. Fr. Robert J. Spitzer, *The Light Shines on in the Darkness: Transforming Suffering Through Faith* (New York: Ignatius Press, 2017), 265, reminds us that for Martin Buber, "thingafication" is the objectification of the "other." Aime Cesaire also uses the term in his *Discourse on Colonialism*, http://abahlali.org/files/_Discourse_on_Colonialism.pdf, 6: "My turn to state an equation: colonization = 'thing-ifiction.'"

69. Johnson, "The King We Need."

70. Johnson, *Taming the Ox*, 51.

71. For a discussion of the moderate reaction to the Vietnam War, see Simon Hall, "The Response of the Moderate Wing of the Civil Rights Movement to the War in Vietnam," *The Historical Journal* 46, no. 3 (2003): 669–701. Hall argues that the more moderate movement wanted to "work within the American political system to bring about change" (670). They adopted what Manfred Berg calls the "separate issues doctrine," arguing that the war and civil rights were entirely distinct issues that should not be mixed (671–672).

72. Simon Hall, *Peace and Freedom: The Civil Rights and Antiwar Movements in the 1960s* (Philadelphia: University of Pennsylvania Press, 2005), 39 ff.

73. Brian Daugherity, "Review of *Peace and Freedom: The Civil Rights and Antiwar Movements in the 1960s*," H-South, https://networks.h-net.org/node/512/reviews/798/daugherity-hall-peace-and-freedom-civil-rights-and-antiwar-movements.

74. For a strong overview of Suzuki's career, see Carl T. Jackson, "D. T. Suzuki, 'Suzuki Zen,' and the American Reception of Zen Buddhism," in *American Buddhism as a Way of Life*, 39–56.

75. Suzuki was a representative at the World Parliament of Religions, along with Soyen Shaku and others. His *An Introduction to Zen Buddhism* from 1934, had great influence on the British and on Americans. The book continued to sell 10,000 copies each year in the 1990s. His influence on "painters, musicians, therapists, and poets" entered American society (Thomas A. Tweed, "Night-Stand Buddhists and Other Creatures: Sympathizers, Adherents and the Study of Religion," in *American Buddhism: Methods and Findings in Recent Scholarship*, eds. Duncan Ryuken and Christopher S. Queen (New York: Routledge, 1999), 71–90, 76). Suzuki's connection to Paul Carus made him the "face" of Buddhism for the West.

76. Pamela Winfield, "Why So Many Americans Think Buddhism is Just a Philosophy," *The Conversation*, January 22, 2018, 2, http://theconversation.com/why -so-many-americans-think-buddhism-is-just-a-philosophy-89488.

77. Moryia Tomoe, "Social Ethics of 'New Buddhists' at the Turn of the Twentieth Century: A Comparative Study of Suzuki Daisetsu and Inoue Shūten," *Japanese Journal of Religious Studies* 32, no. 2 (2005): 283–304, 296.

78. Dharmachāri Nāgapriya, "Poisoned Pen Letters? D. T. Suzuki's Communication of Zen to the West," *Western Buddhist Review* 5, http://www.westernbuddhis treview.com/vol5/suzuki-gentium.html. George Lazopoulos, in his review of Richard M. Jaffe's *Selected Works of D. T. Suzuki*, puts it this way: that in the postwar Orientalist interest in Buddhism, "the still-ancient Orient existed outside history, and Suzuki was a transmitter of its cultural essence," https://lareviewofbooks.org/article/ sage-works-d-t-suzuki/#!

79. Winfield, "Why So Many Americans Think Buddhism is Just a Philosophy," 4–5.

80. "Pawleys Island, South Carolina," blog, http://www.pawleysisland.com/blog/ history-of-the-gullah-culture/.

81. Ralph Steele, *Tending the Fire: Through War and the Path of Meditation* (Los Angeles: Sacred Life Publishers, 2014), 251–252.

82. Ibid., 261.

83. "Pawleys Island, South Carolina": "And thanks to the warm, humid climate of South Carolina and Georgia, diseases such as malaria and yellow fever thrived among the plantations. Most of the African slaves were quite tolerant to these diseases, but their white masters were not. This resulted in the slave-holders moving away from their plantations. . . . In fact, the Gullah people developed their culture not only from their distinct African roots, but also because they had little-to-no contact with white people."

84. Steele, *Tending the Fire*, 31–32.

85. Ibid., 53.

86. Ibid., 54. Steele tells the story of a young white man who believed black people had tails. When he saw a black man come out of the shower with no tail, he cried because he did not know what to think.

87. Ibid., 87.

88. Ibid., 60.

89. Ibid., 88–89.

90. Ibid., 93.

91. Bret Davies, writing on the term "naturalness," in "Naturalness in Zen and Shin Buddhism: Before and Beyond Self and Other Power," *Contemporary Buddhism* 15, no. 2 (2014): 433–447, explains it as "no-thinking-ness" that transcends all analytical understanding. This leads to freedom, naturalness (*jinenn*). As Davis explains, "freedom is understood not as a conquering of nature by means of an assertion of human will, but rather as a return to natural spontaneity by means of an abandonment of . . . willful self-assertion." This freedom is, then, exercised in compassion.

92. Steele, *Tending the Fire*, 95.

93. Ibid., 98.

94. Quoted in Stephen Batchelor, *The Awakening of the West: The Encounter of Buddhism and Western Culture* (Berkeley: Parallex Press, 1994), 274.

95. Ibid., 104.

96. Ibid., 117–118.

97. Ibid., 193.

98. Jaweed Kaleem, "Buddhist 'People of Color Sanghas,' Diversity Efforts Address Conflicts About Race Among Meditators," *HuffPost*, March, 31, 2015, https://www.huffingtonpost.com/2012/11/18/buddhism-race-mediators-people-of-color-san gha_n_2144559.html.

99. Steele, *Tending the Fire*, 194.

100. Ibid., 194–195. Bhante Shuhita Dharma is a fascinating figure. He died in January 2014, and the tributes to him revealed a powerful figure. He had become a Trappist monk at age fourteen, in Teas where he was born. Steele tells us that, after Vatican II, he was sent to study Buddhism in Thailand, Vietnam, India, Bhutan, Taiwan, and Hong Kong. He was ordained in the Theravada, Mahāyāna, and Vajrayana lineages. In a tribute to Bhante in *Lion's Roar*, we learn that he was the first monastic disciple of Ven. H. T. Thích Thiên Ân (himself the first Patriarch of Vietnamese Buddhism in America). See https://www.lionsroar.com/tributes-honor-passing-of-ven-suhita-dharma-first-african-american-buddhist-monk/. He was a social worker who worked with AIDS patients and in prison ministry.

101. Ibid., 194–195.

102. Lion's Roar, "Tributes Honor Passing of Ven. Suhita Dharma, First African-American Buddhist Monk," *Lion's Roar*, January 1, 2014, https://www.lionsroar.com/tributes-honor-passing-of-ven-suhita-dharma-first-african-american-buddhist-monk/.

103. Gaylon Ferguson, see: https://shambhala.org/teachers/acharyas/gaylon-ferguson/ and http://www.naropa.edu/faculty/gaylon-ferguson.php.

104. See Angel Kyodo Williams' website: https://angelkyodowilliams.com/.

105. See, for example, "Joseph Jarman." Interview by Jason Gross, October 1999, http://www.furious.com/perfect/jarman.html. Jarman studied in Japan and the art there, from music to theater, influenced his thought.

106. Steele, *Tending the Fire*, 197.

107. Ibid., 197–198.

108. Ibid., 199.

109. "Martin Luther King, Jr. and the Global Freedom Struggle," *King Encyclopedia*, http://kingencyclopedia.stanford.edu/encyclopedia/encyclopedia/enc_kings_trip_to_india/.

110. Martin Luther King, Jr., *Where Do We Go From Here: Chaos or Community?* (Boston: Beacon Press, 2010), 54. See also Jan Willis' article, "Community of 'Neighbors': A Baptist–Buddhist Reflects on the Common Ground of Love," *Buddhist–Christian Studies* 34 (2014): 97–106 for her understanding of the intersections between King's Beloved Community and the Buddha's teaching.

111. Still Water Mindfulness Practice Center, "Thích Nhất Hạnh, Martin Luther King, Jr. and The Dreams We Hold," http://www.stillwatermpc.org/dharma-topics/thich-nhat-hanh-martin-luther-king-jr-and-the-dreams-we-hold-3/.

112. Alice Slater, "The U. S. Has Military Bases in 80 Countries. All of Them Must Close," *The Nation*, January 24, 2018, https://www.thenation.com/article/the-us -has-military-bases-in-172-countries-all-of-them-must-close/.

113. Lawrence Pintak, "'Something Has to Change': Blacks in American Buddhism," *Lion's Roar*, September 2001, https://www.lionsroar.com/something-has-to-change-blacks-in-american-buddhism/.

114. Ibid.

115. Thích Nhất Hạnh, "For Warmth," in *Call Me By My True Names: The Collected Poems* (Berkeley: Parallex Press, 1999), 15.

116. Jaweed Kaleem, "Buddhist 'People of Color Sanghas,' Diversity Efforts Address Conflicts About Race Among Meditators," *Huffington Post "Religion,"* March 31, 2015, https://www.huffingtonpost.com/2012/11/18/buddhism-race-medi ators-people-of-color-sangha_n_2144559.html?ec_carp=8448305330797211369.

117. Buddhists for Racial Justice, https://northamericanbuddhistalliance.org/calls-to-buddhists/. See also, "Making the Invisible Visible: Healing Racism in Our Buddhist Communities," https://www.spiritrock.org/document.doc?id=9. For a good overview, see Ann Gleig, "The Dukkha of Racism: Racial Inclusion and Justice in American Convert Buddhism," http://www.patheos.com/blogs/americanbuddhist /2016/01/the-dukkha-of-racism-racial-inclusion-and-justice-in-american-convert-buddhism.html. There are many new voices recognizing the intersectionality of race and Buddhism in America, including Pamela Ayo Yetunde (see "Buddhism in the Age of #BlackLivesMatter," *Lion's Roar*, February 8, 2017, https://www.lionsroar. com/buddhism-age-blacklivesmatter/); Lama Rod Owens (www.lamarod.com) and others. They also examine gender, sexuality, and identity.

118. Thích Nhất Hạnh, *The Miracle of Being Awake: A Manual on Meditation for Activists* (Sri Lanka: Buddhist Publication Society/BPS Online, 2006), 23, http://what-buddha-said.net/library/Wheels/wh234.pdf.

119. Ibid., 10.

120. Ibid., 13.

121. Ibid., 4–5.

122. Martin Luther King, Jr., "Why We Can't Wait," in *A Testament of Hope*, 537; Martin Luther King, Jr., "Commitment Card," TeachingAmericanHistory, http://tea chingamericanhistory.org/library/document/commitment-card/.

123. See Adam Lueke and Bryan Gibson, "Mindfulness Meditation Reduces Implict Age and Race Bias: The Role of Reduced Automaticity of Response," *Social Psychology and Personality Science* 6, no. 3 (2014): 1–8.

124. Thích Nhất Hạnh, "Flames of Prayer," in *Call Me By My True Names*, 28.

Chapter 8

The Unbearable Will to Whiteness

Jasmine Syedullah

THE FIRST NOBLE TRUTH

Most times, bearing witness to the unrelenting heartbreak of ignorance, greed, and aversion that greets people of color in predominantly white spaces on a daily basis is, at the very least, overwhelming. For those who "don't see race" or somehow imagine they have escaped the burden of bearing the marks of racialization, bearing witness to this specific feeling of heartbreak is a feat that has proved, for many, nigh unto unbearable. Bodies bend, the breath catches, eyes avert, and in the very moment when the conditions for connection are most critical, the experience of empathy repels and causes some of us to contract.

From a Buddhist perspective, bearing witness to the long-term but everyday effects of racism, patriarchy, and settler colonialism is more than a good idea, it is more than an ethical choice, it is a practice in allowing oneself to be vulnerable to feeling the overwhelming heartbreak of the world, just as it is. Bearing witness in this instance is not a spectator sport. It requires that we bring our full selves to the work of liberation. It asks that we be all in. It is a commitment to be present to the truth of suffering, not suffering treated as a sentimental abstraction or universal analytic, but suffering as an embodied experience, a way to bear witness to the everyday dis-ease in our breath, in our bodies, in our movements, and communities, surfacing in this time, in this place.

The first noble truth of the Buddhist path begins with the truth of suffering. Unlike the Christian tradition, for Buddhism suffering is not, in itself, virtuous. It is not a cross to bear such that something like salvation becomes possible. It is simply the inescapable truth of life. In Buddhist philosophy suffering comes from craving. Craving and attachment to ideals and expectations of what could be, should be, or has been obstruct our perception of things as they are. Beneath craving, as the Tibetans remind us, lies ignorance to things as they are. Ignorance causes craving, craving leads to suffering. As Rick Fields quotes the Dalai Lama in the close of his book, *How the Swans Came to the Lake*, suffering is the inevitable consequence of ignorance. "I believe all suffering is caused by ignorance" the Lama says, "People inflict pain on others in the selfish pursuit of their own happiness or satisfaction."[1] Not knowing the degree of our own ignorance can be a great hindrance to learning to be present to things as they are. Humility in the face of the unknown slows it all down, so that we might watch, in real time, as the movements of the breath, body, heart, and mind stop competing for control and become still, become one. Noticing what all we do not know is a process, a practice of accounting for our place in the world just as it is.

Rather than deliverance from suffering, or *dukka*, "a term translated as suffering, unsatisfactoriness, stress, or more colloquially, 'being out of joint,'" the contemplative practice of sitting meditation associated with Buddhism is a practice in building a relationship with the truth of suffering.[2] This contemplative practice of being with what is has the power to ease an anxious mind, or create a sense of peace, or calm, what some may experience as a break from suffering. Though it is often used as such, meditation is not merely a retreat from the world, permission for avoidance, or dissociation. It is practice in standing with what is.

Contemplative practices sit uneasily alongside other technologies of knowing that are known to the West. Speaking on the meaning of practice, Zen teacher Katsuki Sekida writes, "While philosophy relies mainly on speculation and reasoning . . . we are never separated from our personal practice, which we carry out with our body and mind."[3] Sekida's book, *Zen Training: Methods and Philosophy*, brings practice into conversation with science and social theory and suggests that an understanding of the social and physical world based in an embodied sense-based knowledge of the decentered self is the only way "the fusion of individuals into universal existence" is possible.[4] Sekida writes, "we undertake the practice of zazen, involving as it does many years of tears and sweat. No peace of mind can be obtained unless it is fought for and won with our own body and mind."[5] From the seat of our practice we behold all we hold, all that holds us. Where contemplative practice can take contemporary conversations about racial justice and white supremacy then is toward an unapologetic awareness of the truth of suffering, an embodied kind of practice in becoming more intimate with all supremacy lays to waste, a humble kind of knowing that returns again and again to gather up what is so as to leave nothing behind.

Though the West has midwived the world's most progressive discourse of rights and freedom through revolution, constitutional politics, and international agreements, the most radical notions of freedom are still largely ambiguous. Rather than rooting notions of freedom in embodied realizations of the world as it is, we have historically opted to base imaginations of freedom on idealized abstractly constructed representations of the world that reflect back the will of those who dreamed them into reality. The language of freedom that we hold onto still centers the world as it should be, as it was imagined by those who colonized it, as a fabricated arrangement of abstractly nominated kinships and communities peopled by idealized subjects living outside history, unmarked by gender or race. Such relationships to the world can too easily place freedom outside history and people outside freedom. "When you are born into a national symbolic order that explicitly marks your person as illegitimate," as Lauren Berlant reminds us, you live in a space of ambiguity. "The national body is ambiguous because its norms of privilege require a universalizing logic of disembodiment."[6] Despite its investments in protecting individuals from the tyranny of the state, as philosopher Charles Mills writes in "Race and Global Justice," "the construction of 'Western' political philosophy as raceless has the ideological consequence not merely of misrepresenting its own actual past, but of erecting a convenient cordon sanitaire between it and the oppositional anti-racist tradition of people of color."[7] Since the so-called Western progress has been so blind to those it leaves behind, it is our job to hold it accountable to the truth of the world as it is.

Many of those Western progress has left behind are still here. One need not leave the West to find those who reflect its blind spots. Even within the quarantine of the Western mind/body problem, as it is so called, there lies the ever-emergent Black Prophetic Tradition. This tradition's lineage is one of escape from the brutality of universalizing logics of disembodiment, ghettoized at times and criminalized at others but passed down nevertheless through fugitive protocols of liberation grounded in the diasporic black experience of placelessness and captivity. The Black Prophetic Tradition is what Katherine McKittrick might understand as a "moving technology that can create differential and contextual histories" of liberation.[8] Its logics are racialized and gendered. They are embodied and material, rooted in history while reaching for the infinite possibilities of knowing liberation from the inside out. From political movements for the abolition of slavery in the nineteenth century to the movements for black lives in the twenty-first century, through the witness of David Walker, the confession of Nat Turner, from the dark humor of Malcolm X and the wild hope of Martin Luther King Jr, the truth of suffering becomes a site of contestation over what McKittrick calls "black imaginations . . . of the struggle over social space."[9] Their orientations to both suffering and freedom are deeply marked, not unlike the Four Noble Truths, by a path of practice away from the certainty of suffering toward the uncertainty of liberation by keeping accounts of the world as it is.

While pessimism pervades these projects of liberation, both East and West, and while the Buddhist tradition, the Black Prophetic Tradition, and the philosophy of the Western canon, all begin with some version of "the truth of suffering" their understandings of the best ways out of that truth have divergent implications for the world's intimate relationships to the meaning of freedom. In Arthur Schopenhauer's *The World as Will and Representation*, for example, the German philosopher, and precursor of the more broadly known Friedrich Nietzsche, takes on the problem of suffering as a consequence of the individual's will. Like Buddhists, he argues that suffering is inescapable because the human will is insatiable. Schopenhauer's solution to the problem of suffering is no less than a complete negation of the will to live. Schopenhauer argues that the individual's perspective of the world is bound by one's perception of the world through the will's representation of it. Through the mirror of the will the individual sees the world as mere representations of phenomena, reflections of the self. We are unable to grasp the essential properties of things, he argues, because we constantly perceive the world as it is reflected in the mirror of our endless willing, wanting, or desiring. Individuals do not have the power to see the world as a thing-in-itself and they try to overcome this illusion of perception by attempting to grasp their "essential being." However, the more the individual attempts to make tenable the essence of her being, the more her essential being recedes from her, abandoning the individual to palm "nothing but a wavering and unstable phantom."[10]

Though he convincingly lays out emptiness of the self and virtues of the negation of the will, schooled as he was in colonial encounters with Indian philosophy, he does not offer a practical means by which to arrive at this act of the negation of the will. Schopenhauer's concern with the mind over and against the material world beyond the mind is not unique to his approach to questions of suffering, but is deeply rooted in a Cartesian understanding of what it means to grasp one's own existence. Rather than trust the senses, the body, or the experience of suffering to learn about the meaning of existence beyond the mind, Western philosophers placed value on the cognitive power of the mind's ability to abstract from reality, to reason, to predict, to deduce the meaning of existence as an extension of the will.

Buddhism's premise that all life is suffering long predates those of nineteenth-century Continental philosophy. Sekida's explanation for why we suffer an endless stream of wants and desires, whose satisfactions are passing and whose ramifications for the delusions of consciousness are boundless, differs in a fundamental way from Schopenhauer's thesis. Sekida's *Zen Training* offers an explanation for this state of anxiety in his discussion of the "world of opposition" and rather than an appeal to reason, implores the reader, as a means of transitioning from this state, to become more aware of her emotional responses, desires, and thoughts as they arise and pass away. By calling attention to our process of perception, our experience, we become more aware of our fears, attachments, and desires. Only then can we begin to let these attachments go. The decentralized ego results from this new level of self-awareness. This is then a process of letting go of our attachments, our cause for suffering, in a transition to,

> a state in which you cling to or adhere to nothing. It is not that you are without desires, but that while desiring and adhering to things you are at the same time unattached to them. . . . True freedom is freedom from your own desires.[11]

Sekida calls this movement away from attachment, a movement away from the "habitual way of consciousness," the process of perception whose actions are unaware of themselves and whose telos is inevitably self-serving. "It looks at objects in light of how they can be made use of. . . . This way of treating oneself and the world leads to a mechanical way of thinking, which is the cause of so much suffering of modern man."[12]

Coincidently, the "way out" for Sekida is not an intellectual exercise of overcoming the limitations of the body's inability to grasp the truth of its own existence, and thus leaving the will behind, but rather a daily practice of becoming intimately familiar with every element of its movements. Although both views of suffering within the context of Eastern and Western thoughts recognize that suffering has its basis in wanting and desiring, their respective understandings of the truth of suffering differ. Schopenhauer seems to regard suffering as a personal delusion that can be managed and overcome. Sekida, on the other hand, is not trying to eradicate suffering, but instead offers a means by which one can sit with the truth of life as suffering in order to recognize "pure existence," the experience of perceiving the world, as it is, unobscured by one's desiring the maintenance and protection of one's own interests.

Taking account of the world as it is, of all Western "progress" has laid to waste and left behind is an embodied practice with our shared histories, with both the social construction of the Western philosophical tradition and with it the counter prevailing forces passed down to the present, gaining momentum from both the past progress forgets and the futures it cannot yet imagine. In this particular moment, the Black Prophetic Tradition is bringing contemplative practice to bear on this conversation about whiteness. It is holding a mirror up to the will to whiteness as it exists in the world, as a desire for liberation from suffering driven by what it deems as "noble." The will to whiteness constructs "progress" in its own image, in its own interest. It is the self-persevering pursuit of its own horizon of possibilities, generalized in the form of abstract ideals for application to all who fall within its domain.

These abstract ideals express themselves like vanity distorts beauty, goodness in search of "salvation," refuge in search of dominion, in search of comfort. The will to whiteness is the desire to recover through reason the faith lost to the altar of progress, to recover all that accompanies faith in an all-powerful God. It is a desire to take His place, to become the father of civilization, the judge of the living and the dead.

When those who do not "see race," or are not "sure why we keep having to talk about it," are asked to pay attention to the ways white supremacist, heteronormative, transphobic, ableist, xenophobic, Islamophobic, anti-Semitic, sexist, and classist norms stratify our social structure and place value on the lives of some over and against that of others, we can quickly see just how unbearable a truth suffering is for disembodied individuals to hold. What does their suffering say about the truth of our own existence? They may tremble to ask: How am I to grasp my own responsibility for the conditions in which others live? Rather than relate to the costs their noble pursuits of abstract ideals have on the lives, lands, and cultures, their desires displace and destroy the disembodied turn to themselves. They may temporarily feel rigid or defensive, cold to the truth of their own experience of suffering and to the suffering of others and its effects on their own communities, families, or bodies. Rather than trust their senses they would sooner disassociate from themselves than bear it at all. Some would sooner eliminate every trace of the truth of their own suffering from their sight rather than acknowledge the overwhelming magnitude of its weight on our collective situation, rather than bear the burden of bearing witness to the roots of it all.

Ignorance is universal. Suffering is inescapable. There is, however, a special incentive for those within the US context to remain impervious to its impacts with impunity. The will to whiteness, or one's desire for ever-closer proximity to it, functions as an phantom limb, a proxy for the embodied work of seeing and thus understanding how the particular conquests of land, resources, and people's personal freedoms have shaped the political and social landscape of US racial formations and national identity shape us. No one in the West escapes the mark of race. No one in the West escapes being marked by histories of forced removal or the ongoing genocide of indigenous peoples, their politics, language, and culture. No one escapes the mass conversion of people into property by way of "New World" slavery, or the many generations worth of wholesale exploitation, criminalization, and domestic violence legitimized by immigration policies and border control that have so severely bifurcated US national identity that to live here is to live according to the binary of US racialized meritocracy—the binary marked by those "noble savages" suffering a history of profiling, surveillance, discrimination, and exclusion, and all those on whose behalf this suffering is borne.

Whiteness is more than an individual identity. It is more than an abstract category. It is a desire, a destiny, an investment in a future that partitions the presence of the past in the present to mirror its imagination of itself onto the world for all time. We sense it before we understand it. Whiteness walks into an American Buddhist community and announces itself without speaking a word. It calls our attention and orients our sense of place. We are accounting for it with our language, with our gestures. We anticipate all it means in an instant and yet it has its limitations. My own arrival into white spaces, as a black, dark skinned, woman, signals to those that have already made themselves at home there that I must be in want of or require something, that I must require being welcomed or a pass to enter, to belong. It is an alienating sensation to say the least. While the Eastern attenuation to universality of suffering lays a groundwork for connecting over the gulf of the racial divide that organizes bodies into barriers within this nation, the Western investment in minds over matter makes it difficult for most people to see themselves wielding detachment from identity as a weapon against those whose mere presence marks them in ways they cannot bear to look square in the face. Or at least that is how it feels. It was for this reason that for years my sitting practice was a solo practice, or happened in twos and threes, with a friend, or with my sister, in a park or we might take over some unoccupied room in an empty church or classroom. Because the established practice communities I visited in my early twenties were not a refuge from the unrelenting heartbreak of ignorance, greed, and aversion that so typically greet people of color with the overwhelming burden of predominantly white spaces, secular and otherwise, I choose to suffer my way toward the path of the dharma on my own.

Though it took several years, I eventually found my people. In the last decade or so, increasing numbers of LBGTQIA identified people of color are finding their way, not unlike I had, beyond the bounds of the traditions and institutions of faith into which we were born and raised and are seeking refuge from homophobic and transphobic spiritual communities in places that have been historically understood as more progressive, but predominantly monolithic—middle to upper class, white, and culturally insular. More and more of us are finding ourselves and each other in what are generally speaking, white Buddhist communities. Our arrival, and all it brings up, raises important questions about identity, ownership, race, place, and belonging that are poised to diversify popular imaginations of who represents Buddhism in the United States. As we settle in, however, and make ourselves at home, we set the burden of the overwhelming sense of being black and brown down. We sit with it. We pay attention to it. We give it the time it needs to be felt and learn to understand it as something more complex than a burden. That is when something strange begins to happen. Its weight shifts and it is no longer our individual burden to bear alone. We are learning to share its presence with others, first in people of color spaces, within affinity groups, then in mixed company, in ways that may prove unbearable to some at first. But then we notice when those brave enough to bear it can withstand it, lean in to bear with us. As they begin to feel it all, they feel themselves. They begin to hear the reverberations of racism as they have echoed through their own lives, lineages, and dharma practices, but some still keep their distance. Those of us who can, expand to make room, to offset the weight of the binary, to sit with the unrelenting heartbreak of racial and gender supremacy, class dominance, and cultural exclusion that meets us all right where we live until we know it, if just for a moment, with every breath of our being.

PROPHETIC PRAXIS

In the spring of 2015, I sat down, along with Rev. Angel Kyodo Williams, Sensei and Lama Rod Owens, to eat dinner with the dharma community of the Shambhala Meditation Center of Atlanta. We were there to lead them in the first of four in a series of conversations in three cities that would center the voices and testimony of people of color and queer people of color in Buddhist communities in the wake of the shooting death of Michael Brown and the suffocation of Eric Garner at the hands of police officers in 2014. The conversations would later become a book, published in 2016 entitled, *Radical Dharma: Talking Race, Love, and Liberation*. As we sat around a long t-shaped table, passing colorful platters between us family-style, we got to sharing more than a meal. We opened a dialogue that we would hear echoed throughout our visits to communities in Boston, Brooklyn, and Berkeley. It was a cautious, hesitant conversation about the dharma of hierarchy within many Buddhist communities, and several of us were concerned for the ways our deference to hierarchy hindered the path of collective liberation. It was a difficult conversation about the patriarchal hierarchies of the traditions in which we sit, practice, and come together and what it means to enter them as people marked by difference, as people routinely policed and criminalized for speaking truth to power, as those routinely deferred access to power, legitimacy, and protection—not just in our sanghas, but in society at large. While some predominantly white dharma communities (PWDCs) recognize their homogeneity and insularity is a problem, they are still grasping to understand how to shift. They are realizing that knowing they have a problem is not enough to know how to change course, and how hard it is to shift when the greatest insights are coming from the most marginalized perspectives.

We had not planned to record the dinner conversation but when the direction it took fed directly into the reason we were there we quickly pulled out a cell phone. This was not a conversation we wanted to lose. The transcription of the recording picks up just as one woman asked, "So is this desire to be more diverse—that doesn't necessarily run counter to this, to our culture of hierarchy, does it?"

The simple answer, as Lama Rod responded that night was, "I believe it does." There was silence in the room as we waited for him to explain. Many of the attendees had just been sharing how beloved the hierarchy of the Shambhala community was to them. They were curious how it could also be a hindrance to the desire for diversity. Lama Rod went on to say, "I believe when you're reproducing systems of power and hierarchy *that* directly pushes back on inviting groups into the community that have traditionally been very traumatized by power and hierarchy." As a black academic I knew this all too well. Not only do investments in hierarchy create cultures that are insular, they are also more likely to protect the integrity of the structures that house them than the safety and well-being of those who abide within them, particularly when an individual's safety and the integrity of the governing structure are at cross-purposes.

As I write this chapter, the integrity of the Shambhala community was rocked as a report was released on June 28, 2018, the second of such a report which was part of a larger initiative to break the silence of sexual abuse survivors within the community. This report shed light on a specific history of sexual abuse allegations against Mipham Rinpoche, the Sakyong, or king, of one of the largest Buddhist organizations in the West, Shambhala International. In addition to the tremendous crisis of faith catalyzed by the revelations of the report, the challenge we are seeing in so many corners of Western culture right now from the movement for black lives to #metoo is the explosive tension between how desires for diversity expressed within institutions built upon practices of insularity, hierarchy, and exclusion can grow more inclusive even as they fight to maintain the way things have traditionally been done. As Lama Rod explained in a dharma talk at New York Insight Meditation Center shortly after news of the controversy surrounding the Sakyong spread, "hierarchy isn't wrong, it is a problem when it's protecting itself." He shared his own experience of becoming aware of the sexual misconduct of his own teacher, Lama Norlha Rinpoche, who founded a monastery in Wappingers Falls, NY, and was forced to retire after allegations against him were finally made public. "You should be practicing dharma to be free," Lama Rod reminded us, "not to belong to something or protect them."

While PWDCs extend open invitations to those long differed access, the implicit possessive investments, as George Lipsitz termed them, in patriarchy and whiteness that organize the community, prevail. It is an internal contradiction that propels many of us who are changing the demographics of US Buddhism one by one, are contending with in a variety of ways. What desires for diversity demand is a deeper structural shift than can be attained by ways of increased female leadership, more participation of people of color, and the additive inclusivity of queer friendly, inclusive guidelines for community building. In dharma communities and in other sites of collective social networking, it will require a shift in how we pay attention to the embodied truth, our own and others, of suffering, belonging, and exclusion that have historically organized our ideals of freedom, safety, and justice. It shifts not only what we build but how we feel we should be building it. As Rev. Angel reflected that day back in 2015 around the table at the Shambhala Meditation Center of Atlanta, "If the historical structures have endured to benefit particular people—if those remain in place, they continue to benefit particular people until they are reorganized. Which is what happened in the [U.S.]. We had to have laws that reorganized the way in which property was handled, the way in which access was handled. Things had to be reorganized in order to change [the structure of] power."

BEINGS ARE NUMBERLESS

Are the structures of power embedded in the architectures of Western Buddhist communities shaped by the will to whiteness? There is not one answer, but many. A whole complex history of the colonization of cultures, the migration of transmission, and the breaks in lineage that collide in overlapping investments in patriarchy East and West across TransAtlantic gravesites and Pacific war burial grounds, layer upon layer of Western orientalism and white supremacy, all thoroughly combine to complicate contemporary analytics of power, privilege, race, gender, resistance, and authority in the context of "Buddhism in America." In Richard Hughes Seager's book by the same name he writes,

> American Buddhism resembles an extensive web or network of monasteries, temples, and centers cross-cut by lines of affiliation that are often difficult to trace clearly . . . [it] is characterized by variety and complexity at a time when the nation's ideals are increasingly being recast in terms of multiplicity and autonomy at the local and regional levels. . . . The most prominent feature of American Buddhism for the last three or so decades has been the gulf between immigrants and converts, created by a range of deep cultural, linguistic and social differences . . . here the contrast between tradition and innovation often appears in particularly high relief.[13]

On the level of representation, innovation looks like the rise of people who have been long marginalized within US Buddhism to positions of leadership. The forward looking gaze of the newly renamed March 2016 premiere issue of *Lion's Roar*, formerly *Shambhala Sun*, features representations of the "new faces of Buddhism" in its cover art.[14] The magazine's editors selected a colorful assembly of dharma teachers, white, black, and brown, both those born in the United States and those who brought Buddhism to this country with them, all of whom are leading the charge to engage directly with matters of race, diversity, and difference in the practice of liberation in Western Dharma. Their arrival begs questions about where they have been, who they are replacing, and why their arrival matters now. How are these faces new if the practice originally belongs to those who were brown? How does the East/West narrative make disappear much of what these encounters surely surface? There is a clear and present multicultural optimism shining through the issue's recognition of these teachers but so too is there a deeper witness of an emergent alignment and mutual understanding between teachers that the future of American Buddhism is the culmination of postcolonial liberation, black liberation, and the negation of the will to whiteness.

For those paying attention, the proverbial writing is on the wall, and a deeply prophetic perspective on the practice is cohering from multiple directions at once. It may be precisely what Buddhism needs, as Anam Thubten, founder of the Dharmata Foundation, writes in the March 2016 issue of *Lion's Roar*, "to fulfill the needs of our contemporary society so it can be a rich, living spirituality instead of just another conventional religious tradition."[15]

The question of who represents US Buddhism then has increasingly required an expanding examination of how the intersectional and interdependent insights of dharma practice sit within the settler colonialism, heteropatriarchy, and white supremacy of US empire, economy, and governance. With the increasing number of Asian American, Latinx, and Black American practitioners rising to prominent roles of dharma leadership in Buddhist communities, the question is how their presence is not only diversifying racial representations of Western Buddhism, but also actively working to bring hard-won practices of liberation from their own prophetic and contemplative traditions—generations of practice in knowing what time it is and what these times call for, knowing how to survive forced migration, exploitative labor, genocide, colonization, intimate violence, and state-sanctioned violence. Indeed, how do we diverse groups bring "all our relations" to bear on the timeless truth of the dharma and what does our welcome require of those already at home on the cushion?[16]

This point of convergence between black and brown lineages of collective resistance to racial terror and the variations of lineages of Buddhism that have migrated to the United States over the last half century from India, China, Sri Lanka, Korea, Japan, Vietnam, Thailand, Tibet, Myanmar, Indonesia, Cambodia, and, the places of their forced migration throughout the Caribbean, the Americas, and Europe, has an important impact on this land in a way that is both new and simultaneously mediated by a much older politics of encounter. It is a point of convergence mediated by a racialized and weaponized set of priorities, perspectives, investments, desires, and feelings that are born of a colonial experience and fascination with the "East," by the "West." Thinking with social theorist Edward Said, Joseph Cheah writes, "The legacy of Orientalism in convert Buddhism can be traced to . . . Orientalist racial projects, vestiges of white supremacy ideology [that] can still be detected today in the controversy surrounding who represents 'American Buddhism.'"[17]

Cheah's book *Race and Religion in American Buddhism* argues that in order to understand the story of Buddhism in the West, one must not only trace the anthropological and Christian missionary origins of its arrival or its slow integration into American culture through the counterculture of the early-nineteenth-century romantics and mid-twentieth-century Beats, but also recognize how whiteness has colored this story in ways we may be only just beginning to name. As Cheah writes, "in most instances, white supremacy operates in the United States as an invisible standard of normality for many white Buddhists and sympathizers."[18]

On the ground, this structural tendency toward replicating the feelings, attachments, and investments of white supremacy, the will to whiteness, within what Cheah refers to as "the orientalism of convert Buddhism" can be difficult to distinguish from the cultural hierarchies of gender, ethnicity, and power already embedded within the practices of Buddhism rooted in the social order of their places of origin. In fact, to render the white supremacy of American access to the dharma visible requires a deeper conversation about the interlocking structures of dominance and discipline that undergird everyday understandings of liberation, both East and West. It requires that we ask big questions about the mutually reinforcing movements of Enlightenment logics and what Lisa Lowe terms "the economy of affirmation and forgetting"[19] that relay between multiple scales of injury incurred through the plunder and theft of colonial encounter. It requires that we, who call ourselves Americans, and even those of us who simply live within its borders, not only notice that we are living among the bounties of colonial violence, empire, and war, but sit and stay noticing, experience noticing, and practice it, not only on the cushion but in our daily lives. To paraphrase Rev. Angel Kyodo Williams' Sensei in a recent talk at Omega Institute to a convening of spiritual retreat center leaders, it is a conversation that requires that we see the violence of appropriation in its historical context, not simply as a singular injury that lives in the past, but one which we continue to feed off of in our willful ignorance to its perpetuations of harm in the present.

I VOW TO TRANSFORM THEM

How might we, who live here on stolen land, sit with the white supremacy constitutive of the trade routes of transmission that have brought the

Buddha's teachings to us and brought us to the cushion? How might we who benefit from the bounty of genocide and the afterlife of slavery, from what native studies scholar and activist Andrea Smith calls, the "interrelated logics" of American slavery, genocide, capitalism, orientalism, and war sit with the truth of suffering? How are American Buddhist communities "digesting," as Rev. Angel recently noted in an interview, "the material of how intolerable it is to be so intolerant?"[20]

Rather than a call to oneness that occludes historical legacies of racial dominance, patriarchy, settler colonialism, and xenophobia, I am inspired by this call for a radical dharma, a practice of becoming present to the discomfort of being one, to consider how to sit, in real time, with the unbearable forms and blinding emptiness of white supremacy in our practices of liberation. In his short contribution to the conversation between ethnic Buddhist teachers in America and American Buddhist Teachers-of-Color, Anam Thubten wrote that the timeless truth of the Buddhist tradition is about finding true joy by freeing ourselves from the internal world of concepts and beliefs that veils the indescribably beautiful nature of our lives. He makes the point that *the world is in an unprecedented phase in which change that used to take centuries is happening in a very short period of time*. It is time for us to see that humanity and our natural world are intrinsically sacred so we can respect and love each other and save this kind and unbelievably magical Mother Nature.[21]

More than a melting pot, this articulation of the dharma announces the nuance of the urgency of the current moment and all that its desires for diversity bring crashing together. Rather than close down or finally settle a conversation about who decides what the truth of the dharma is and where we ought to look for authentic representations of it, Anam Thubten invites us into a practice of conversation about the dynamism of diversity, about how convergence makes awakening to the "intrinsically sacred" truth that resonates across differences more possible. Like all wisdom traditions, the truth cannot be caged, or bound, not even by its place of origin, not even by the lives of those diasporic spaces and peoples it moves, those who change it in their very turns toward it. It moves impeded only by our own desire to hold it as our own.

This alchemy of place and practice has mixed New World discourses of liberation with the wisdom traditions of contemplative practice to forge new dharma communities. Rather than a relativist consumer-oriented celebration of multiculturalism, what is emerging in these spaces of convergence is transforming the depths of our modern attachments to individualism and investments in self-preservation, giving way to new ways to cross lines of difference to build toward a practice of liberation that is unbound. As a consequence of its arrival in the American context, by way of both immigration and conversion, poetry and profit, Buddhism is being made to encounter itself in new ways—lineages indigenous to the Asian continent, long distanced from each other by differences in dharma discourse and practice will inevitably encounter each other here in ways otherwise unthought and unexpected. Convergences both intermareal and cross-cultural are turning the appearance of the dharma from distinctly different landscapes of practice back onto each other. Returning to practices anew, as Richard Hughes Seager writes in *Buddhism in America*, there are even those "Buddhists, both European American and Asian American [who] are beginning to mix elements of practice drawn from the different traditions of Asia that are now found in this country."[22]

In my own experience as part of *the* newDharma Community, founded by Rev. angel Kyodo williams, Sensei, I trained with one of the first black female Zen teachers to receive transmission in this country. Rev. angel Kyodo williams Sensei and the dedicated practitioners of her Center for Transformative Change, a dharma-based activist organization led by women, were my first dharma home. We were an unusual Sangha—Black, Asian, Latinx, and White, representing a spectrum of sexual orientations and mostly cisgendered, men and women who lived and worked together in a practice space and intentional collective, first in Oakland then in Berkeley, California. The newDharma liturgy is firmly rooted in the Zen Tradition, and as such borrows heavily from the Zen Peace Maker liturgy. But it also includes aspects of practice adapted from Tibetan Buddhism and inflected by the prophetic spirituality of black liberation movements. We sing The Heart Sutra and hold dance practice along with yoga and martial arts in the Zendo. When we who represented four continents of multiple heritages, when we who each hailed from multiple lines of flight from intersecting structures of violence and oppression, stood together to dedicate the merit of our recitations of the Heart Sutra, "in grateful thanks to our many ancestors along the way," when we asked that "the benefits of our practice be extended to all our relations" proclaiming "may we realize the awakened way together," the space of our practice of necessity expanded.[23] In one instance it expanded to include not just us in the room but also those gathered a few miles away in vigil and protest, awaiting news of an indictment or absolution of guilt for the man videotaped shooting a twenty-two-year-old Oscar Grant in the back, killing him during an arrest in the Fruitvale Station Bart station on early New Year's Day, 2009. It expanded to include the man accused of shooting him as well. In another instance it expanded from us in the room to include both the tents of protesters and houseless activists that mobilized the Occupy Movement to fill our city's common places with demands to heed the 99 percent *and* the gentrifying developers and city planners who would eventually make the very practice hall we called home too costly to continue to house our sangha today. Who all? This collective speaks to the way in which "all our relations" might in any instance include not an abstract, idealized, or distant concept, but an everyday practice of extending toward those who helped us become more present to what all was present in our walking meditations through the streets of North Oakland and South Berkeley. It was a daily act of reckoning with Who All's liberation still does not matter enough to matter to all our relations right here, right now. It is a practice of noticing that there is a political context to where we sit, a long-standing relationship with all those who have sat here before us. I would ride my bike to and from practice, across the Oakland/Berkeley border, chanting the Four Great Bodhisattva Vows and feel the ground shift beneath me, feel the world shift me, from breath to bone.

Early on in my practice, my teacher noticed that the mudra I held was not one she had taught me. She asked where I had learned it. I explained that the mudra I practiced was from the university class in which I had first learned to sit. She said it was monastic, meant for those dedicated to sitting for long periods of time away from their communities and families completely enveloped in zazen. The mudra she taught me that day she taught precisely because we were, as she said, in an urban practice center. We were only here for a brief time before we would have to integrate what all we practiced on the cushion into our lives. Fearless warrior practice, she called it. This practice in presence to place, to when and where we are, is not new to people of color, though it may be new to US Buddhism. It lives in the testimonies and memoirs of those descended of runaways, freedom fighters, fugitives, and maroons. It lives in the ways they tell time with their relationships to each other, to the land, to freedom, to the knowledge that there is a place beyond bondage, beyond even death. Though my own journey to Buddhism began in earnest in school, I had first meditated in church. My father led pilgrimages to Taize, a Catholic French monastery that was established as a refuge to those fleeing the Holocaust during World War II. By the time I visited as a teenager in the 1990s, it was an inter-denominational Christian worship practice that centered meditation and chanting and was flooded week after week with youth in search of spiritual awakening. It was the medicine my aching adolescent soul needed to push past my own rebellion from institutionalized religion to find home in spiritual community and the alchemy of collective witness to trauma and healing.

SWEET HONEY IN THE ROCK

As the shackles of American slavery began to weaken their hold, the concepts of freedom that cascaded forth from the words and witness of the refugees of the Plantation South were soaked in generations of unspeakable trauma, the trauma of bearing witness to the subjection of one's life relations, and loves to the will of another. For these fugitive communities, freedom was not a place free of suffering, but a necessary practice in struggling with conditions of impossibility, uncertainty, the unknown.

What has become clear to me through my own practice and study of those for whom freedom is a constant struggle, as activist academic Angela Davis reminds us in her 2016 book of the same name, is that the flight toward freedom is not free from suffering. Suffering freedom in this way was not a romantic journey or salvific mission. It represents neither an escape from reality, nor an intellectual transcendence of the muddy waters and rough ground of everyday life. In this moment it is what one might call an embodied practice of liberation from the will to whiteness.

NOTES

1. Rick Fields, *How the Swans Came to the Lake* (Boston: Shambhala Publications, 1992), 378.

2. Richard Hughes Seager, *Buddhism in America* (New York: Columbia University Press, 1999), 15.

3. Katsuki Sekida, *Zen Training: Methods and Philosophy* (New York: Weatherhill, 1985), 29.

4. Ibid., 170.

5. Ibid., 171.

6. Lauren Berlant, *The Queen of America Goes to Washington: Essays on Sex and Citizenship* (Durham, NC: Duke University Press, 1997), 238.

7. Charles Mills, "Race and Global Justice," in *Domination and Global Political Justice: Conceptual, Historical, and Institutional Perspectives*, eds. Barbara Buckinx, Johnathan Trejo-Mathys, and Timothy Waligore (New York: Routledge, 2015), 181–205, 194.

8. Katherine McKittrick, *Demonic Grounds: Black Women and the Cartographies of Struggle* (Minneapolis: University of Minnesota Press, 2006), xii.

9. Ibid., 9.

10. Arthur Schopenhauer, *The World as Will and Representation*, vol. 1 (New York: Dover Publications, Inc., 1969).

11. Sekida, *Zen Training*, 94.

12. Ibid., 169.

13. Seager, *Buddhism in America*, 233.

14. The first of its kind since the magazine's name change from *Shambhala Sun*.

15. Lion's Roar, "Hear the Lions Roar," *Lion's Roar*, March 2016, 41.

16. In this chapter, I use the term dharma to refer to the teachings of the Buddha in a broad sense. Though the history of Buddhism's arrival in the United States, as Richard Seager reminds us, reflects "the variety and richness of the Buddhist traditions . . . the major story in America was the way a free-floating dharma discourse . . . was becoming grounded in a wide range of new dharma institutions" (8).

17. Joseph Cheah, *Race and Religion in American Buddhism: White Supremacy and Immigrant Adaptation* (New York: Oxford University Press, 2011), 3.

18. Ibid., 4.

19. Lisa Lowe, *Intimacies of the Four Continents* (Durham, NC: Duke University Press, 2015).

20. Angel Kyodo Williams, "The World Is Our Field of Practice," an interview with Krista Tippett, *On Being*, National Public Radio, April 18, 2018, https://onbeing.org/programs/the-world-is-our-field-of-practice-apr2018/.

21. Lion's Roar, "Hear the Lions Roar," 41.

22. Seager, *Buddhism in America*, 14.

23. "Dedication of Merit," new Dharma Community, led by Rev. Angel Kyodo Williams (Oakland, CA: Sensei, 2004).

Chapter 9

Making Consciousness an Ethical Project

Moral Phenomenology in Buddhist Ethics and White Anti-Racism

Jessica Locke

INTRODUCTION

In Buddhist ethics and whiteness studies, we can find rich discussions of the problems and possibilities that stem from the perceptual habits that ground our ways of having a world. While the content of these traditions, on the face of it at least, appears to deal with radically different problems, they both point to the depth of the ethical ramifications of our phenomenological rapport with the world. The entire Buddhist path is predicated upon human beings' ability to work to transform our phenomenological orientation in order to extirpate ourselves from the fundamental ignorance that causes our suffering and our ethical failures. Anti-racism likewise hinges upon not only the possibility but the necessity of working to revise racialized perceptual habits and thereby challenge the racist valuations that arise within and because of white supremacy.

In what follows, I use moral phenomenology as the unifying concept through which to read Buddhist ethics and whiteness alongside one another. My aim is to draw forth the structural similarities between the Buddhist account of releasing oneself from the self-cherishing attitude and the anti-racist task of challenging racialized perceptual habits. The latter task is especially urgent for white people, for whom whiteness is often difficult to single out as a subjective structure of experience. Whereas people of color are much more aware of white privilege, racism, and the way norms of whiteness function as a standard of value in American culture, white people more often lack perceptual attunement to our own privilege, to racialized dynamics in society, and indeed to our own racialized styles of thinking and perceiving. For this reason, much (but not all) of my analysis of whiteness as a moral-phenom-enological problem will problematize it within white peoples' experience.

My approach to these moral phenomenologies is not just descriptive. Ulti-mately, reading these moral phenomenologies alongside one another helps draw into focus the available trajectories for working on the structure of con-scious experience to change ourselves at the dispositional level. The aspira-tion to cultivate ethical subjectivity and transform consciousness in this way is bold; it asks much more of us than subscription to moral norms. Instead, it makes experience itself an ethical project. While the task of transforming our way of having a world sounds impossibly vast or possibly even naïve, both Buddhist ethics and anti-racism demonstrate how indispensable this form of ethical self-cultivation is to our flourishing.

MORAL PHENOMENOLOGY AND THE
ETHICAL RAMIFICATIONS OF EXPERIENCE

Moral phenomenology addresses the ethical salience of experience itself. The qualities of my experience—the valuations that I bring to the objects of my experience and my affective responses to those things—comprise the scene in which my moral life unfolds. I am disposed to the world—pushed and pulled by certain ideas, objects, people, and courses of action—because of the meanings that supervene on all of these things. These meanings guide my navigation of the world; they comprise the frames of reference within which I think, feel, and act. The values and significances that populate my world come to me with a "wake of historicity," as Merleau-Ponty would say;[1] they are invested in the objects of experience by way of perceptual habits that sediment over time through repeated engagement and practice. This kind of habituation finds myriad instantiations in our perception. One would not have to search too long to find two Americans who perceive a semi-automatic weapon according to vastly different perceptual habits: such a weapon is either revolting—a grotesque, infuriating symbol of the NRA's cold-blooded grasp on American policy and public safety—or it is evocative of American independence, self-determination and freedom from the always-lurking threat of tyranny or threat of the "Other."

While the significance of our world seems seamless and totalized, in fact the specificity of its meaning for us is underwritten by the subjective styles by which we experience it. Our perceptual habits draw forth the meaningful particularities of our world. In this sense, we see ourselves reflected within the world that we help to constitute; the significances that stand out to us as meaningful are not objective facts of our world per se but rather are given to us through the subjective structures that we provide for having a world at all. Nonetheless, the subjective contribution we make toward its appearance for us is hidden behind its seamlessness and totalized quality. We do not see our perceptual habits but rather we see and experience *through* our perceptual habits, and our ethical lives—every choice we make and even how the terms of our choices appear to us as such—are grounded first and foremost in perception.

What moral phenomenology highlights for us, therefore, is that how we comport ourselves in the world is profoundly conditioned by the habitual, phenomenological structures that run much deeper than our explicit intellectual commitments. Our ethical flourishing and the fullness of our character are not matters of subscribing to a "correct" view at an intellectual level, and we cannot eschew ethical infelicities simply by intellectually assenting to a philosophical or a political tenet. The real ethical work that moral phenomenology suggests lies in addressing the contradiction between our reflective, consciously avowed values and our pre-reflective, unconscious feelings and responses that comprise the conditions under which we gear into our ethical lives.

UNDOING THE HABIT OF SELF-CHERISHING: MAHĀYĀNA BUDDHIST ETHICS

In the traditional Buddhist iconographic representation of the human condition known as the Wheel of Life, the cyclic suffering of our existence turns on the "hub" of the so-called three poisons—the afflictions of passion, aggression, and ignorance, represented by a rooster, a snake, and a pig, respectively. In many renderings, the rooster and the snake are depicted emerging from the mouth of the pig, symbolizing how passion and aggression are in fact products of our fundamental ignorance (Sanskrit: *avidya*). This ignorance names our fundamental, primal misapprehension of the way things truly are—interdependent and impermanent.[2] We hypostasize the content of our experience and our own atomic, individualized selfhood, projecting upon them a permanence and a substantial reality that they in fact lack. Then, based upon that misapprehension, we perceive and experience the world through a structure of subject-object duality.

Clinging to the self and phenomena as permanent entities skews our experience. Everything that we perceive is understood relative to the reified self as either worthy of desire and pursuit (passion, the rooster) or revulsion and avoidance (aggression, the snake). This is a mediated world "full of symbolic representations," as twentieth-century Tibetan teacher Traleg Kyabgon puts it.[3] By clinging to the self and to the meanings and values that we project onto the content of our world as intrinsically existent, we establish a highly polarized, ego-centered frame of reference that serves as the map with which we navigate our world.

We interrogate the world through a perceptual habit of this clinging to "permanent essences," and this imputation of intrinsic reality of a self and a world produces an ethical orientation that is an expression of confusion. By postulating a substantial self dialectically opposed to a solid world "outside," populated by essential objects to which we are either attached or from which we are repulsed, we engage in an exhausting, never-ending drama of fighting to defend or fortify ourselves. As Traleg Kyabgon puts it, "We do objectify things in the sense of seeing everything in a dualistic fashion—subject and object, perceiver and perceived—but we also fail to objectify things, and so end up *seeing it all too personally.*"[4] In postulating a fixed, objective world, we effectively give ourselves a profoundly subjective world with ourselves placed at the center of it.

This dualistic way of taking up the world is the origin of suffering, the central problem addressed by Buddhist ethics.[5] Fundamentally, the Buddhist ethical approach to ending suffering and promoting human flourishing problematizes the conventional phenomenological orientation that is the cause of our suffering. It calls us to transform that orientation in the interest of ethical self-transformation. Following Jay Garfield,[6] I read this ethics as a moral phenomenology;[7] it calls for a process of ethical self-cultivation that moves the practitioner from a state of deluded egocentrism toward a liberated state of non-clinging, allowing her to become fully open to and skillful in the task of benefiting sentient beings. When we posit the "I" as our own mobile center of the universe, we automatically develop the instinct to protect and privilege its interests, producing an orientation classically termed "self-cherishing." The twentieth-century Tibetan scholar Geshe Lhundub Sopa is unsparing in his emphatic warnings about the perils of self-cherishing, which he refers to as "the real enemy" and as a "demonic attitude" through which both "you and others will be harmed by your egocentric behavior."[8] Self-cherishing harms us because it reinscribes the reification of self and other, thus entrenching us ever more deeply in ignorance and prompting us toward exclusive self-concern and indifference to the interests of others.

Self-cherishing is therefore an ethical problem with epistemological roots, and Buddhist ethics addresses it by asking us to unweave the habits of perception that polarize our experience. In Mahāyāna Buddhism, this takes the form of cultivating *bodhicitta*, the "awakening mind" (Tibetan: *byang chub kyi sems*). *Bodhicitta* names the realization of the selflessness of one's own identity and the emptiness of all phenomena, together with the compassionate intention to become enlightened in order to benefit sentient beings. Altogether, this marks a total dissolution of the self-other binary that motivates self-cherishing. Of course, this binary is already refuted by Buddhist metaphysics; philosophically speaking, this is the "View" to which all Mahāyāna practitioners subscribe. Simply subscribing to this view does not quite suffice as a method for extirpating ourselves from ignorance, however. The view of emptiness and the ethical comportment that pairs with it have to be integrated at a deep, intrapersonal level, and that requires an ongoing practice of working with phenomenological habits.

The Tibetan Buddhist Mind Training (Tibetan: *blo sbyong*) tradition is dedicated to the project of cultivating *bodhicitta*. The *Wheel-Weapon Mind Training*, a text attributed to the eleventh-century Indian sage Dharmarakṣita, is an especially provocative example of this moral-phenomenological training.[9] One of its most prominent tropes is the repeated listing of various types of suffering, such as social alienation, mental anguish, sickness, failure (both worldly and spiritual), destitution, unwieldy mental states, and the list goes on, and then pairing them with a meditation upon the sort of ego-clinging that is its cause. For example, one such verse reads: "When there is disagreement as soon as my companions gather, it is the weapon of my own evil deeds turned upon me for peddling my discontent and evil disposition everywhere. From now on without any ulterior motive, I shall behave well toward all."[10] The primary exercise here is a reorientation of the practitioner's understanding of her own suffering. Rather than seeing it from the standpoint of being victimized by something "out there," again and again the practitioner locates the cause of suffering in herself, in her own ego-clinging mind, and commits herself to reversing this tendency by doing the opposite of the habitual behavior that led to the suffering in the first place.[11]

The text goes on to celebrate the value of suffering and its role in pointing out to us the fact of our self-cherishing. In wonderfully florid language, the text supplicates for the destruction of ego-clinging: "Roar and thunder on the head of the destroyer, false construction! Mortally strike at the heart of the butcher, the enemy, Ego!"[12] This move—of turning our attention toward the ego-centricity of our phenomenological orientation to the world—interrupts the conventional attitude of experiencing the world antagonistically, from the "zero point" of our own atomistic selfhood. In his commentary on this text, Geshe Lhundub Sopa summarizes this instruction as follows: "We usually blame countless external causes [for our suffering], but now we should place the blame only on the view of a real personal identity and the self-cherishing attitude. Nobody and nothing else should be blamed."[13] This is not a moralistic instruction toward self-flagellation. It is a method for training the mind away from our habitual responses to suffering. It hinges first and foremost upon the exercise of stepping outside of our ordinary ways of navigating the world and contesting the objectivity of the assumptions and values that supervene on our experience. There is nothing esoteric about this mind training practice; it engages with our most mundane irritations, social obstacles, and personal challenges, explaining them in a way that reveals their potency as nearly endless objects of moral-phenomenological practice, so long as we relate to them skillfully.

At one point, the text acknowledges the profound effects of our habituation in creating the conditions for our suffering: "Habituated to attachment and aversion, I revile everyone opposed to me. Habituated to envy, I slander and deprecate others."[14] The Tibetan verb that is the root of the term "habituated" in this verse is *goms*, which is also the root of the verbs "meditate" and "cultivate." Indeed, elsewhere in the text, this verb is used in a highly phenomenological sense to describe the consequences for "cultivating impure vision" and the need to "cultivate only pure vision."[15] The difference between these two uses of the root verb *goms* involves a subtle but revealing detail of Tibetan grammar. *Goms* can take a volitional or a non-volitional valence, distinguished by a difference in spelling; to be "habituated" is to dwell within the dualism and afflictive emotions of our confusion non-volitionally, whereas "to cultivate" involves a volitional engagement and intervention upon the structure of our experience. The moral-phenomenological lesson here is that the habitual structures that we dwell within come together through a process of cultivation that is accessible to us if we actively engage with it. Meditation and the moral-phenomenological self-cultivation of Buddhist ethics writ large are volitional acts that can become part of the non-volitional, background structure of our experience. This grammatical quirk in Tibetan points to the link between the "active" and "passive" aspects of our subjectivity that Buddhist moral phenomenology exploits.

Altogether, the *Wheel–Weapon* is an extended exercise in reframing the significance of suffering, making suffering an instruction that points back at us, at the practitioner, to our own attitudes and ways of experiencing the world. This exercise restructures those habitual patterns that define and condition our suffering and self-cherishing. This practice of mind training is a rigorous method for eradicating the orientation that has proceeded from the reification of self and other and for setting the practitioner aright with a more epistemologically and ethically felicitous orientation. It shows how true ethical flourishing relies upon a process of transforming the practitioner's way of having a world through a practice of de-habituation from ignorance and toward *bodhicitta*.

CONTESTING HABITS OF WHITENESS: MORAL PHENOMENOLOGY IN WHITE ANTI-RACISM

bell hooks argues that it is necessary "for concerned folks, for righteous white people, to begin to fully explore the way white supremacy determines how they see the world, even as their actions are not informed by the type of racial prejudice that promotes overt discrimination and separation."[16] She notes that well-meaning white people face an obstacle in recognizing the elements of our own experience—the ways we perceive and navigate the world, the subtleties of our values and feelings—that are, in fact, rooted in racism and therefore play a collaborative role in white supremacy. Even if white people disavow the harms caused by racism, we often unwittingly re-enact those harms by embodying a stance of white normalcy to which we have become habituated by our culture. This recalls James Baldwin's assertion that white people are "trapped in a history which they do not understand; and until they understand it, they cannot be released from it."[17] For white people to truly engage with anti-racism means not just addressing overt bigotry or structural racism but what hooks calls the "encompassing and profound reality" of the holistic, world-forming impact of white supremacy, which carries the past into the present at each instant, in our social discourse as well as our subjective experience within which white supremacist values and attitudes supervene, though they may not be obvious as such.[18]

hooks goes on to call for "a paradigm, a practical model for social change that includes an understanding of ways to *transform consciousness* that are linked to efforts to transform structures."[19] The moral-phenomenological significance of a practical model for transforming consciousness is what I examine in the following section.[20] My objective in drawing out this moral phenomenology is to go beyond a diagnosis of whiteness as a totalized phenomenological and social structure and to move toward a more proactive engagement with the possibilities for transforming consciousness on the order of what hooks says is necessary.

Whiteness provides a set of norms, meanings, and values based upon a centering and valuation of whiteness and white people and a decentering and devaluation of blackness and black people. There is nothing essential or ultimately ontologically *true* about whiteness or white normalcy, but even in its contingency it is a powerfully regulative norm of social discourse and embodied subjectivity. As George Yancy puts it, whiteness is a *"relationally lived* phenomenon"; it is not a metaphysical reality.[21] People of color are marked and "Otherized" by the norms of whiteness; Yancy describes the experience of being black under the white gaze as an invasion, a distortion, and as a rupture of one's own body schema.[22] Conversely, white people experience whiteness as an absence, as being the unraced "norm" against which blackness and all other racial categories are dialectically known, raced, marked, and named. Whiteness remains unmarked, while blackness becomes the object of the white gaze. Black "Otherness" is marked, disciplined, and made to stand out as "abnormal"—outside the norm of whiteness—while whiteness remains "unremarkable." Yancy illustrates this point by recounting an encounter at an annual meeting of the American Philosophical Association, in which a white philosopher admonished Yancy not to use African American vernacular in his writing and remarked that Yancy "[speaks] very well." The implication was that Yancy was out of turn in using a writing style that did not conform to "standard" American English and that, from the unspoken but centered standpoint of the white philosopher's authority on language, style and professional mores, Yancy's blackness marked him as problematic and at the margin of the profession.[23] For a white person, the experience of being centered as "the standard" in this way elides the contingency of the highly polarized valuation conferred upon us. As Sara Ahmed puts it, whiteness "becomes the very 'what' that coheres a world" but also functions as "a category of experience that *disappears* as a category *through* experience."[24] Whiteness orients subjects and dictates how they inhabit and navigate their world, but it does so while disappearing into their implicit, background experience.

In taking the valuations that define our experience of the world as objective and failing to appreciate all the ways in which our subjectivities are constituted in contradistinction to the violently targeted "Other" of blackness, white people are indeed beset by a specific and pernicious form of ignorance. This is the "white ignorance" that Charles Mills defines as "a particularly pervasive—though hardly theorized—form of ignorance."[25] This ignorance yields an inaccurate rendering of the world, because the biases that inhere in white ignorance entail *not* seeing what is there but instead "seeing" a fictionalized Other. On the other end of this fictionalization is, of course, a person of color who can and does realize that "they are not seen at all."[26] The regulatory work being done by whiteness is thus not equally invisible to everyone; as Ahmed points out, privilege is only invisible to those who have it.[27] White ignorance is not simply one standpoint among others; there is a veridical viewpoint that this white ignorance precludes, a knowledge to which those situated outside the "zero point" of white normalcy have access.[28] Phenomenologically speaking, the norms and valuations of whiteness become sedimented in perceptual habits as preferences toward whiteness and aversions toward blackness. These perceptual habits are often so seamlessly integrated into the lifeworld of the perceiving subject that he does not even realize they are at play, though for the well-meaning, liberal white person, they undercut his explicitly held beliefs about race.

Implicit bias is a telling example of how this process of undercutting functions. In the years since the Civil Rights era, the number of white people in the United States who avow racially discriminatory views has declined.[29] However, as many social-psychological studies across decades suggest, even well-meaning, liberal white people still perceive and respond to people of color in a racist, biased way. While on the whole it has become far more taboo to be explicitly bigoted (notwithstanding the recent resurgence of flagrant white supremacist rhetoric in the era of Donald Trump's election and presidency), and while more and more white Americans now profess racially egalitarian values, in point of fact, even these white people still instantiate racist views in their lived experience and social comportment. For example, in their study of bias in hiring decisions, Dovidio and Gaertner assigned white people who had claimed not to hold racially discriminatory views the task of rating the resumés of hypothetical job applicants. In cases when the standard for judging qualifications was ambiguous, the study subjects demonstrated a bias in favor of candidates with stereotypically white-sounding names and against candidates with stereotypically black-sounding names.[30] That is, "moderate qualifications are responded to as if they were strong qualifications when the candidate is white, but as if they were weak qualifications when the candidate is black."[31] Despite professing liberal, egalitarian ideals, these subjects saw potential job applicants through a gaze that inflected black applicants with disfavor and projected preference for white applicants. The gaze with which these study subjects met their world (and these potential job applicants) constitutes an ethical failure, a mismatch between their explicitly held morals and their actual, practical discourse with the world and with others.

What this shows is that even if white people intellectually assent to anti-racist politics, we are still subject to the powerfully influential historicity of white supremacy that shows itself in pervasive, unconscious racist perceptual habits that influence feelings about and behavior toward people of color. Examining an encounter with a white woman in an elevator whose discomfort with being alone with a black man was palpable, Yancy writes that even if she comes to "judge her perception of the Black body as epistemologically false, . . . her racism may still have a hold on her lived body. I walk into the elevator and she feels apprehension."[32] Conceptually agreeing with racial justice does not undo all of the subtleties of the embodied, affective, symbolic, and perceptual facets of racial bias that have sedimented as part of our phenomenological rapport with the world.

Implicit bias is a manifestation of a phenomenological orientation conditioned by the standards of norms of whiteness that distort perception. Through this distortion, what is seen is not the black person but the racism of the white gaze itself. On this point, Yancy writes, "The white gaze defines me, skewing my own way of seeing myself. But the gaze does not 'see' me, it 'sees' itself."[33] That the white gaze is polarized at all is not obvious to the white person, however. The error and distortion rendered by the white gaze is belied by its totalizing function, and what is given through the white gaze, while clearly both product and reproduction of a cultural patrimony of white supremacy, is experienced as ahistorical and objective. What appears vis-à-vis the white gaze arises within the seamless, totalized lived experience of the white subject. Again, we return to bell hooks: "When liberal whites fail to understand how they can and/or do embody white-supremacist values and beliefs even though they may not embrace racism as prejudice or domination . . . , they cannot recognize the ways their actions support and affirm the very structure of racist domination and oppression that they profess to wish to see eradicated."[34] Problematizing racism and white supremacy in the world and in American society does not equate to routing the effects of white supremacy in one's own thinking, perception, and ways of having a world.

For the white subjects in the implicit bias studies to truly live out their ideals of racial equality, they must not only ascribe to those politics in a nominal fashion but also work to inculcate those valuations at the level of their structures of perception, so that in their everyday discourse, their perceptual practices, and their various forms of bodily comportment they do not reinscribe and re-enact the long history of white supremacy that they claim to disavow. White anti-racism must go beyond offering "corrections" to mistaken views about race and offer practical ways for transforming consciousness. This is why Shannon Sullivan argues that the unconscious habits of white privilege are not simply the result of naïveté that can be cast out by informing a white person of the factual errors embedded in her assumptions about race.[35] There is something durably pernicious about the unconscious habits of white privilege such that even well-meaning and well-informed attempts to rout it often miss the mark. Simply acknowledging the fundamental fictitiousness of racial categories or the injustice of white supremacy, for example, is not enough to unfurl the tapestry of racialized habits of perception. Metaphysics and intellectualization are not enough, an insight that is the subtext of hooks' call for a pedagogy that can transform consciousness to address the "encompassing and profound reality" of white supremacy at the level of how we see and experience the world.

An example of a pedagogy in this vein comes from Patricia Devine and her colleagues at the University of Wisconsin-Madison, who developed a multifaceted implicit bias intervention program.[36] The program included five types of interventions: stereotype replacement, counter-stereotypic imaging, individuation, perspective taking, and increasing opportunities for contact that together produced "encouraging evidence . . . in promoting enduring reductions in implicit bias."[37] Each of these interventions, while mutually reinforcing, takes a distinct approach to undermining negative stereotypes of blackness.[38] To delve into but one example, the intervention of counter-stereotypic imaging provides rich fodder for moral-phenomenological analysis. This intervention utilizes the explicit thought process of "mental imagery" to show that implicit stereotyping processes are malleable and indeed more "interdependent" with explicit thought processes than they might otherwise appear.[39] Subjects were asked to repeatedly and in detail draw forth "positive exemplars" whose identity or characteristics cut across conventionally negative valuations of blackness. These exemplars could be "abstract, embodying a specific quality (e.g., smart Black people), famous (e.g., Barack Obama), or non-famous (e.g., a personal friend)."[40] In subsequent tests of their implicit bias, these subjects showed a diminished proclivity for racial stereotyping, effectively showing that a practice of counter-stereotyping—together with the full complement of other interventions prescribed by the program—can make a racial stereotype less hegemonic in dictating how one thinks about and perceives members of an out-group.

At first blush, this intervention may appear shallow or tokenistic. After all, having the "positive exemplars" of Barack and Michelle Obama in the White House for eight years quite manifestly did not "end" racism in the United States.[41] From a moral-phenomenological standpoint, however, actively engaging in a practice of counter-stereotyping goes much deeper than tokenizing or making an empty gesture toward the value of diversity. What makes this intervention more meaningful and fruitful than that is its repeated, sustained practice and its active confrontation with habitual thinking as such. Rather than papering over racialized perceptual habits, it seeks to displace them by developing a rich, detailed competing narrative about blackness. What is underway in a practice of mental imagery such as this is a regime of de-habituation; it uses explicit thought processes to intervene upon implicit values, and its primary tool is affective and aesthetic rather than strictly rational or argumentative. It uses the intimacy of a visualization process to disrupt the totalization of a single, stereotypical perceptual habit over and over again. The stylizing function of the white gaze is confronted by a competing narrative that foregrounds black positivity. This process interrupts the seamless totalization of the white gaze, and, as a result, the valuations of whiteness become less hegemonic.

In similar fashion, other recent social-psychological research has studied the effects of a traditional Buddhist meditation technique known as loving-kindness meditation upon implicit bias with promising results. Loving-kindness meditation can take several forms, but a classic technique is to visualize a specific person and mentally repeat to oneself again and again phrases such as, "May you be at ease and happy."[42] At the University of Sussex, Alexander Stell and Tom Farsides found that practicing loving-kindness meditation toward a member of a racial out-group increased explicit, controlled cognition and decreased automatic, implicit cognition, resulting in a diminution of implicit bias toward the target group, as measured by the Implicit Association Test.[43] (In this particular study, the loving-kindness was practiced with a specific black person in mind and resulted in decreased implicit bias toward black people in general.) Put more simply, this evidence suggests that this loving-kindness meditation makes subjects less beholden to their "knee-jerk," stereotypical responses. Utilizing Buddhist meditative techniques in this specifically anti-racist way highlights the moral-phenomenological ramifications of actively countering stereotypical thinking and habituated responses. On the whole, studies such as these point to the potential of "Buddhist-inspired," contemplative anti-racist pedagogies to help reshape the racialized perceptual habits that cannot be accessed by intellectual learning alone.

Nonetheless, the potential gains of anti-racist pedagogies such as these are still, admittedly, modest, and we should not become too grandiose in our hopes that something like a solitary practice of counter-stereotypic mental imagining can "solve" racism. While this research on implicit bias does indicate the malleability and mutability of our phenomenological structures, it also underscores what an incremental and long-term commitment the revision of these structures will require. Even Devine's report warns that "*effort* [is] necessary for implicit bias reduction" and "it is also likely that there is no single 'magic bullet' that, by itself, prompts the regulation of implicit bias."[44] The weight of a lifetime's sedimentation of whiteness is certainly heavy, which is why even those of us who want not to be racist still may find ourselves manifesting racialized perceptual habits in our quotidian discourse.

Nonetheless, research such as this gives us meaningful insight into the moral-phenomenological project of transforming consciousness in the interest of anti-racism. These findings highlight the revisability of our perceptual processes. The phenomenological structures through which we have a world are indeed historical. These perceptual habits are not primordial, and the fact that they have a history should also draw our attention to their futurity. Specific, targeted interventions such as counter-stereotyping practice show that all experience changes us, and what we choose to bring into our milieu can work either to further entrench or to undermine the totalization of our racial categories. Doing so is not tantamount to disavowing whiteness or casting off white privilege, which is simply not possible to do in a racist society. Rather, it is a way of consciously naming how one's position is conditioned by whiteness and becoming less embedded in the ignorance that it entails.

THE MORAL-PHENOMENOLOGICAL VALUE OF NAMING AND DE-CENTERING OUR ORIENTATION

Reading the moral phenomenologies of Buddhist ethics and white anti-racism alongside one another highlights the value of naming our phenomenological orientation *as* a phenomenological orientation and then working to displace its centrality in our way of having a world. Naming the self-cherishing attitude as such—as the product of the avoidable ignorance of a reified self-other binary—uproots phenomenological structures and calls into question the objectivity of what is given in experience. The entire 2,500-year history of

Buddhist practice hinges upon the human capacity to accomplish this profoundly radical moral-phenomenological shift. Likewise, for white people, the practice of taking stock of and challenging how whiteness inflects our way of having a world is required if we are truly to decenter white supremacy in our own thinking as well as in the broader culture. Refusing to own the specificity of one's orientation as a white person only reinforces the status of whiteness as the basic standard of "the human" and the "Otherness" of anything defined in contradistinction to whiteness.

Traleg Kyabgon reminds us that "our nature is one of tremendous potentiality, but a potentiality seldom explored. Due to our habits, we have done almost every conceivable thing *except* take full advantage of our potentiality. In fact, we have achieved the opposite, firmly putting a lid on our potential."[45] Exploring the tremendous potentiality of our subjectivity does not begin and end with embracing an intellectual anti-foundationalist metaphysical point about the fluidity of subjectivity. Such an exploration likely begins with an admission that the terms of our experience are mutable, but the real ethical work lies in taking up a practice of working on those terms in the interest of ethical self-cultivation. We can understand the temporality and historicity of our subjectivity as invitations to their revision, but we also must take responsibility for the hard, incremental work required to accomplish such revision. This recalls the famous line from the twelfth-century Tibetan lama Gampopa, who admonished his students to practice with such urgency "as if a snake had crawled into your lap or your hair had caught fire."[46] Self-cherishing has deep roots, and the opportunity that we have to practice the Buddhist dharma is precious. If nothing else, what Buddhist ethics can help the aspiring white anti-racist appreciate is the need for a long, sustained commitment to this practice. There are no instantaneous "fixes" for moral-phenomenological infelicities; these are structures of our consciousness that have come together over a long history and require dedicated practice in order to challenge.

Those who are pessimistic about the likelihood that white people will engage deeply with their own moral phenomenology cannot be blamed for drawing that conclusion; the phenomenon of white fragility speaks to the unwillingness of many white people to earnestly examine the racist norms that structure our thinking and perception. Not only must a white person be willing to contest their privileged, centered position in the epistemic, social and economic regime of whiteness; they must also submit to the disorientation and dissolution of their self-constitution that accompanies phenomenological self-transformation. Even the most committed white anti-racist must be prepared for the potential uncertainty and groundlessness that come with being de-centered from one's conventional orientation to the world.

This brings to mind a notable distinction between Buddhist ethics and white anti-racism, which is the motivation to practice. The lodestone and primary driver of Buddhist practice is the painful, lived reality of suffering. We are all ensconced in suffering, and it is up to us and us alone to find a way out of it. This gives us a powerful reason for us to address our ignorance. Many Buddhist texts foreground the painful reality of the human condition in order to encourage the practitioner to exert herself on her path of practice. For example, the popular Tibetan teaching known as the Four Reminders outlines four key points that are meant to help motivate the practitioner: the difficulty of attaining the freedoms and advantages of human life, the reality of death and impermanence, the defects and suffering endemic to our cyclic existence, and the weight of karmic cause and effect. The second of these, the contemplation of death, deliberately evokes fear in order to spur the practitioner to take seriously the opportunity she has to practice. In her book on the Four Reminders, the contemporary Tibetan teacher Jetsun Khandro Rinpoche writes, "Reflecting on the impermanence of all phenomena should give rise to a sense of fear—not a paralyzing fear that keeps us from generating positive tendencies or bringing our potential to fruition, but a *genuine sense of urgency* in the face of impermanence."[47] Buddhist literature frequently invokes the value of this fear (Sanskrit: *saṃvega*), which Lajos Brons defines as "a religiously and morally motivating state of shock or agitation."[48] This fear can be highly productive inasmuch as it "produces and deepens insights in the nature of suffering and the brevity and irretrievability of an individual's life," which makes suffering intolerable and motivates the practitioner to decrease suffering in oneself and in others.[49] All this is to say, Buddhist practitioners are given many opportunities to consider the urgency of the moral-phenomenological task before them. Although this task may be intensely challenging at times, it is framed as the only viable alternative to an endlessly repeating cycle of suffering. Buddhist practitioners are responding to a real and urgent existential problem.

White people likewise need to generate a motivational state similar to the Buddhist use of fear, a "white *saṃvega*." The subjects in Dovidio and Gaertner's study on implicit bias espouse ethical ideals of racial equality but then fail to enact them in their lived, embodied social discourse. Is this not a profound failure to achieve ethical flourishing? What I think this indicates is that altruistic motivation and positive emotions such as compassion—while good and likely necessary—may not on their own prompt the kind of deep self-examination and self-critique required for finding and challenging the parts of our moral subjectivity that go against how we see ourselves or how we wish to be in the world. For those of us who wish not to collaborate with white supremacy, the extent to which any of us are able to remain unaware of or indifferent to the racist patterns and habits that structure our experience of the world should be deeply disturbing, provoking a genuine sense of urgency to unseat the embodied, affective, perceptual habits that are undermining our explicitly held ethical values. In the same way that Khandro Rinpoche qualifies the difference between fear that paralyzes us and fear that motivates us, white people must learn to discern the difference between fearing racism because it is taboo to be racist (and therefore avoiding the topic altogether) and fearing racism because it stands between us and the values by which we wish to be guided in our ethical lives and that we wish to see manifest in our communities and society.[50] Cultivating this motivational fear is a moral-phenomenological exercise in itself, inasmuch as it reorients the significance of white people's relative comfort within white supremacy—both material and epistemic—as in fact an obstacle to flourishing.

In sum, these moral phenomenologies of Buddhist ethics and white anti-racism offer a vivid, highly relevant illustration of what it means to transform consciousness. The Buddhist project of releasing oneself from self-cherishing can sound archaic, grandiose or simply beyond reach of any normal person in a way that elides the quotidian intimacy of what *bodhicitta* might mean in our ordinary discourse, while the project of challenging racialized perceptual habits likewise might seem impossibly unrealistic or too personally taxing to attempt. Nonetheless, this comparative moral-phenomenological analysis shows us that by engaging wholeheartedly in practices that uproot our ordinary, habitual orientations, we can exploit the always-unfinished trajectory of our ethical subjectivity.

NOTES

1. Maurice Merleau-Ponty, *Husserl at the Limits of Phenomenology*, trans. Leonard Lawlor (Evanston, IL: Northwestern University Press, 2001), 6.

2. Buddhist metaphysics describes the "way things truly are" by way of the doctrine of interdependent origination (Sanskrit: *pratītyasamutpāda*; Tibetan: *rten cing 'brel bar 'byung ba*), which holds that all psychological and material manifestations arise in dependence upon the causes and conditions that bring them about. Nothing exists as a separate, inherently existing entity; everything exists interdependently.

3. Traleg Kyabgon Kyabgon, *Karma: What It Is, What It Isn't, Why It Matters* (Boston: Shambhala Publications, 2015), 113.

4. Ibid., 111 (emphasis added).

5. "Suffering" here is a translation of the Sanskrit *dukkha*, which otherwise can be rendered as "dissatisfactoriness." The suffering of the human condition encompasses the trials of old age, sickness, and death, but it also includes the subtler fact that there is no ultimate, lasting satisfaction to be found in human life, at least as most of us conventionally approach it.

6. Jay L. Garfield, "What Is It like to Be a Bodhisattva? Moral Phenomenology in Śāntideva's Bodhicaryāvatāra," *Journal of the International Association of Buddhist Studies* 33, nos. 1–2 (2012): 333–357; Jay L. Garfield, *Engaging Buddhism: Why It Matters to Philosophy* (Oxford: Oxford University Press, 2015).

7. This is not an uncontested reading of Buddhist ethics. Damien Keown (2001) and Charles Goodman (2009) have each advanced influential readings of Buddhist ethics as iterations of virtue ethics and consequentialism, respectively. While each of these readings is illuminating in its own right, I am convinced by Garfield's argument against the tendency to read Buddhist ethics through a Western paradigm. He argues that the virtue ethical or consequentialist moments that we might find in Buddhist texts are not definitive of the overall work of Buddhist ethics, which Garfield argues differs in kind from mainstream Western ethical thought and is defined by its unique commitment to the transformation of the practitioner's experience of the world at a phenomenological level. Damien Keown, *The Nature of Buddhist Ethics* (New York: Palgrave, 2001); Charles Goodman, *Consequences of Compassion: An Interpretation and Defense of Buddhist Ethics* (Oxford: Oxford University Press, 2009).

8. Geshe Lhundub Sopa, Leonard Zwilling, and Michael J. Sweet, *Peacock in the Poison Grove: Two Buddhist Texts on Training the Mind* (Boston: Wisdom Publications, 1996), 123.

9. I am grateful to Khenpo Tsondru Sangpo of Ka-Nying Shedrub Ling monastery in Boudhanath, Nepal, for the generous and detailed personal instruction he gave me in this text.

10. Dharmarakṣita, "The Wheel-Weapon Mind Training," *Peacock in the Poison Grove: Two Buddhist Texts on Training the Mind*, translated by Leonard Zwilling and Michael J. Sweet (Wisdom Publications, 1996), p. 71, verse 24.

11. This is, admittedly, a provocative view, as it has the appearance of victim blaming. It is important here to recall that this text is trained upon the moral-phenomenological problem of self-cherishing, so it simply does not anticipate the modern, Western reader concerned about the possibility that there might be blameworthy causes of suffering outside of one's own psychology, such as social injustice. The text assumes that the most pressing problem of human life is a moral-phenomenological one, and its pedagogy is exclusively concerned with addressing that problem alone. Nonetheless, while traditional texts such as the *Wheel-Weapon* do contend that the ultimate source of our suffering is located in our own psychology, in the 'ur' habit of self-cherishing, it does not follow that Buddhist ethics generally instructs that we should ignore the problem of injustice or that a victim of racial oppression simply needs to change her way of thinking to free herself from her suffering. For example, contemporary Buddhist theorists such as Rev. Angel Kyodo Williams, Lama Rod Owens, and Jasmine Syedullah have advanced theories of racial justice grounded in the Buddhist "view," using the term "radical dharma" to refer to the path of seeking outer and inner liberation—that is, worldly and spiritual, personal and social—which they argue are in fact inseparable (Rev. Angel Kyodo Williams, Lama Rod Owens, and Jasmine Syedullah, *Radical Dharma: Talking Race, Love, and Liberation* (Berkeley: North Atlantic Books, 2016).

12. Dharmarakṣita, "The Wheel-Weapon Mind Training," *Peacock in the Poison Grove: Two Buddhist Texts on Training the Mind*, translated by Leonard Zwilling and Michael J. Sweet (Wisdom Publications, 1996), p. 85, verse 55.

13. Sopa, Zwilling, and Sweet, *Peacock in the Poison Grove*, 173.

14. Dharmarakṣita, "The Wheel-Weapon Mind Training," *Peacock in the Poison Grove: Two Buddhist Texts on Training the Mind*, translated by Leonard Zwilling and Michael J. Sweet (Wisdom Publications, 1996), p. 101, verse 85.

15. Ibid., 135, verse 15.

16. bell hooks, *Talking Back: Thinking Feminist, Thinking Black* (Toronto: Between the Lines, 1989), 196.

17. James Baldwin, *The Fire Next Time* (London: Penguin Books, 2007), 16–17.

18. hooks, *Talking Back*, 201.

19. Ibid., emphasis added.

20. Although this chapter focuses specifically upon the moral phenomenology of whiteness, I am not arguing that whiteness is only a moral-phenomenological problem. However, I do maintain that, especially for white people, taking seriously the task of challenging white supremacy at a systemic level requires coming to see the breadth and depth of these systems, including their relationship to our own psychology and moral-phenomenological formation. hooks affirms this point as well: "For our efforts to end white supremacy to be truly effective, individual struggle to change consciousness must be fundamentally linked to collective effort to transform those structures that reinforce and perpetuate white supremacy" (hooks, *Talking Back*, 203).

21. George Yancy, "Whiteness: 'Unseen' Things Seen," in *Black Bodies, White Gazes: The Continuing Significance of Race* (Lanham, MD: Rowman & Littlefield, 2008), 34.

22. George Yancy, "Whiteness and the Return of the Black Body," *The Journal of Speculative Philosophy* 19, no. 4 (2005): 215–241.

23. Yancy, "Whiteness: 'Unseen' Things Seen."

24. Sara Ahmed, "A Phenomenology of Whiteness," *Feminist Theory* 8, no. 2 (2007): 149–168, 150 (emphasis added).

25. Charles W. Mills, "White Ignorance," in *Race and Epistemologies of Ignorance*, eds. Shannon Sullivan and Nancy Tuana (Albany, NY: SUNY Press, 2007), 11–38, 15.

26. Ibid., 18.

27. Sara Ahmed, "Declarations of Whiteness: The Non-Performativity of Anti-Racism," *Borderlands* 3, no. 2 (2004), http://www.borderlands.net.au/vol3no2_2004/ahmed_declarations.htm.

28. The pervasiveness of white ignorance is not uniform throughout a culture, however. Mills is careful to point out that whiteness intersects with the multiplicity of identities and standpoints that various individuals embody and live out, such that "speaking generally about white ignorance does not commit one to the claim that it is uniform across the white population." Further, white ignorance is not necessarily "confined *to* white people," and "it will often be shared by nonwhites to a greater or lesser extent because of the power relations and patterns of ideological hegemony involved" (Mills, "White Ignorance," 22).

29. For example, the so-called Princeton Trilogy, a series of surveys of Princeton students, indicates a diminution over time of white students who espouse negative, stereotypical views about black people (Patricia G. Devine and Andrew J. Elliot, "Are

Racial Stereotypes Really Fading? The Princeton Trilogy Revisited," *Personality and Social Psychology Bulletin* 21, no. 11 (1995): 1139–1150).

30. This is a classic and well-known study of implicit bias, but many more studies have examined its prevalence in areas from jurisprudence to nonverbal communication in casual interpersonal encounters. In a more recent meta-analysis, Pearson, Dovidio and Gaertner review and evaluate several (Adam Pearson, John F. Dovidio, and Samuel L. Gaertner, "The Nature of Contemporary Prejudice: Insights from Aversive Racism," *Social and Personality Psychology Compass* 3 (2009)).

31. John F. Dovidio and Samuel L. Gaertner, "Aversive Racism and Selection Decisions: 1989 and 1999," *Psychological Science* 11, no. 4 (2000): 315–319, 318.

32. George Yancy, "The Elevator Effect," in *Black Bodies, White Gazes: The Continuing Significance of Race* (Lanham, MD: Rowman & Littlefield, 2008), 5.

33. Yancy, "Whiteness and the Return of the Black Body," 230.

34. hooks, *Talking Back*, 193.

35. Shannon Sullivan, *Revealing Whiteness: The Unconscious Habits of Racial Privilege* (Bloomington: Indiana University Press, 2006).

36. Patricia G. Devine, Patrick S. Forscher, Anthony J. Austin, and William T. L. Cox, "Long-Term Reduction in Implicit Race Bias: A Prejudice Habit-Breaking Intervention," *Journal of Experimental Social Psychology* 48, no. 6 (2012): 1267–1278.

37. Ibid., 1276.

38. Briefly, the intervention of stereotype replacement involves recognizing when one has a response that is based on a stereotype, labeling it as such, and replacing it with an unbiased response. Counter-stereotypical imaging, discussed above, involves "imagining in detail counter-stereotypic others." Individuation involves intervening upon stereotypic inferences about a target group member by obtaining specific, personal information about that person. Perspective taking involves "taking the perspective in the first person of a member of a stereotyped group," which "increases psychological closeness to the stigmatized group." Finally, increasing opportunities for contact involves cultivating more direct contact with members of the "out-group," which alters the "cognitive representations of the group" and "[directly improves] evaluations of the group" (Ibid., 1271).

39. Irene V. Blair, Jennifer E. Ma, and Alison P. Lenton, "Imagining Stereotypes Away: The Moderation of Implicit Stereotypes through Mental Imagery," *Journal of Personality and Social Psychology* 81, no. 5 (2001): 828–841, 837.

40. Devine et al., "Long-Term Reduction in Implicit Race Bias," 1270–1271.

41. In fact, the news commentator Van Jones even posited that the election of Donald Trump was a manifestation of "whitelash," a reaction on the part of white Americans to a black president and an apparently transforming racial landscape (Josiah Ryan, "'This Was a Whitelash': Van Jones' Take on the Election Results," *CNN*, November 9, 2016, https://www.cnn.com/2016/11/09/politics/van-jones-results-disappointment-cnntv/index.html.

42. Jack Kornfield, *The Art of Forgiveness, Lovingkindness, and Peace* (New York: Bantam, 2008), 120.

43. Alexander J. Stell and Tom Farsides, "Brief Loving-Kindness Meditation Reduces Racial Bias, Mediated by Positive Other-Regarding Emotions," *Motivation and Emotion* 40, no. 1 (2016): 140–147.

44. Devine et al., "Long-Term Reduction in Implicit Race Bias," 1277.

45. Kyabgon, *Karma*, 137.

46. Sgam-po-pa, Khenpo Rinpochay Könchok Gyaltsen, and Trinlay Chödron, *The Jewel Ornament of Liberation: The Wish-Fulfilling Gem of the Noble Teachings* (Ithaca, NY: Snow Lion Publications, 1998), 215.

47. Khandro, *This Precious Life: Tibetan Buddhist Teachings on the Path to Enlightenment,* rev. ed. (Boston: Shambhala Publications, 2005), 50 (emphasis added).

48. Lajos Brons, "Facing Death from a Safe Distance: Saṃvega and Moral Psychology," *Journal of Buddhist Ethics* 23 (2016): 83–128, 84.

49. Brons, "Facing Death from a Safe Distance," 120. I thank Stephen Harris for a helpful discussion of *saṃvega* and for pointing me toward Brons' work on this concept.

50. There is already valuable work in critical race studies on the value of negative affect in anti-racism; for example, Alexis Shotwell's work on the value of shame in white anti-racist praxis illuminates the difference between the paralysis of white guilt and the productiveness of white shame (Alexis Shotwell, *Knowing Otherwise: Race, Gender, and Implicit Understanding* (University Park, PA: Penn State University Press, 2011)).

Chapter 10

"bell hooks Made Me a Buddhist"

Liberatory Cross-Cultural Learning—Or Is This Just Another Case of How White People Steal Everything?

Carol J. Moeller

INTRODUCTION

A central feature of white settler colonial subjectivity is forgetting; we live whiteness in part as active ignorance and forgetting. . . . But we don't just have a knowledge problem—we have a habit-of-being a problem; the problem of whiteness is a problem of what we expect, our ways of being, bodily-ness, and how we understand ourselves as "placed" in time. *Whiteness is a problem of being shaped to think that others are the problem.*[1]

As Alexis Shotwell writes, oppressive legacies continue to live on in us, and—whatever our explicit intentions—we tend to reproduce these practices: colonialist-sexist-racist-capitalist-neo-liberal-able-ist heteronormative practices. Many respond to the concern about this reproduction of oppression with efforts to purify ourselves of them. Yet such ideals of purity are part and parcel of these bad ideologies. Instead, as Shotwell argues, we must work directly with our compromised imbrication in oppressive patterns. She offers critiques of purity, distributed ethics, attention to multiplicity of activist practices, and awareness of our interconnectedness to approach decolonization.

bell hooks, Chandra Mohanty, and others devoted to liberatory critical consciousness have taught me and others much about how to live differently, doing so with much explicit attention to legacies of oppression. Buddhist and other mindful practices can teach ways of thinking, being, and relating to the world that dovetail with these. I connect these ways of learning and being, specifically here for whites and others of settler "habits-of-being," as

Shotwell notes. Racism, colonization, and other relations of minoritization are often thought to be of interest only to minoritized group members. As in the quote above by Shotwell, whites are "shaped to think others are the problem."

Here, I consider practices of critical consciousness, Buddhism, and mindfulness (more generally) in relation to whiteness. Imperialist/pseudo-versions of both mindfulness practices (whether Buddhist or non-Buddhist) and "critical consciousness" practices can serve to reinforce habitual oppression and other "habitual tendencies" that perpetuate hegemonic patterns. Liberationist, genuine versions of each, in contrast, can be helpful in enabling one to live differently, to, as Sara Ahmed writes, "not produce what we inherit."[2] They invite us to live differently, teaching, showing, and embodying ways to do so. Dzigar Kongtrul Rinpoche draws from the concept of "radical openheartedness,"[3] which is the Tibetan Buddhist notion of "Tsewa" (in Tibetan transliteration: brtse ba, in Tibetan script:བརྩེ་བ). Might this concept be drawn from to transform the world such that everyone may flourish? In particular, I draw upon:

1. My own experience with Buddhist practice, particularly Tibetan Buddhist practice and study, as a student of Mindrolling Jetsun Khandro Rinpoche and Dzigar Kongtrul Rinpoche.[4]
2. Feminist anti-racist counter-hegemonic praxis, developing "critical consciousness,"[5] particularly through mentoring by bell hooks[6] and Chandra Talpade Mohanty.

APPROACH AND METHODS

Neither attempts at Buddhist practice nor efforts at what Paulo Freire terms "education for critical consciousness" inherently and automatically challenge white supremacy. Rather, imperial forms of each are common. In both areas, one may have tendencies to "talk the talk" without "walking the walk"—leaving a significant gap between theory and practice. Moreover, many use Buddhist teachings in service of their own egos. Many engage in cultural appropriation and "other-izing" fascination with Eastern spiritual traditions, as with Native American/First Nations traditions, without treating people of those traditions with respect and without doing social justice work to challenge unjust conditions under which actual people connected to these traditions actually live. How many of us have dreamcatchers in our homes or cars, without having even cursory knowledge of the origins of dreamcatchers, and without working diligently for such Native American/First Nations movements as land rights or against violence targeting Native Americans?

As Audre Lorde notes with respect to relations of oppression (in which she calls a "market fundamentalist culture"—geared toward the profits of the few rather than the flourishing of all), one is not trained to relate to others across differences as equals. Rather, one is conditioned to ignore, copy, or destroy difference.[7] Whereas exploitative and distorting approaches under conditions of oppression may reinscribe rather than transform oppression, liberatory approaches may enable us to live differently in ways that interrupt patterns of white supremacy and coloniality, in intersection with all forms of minoritization and oppression.

I suggest that pseudo-Buddhist/mindfulness and pseudo-critical consciousness views and practices can be mutually reinforcing in the negative, re-inscribing the very ignorance and oppression to which they claim to be antidotes. In challenging these, I suggest parallels between transformative versions of each. I draw from Johnnella Butler's terminology of the "true-true" for versions of Buddhism/mindfulness and critical consciousness that truly de-mystify rather than obscure oppressive relations that enable "critical unforgetting" rather than that "central feature of white settler colonial subjectivity [that] is forgetting."[8] Shotwell invokes Roxanne Dunbar-Ortiz's discussion of Andre Brink's reminder that the opposite of "truth" from the Greek is not "lie" but rather "forgetting," demonstrating how active forgetting is crucial to the maintenance of colonial and oppressive relations.

I invoke Johnnella Butler's[9] phrase, the "true-true." Butler develops her notion of the "true-true" in the context of African American literature and criticism, developing central themes of wholeness, double-consciousness, and rememory. Butler writes, "Through dialogue, rememory is engaged and double consciousness mediated, yielding epistemic knowledge from identity that is multiple. As a dialogic strategy, rememory investigates the binaries of the general and the particular, the past and present, the present and the projected future; it analyzes interconnections, contradictions, overlaps, and intersections that become apparent when historical and folk narratives, literature, music, politics, economics, visual arts, and theory and life events are read next to one another."[10] Butler works with W. E. B. DuBois' multilayered interdisciplinary approaches to the diverse lived experience of black people. Whereas many have interpreted DuBois' "double consciousness" as a sharp dualism, Butler reveals its dialogical and whole quality.

Butler invokes a Bakhtinian notion of truth as dialogic. "Truth," according to Bakhtin "is not born nor is to be found inside the head of an individual person, it is born *between* people collectively searching for truth, in the process of their dialogic interaction."[11]

As Butler writes, "One has to take risks in order to get to the true-true— that is, the objective truth as it is experienced, felt, represented, and as it affects you and others. The dialogic strategy of rememory allows for critique

of the binary of double consciousness and makes wholeness—or compre-
hending and engaging the world from the vantage of agency—possible."[12]
Butler examines the layers of complexity of perspectives in focusing on the
"true-true."

Both Buddhist and critical consciousness approaches recognize that the
world is more complex and less transparent than is often thought. I consider
both liberating and distorting versions of Buddhist and mindfulness practices
and both liberating and distorting versions of critical consciousness practices.
Cross-cultural engagement can be fraught with such issues as exploitation
and cultural appropriation, such that whiteness consumes "the other" without
accountability. Respectful cross-cultural engagement with accountability,
across various borders, is precisely what is required to intervene upon rather
than simply reproduce white supremacist, capitalist, hetero-normative, ableist, patriarchy.

HOW DID BELL HOOKS MAKE ME A BUDDHIST?

In *Training in Tenderness: Buddhist Teachings on Tsewa, the Radical Openness of Heart that Can Change the World*, Tibetan Buddhist teacher Dzigar
Kongtrul writes of Tsewa, which is a "radical openness of heart," not as a
remote esoteric concept, but as a warm heart that each of us has, whatever
challenges we may face of ignorance, violence, hatred, exploitation, and
abuse. Kongtrul uses the Tibetan term Tsewa rather than English words
because the English candidate terms (such as love and compassion) tend
to have many associations that complicate the intended meaning from the
Tibetan Tsewa (Tibetan transliteration: *brtse ba*, in Tibetan script:བརྩེ་བ).

Kongtrul's work on Tsewa touches—directly and indirectly—on critical
consciousness ideas and methods I encountered with bell hooks. Kongtrul
specifically challenges a "capitalist mentality," which encourages us to
be cynical and look out for our self-interests first and foremost.[13] Dzigar
Kongtrul notes that while many today find diversity threatening, diversity is
in fact a great strength. He writes, "The only way forward is for people to
bind themselves closer together than ever before. The glue that will bind us
has to be our common tenderness of heart. . . . With that view, our diversity
will only be an advantage, an aid to our individual and collective growth."[14]
Kongtrul notes how people with various heritages and ethical and spiritual
traditions extending around the globe have greater contact and interaction
than ever before. I discovered Kongtrul, my own Tibetan Buddhist teacher for
the past twelve years or so, as well as Mindrolling Jetsun Khandro Rinpoche,
my primary teacher, through a somewhat circuitous path. bell hooks played
a considerable part, exposing me to Buddhism and—through her connection

to Buddhism—exemplifying a combined critical consciousness and mindful spiritual outlook that was, and continues to be, life-sustaining. It has now been thirty years since I first connected with radical educators such as Chandra Mohanty, Adrienne Jones, and bell hooks. In these thirty years of activism, working in higher education, and living life generally, I continue to build on lessons from these mentors. The lessons are not only regarding how to transform one's thinking, but also one's whole self in the interests of liberation.[15] Following Shotwell's terms, their approaches to liberation go beyond the "knowledge" problem with whites to the "habit of being" problem.

bell hooks introduced me to Buddhism originally by quoting Thích Nhất Hạnh often, referring to him as an exemplar of how to respond to the world. (I was bell hooks' student at Oberlin College in the late 1980s.) She invited us to consider the teachings of Thích Nhất Hạnh, a Vietnamese Buddhist monk, who led a nonviolent, Gandhian-style resistance movement to the war in Vietnam. Thích Nhất Hạnh defines mindfulness as "keeping one's consciousness alive to the present reality."[16] He does not see this mindful mode of consciousness as in tension with a busy, complex life. He suggests that mindfulness can be cultivated through practice in any situation. He writes:

> keep your attention focused on the work, be alert and ready to handle ably and intelligently any situation which may arise—this is mindfulness. There is no reason why mindfulness should be different from focusing all one's attention on one's work, to be alert and to be using one's best judgment. During the moment one is consulting, resolving, and dealing with whatever arises, a calm heart and self-control are necessary if one is to achieve good results.[17]

Hạnh's teaching includes mindfulness in situations of great pain and devastation. For example, he taught the importance of meditation during such activities as removing dead bodies from bombed areas in Vietnam. In the activist tradition of "engaged Buddhism," he led over 10,000 people in rebuilding bombed villages, setting up medical care, teaching children, and organizing food cooperatives, all in a spirit and mode of compassion. Refusing to take sides in the conflict, he[18] argued that "both sides were but the reflection of one reality, and the true enemies were not people, but ideology, hate, and ignorance."[19] Martin Luther King, Jr. was so moved by Hạnh's philosophy and efforts that King nominated him for the Nobel Peace Prize and publicly denounced the Vietnam conflict during a press conference with Hạnh. King endorsed Hạnh's mindful approach to activism, which eschewed any bitterness, hate, or polarization of people into "us and them" thinking. As young activists and undergraduate students at Oberlin College, many of us did not want to hear about hooks' Buddhist lessons—that we critique others' ideas without judging the person presenting the idea, for example. We were "twenty-somethings" and thought ourselves the vanguard of social change; hooks' challenges to our judgmentalism sounded accommodationist. It was only later that I started reading Thích Nhất Hạnh and other Buddhists and became ready to hear those lessons from hooks that had been so jarring to my young activist ears.[20]

From years (now decades) of reflecting upon hooks' lessons in embodying critical consciousness through "education as the practice of freedom"[21] I can better understand the impact of hooks' pedagogy. Here are some ways I experience hooks as embodying her ideas.

She shares/shares *and* embodies her love, honesty, integrity, struggle, and commitment to live in accord with the examples of Thích Nhất Hạnh, Paulo Freire, and other moral-political-spiritual leaders.

She centers critique of "white supremacist capitalist patriarchy"—refusing to focus on any single issue in isolation.

She speaks/spoke often of ways we are wounded by oppression in its various forms and specifically in families of origin and other situations in which we may have encountered interpersonal and/or other forms of violence. She explicitly focused on her notion of "self-recovery" and often asked how to deal with being "wounded in the place we would know love." bell hooks helped to cultivate our thirst for theory and praxis that transforms us and the world and that did not divorce spiritual, political, ethical, emotional issues or aspects of life. I sat in on her Reading Fiction introductory-level course, which she organized around the theme of self-recovery.

I recall another student and I "venting" with criticism at a professor from a minoritized group. One of us said that the professor was "out of control" with his emotionally charged interactions with us. hooks refused to jump on our bandwagon of judging the professor, reminding us instead of how wounded people tend to be, and how charged our interactions can be across minoritized groups. She said that the student was "out of control," with the student's own pain and upset. (To be clear, these were not incidents of harassment or assault, but rather arguments and hurt feelings about why this professor— who we saw as a mentor—was failing to be supportive and radical in ways that we wanted.) In contexts with few faculty from minoritized groups, the stakes of mentor relationships were very high. She offered perspective—that we lacked utterly—of how our professors and other mentors were imperfect human beings, thinkers, and teachers, negotiating contexts of oppression in often uncharted territory. hooks always encouraged us to be aware that people tend to be walking around with a lot of pain and deserve compassion rather than judgment and rejection. Often when I saw her, even many years after being a formal student of hers in a classroom at Oberlin College, she would ask me, "Carol, how is your heart?"

She asks us to envision liberationist futures in which everyone may flourish, and in which love and solidarity shape the fabric of the world. She often quoted Ernesto Che Guevara's powerful message: "At the risk of seeming ridiculous, let me say that the real revolutionary is guided by a great feeling of love."[22]

I recall walking with her at the Feminist Expo in Baltimore, Maryland (April 2000). To me privately and later in the session she led, she noted that many people at the conference were not very friendly, that few people said "hello" in response to her "hello" in passing, until they realized who she was, in the context of her session and book signing. She seemed pained that in the rush and anonymity of the conference, the culture seemed be so isolating and unwelcoming. Speaking of her book on love,[23] she stressed how love needs to be foremost in the fabric of our lives, and that supposedly feminist spaces would do well to embody values asserting that everyone matters.

hooks has a way of honoring everyday people, even as she acknowledges that we all tend to be deeply shaped by white supremacist capitalist patriarchy. She used to quote the following line from Paulo Freire, "We cannot enter the struggle as objects in order to later become subjects."[24] She reminds us that we are all subjects of our own lives, and that it is up to us to grow and change and engage in "self-recovery," engaging in transformation rather than play out weary parts assigned to us in our inegalitarian world.

"TRUE-TRUE" MINDFULNESS AND BUDDHIST PRACTICE

Years of activist and academic challenges brought bell hooks' lessons to mind repeatedly, which encouraged me to explore Buddhism. In my own story, I encountered Ellen Langer's secular psychological research on "mindfulness" (building it centrally into my dissertation in philosophy) long before I became an active student and member of a Buddhist community. I speak to both contexts here. Qualities of "mindfulness" and attention are relevant not only to Buddhist practitioners but to everyone. In this next section, I introduce a secular, general version of mindfulness from Langer's psychological research.

Langer's Psychological Research on Mindfulness

According to Langer's extensive research, there are empirically identifiable phenomena she calls mindfulness and mindlessness. Langer's book *Mindfulness* is a synthesis and "translation of over fifty experiments and an attempt to demonstrate their implications beyond the lab, both in literature and in daily life."[25] Mindlessness tends to take three main forms: (1) entrapment by categories, (2) engaging in automatic behavior, and (3) acting from a single perspective, "acting as though there were only one set of rules."[26] Langer writes, "Mindlessness sets in when we rely too rigidly on categories and distinctions created in the past. We build our own and shared realities and then we become victims of them."[27] (Connections with various manifestations of hegemonic culture are easy to make here.)

In contrast, mindfulness has three key qualities: (1) creating new categories and distinctions, responsive to particulars of context, (2) acting consciously with awareness of options, open to new information, (3) acting with awareness of various views, aware that one is operating in line with one way among many (still, doing the best we can with what we see, we do so humbly, with awareness that we do not have all the answers).

When one is mindful, one is alive to salient features in the present moment, which enables more effective responses to situations than mindlessness. Further, mindfulness contributes to vitality, enjoyment, psychological well-being, and overall health. The deadening consequences of mindlessness include fatigue, burnout, and diminished creativity and effectiveness. Langer's research includes many experiments in which elderly people are asked to engage in simple activities that promote mindfulness, while a control group does not. The mindful tasks can be as simple as caring for a plant, making such decisions as where to place it and how much to water it. In the control group, each member is given a plant but told not to worry about its care and that the staff will care for it. After a period of time with daily mindful activity, the mindful group demonstrates striking degrees of improvement, such as decreases in illness and depression and increases in alertness, activity, happiness, and even longevity.

Mindful modes include openness to learning, being flexible, not being trapped in rigid categories, and rejecting good/bad outcome-oriented modes (making people change, agree with our agenda, etc.) in favor or a process-oriented approach to learning which recognizes and respects that everyone is engaged in a *process* of learning. A certain kind of humility is required since none of us have all the answers. Whatever our views and social locations, we all have much to learn, and learning comes most easily from mindful modes. Returning to bell hooks' lessons, she taught us that thinking of certain groups or people as "the enemy" may seem comforting for a while, making things seem clearer, such as who is trustworthy and who is not. However, it backfires if we fail to acknowledge how we too are all full of contradictions and blind spots.

Buddhist Notions and Practices Relating to Mindfulness

In this section, I address specifically Buddhist contexts in which "right mindfulness" is situated in the contexts of the Four Noble Truths of Buddhism. It is important to note that the Buddhist Four Noble Truths and the EightFold Path are huge topics. They are not simply propositions to be reflected upon and considered abstractly, but should be approached through a lifetime of study, hearing, contemplation, and meditation. To put it simply, the Four Noble Truths are as follows:

1. Suffering is pervasive.
2. Suffering is caused by attachment and craving.
3. Suffering can cease.
4. The EightFold Path leads to liberation from suffering.

"Right mindfulness" is only one Fold of the EightFold Path to liberation from suffering taught by the Buddha. For liberation, "right mindfulness" must be combined with the other seven dimensions of the Path to Cessation of Suffering. These are:

1. Right View
2. Right Resolve
3. Right Speech
4. Right Action
5. Right Livelihood
6. Right Effort
7. Right Mindfulness
8. Right Meditative Concentration (samadhi)

It is worth quoting Matthieu Ricard at length for this authentic Buddhist context and the complexities of mindfulness. In response to a Buddhist scholar suggesting that a high-rope walking acrobat holds mindfulness, Ricard writes:

A clearer example [that a high-rope walking acrobat, moving one-pointedly across a wire] might be that of a sniper waiting for his victim: he can be one-pointedly concentrated, abiding unwaveringly in the present moment, calm and poised. The sniper is able to maintain his attention over time and bring it back to his target as soon as it wanders. To succeed in his ominous goal, he has to ward off distraction and laxity, the two major obstacles to attention.

Bare attention, as consummate as it might be, is no more than a tool that can certainly be used to achieve enlightenment and is needed for this purpose, but which can also be used to cause immense suffering. Obviously, what is entirely missing is the ethical dimension of a mindfulness that deserves the qualification of "wholesome" and can lead to enlightenment.

In addition to directing the attention (manasikara in Pali, manaskara in Sanskrit, and yid la byed pa in Tibetan) to a chosen object and maintaining the attention on this object (respectively sati, smriti, and dran pa), genuine mindfulness must include an understanding of the nature of one's mental state (sampajanna, samprajnana and shes bzhin), free from distortions, as well as an embedded

ethical component that enables one to clearly discern whether or not it is beneficial to maintain our present state of mind and behavior.[28]

So, mindfulness requires: (1) focusing and keeping attention on a certain
object, (2) awareness of one's mind as clear of obscuring influences, and
(3) embodying ethical reflection and clear discernment upon one's mind and
behavior. On this Buddhist view, mindfulness is not simply "bare attention" but
must include beneficial mind and actions. Further, mindfulness is necessary to
ethical practices; one must attend to the right things in the right ways to be ethical. Ethical orientation and mindfulness are co-constitutive; we need be ethically oriented to be mindful, and we need to be mindful in order to be ethical.[29]

> To these three, one also adds "concern" (Pali, appamadena, Sanskrit. apramada,
> Tibetan bag yod) which is to constantly maintain the ethical dimension of mind-
> fulness and vigilantly guard the mind from falling into unwholesome thoughts
> that lead to unwholesome actions.
>   The practice of mindfulness thus needs to be guided by right view and insight
> (such as the understanding that all phenomena are empty of independent exis-
> tence), and motivated by the right intention, such as the aspiration to achieve
> enlightenment for the benefit of all beings.

Thus, one must hold this "concern," being conscientious, keeping oneself
from being distracted by unvirtuous thoughts and actions. This helps one
maintain an ethical orientation, undistractedly better able to work for true
benefit of oneself and others that all beings may be liberated.

> It is quite true that a meditator resting in pure awareness and perfect understand-
> ing of the fundamental nature of mind, unaltered by mental constructions, will
> be unable to pull the trigger and kill someone. This kind of luminous awareness
> is a state of wisdom and is the natural state of a mind that is entirely free from
> ignorance and mental toxins and spontaneously imbued with unconditional
> altruism and compassion. Such a state is the result of having achieved inner
> freedom and should not be confused with mere mindfulness and bare attention.

With Ricard's clarifications, we can segue into some of the non-liberating
ideas and practices of "mindfulness" that are divorced from this ethical context and larger Buddhist View.

NON-LIBERATING APPROACHES TO BUDDHIST
AND OTHER MINDFULNESS PRACTICES

Ricard has analyzed and applied Buddhist views of mindfulness as including ethical orientation and Buddhist views on the nature of mind, reality,

interdependence, and the notion that all beings have value and that their/our liberation requires pursuit. Removed from this context, notions of mindfulness lose much of their sense. So too do Ron Purser and David Loy critique certain notions of "mindfulness" as commodified in accommodationist ways—shoring up institutions and practices that would best be subjected to critique from Buddhist views.

The very term "mindfulness" has been problematically commodified, divorced from Buddhist discipline and ethics, appropriated by corporate culture, and even applied to questionable ends, such as in "mindful sniper" blogs. As Ron Purser and David Loy write:

> While a stripped-down, secularized technique—what some critics are now calling "McMindfulness"—may make it more palatable to the corporate world, decontextualizing mindfulness from its original liberative and transformative purpose, as well as its foundation in social ethics, amounts to a Faustian bargain. Rather than applying mindfulness as a means to awaken individuals and organizations from the unwholesome roots of greed, ill will and delusion, it is usually being refashioned into a banal, therapeutic, self-help technique that can actually reinforce those roots.[30]

"McMindfulness" dilutes much of the context and substance of mindfulness, divorcing it from the substantive Buddhist views of how to live, how to know, what the world is like, how suffering occurs and continues in cyclical fashion.

Even among supposed Buddhist practitioners, ideas and practices of Buddhism may be distorted and appropriated to serve one's own ego and advance self-interested arrogance, pride, and other aspects of what Chogyam Trungpa calls "Spiritual Materialism."[31] Contemporary Tibetan Buddhist Teacher and filmmaker Dzongsar Khyentse remarks on some of these tendencies to distort, misuse, appropriate, and apply "imperial" approaches to the Buddhist Teachings. He writes, "I find heartbreaking the imperialist attitude that arrogantly isolates one aspect of Eastern culture, analyzing it at a careful distance, manipulating and sterilizing it to fit Western agendas, and then perhaps concluding that it is now suitable for consumption."[32]

He notes that such twistings of the Buddhist Teachings may aggravate the very egoistic tendencies Buddhist practices are meant to cut through. Continuing directly from the previous quote, Dzongsar Khyentse Rinpoche writes "This is cherishing of ego. For even if we think we want to practice the Buddhist path to give up our ego-clinging is not easy, and we could well end up with our own ego's version of dharma—a pseudo-dharma which will only bring more suffering instead of liberation."[33] Pseudo-dharma, contrived and affected Buddhist identification, and "McMindfulness" each reinscribes white supremacist and other oppressive patterns rather than producing liberation from these patterns.

hooks' conceptualization of imperialist patriarchal white supremacist capitalist cultures are well known for decimating minoritized peoples, all the while exoticizing and absorbing anything seen as beneficial to them—appropriating from the ruins that we have produced. As a professor, scholar, and writer, hooks made/makes that point consistently. She is aware of how whites are prone to "groove on" culture from minoritized groups but reject its demands that we grow and examine ourselves. She famously speaks of majoritized people's tendencies to "eat the other" without becoming critically conscious in engaging with the work of "the other." As character Kima Greggs says to Ellis Carver in HBO television show "The Wire" (upon seeing white young people wearing and speaking in ways that seemed to appropriate urban black speech and clothing), "White people steal everything." How does that trajectory—of white people stealing everything and denying complicity in racist violence—operate with Buddhism and race? With Tibetan Buddhism, it was the Chinese rather than the US or European colonial powers that committed genocide, which Involved killing one-sixth of Tibet's population, destroying the majority of Tibet's sacred sites, objects, and texts, and seizing the land. However, US hands are by no means clean. The United States, like those other colonial powers, refused to come to Tibet's aid when the Dalai Lama requested diplomatic and other assistance well before the Chinese invasion. Many Tibetan Buddhist teachers, scholars, and practitioners in exile have come to other parts of Asia, the Americas, Europe, Africa, and Australia and established centers and followings. Indeed, many regard it as a great irony that China's efforts to destroy Tibetan Buddhism instead resulted in the spreading of Tibetan Buddhism throughout the world. The Dalai Lama, who China had sought to kill, not only survived but became widely recognized as a world leader.

Nonetheless, US Tibetan Buddhist communities have complicated relationships to race. In my Tibetan Buddhist community, the leader is a *Tibetan* Tibetan Buddhist teacher (rather than an Anglo- or European teacher of Tibetan Buddhism). She is a member of the Tibetan refugee community in India. The leadership is not white. The community of practitioners is mostly white, though not exclusively. How much do we acknowledge, though, that we are largely citizens of a settler nation? On a level of material and political power, our social identities are more analogous to the Chinese oppressors than to the Tibetans with whom we seek to align ourselves. How are we like whites who attend Native American ceremonies and receive benefits without acknowledging our complicity with the genocide of Native people?

Jetsun Khandro Rinpoche, my primary Buddhist teacher, often nudges her students, revealing ways that we treat Buddhism as a commodity to inflate our egos, rather than—as the teachings are intended—to lessen our self-absorption. She challenges our affectations, such as wearing prayer beads apparently as jewelry rather than as practice tools. Even in our meditation postures, she notes that we can be "puffed up" with pride and arrogance. She notes our tendencies to embrace solid identities, such as "I am a Buddhist," with an arrogant mentality. She tends to call us rather "practitioners," which emphasizes how we are in process, learning and practicing the teachings. Tibetan Language Institute director David Curtis notes that the Institute gets more frequent requests for Tibetan images for tattoos than for Tibetan language instruction for Buddhist study. Often images and symbols associated with Buddhism are used as decorations which may be seen as degrading or objectifying Buddhist iconography. Dibyesh Anand has done really important work regarding a postcolonial analysis of the "poetics of 'Exotica Tibeta' (a shorthand for the exoticized—both positive and negative—Western representations of Tibet)."[34]

In my Buddhist community, examples of everyday racism abound. People of color report being mistaken for each other, though they look nothing like the other person. One woman of color relates an uncomfortable exchange, in which a white woman called her by the name of another woman of color, then, when corrected, went on and on with apologies and explanations, apparently wanting the woman of color to absolve her somehow of her mistake.

In one forum at a retreat, a woman of color of my Buddhist community articulated her concerns about our lack of diversity, pointing to the barriers of class, race, and culture that stand in the way of many participating in our retreats. Others point out that our community is flexible with payment for retreat, giving scholarships and payment plans. This response seems insufficient. She asks how others are even to know that the Buddhist community would have something to offer them if they are not already familiar with it. She reminds us that taking time off work and other responsibilities to explore Buddhism in retreat is not an option for many.

Within Buddhism, as with other philosophies and wisdom traditions, there is also respectful ethical cross-cultural engagement. For one exemplar of liberatory, respectful cross-cultural learning, consider a US white man, Gene Smith, who used his position as a US citizen and his access to (ever increasing) technology to help preserve precious Tibetan Buddhist texts. With the Chinese invasion and genocide, the Chinese attempted cultural and religious genocide as well, destroying most of the sacred texts, objects, temples, monasteries, and libraries. Tibetans in exile literally walked across the Himalayan Mountains to escape, carrying what they could of sacred texts. As Smith learned of this destruction of sacred texts and sites and of the chaotic dispersal of surviving texts, he took it upon himself to coordinate preservation—and later digitalization—efforts. With a note of introduction from his own Tibetan Buddhist teacher, Smith traveled to remote sites to collect copies of these sacred texts, eventually preserving them digitally through the Tibetan

Buddhist Resource Center. He also helped preserve the printing woodblocks so that the Tibetan Buddhists could continue to use their traditional technology to print texts. Smith lobbied the US government and arranged to have the US government through the Library Congress "repay" the sharing of priceless wisdom with material resources needed by the Tibetans in exile.[35]

Note that Smith did not selfishly benefit from Tibetan Buddhist teachings. He used the privilege and connections he held to be of service to the Tibetan people. He regarded Tibetans as subjects of their own lives and wisdom traditions, even amid the horrors they were facing. Rather than seeing them as objects of sympathy, he valued them as subjects, partnering with Tibetan Buddhists to help preserve their precious teachings, and working with the US government to arrange access to material resources. This approach opposes the usual dynamics of cultural appropriation in which majoritized groups take cultural and knowledge resources from minoritized groups with neither consent, nor credit, nor reciprocity.[36]

"TRUE-TRUE" "CRITICAL CONSCIOUSNESS"/ LIBERATING PHILOSOPHIES

In previous sections, I have hinted at what bell hooks calls, following Paulo Freire, "education for critical consciousness." As with hooks' example, it is important that critical consciousness not be single-issue focused; rather, critical consciousness must deal with a multiplicity of issues—how gender is racialized in particular ways, how race is gendered, how heteronormativity takes particular forms in relation to gender, race, disability, and so on.

The term "intersectionality" has caught on recently to signal this mutual imbrication. There are critics from a variety of perspectives who critique the concept of "intersectionality" and how the concept is used. Michael Hames García, in *Identity Complex*,[37] prefers to speak of "multiplicity" partly because even the "intersectionality" metaphor preserves the notion of multiple distinct vectors crossing each other, whereas the multiplicitous imbrication of such factors as colonialism, gender, race, sexuality, disability, and citizenship status is much deeper than that.

Critical consciousness, at its best, strives to keep asking questions across difference and does not pretend to have settled everything. Here, I would like to foreground notions of activist-accountable scholarship/praxis that avoid insular academic discussions in order to keep open these questions, across various borders. I borrow from a framework of recommendations provided by Chandra Mohanty,[38] as presented at a conference of the Future of Minority Studies Project. Mohanty notes that collaborative work across various borders is crucial to producing knowledge that goes beyond narrow reference points. She gives four main points of guidance for those attempting activist scholarship to think and work across barriers and to increase accountability to communities, groups, and the larger world upon which we are reflecting and into which we wish to intervene.

1. Chandra Mohanty states that "people who do activist scholarship need to be attentive to accountability."[39] She asks which communities we locate ourselves in, and to whom do we hold ourselves accountable.
2. Mohanty notes that one must "speak truth to power, speak to/of injustice."[40]
3. Mohanty claims that we must vigilantly ask ourselves "what kinds of knowledge are we producing . . . do [these knowledges] reproduce colonization or are they de-colonizing and democratizing?"[41]
4. Being accountable in such ways "involves a radical bringing of our whole selves . . . mind, heart, hands, body"[42] across lines of difference. Mohanty notes that with such deep "whole self" engagement, we have greater opportunities to learn from tripping up, to catch on to our mistakes and improve our praxis, being more responsive and accountable to others. If not, if we confine ourselves to divisions and insular spaces, we may talk to ourselves and with others who share our reference points, not realizing the limitations arising from this insularity.[43]

Mohanty's suggestions on accountability across difference are fruitful. Often in higher education, K–12 environments, nonprofit contexts, or advocacy situations, we may fail to notice how insular our spaces can be and how we may see "expertise" in people who have certain credentials and academic training without necessarily having worked and lived with the challenges. One colleague, Dr. Hasshan Batts,[44] is a prison survivor and now holding a doctorate in social work and doing community organizing around incarceration and re-entry. He notes that many want to exploit his story without really respecting him as a thinker and knowledge producer. He uses the reminder that people "closest to the pain" need to be respected as knowers.

Chandra Mohanty's four lessons above may be applied broadly. Here, I use them to speak briefly to some of my working and living contexts:

On Mohanty's Questions on Accountability

As Audre Lorde writes in her oft-quoted passage about "the Master's Tools," "The more one depends on the Master's House for support, the less one hears what he doesn't want you to hear." Much has been written about how neoliberalism, disciplinary practices, elitism, and other factors have shaped even feminist, ethnic, and other minoritized studies to moderate and "ghettoize" them and their impact. It is crucial that my relationships of accountability do not rest in academia. How are we involved in activist, neighborhood, and community settings, across diverse groups, in everyday language, working for change? Politics of place, land, and space are critical. I write from unceded Lenape land, in a nation built upon stolen land and labor, in a country which every day violates international standards of human rights. How does one use privilege and citizenship status for justice?

On Mohanty's reminder to "speak truth to power, speak to/of injustice"

   The un-forgetting practices Shotwell describes are crucial, as are the collaborations across difference, thinking across boundaries.

On Mohanty's question "What kinds of knowledge are we producing . . . do [these knowledges] reproduce colonization or are they de-colonizing and democratizing?"

   I ask how my teaching, writing, and being depart from and critically engage with patterns of oppression. I cannot claim to have any definitive answers.

On Mohanty's claim that this work "involves a radical bringing of our whole selves . . . mind, heart, hands, body . . ." across lines of difference

   In both activist and other relationships, how do we go beyond content to deep relationships which enable practices of freedom? In working among whites and across various forms of difference, with deepening dialogue and accountability, I trip up, and I learn.

NON-LIBERATING ATTEMPTS AT "CRITICAL CONSCIOUSNESS"/LIBERATING PHILOSOPHIES

Throughout this chapter, I have suggested that bell hooks, Buddhist, and other mindfulness practices, and critical consciousness offer ways of being that may transform oppressive patterns into liberatory practices. Yet, not all attempts at these are fully counter-hegemonic. There are pseudo, imperialist, or superficial versions that fall far short of the "true-true" liberatory versions. At this juncture in the chapter, I point to some versions of such efforts at critical consciousness that fall short.

   Readers have their own insightful examples of what I call "non-liberating attempts at critical consciousness." In fact, we might even call them pretenses of critical consciousness. Within this context, here are some examples:

a. "saying the right things" but having big gaps between ideas and practise;
b. in academia or even social service (nonprofit industrial complex), not being accountable to those "closest to the pain," using stories of "others" while treating them as objects rather than subjects;
c. operating in insular spaces, failing to be accountable to the larger constituencies and social movements with which one claims to be aligned;
d. re-capitulating white-centeredness, white neurosis, anxiety, perfectionism, and emotions as deflection away from accountability;
e. caught in single-issue focus or only superficially engaging with multiplicity of minoritization;
f. using notions like "intersectionality" without referencing and crediting the wealth of (especially) women of color activism from which these ideas emerged.

Readers may recognize these sorts of limited approaches to critical consciousness and have more types to add to my list. Points (e) and (f) may require more elaboration. Regarding (e) and (f), Sirma Bilge and Patricia Hill Collins note how those using the term "intersectionality" often make a superficial reference to Kimberlé Crenshaw's published work, using that term without recognizing how the concept is built upon women of color activism and theoretical work, particularly from black lesbian feminists. Further, many water down "intersectionality" to mean any way of referring to multiple vectors of oppression, whereas early formulators of such theory, such as the Combahee River Collective statement,[45] had a strong critique of capitalism. This problem regarding the underappreciation of original sources is also present in "affect studies." Michael Hames-García[46] marks a similar argument regarding "queer theory," that is, how the use of "queer theory" often makes invisible the queer people of color who are the agents of the critical thinking and activism that actually challenge heteronormativity, racism, sexism, classism, and other forms of oppression long before "queer theory" came into institutional formation.

"TRUE-TRUE" BUDDHIST/MINDFULNESS
PRACTICE WITH CRITICAL CONSCIOUSNESS

Throughout this chapter, I have spoken of Buddhist/mindful practices and critical consciousness practices as not merely academic—not merely "book learning"—but as embodied, concrete interactions. I suggest that there are parallels between Buddhist practice and counter-hegemonic critical consciousness practice, particularly in realms beyond classroom contexts. bell hooks, Chandra Mohanty, and other teachers and colleagues in feminist, anti-racist contexts challenge us to live our ideals. Similarly, Buddhist practice is not simply about believing certain ideas as it is about living the teachings, watching our minds, letting go of "self-importance" or "self-cherishing." (Dzigar Kongtrul uses the translation "self-importance" for the Tibetan term, "dak che dzin."[47] The opposite of this mindset is "zhen che dzin," which means "holding others as important and dear."[48]) I have learned much particularly in working closely with a teacher and in a Buddhist community, in which we are "called out" on problematic imperialist ways of relating to Buddhism (such as being fascinated with esoteric practices rather than engaging with the substance of the teachings, or engaging in "spiritual materialism,"[49] which is Chogyam Trungpa's term that marks how we use Buddhism to enhance the ego rather than to lessen its hold on us.

In each case (genuine mindfulness/Buddhist practice and counter-hegemonic praxis): one consciously undertakes to live differently.

1. One recognizes that one's very self (body, mind, nervous system, desires, imagination) has been colonized, partly constituted by causes and conditions of oppression. As Sara Ahmed writes, we must learn not to "reproduce what we inherit" in the sense of oppressive patterns.[50] In Buddhist contexts, one may speak of "habitual tendencies," which tend to reproduce our ways of being into patterns for the future. These are not deterministic patterns as is sometimes thought, where Buddhist notions of karma are seen as fatalistic. One need not believe in an esoteric metaphysics to see that one tends to behave similarly (whether at the individual level or collective level) unless one does things differently. Karmic patterns have a momentum to them, that—if not interrupted by awareness, practice, and different behavior—continue.

2. Yet each (critical consciousness and Buddhism) embodies a view that change is possible—in fact, each uses terms like "liberation," "Enlightenment," even "colonizing" and "de-colonizing." In fact, within a Buddhist context, Dzigar Kongtrul has spoken of "colonizing" and "de-colonizing."[51]

3. Each requires a deep sense that one must take responsibility for oneself and consciously undertake change. As classic Buddhist philosopher Vimalamitra writes on "samsaric pursuits," "It only ends when you stop."[52]

4. In each case there is a metaphysics, a deep view of the nature of reality, that speaks to the lived world as being dynamic, complex, and continually changing. In Buddhist terms, there are dynamic processes of causes and conditions that are of "interdependent origination."

5. Each embodies a view that the world is not immediately transparent, that clarity requires "attention" and that mundane, conventional

understandings of reality often obscure more than they reveal. As Iris Murdoch writes, "the reward of attention is knowledge of reality."[53]

6. There is epistemology (theory of knowledge) which brings attention to the knower, seeing each of us as (often) caught up in one's own perspective in ways that may be distorting, so that clarity—about oneself and the world—may require deep critical self-reflection.

7. Each offers a way out, yet, as a line from Robert Frost states, "I can see no way out but through."[54] Genuine transformation must be from immanent critique rather than from some false transcendence of a "God's Eye perspective."

8. One surrenders to grow in—and as—a "beloved community." Whereas some think Buddhism encourages obliviousness to the needs of others, this is a gross misunderstanding. Even yogis in retreat for decades strive to benefit beings.

9. Buddhist practice and "education for critical consciousness" offer ideas, practices, "how-tos," communities of practice, importance of "critical self-reflection," importance of taking responsibility for oneself, embracing embodied practices of transformation in relation to others.

10. Notions of "radical openness"[55] (hooks' phrase) and "radical openheartedness" (Kongtrul's term)[56] offer similar or complementary outlooks, virtues, and exemplars. These include such features as epistemic humility, critiques of exoticization, critiques of cultural appropriation, and holds that one must make changes in the world, not simply in one's own thinking.

11. In both genuine mindfulness and critical consciousness practices, people cite the experience of working with a teacher as crucial to development. Those on these paths often see awareness as arising not simply from abstract ideas but rather from being with others who can challenge us to grow. Within a Buddhist context, one may undertake commitments with a Teacher to "take Refuge" and take a "Bodhisattva Vow." Many Buddhist writings refer to the Student/Teacher relationship, emphasizing the role of experiencing a teacher with direct realization of the teachings.[57]

12. In each case, such a Teacher does not just convey content, such as ideas or beliefs, but rather a whole spirit/body/mind way of being in the world. My root Teacher Khandro Rinpoche speaks of her desire that we cultivate "supple and flexible body, speech, and mind." She urges us to learn from the monastics (monks and nuns) who have undertaken lifelong commitment and training, for how they move, how they speak, how they serve, and how they conduct themselves generally. They are present, doing what is helpful, without personal drama or display or arrogance.

13. Both Buddhist practice and education for critical consciousness direct us to what really nourishes us—connection to others, values, meaning,

having a positive impact upon the world, being of genuine service to others.

14. Each promotes views of human equality and the notion that each person is worthy of dignity and respect. Buddhist teachings hold that all sentient beings have "Buddha Nature"—"basic goodness." According to a classic Buddhist metaphor, just as the sun is still there, even when blocked by clouds, Buddha Nature is still there, even when obscured by emotional and mental (and behavioral) obscurations.

CONCLUSION

Simone Weil writes, "How were the factors of oppression, so closely bound up with the actual mechanism of social life, suddenly to disappear?"[58] Elsewhere, I have written of my own original view of "moral attention" and later "critical moral attention." I suggest ways of working with social locations as a point of entry into understanding the world, taking greater responsibility for who we are and who we might become—individually and collectively. To do this, we must engage critically with our own and others' views and experiences, using these as "raw material" for growth.[59]

I present these discussions of Buddhism/mindfulness and critical consciousness approaches as active methods engage in liberatory cross-cultural learning that resists white supremacist patterns of "eating the other" in favor of deep transformation of self and work across borders, and with accountability. This critical approach is crucial to anti-oppressive work. Racism—as well as other kinds of oppression—tends to make one unaware of one's unawareness.

M. Jacqui Alexander once remarked that we need to value those who are "living archives" of movement and thinking history. At the risk of seeming like a star-dazed nostalgic, I have offered these reflections based upon what I have learned from bell hooks, Chandra Mohanty, Jetsun Khandro, and Dzigar Kongtrul. I am thankful to bell hooks, Chandra Mohanty, and Satya Mohanty who spoke to me for many years, especially in many moments that I was tempted to leave graduate school or academia. To these I could add many other mentors and co-theorizers, such as Satya P. Mohanty, Paula Moya, Michael Hames-Garcia, and Linda Martin Alcoff (the four cofounders of the Future of Minority Studies Project) and my many Future of Minority Studies Project[60] mentors and colleagues.

I credit early teachers, hooks and Mohanty, in particular, with offering glimpses into a radically openheartedness-way-of-being, and Buddhist teachers Jetsun Khandro Rinpoche and Dzigar Kongtrul Rinpoche with enabling me to develop engagement with and accountable to others within the context of Buddhist practice. Whether working with liberatory knowledge specifically in the context of social justice movements (as from hooks) or with liberatory knowledge more generally located in a view of how humans can be trapped in habitual tendencies that keep us stuck (as Buddhist—and other—teachings reveal), one can mis-use these and fall into being just another white person stealing or appropriating everything. In contrast, one can develop authentic practices which help to cultivate genuine liberatory knowledge and ways of being. Engaging across various borders tends to be crucial to cutting through the "colonizing" tendencies. In short, by engaging across various borders, this enables alternatives, which can amount to genuine cross-cultural learning.

For further learning, I point to the important project that Chandra Mohanty and Linda Carty are leading, which is called Feminist Freedom Warriors. In both the book[61] by the same title and in the website of digital interviews (feministfreedomwarriors.org), they offer windows into the "living archives" of such scholar-activists as Angela Davis, Minnie Bruce Pratt, and Beverly Guy-Sheftall. They embody and model what I point to here—radical un-forgetting (as Shotwell describes), working with respect across difference, collaborating in imagining and building a liberatory world.

Engaging across various borders is crucial to cutting through "coloniz-ing" tendencies, which can amount to genuine cross-cultural learning. As Sean Tecumseh Teuton argues, "If we imagine a decolonized world—for we must—the free exchange of knowledge is not only a benefit to particular nations but also to the goal of greater human inquiry."[62] Teuton advocates for exchange of ideas across various borders but notes how oppression has com-plicated that. He argues for "cultural interaction as a form of cross-cultural inquiry,"[63] pointing to Satya P. Mohanty's formulation of "multiculturalism as epistemic [knowledge-seeking] cooperation."[64] Satya Mohanty endorses John Dewey's claim that human cultures are "experiments in living." My hope is that this discussion of critical consciousness, Buddhism, mindfulness, and whiteness suggests de-colonizing directions. Teuton argues for decolo-nization as necessary to how all of our interests lie in finding better ways to live.[65]

NOTES

1. Alexis Shotwell, *Against Purity: Living Ethically in Compromised Times* (University of Minnesota Press, 2016), 38.

2. Sara Ahmed, *On Being Included* (Durham, NC: Duke University Press, 2010), 182.

3. Dzigar Kongtrul, *Training in Tenderness: Buddhist Teachings on Tsewa, the Radical Openness of Heart that Can Change the World* (Boulder, CO: Shambhala Publications, 2018).

4. Preliminary notes: I speak from my own perspectives as a student of "critical consciousness" and of "Buddhism." I tell my own story. I am not authorized by bell hooks (or Chandra Mohanty or other teachers I reference) or by my Buddhist teachers Mindrolling Khandro Rinpoche or Dzigar Kongtrul Rinpoche (each has senior students of many decades who are authorized as teachers—I am not that). None have reviewed or legitimated this chapter. I speak for myself only, of what I have learned, however limited, in the thirty years of engaging with "counter-hegemonic teachings" and sixteen–seventeen years of working directly with Mindrolling Khandro Rinpoche, being active in her global community of students, and frequently attending her intensive retreats, first in Baltimore and then at Mindrolling Lotus Garden in Stanley, Virginia (www.lotusgardens.org), and with Dzigar Kongtrul Rinpoche for fourteen or so years at Mindrolling Lotus Garden with his teachings, through reading his many books, listening regularly to his and his students' weekly "Link" program over the phone and then internet (thanks to friend Desiree Mitchell for alerting me to these Link programs). See Mangala Shri Bhuti's official website (http://www.man galashribhuti.org/TheLINK). Other Buddhist teachers who have particularly influenced me include Sakyong Mipham Rinpoche, the late Chogyam Trungpa, and the Dalai Lama.

5. Also, frequent reference points for me include the work of Audre Lorde (primarily through her writings), with Chandra Mohanty—also my professor at Oberlin and now longtime colleague and friend—and the Future of Minority Studies (FMS) Project. FMS describes itself as a "a mobile inter-institutional think tank" devoted to substantive conversation on relationships between minoritized peoples, knowledge, and democracy (see http://fmsproject.cornell.edu).

6. bell hooks leaves her name uncapitalized, saying at one point that she does this out of respect for the unlettered wisdom of her ancestors.

7. Audre Lorde, "Women Responding to Racism," in *Sister Outsider* (Freedom, CA: Crossing Press, 1984).

8. Shotwell, *Against Purity*, 38.

9. Johnnella E. Butler, "African American Literature and Realist Theory: Seeking the 'true true,'" in *Identity Politics Reconsidered*, eds. Linda Martín Alcoff, Michael Hames-García, Satya P. Mohanty, and Paula M. L. Moya (New York: Palgrave, 2006), 171–192.

10. Ibid., 175.

11. Ibid., 175.

12. Ibid., 176.

13. Kongtrul, *Training in Tenderness*, 6.

14. Ibid., 103.

15. I am not claiming to have "arrived" at some high level of development but rather to be walking along these paths. As Highlander School founder Myles Horton and radical educator Paulo Freire title a book of their own work, *We Make the Road by Walking*. In a world where patterns of equality do not predominate, efforts at learning and living in egalitarian conditions of mutual respect are somewhat uncharted territory. Myles Horton and Paulo Freire, *We Make the Road by Walking: Conversations*

on Education and Social Change, eds. Brenda Bell, John Gaventa, and John Peters (Philadelphia, PA: Temple, 1990 reprint edition).

16. Thích Nhất Hạnh, *The Miracle of Mindfulness: A Manual on Meditation*, trans. Mobi Ho (Boston: Beacon Press, 1975), 11.

17. Ibid., 14.

18. "Thích" is his surname, since in Vietnamese names, the surname occurs first.

19. Ibid., vii–viii.

20. Portions of this chapter appear in my "Moral Attention: Toward a Liberationist Ethics of Everyday Life," (PhD dissertation, Philosophy, University of Pittsburgh, 1998).

21. Paulo Freire's phrase.

22. Ernesto Che Guevara, *Socialism and Man in Cuba* (New York: Pathfinder Press, 2009, originally published in 1965).

23. bell hooks, *Salvation: Black People and Love* (New York: William Morrow, 2001).

24. bell hooks, *Teaching to Transgress* (New York: Routledge, 1990), 15.

25. Ellen J. Langer, *Mindfulness* (Reading, MA: Addison-Wesley Publishing, 1989), 2.

26. Ibid., 16.

27. Ibid., 11.

28. Matthieu Ricard, "A Sniper's 'Mindfulness,'" blog, http://www.matthieuricard .org/en/blog/posts/a-sniper-s-mindfulness (accessed May 15, 2018).

29. Thanks to Emily McRae for clarifying this point.

30. Ron Purser and David Loy, "Beyond McMindfulness," *HuffPost Blog*, originally posted July 1, 2013, updated August 31, 2013, https://www.huffingtonpost.com /ron-purser/beyond-mcmindfulness_b_3519289.html# (accessed May 15, 2018).

31. Chogyam Trungpa, *Cutting Through Spiritual Materialism* (Boulder, CO: Shambhala Publications, 1972).

32. Dzongsar Khyentse Rinpoche, as cited in "Tibetan Buddhism in the West," in *In the Presence of Masters*, ed. Reginald Ray (Boulder, CO: Shambhala Publications, 2004), 241.

33. Ibid.

34. Dibyesh Anand, "Archive and the Poetics of 'Exotica Tibet,'" in *Tibetan Borderlands*, ed. P. Christiaan Klieger (Leiden, The Netherlands: Brill, 2006), 49–66.

35. See *Digital Dharma*, a documentary about this process. See http://DigitalDharma.com for more information and access to the documentary video.

36. In one extreme of these "imperialist" dynamics, I must note stories I have heard of some US pseudo-gurus who claim to be enlightened masters and instead manipulate, control, and exploit people in cult-like situations. See Martha Sherrill, *The Buddha from Brooklyn* (NY: Random House, 2000) for a journalist's account of a US teacher, recognized by a Tibetan lama, who Sherrill alleges engages in various questionable practices.

37. Michael Hames-García, *Identity Complex* (Minneapolis, MN: University of Minnesota, 2011).

38. Chandra Talpade Mohanty, Future of Minority Studies Annual Colloquium, Comments as Moderator of Panel, "Minority Identity and Inequality: Three Social Science Research Projects," July 31, 2010, Ithaca, NY (my own transcription—verified by and used with permission from Mohanty).

39. Mohanty, "Minority Identity and Inequality."

40. Ibid.

41. Ibid.

42. Ibid.

43. Ibid.

44. See http://www.hasshanbatts.com.

45. Combahee River Collective, "A Black Feminist Statement," in *Capitalist Patriarchy and the Case of Socialist Feminism*, ed. Zillah R. Eisenstein (New York: Monthly Review Press, 1979), 362–372.

46. Hames-García, *Identity Complex.*

47. Dzigar Kongtrul, *The Intelligent Heart: A Guide to the Compassionate Life* (Boulder, CO: Shambhala Publications, 2016), 4.

48. Ibid., 6.

49. Trungpa, *Cutting Through Spiritual Materialism.*

50. Ahmed, *On Being Included*, 182.

51. Dzigar Kongtrul, talk given at Mindrolling Lotus Garden, Stanley, Virginia, July 2015 (my own transcribed notes).

52. Vimalamitra as cited in Erik Pema Kunsang (compiler and translator), *A Tibetan Buddhist Companion* (Boulder, CO: Shambhala Publications, 2003), 163.

53. Iris Murdoch, *Sovereignty of Good* (London and New York: Routledge, 1970), 87.

54. Robert Frost, "A Servant of Servants," in *North of Boston* (New York: Henry Holt, 1915), 28–29.

55. bell hooks, numerous classes at Oberlin College in 1987, 1988.

56. Kongtrul, *Training in Tenderness.*

57. For one beautiful expression of this reflection on student–teacher relationships, see Dzongsar Khyentse's episodic memoir blog www.mugwortborn.com. See the photo of him and other young monks with Dilgo Khyentse Rinpoche, in "The Purpose of this is to Introduce My Teachers," posted March 9, 2016.

58. Simone Weil, *Oppression and Liberty*, trans. Arthur Wills and John Petrie (New York and London: Routledge and Kegan Paul, 1958).

59. These formulations rely on the work of Paula Moya and Satya P. Mohanty, as well as other members of the Future of Minority Studies Project, with whom I have had the great fortune to work and think and be with for many years.

60. For more on FMS see http://fmsproject.cornell.edu.

61. Chandra Mohanty and Linda Carty, eds., *Feminist Freedom Warriors* (Chicago: Haymarket, 2018).

62. Sean Tecumseh Teuton, "Internationalism and the American Indian Scholar," in *Identity Politics Reconsidered*, eds. Linda Martin Alcoff, Michael Hames Garcia, Satya P. Mohanty, and Paula M. L. Moya (New York: Palgrave, 2006), 264–284.

63. Ibid., 273.

64. Satya P. Mohanty, *Literary Theory and the Claims of History* (Ithaca, NY: Cornell, 1997), 241–247.

65. Thanks to Robert LaRue, Sarah Goletz, Amy Phillips, and Abby Feight for reading and offering feedback on earlier versions of this chapter, and to Kin Cheung, who alerted me to the "mindful sniper" blogs. Particular thanks to bell hooks, Chandra Mohanty, Jetsun Khandro Rinpoche, Dzigar Kongtrul Rinpoche, Satya P. Mohanty, and my friends and colleagues of the Future of Minority Studies Project, the Transformational Intergroup Dialogue Network, ACT UP, Queer Nation, Women for Racial and Economic Equality, Make the Road, PA, Amor y Rabia, and other activist networks to which I belong. Ideas arise in movements. Particularly with my Future of Minority Studies folks, it is impossible to properly give credit to those who have so shaped my ideas in collaboration. The limitations of this work, of course, are entirely mine. Thanks to George Yancy and Emily McRae for their insights and for incredible patience and support.

Chapter 11

Excoriating the Demon of Whiteness from Within

Disrupting Whiteness through the Tantric Buddhist Practice of Chöd *and Exploring Whiteness from Within the Tradition*

Lama Justin von Bujdoss

Explorations into whiteness within the context of Vajrayana or tantric Buddhism are a recent phenomenon and more focus in this area is sorely needed. Thankfully, reflections on this topic appear to be largely a product of the direction in which Western Buddhism is moving, especially by Buddhist teachers, communities, and scholars who are motivated by engaged Buddhism. The purpose of this chapter is to frame the exploration of whiteness *within* the tantric Buddhist tradition. I argue that whiteness, while deeply rooted within the context of power dynamics around race and various colonialisms, can be, and perhaps ought to be, treated as a unique expression of the neurotic mind, interfacing with and expressed as a particular *klesha* pattern: a by-product of the reactive mind, rooted in ego-clinging.

In particular, I will look at whiteness as an expression of the demons of self-clinging as found within the Tibetan Buddhist *chöd* tradition of Machik Labdron. This tradition is rooted in an amalgam of the Mahāyāna Buddhist practice of the Perfection of Wisdom (Sanskrit: *Prajnaparamita*) and various tantric Buddhist practices brought from India to Tibet by the famed Indian Buddhist yogin, Padampa Sangye. Unique to the practice of *chöd* are visualizations in which one offers one's own body to be consumed by demons and various forces that obstruct one from realizing enlightenment. I will examine texts attributed to Machik Labdron, the eleventh-century female Tibetan progenitor of this tradition as well as later commentarial

207

and liturgical samples from the third and eighth Karmapas, Rangjung Dorje and Mikyö Dorje, respectively. I will show that whiteness is a manifestation of ego-clinging and a constellation of a variety of *kleshas* (or afflicting emotions) and "demons"—in the parlance of the *chöd* tradition. I will also explore models through which traditions of Buddhist practice can be empowered to approach, expose, and exorcise whiteness within the current context of Buddhism. I conclude with two contemporary *chöd* texts I composed in 2015 for workshopping at the Second Annual Buddhism and Race Conference at Harvard Divinity School, and in 2016 at the request of an enthusiastic friend who found meaning in the first text and desired a daily practice to be written. These texts are presented here in an effort to further unify this unique tantric Buddhist practice with the exploration of whiteness and the suffering experienced within the modern charnel grounds of American culture.

I am also seeking to embed awareness of whiteness not only as an organizational impediment to the creation of effective Buddhist communities, but to also highlight whiteness—especially as it arises unconsciously—as an impediment to realization within the specific context of Buddhist praxis. Embedding an awareness of whiteness within the world of Buddhist praxis necessitates ownership of whiteness, especially so that it can become an aspect of contemplative self-reflection. It can be argued that active engagement/cultivation of awareness of whiteness and other forms of unexamined dominance (maleness, patriarchy, able-bodiedness, etc.) ought to be absorbed into the canon, and that *failure to do so is a failure to adapt* and *therefore secures the tradition's seat at the table of waning relevance.*

I feel the need to disclose that I am writing from the intersection of being a cisgender white male. I am also a Buddhist teacher, a practitioner of Buddhism and a chaplain, not a scholar. My voice is that of a loving critic of a tradition that I participate within. Yet, I cannot simply sit on the sidelines when it comes to the way in which my tradition does not truly acknowledge the deep impact that whiteness and other forms of oppression have on everyone whether we are conscious of the impact and range of such oppression and our complicity in propagating such oppression or not. When a deep sense of alarm and inner conflict arises around how reluctant many Tibetan Buddhist communities are to accept that whiteness is something worth addressing, I feel the need to speak up. It also feels important, if not vital, to keep reminding Buddhist communities and individual practitioners that keeping our eyes open to whiteness ought to be seen as a form of dharma practice, and that such an engaged practice is actually part of the amazing power that dharma has to effect awakening.

THE COMPLEXITIES OF WHITENESS IN
VAJRAYANA: INTERSECTING COLONIALISMS

Buddhism, like a great many things, was "discovered" and became an object of curiosity, study, and appropriation by the Western world. Inspired by a sense of adventure, and perhaps some degree of unhappiness with some of the ways that the Victorian era and the nascent era of modernity created a new sense of being that was not satisfying, a series of curious Europeans set out to explore, record, and bring back initial fragments of the Buddhist tradition. The Western world at the time was hungry for the "exotic" and this inner-spice-trade, as it were, cannot easily be separated from Western colonialism and its related assumptions that other cultures, not only natural resources, were free for the taking. In this way Buddhist art and texts were collected and brought to the major museums just as was done in earlier phases of cultural collection ostensibly for objective study.

Over the past thirty years a steady stream of academic research has revealed some of the dynamics involved in the "discovery" or "creation" of Buddhism by early adventure—"scholars" and missionaries who helped create images of what Buddhism might look like. Philip Almond, in the introduction to his important work "The British Discovery of Buddhism" suggests:

> Buddhism, by 1860, had come to exist, not in the Orient, but in the Oriental Libraries and institutes of the West, in its texts and manuscripts, at the desks of the Western savants who interpreted it. It had become a textual object, defined, classified and interpreted through its own textuality. By the middle of the century, the Buddhism that existed "out there" was beginning to be judged by a West that *alone* knew what Buddhism was, is, and ought to be. The essence of Buddhism came to be seen as expressed not "out there" in the Orient, but in the West through the West's control of Buddhism's own textual past.[1]

Indeed, despite claims of objectivity in studying Buddhism it is not only possible, but likely, that a variety of assumptions and generalizations imposed by Western scholars very much impacted early scholarship on the subject. In a significant way, Buddhism has always struggled to some extent in relation to the ideas about it. The works of Donald S. Lopez Jr., Christian K. Wedemeyer, and Bryan Cuevas, to name a few, highlight in their respective areas of study just how the creation of what Buddhism is, or has become, is often partially a product of the person wanting to learn about it. Christian K. Wedemeyer's *Making Sense of Tantric Buddhism: History, Semiology, and Transgression in the Indian Traditions* offers a lucid and profound exploration of the various ways that tantric Buddhism has been narrated over time, in many ways (and perhaps in all attempts) to make tantric Buddhism conform to the assumptions of the person studying the tradition.[2] In some cases, as in the case of the exegesis of tantric Buddhism, it seems that aspects of the tradition elude objective understanding and that all we can settle upon is that how we understand the tradition is always in flux. The images which we create about the Buddhist tradition are often created in a way that reflects more than pure, scientific objectivity (if that is even possible), but rather the reflected images that are useful to us and the existential proclivities of the day. This can be seen through the way Buddhism has been affected by the cultures to which it has been introduced. As Buddhism spread through Tibet, China, Japan, Korea, other parts of Asia, and even to the West, the local politics, art, music, literature, and other forms of cultural expression helped create the wealth of diversity one finds in global Buddhism. More often than not, there is no singular Buddhism, but rather a series of *buddhisms* that speak to the varied needs that concern us. In this way, there is a certain constant thread of colonialism, at least potentially, in which the crafted images of the *buddhisms* that we need to exist in a particular way to fit our narrative—accidentally, and in some ways intentionally—seek to support our prevailing views and that of our culture. As such, it is not surprising that a number of the *buddhisms* we see around us reflect the same white supremacy that we see within the larger American culture.

In "Black Looks: Race and Representation," bell hooks reflects:

> Socialized to believe the fantasy, that whiteness represents goodness and all that is benign and non-threatening, many white people assume that this is the way black people conceptualize whiteness. They do not imagine that the way whiteness makes its presence felt in black life, most often as terrorizing imposition, a power that wounds, hurts, tortures is a reality that disrupts the fantasy of whiteness as representing goodness.[3]

Socialized views and assumptions naturally impact the way that some of the various *buddhisms* have come into being. That bias works its way into Buddhism is not surprising given some of the dynamics that were at play in the early days of how Buddhism was introduced to the West. Of course, a common (and convenient) narrative around the spread of Buddhism to the West is rooted within the tradition itself, in which such transmissions of dharma are seen as an act of perfect compassion: Buddhism spread to the West as the karmic causes and conditions and the merit of the early Western practitioners co-created this miracle. Upon closer examination, it is important to note the hand of whiteness in this first wave of dharma students and their views. Class privilege, including the increased ability to have leisure time to access dharma and to acquire financial support and real estate for early dharma centers, was not insignificant. They were likely aided by their location in relationship to the privilege and benefits of whiteness which informed basic assumptions about how sangha organizes itself, how and to whom dharma should be taught, and what cultural forms of expression are preferred over others. This is not to deny their important and groundbreaking work, but to keep our eyes open to how socialized patterning, especially unquestioned patterning, has a way of replicating itself. These dynamics seemed especially at play within the way that the Tibetan Buddhist tradition spread, and in relation to the willingness of early Tibetan teachers to rely upon the prevailing benefits of whiteness, particularly the social status it conferred and the increased access to material wealth and real estate, as useful tools for preserving a cultural tradition that remains at risk of extinction.

White privilege and whiteness inherent in the early transmission of Buddhism to the West seems easily (and conveniently) masked by the label: "merit." This can easily be the case as in the Buddhist context; one of the benefits of accumulating merit through positive acts is having access to leisure, wealth, and means through which one can have the time and the space through which to connect with Buddhist teachings. Whiteness can be further white-washed and cleaned-up, by inadvertently being justified as an expression of "skillful-means." Skillful-means (Sanskrit: *upaya*) in this context is the process whereby one uses diverse means to effectively bring benefit to others with a conscious intention rooted in compassion *and* is able to affect such positive outcomes. Not that white privilege is a skillful way to accomplish Buddhist goals in benefitting others, but, when you benefit from white supremacy it is easier to get certain things done. Even when you are not aware of how and why these seemingly miraculous benefits arise. This is especially the case in a culture in which unexamined white supremacy is still powerful. In this way, there seems to have been a transactional relationship in which the benefits of whiteness became hard to remove from some aspects of the way that Buddhism and all of its subsidiary *buddhisms* continue to manifest within the arena of American culture.

DIAGNOSING AND UNDERSTANDING WHITENESS FROM WITHIN THE TRADITION: WHITE DEVILS

That the underlying benefits associated with whiteness helped the tantric Buddhist tradition take root in the West is not surprising, but for a tradition that is not compelled to explore whiteness and its effects we might ask, how best can we understand it? More to the point, how can we understand whiteness within the context of the tradition so as to better understand how dharma practice can aide in addressing the dynamics that create whiteness and racial bias?

Within the *Machik Namshe*, or *Machik's Complete Instructions*, a collection of instructions on *chöd* practice structured according to a question and
answer format that has become a mainstay of the tradition, we find a section
of the text called *The Questions of Gangpa Muksang*. This section of the
larger text offers a wonderful description of the various demons and gods that
one encounters within the practice of *chöd*.

These demons and gods tend to represent what we might call the dynamics
of neurosis and ego-clinging that prevents us from recognizing the essential
nature of our mind, and simultaneously, the arising of the phenomena that we
experience. They represent internal processes through which we relate to the
outer world—the ways in which we create and recreate identity. Within the
context of the Tibetan cultural framework, these figures were also external-
ized to represent the occasional real ghost, demon, or god. For our purposes
I would like to avoid the lengthy, albeit sorely needed work around the
cross-cultural dynamics related to how the modern Western practitioner of
Vajrayana understands and copes with ghosts, demons, and gods, and stick
to an exploration of how whiteness can be seen in relation to the Four Devils
described by Machik Labdron in the *Machik Namshe*.

Within the context of the practice of tantric Buddhism, the practitioner is
asked to bring the full range of their experiences to contemplative practice. In
this way nothing is necessarily off the table, and in some cases the practice can
get radical. This potential of radical practice allows one to use anger, desire,
attachment, and aversion and the entirety of the range of human experience as
the back-drop for investigating the nature of mind. The practice of *chöd* is no
different in that the practice has historically been done in physical places of
great fear. In Asia these places might include charnel grounds, places of death
or natural disaster, or places believed to be haunted. Here such sites could
include sites of lynchings, slave burial grounds, and civil war sites, as well as
more recent contemporary locations of racial violence for example. The use
of locations of fear and difficult emotion is almost homeopathic in the sense
that the practitioner of *chöd* uses the self-clinging and self-cherishing behind
fear and violence as the location through which one focuses the practice of
offering oneself to one's own demons. Just as tantra uses the range of human
experience, *chöd* allows us to use place and the power of place as a way to
heal ourselves and potentially the environment.

Generally, demons within the practice of *chöd* are meant to be fed, paci-
fied, and thus freed. In other words, through the process of systematic reorientation through the cultivation of insight and awareness around how these
devils/demons block the opportunity for realization to arise, we learn how to
be free of them. Realization in this particular context refers to the development of the ability to rest naturally in a state of ease and radical acceptance of
things as they arise. Another experience that also begins to arise at this point

is a deep-seated sense of compassion and empathy for others—for at last we finally become able to clearly see how deeply connected our suffering is in relation to our ignorance.

When asked specifically about these devils, Machik clarifies by suggesting:

> Son, Listen. These are the characteristics of devils (Tibetan: *bdud*). That which is called "devil" is not some actual great big black thing that scares and petrifies whomever sees it. A devil is anything that obstructs the achievement of freedom. Therefore, even loving affectionate friends become devils [with regard to] freedom. Most of all, there is no greater devil than this fixation to a self. So, until this ego-fixation is cut off, all the devils wait with open mouths. For that reason, you need to exert yourself at a skillful method to sever the devil of ego-fixation. As adjuncts, there are three devils that are born from ego-fixation; thus we have the four devils that must be severed. These are their names:
> Devil of the Material and Devil of the Immaterial;
> Devil of Exaltation and Devil of Inflation.
> Those are the four devils of ego-fixation.[4]

Material Devil

Machik goes on to describe to Gangpa Muksang the specific qualities of the four devils. The Material Devil is rooted in materiality, or that which is observed within our visual field, as well as our subsequent attraction or aversion to material phenomena. This devil is also described as the devil of "dualistic grasping" because

> one is attached to the [perceived] real existence of a sense object, and the sense organs get caught in the actual object of [attraction or] aversion. This creates the condition for harming sentient beings and thus becomes the bondage to cyclic existence. For that reason, it is called a devil.[5]

The means through which severance of the Material Devil occurs is through learning how to eliminate clinging and attachment as well as aversion and dislike through familiarizing oneself with "natural emptiness without attraction or aversion to form." She goes on to remind Gangpa Muksang:

> You cannot stop form from appearing, [but realize that it is] mere appearance without grasping on to its valid existence. By eliminating clinging to that mere appearance, you will be liberated from form, noble son. It is the same with sound, smell, taste and texture.[6]

Whether we make our homes in dense urban areas, smaller cities, rural locations, suburbia, or various combinations of these and other locations, we are surrounded by constant appearance. The pulsating waves of appearance, one thing after another, is hard to deny; the point that Machik makes is not rooted in the denial of appearance, but rather the way in which we tend to make the experience of conventional reality feel as if it has inherent existence. At issue is the need to make assumptions, to project relational patterns around how this multiverse of appearance manifests and the belief that such appearances are true. Machik is reminding us that falling into habitual reactions based on appearance and reactionary judgments becomes an act of violence with regard to what is naturally arising in the moment. The appearance of black bodies is appearance, free and naturally arising. Feeling the need to call the police or react with fear or anger is an example of falling into patterns of aversion with regard to the materiality of blackness. Discrimination, sexism, homophobia, racism, cognition of hierarchies, basic patterns of assumption are all the entourage of this devil.

Immaterial Devil

Machik then describes the Immaterial Devil, which she states, "does not appear as an actual object of the senses," but

> rather, it is any of the good or bad concepts that arise in your mind. They are called demons (*'dre*) when you apprehend them as frightful appearances that cause terror, and called gods when you apprehend them as pure appearances that cause cheerful and pleasurable experiences. In that way, the mental grasping at the two concepts of good and bad conditions the mind to become afflicted with emotion. Although afflictive emotion is without materiality and there is no real, actual object, it has the ability to inflict harm by causing you to stray into unvirtuous actions, so it is called a devil.[7]

She then reminds Gangpa Muksang that the very mind that can inadvertently become the ground, or host, to such conceptual elaborations is inherently pure and without a shred of duality. As such she reminds the practitioner of *chöd*:

> Don't try to block the sensations and such that arise in the mind. Also, don't block any of the various good or bad thoughts and memories. Don't even entertain any notions about them. Whatever thoughts and memories arise, don't hold on to them by dwelling on them. Mind is the clear nature of vast space, and any thought or memory whatsoever can arise within it.[8]

She concludes her description of the Immaterial Devil by pointing out that letting the mind rest in its own nature, just as it is, renders the Immaterial Devil no longer an obstacle, but rather an experience of non-dual clarity.

The terrorism inherent in conceptual elaboration and the need for full blown construction of systems of hierarchy is part of the dynamics at play with the Immaterial Devil. This is where whiteness becomes an insidious problem. If in the beginning, the seeds of recognizing difference within the arising of pure appearance increased the probability of habits rooted in ignorance, here we begin to see the danger of allowing an industry of further discrimination to churn out increasingly real and intractable assumptions about the world around us. This includes assumptions and emotions regarding the black body and embodied people of color. The Immaterial Devil grows stronger when we do not examine why we have created the systems around how we organize ourselves. It grows stronger when we do not uproot and question the commonly held narratives around how and why dharma has been transmitted to the West. It grows more calcified when we do not ask why our sanghas are so white, why the majority of our teachers are white, and why we have created organizational structures that appear to benefit white practitioners and teachers over people of color. When we do not ask, can there possibly be a better way? Or, how has this become the only way? We lose our agency and only seek to co-create ideas of dharma transmission and lineage that privilege the few over the many. The Immaterial Devil perpetuates terrible violence. It denies diverse voices, it lowers those with less means, it favors the powerful, property, and wealth. It also creates narrative models of success within the dharma and non-dharma world based on dynamics rooted in white supremacy.

Devil of Exaltation

The Devil of Exaltation, Machik tells us, is rooted within the seductive attachment to experiences, concepts, or anything which gives rise to tremendous joy. The root of such elaborate exaltation might be connected to wealth, fame, prestige, the accumulation of magical powers from successful practice (Sanskrit: *siddhis*), or even the dawning of realization itself. Continuing in the manner of a doctor she offers the following diagnosis related to the Devil of Exaltation:

> Delighting and exalting in any of these causes great arrogance and pride and becomes an obstacle on the path to freedom, so it is called a devil.[9]

The treatment of such an obstacle is rooted, as with the others, in maintaining a relationship to dharma practice that stresses a continuous coming back to familiarizing oneself with the essential, basic non-duality of mind. The fastidious and concerned teacher that she is, she reminds us that

> since neither the mind has even a hair's tip worth of permanent, true existence, understand it as an illusion or a dream. Practice as if it were an illusion or a dream. Rest in the state of emptiness, free of all [dualistic] extremes of a mind

gloating about its qualities or its objects. In that way, as you meditate in the illusory, dreamlike nature of all phenomena within great emptiness free of extremes and integrate it into the path, the dreamlike devil of exaltation will be severed, and the welfare of all illusory, dreamlike beings will come to pass, noble son.[10]

Here Machik points out the fundamental seduction inherent in the arrogance and pride of believing that we are special or deserving when we benefit from privilege, unconscious bias, and patterning. One must maintain awareness of the ease through which we bolster egotism around the "auspicious conditions" around having access to dharma, especially when the convenience of these narratives of merit and positive karma may actually activate whiteness. In this way, conceptual elaborations regarding our storehouse of positive karma can easily allow us to get caught up in the hype around that to which we have access. It can be easy to accidentally mythologize our experiences at the expense of the way we relate to others. In some cases, the very access to dharma may have been expedited by the privileges we enjoy based on our race, or gender, or sexual orientation.

In fact, it behooves us to examine whether the narrative of merit has a shadow side—a side that perpetuates unsaid assumptions about whole populations that seemingly lack the merit to have equal access to dharma and all of its benefits, while ignoring the degree to which cycles of oppression are related to the way things appear in reality. Such models of merit, when distorted by grotesque biases, weaponize access to dharma, privileging those with means, those who want to adopt traditional Buddhist cultural systems of organization and etiquette to escape their current locations in relation to their role as oppressor, and those who wish to serve some larger purpose toward the growth of the sangha. Celebrating high position, special access, and contentment with dharma structures that benefit a small segment of society is ultimately a failure of integration of the universal compassion of the bodhisattva. Under such circumstances, when we puff ourselves up and use the dharma to defend our limited activities we are just fooling ourselves and are merely covering the systematic oppression of others with the exotic brocade of Buddhist praxis and carrying on with limited, ignorant behavior.

Devil of Inflation

The final of the four devils is the Devil of Inflation. Machik Labdron reveals to Gangpa Muksang that this forth devil is actually the root of the three preceding devils as it relates to the very dynamic of ego-cling—the core root of our suffering.

Given that ego-fixation is the root of all problems and the cause of wandering in cyclic existence, it is therefore the devil that withholds the attainment of freedom. Thus it is called the devil of inflation or the devil of ego fixation. The mind that holds on to a self where there is no self has become afflicted. Then discursive thought holds on to any good or bad mental arising and fixates on it as true existence. That is called inflation.[11]

She concludes her discourse on the four devils by further clarifying:

Once you are free of the inflation of fixating on true existence, you will encounter the untrue, space like absolute. This severs the devil of inflated object. If the devil of inflated object is severed, then all devils that arise from afflictive emotion are severed. When there is ego, then there is the devil. When there is no ego, there is also no devil. In no-ego there is no object to be severed, and so no fear and no terror. That timeless wisdom of awareness free of extremes expands intelligence to [encompass] all knowledge. This is called the fruition of liberation from the four devils.[12]

Shortly afterward, Gangpa Muksang then poses the question regarding when these devils are to be made the objects of severance and as to whether or not there is a particular sequence in which to treat them. Machik Labdron indicates that the Material and Immaterial Devils arise instantaneously at all moments. That is because we are always interacting with visual phenomena and are always afforded the opportunity to then engage in subsequent dualistic responses to whatever it is that is arising within our field of experience. Our judgments, assumptions, and biases, ranging from near instantaneous unconscious reactions, to those patterned ways of relating to the world based on conditioning, often reinforced by the various communities with which we operate within, whether family, larger cultural identifications, as well as the historical narratives to which we link our own existence, are all based on how (or whether) we are reacting to what is arising in the moment.

The Devil of Inflation is where the main object of spiritual practice is rooted in that the very ego-clinging creates the ripe fields of activity of the Material and Immaterial Devils. After all, when there is a fundamental disruption of the individual narrative of the self, and the resultant clinging to that narrative (ego-clinging), as well as the constant creation of the world in relationship to our own image, there is no "other" to fret over with a mind of elaboration. The arising of the field of appearance becomes an experience of pure being without the need for inflamed discursiveness or assessment of that which becomes.

This is exactly when the Devil of Exaltation becomes most tricky to navigate, as this is when the arising of the experience of greater insight becomes an attractive place to puff ourselves up, and when the prophecy of white supremacy is at its most seductive for white folks.

WHITENESS AS A KLESHA

In volume 14 of Jamgon Kongtrul Lodro Thaye's (CE 1813–1899) *Treasury of Precious Instructions*, the volume dedicated to the practice of *chöd*, we find the great meditation master and scholar, the Third Karmapa, Rangjung Dorje's (CE 1284–1339) wisdom on the matter in a text called *The Great Bundle of Precepts on Severance Outline and Complete Explanation*:

> when you realize as inflation any concepts composed of dualistic fixation, you realize the coarse apprehended objects without fixation. Severing that inflation cuts off the four devils. For example, when the fire inside is extinguished, the smoke in the crevices of the wall naturally subsides. Furthermore, like cessation or the nirvanic peace of the shravakas, mere objective appearances are not stopped. The objects of form and so on continue to appear, but their essence remains the empty nature of phenomena. Like a rainbow in the sky, the appearance has no nature of its own. Just so, the noble ones see this as totally obvious, while ordinary individuals know it to be so if they examine and investigate by means of scripture and reason. In the Heart Sutra it is explained, "Form is empty; emptiness is form." For example, it is like a skilled illusionist in whom thoughts of attachment to the created illusions do not occur. Therefore, other than realizing that the four devils that come from inner inflation are not truly existent, it is not that the dualistic intellect has something to sever. The realization that things and fixations are rootless means that form and so on are liberated in their own ground. That is the perfection of wisdom. Therefore it is said, "Rest within the state free of dualistic fixation."[13]

It should be clear by now that the very existence of whiteness is a function of ignorance—a function of being unable to fully manifest the radical clarity and honesty of awareness as well as the cultivation of a heart of compassion that allows us to operate motivated from a place of appreciating the universal basic goodness inherent in all beings. Whiteness is rooted in not taking the time to apply insight practices in an even manner outwardly *and* inwardly. Whiteness benefits from not being questioned, and it benefits those who propagate it in ways both obvious and subtle. It affects the way white people act, what we believe we feel we and our dharma organizations are entitled to, as well as our application of ethics. Whiteness has a tendency to bend ethics to benefit those in power, providing special access to the wealth, the bodies, and power over others.

Whiteness, when not examined, when left unclaimed, and its existence denied in dharma, has the power to severely undercut the benefit inherent in dharma. It is a poison; until those fearful of acknowledging the existence of whiteness, white privilege, racism, sexism, and patriarchy can finally see these things within themselves and recognize them as valid places for applying Buddhist practice, they are denying the existence of a poison within them and the effect it has on others. Whiteness is undeniable just as *kleshas* (afflictive mental states) or the three poisons (the afflictions of ignorance, attachment, and aversion) are undeniable, just as the effects of fundamental ignorance are undeniable.

In a text titled *Practice Manual on Severance* in the same collection, Rangjung Dorje continues:

> We have all failed to cut off these inflated thoughts throughout cyclic existence without beginning. Based on thoughts fixated on rejecting and accepting samsara and nirvana we experience the tangible objects of form, sound, smell, taste, and texture directly with our senses, and intangible positive and negative mental sensations. Without realizing it, they become binding, and through that power they become the devils of the death lord, the afflictive emotions, and the aggregates. Fixation on exaltation based on attachment to the path's meager qualities is the devil of being a god's child. Once you understand that this has occurred from incorrect thinking about all of these, the remedy is to be without the embellishment of conceptual thought. In the ultimate sense, there is no established existence whatsoever to the harm and harming of gods and demons, self and others, and samsara and nirvana.[14]

Karmapa Rangjung Dorje's equating the four devils with afflictive emotions makes a connecting link between the fundamental ignorance that is the source of afflictive emotions and afflictive mental states which are known as *kleshas* and what we understand to be whiteness.

In Buddhist psychology *kleshas* are defined as afflicting or disturbing emotions which are rooted in a misapprehension of reality as it arises and is misperceived through the fundamental three poisons or three unwholesome roots (Sanskrit: *trivisa*). These three poisons (ignorance, attachment, and aversion) function as impediments that prevent us from enlightenment as they relegate experience to samsara.

I would go further by suggesting that whiteness must be seen as an expression of our *kleshas*. Using Machik Labdron's model of the four devils, it becomes clear that the six root *kleshas* of the *Abidharma-kośa*—Attachment, Anger, Ignorance, Pride/Conceit, Doubt, and Wrong View—expand outward in the negative from ignorant interaction with external phenomena, quickly creating a samsaric world-system from which billows a multitude of mental afflictions derived from the three poisons. These include Attachment, Ignorance, and Anger as well as the blending of these three. The multitude of blended poisons creates the conditions for afflictions like excitement, avarice, power lust, glory seeking, low self-esteem, self-hatred, resentment, passion for power and greed, pretension, and disrespect to name just a few.[15] Such afflictions are clearly ripe building blocks not just for whiteness, but for

full-blown racism, sexism, homophobia, and a variegated display of intoler-
ances. Indeed, the devils of ignorance create whiteness, and similarly the
unexamined bias and ignorance of whiteness furthers our own limited way of
interacting with the world both externally and internally.

It feels vitally important that the contemporary Buddhist world begins to
see that there is a tremendous deflection inherent in reducing an exploration of whiteness and its retinue of related devils to the imposition of liberal
politics. In fact, the heart of the *chöd* tradition begs us to disrupt, to cut, to
disembowel and halt with extreme power and energy, the root ignorance that
makes it feel as if we are truly special and unique and that the rest of this
vast universe only exists in relationship to us, to serve us or to be used by us
for our own immediate gain. The question is: Can we step up? Can we commit to doing the work to practice dharma authentically with everything that
arises? Or are we just going to pay lip-serve to such exhortations and remain
duplicitous in relationship to perpetuating the suffering of others? If this is
the case, then we must accept that we are not fully practicing the dharma and
must accept our complicity in hypocrisy.

NEW DIRECTIONS AND AVENUES
FOR DISRUPTING WHITENESS

It seems that American Vajrayana Buddhism lacks the means of thorough
self-reflective internal theological debate. Perhaps this is partially due to the
fact that as a relatively new faith tradition in the United States it has not been
fully claimed with authority by its Western practitioners/teachers who worry
about having the authority to do so, and the reluctance of Asian lineage hold-
ers to let go of the reigns and trust their students to self-govern and attend
to the needs that exist here on the ground. This feels particularly vital as this
ground, this American soil, has been, and remains witness to a seeming endless display of violence committed by people enflamed by ignorance.

Just as the Indian Prince Siddhārtha demonstrated the mudra of *bhumisparsha* (the physical gesture of touching earth to remain witness to his
enlightenment experience), it feels not just pertinent but absolutely necessary
that we return to this earth, to this soil, this concrete and asphalt, which has
been mixed with and stained by the blood and tears of many different peoples
for the benefit of white-dominant economics, land acquisition, power con-
solidation, harvest of natural resources, and, especially at this particular time,
injustice surrounding immigration policy. In this way, racism and colonialism
need to be owned in an American Buddhism. The full range of the brutality
and the terror of an unchecked whiteness is part of the ground from which our
collective spiritual practice necessarily arises.

The power of spiritual bypassing, or the use of spirituality to avoid the problems with which we struggle with internally and relationally can become a major impediment. This is especially the case when needing to own up to the dynamics at play here within general American culture and the dialogue between intersecting cultures, especially when it comes to Buddhist practice. Having spent a considerable amount of time in Asia, where most of my Buddhist spiritual formation occurred, it is easy to try to distance myself from the patterns of violence and oppression that exist in the United States and concern myself with what is often erroneously regarded as *pure* (i.e., Asian) Buddhism. It is worth considering that pure Buddhism is generally found when we stop, and, in our own way, engage in the mudra of bhumisparsha to touch the ground as witness and anchor the practice of Buddhism within our own story, to use our own illusory narrative and its valence as a subject for the work of spiritual practice. This necessitates a resourcefulness in which we use everything, which in the case of whiteness includes the ways that we harm and have been harmed by unexamined whiteness. As a result, when we are touching the ground, we are touching the literal Earth which is convulsing under the strain of environmental degradation due in part to unexamined whiteness, and we are also touching our own emotional and spiritual ground which has also been affected by unexamined whiteness. This exploration into one's own whiteness is often accompanied by a deep pain rooted in oppression and the same fundamental ignorance of which Machik Labdron and Rangjung Dorje describe.

Such being the case, perhaps the experience of enlightenment is only possible in American Vajrayana Buddhism when the ways that fundamental ignorance and the assumptions around identity and power that arise from such ignorance become part of the focus of practice. This is not to say that this is the totality of the path. However, it is clear that it is a much more significant part of the path than many would like to acknowledge. After all, if we do not wish to develop awareness of our unconscious biases and our unexamined assumptions around why the world appears to be the way that it is, that enlightenment just happens without any real effort, then we are participating in an escapist hallucination. If only it were that easy. Just as we cannot afford to neglect the environmental crisis, we cannot afford to fail to claim whiteness and its effects on others. To not do so is a violation of the ethical foundation upon which Buddhism is built.

From within the location of the tantric Buddhist imperative, there are a few constructive models that can aide in the embrace of the meat of whiteness as a place where we sink the teeth of our practice: samaya activity. Within tantric Buddhist praxis, once having been initiated into a particular practice, and having received instructions and the permission to engage a number of practices, there is often a samaya, or commitment to a particular type of activity, which can take the form of maintaining a specific view regarding how one interacts with the world as it arises. Sometimes there are specific lists of samaya vows, other times samaya activity is described in a more general way. Whichever the case, adherence to samaya vows or samaya activity is considered vital to maintaining the power of the practice. It is both an expression of one's commitment to practice as well as a powerful technique to help apply the full range of tantric practice to the full range of life.

In the *chöd* practice attributed to the Eighth Karmapa, Mikyö Dorje, which was compiled by Karma Chagme, titled, *The Method for Accomplishment on One Seat*, there is a portion in which the samaya conduct for *chöd* is described as follows:

I am a wrathful Labdron with a black complexion.
On my crown is Buddha Shākyamuni, the three precious jewels.
At the throat is the holy Lama Dampa in the aspect of an Indian.
At the heart are the sublime deities, the five family dakinis,
And at the navel is the activity dakini with a green complexion.
As I am the actual Dakini Machik Labdron,
I have no concern, conscience or fear outside.
I have no attachment, anger, happiness, sorrow or worldly concerns inside.
There is no distinction between enemies and friends, everyone
    is the same because they are my father and mother.
There is no distinction between gods and demons, they are
    all the same because they are my concepts.
There is no distinction between clean and unclean,
    everything is same and experienced as amrita.
There is no distinction between comfort and discomfort,
    everything is the same because it is my own mind.
There is no distinction between this life and the next because
    I am already a Buddha.
My natural mind is the unborn Machik Labdron.
This itself, left uncontrived is Dharmakaya.
I am joyful because I have found Dharmakaya within myself.
All these appearances are unreal because they are empty;
Indistinguishable, like a dream that I dream.[16]

As we see, one who is fully committed to this practice makes a concerted effort to regard oneself as no different than Machik Labdron and to hold a certain "divine pride" or "pure view" in which one represents a continuity of the expression of non-dual liberated mind, free from all of the conceptual elaborations that cause the various sufferings created by the four devils expressed earlier in the *Machik Namshe*. When one arises like this one arises unimpeded, uncontrived, fresh, and able to radically accept whatever arises without the need to craft endless narratives. In this regard, we need to practice from a place of dedicated, direct authenticity and agency. We must bring that which arises upon our soil to our practice and not back down. More importantly, we must write new practices that speak to our unique needs. This is not to say that the older accepted practices found within the canon of tantric Buddhism need to be replaced; this is to insist that as a living lineage we must *continue*. We must continue the work to uproot ignorance. Our various tantric Buddhist lineages must continue to grow to meet the needs of all that feel inspired to walk the path—and therefore, practice texts must be included to address oppression, that is, to continue to manifest the power and inspiration of the dharma as it disrupts whiteness. Failure to do so is both a violation of the larger Buddhist commitment to an ethics rooted in the alleviation of suffering of all sentient beings, as well as the more specific failure to manifest an authentic tantric Buddhist praxis in which we learn to directly work with our *kleshas* and the subsequent limited view that arises when we do not interrogate our assumptions about Buddhist practice.

As far as the composition of new practices and working to revitalize the canon, I have composed two ritual texts aimed at bringing the work of engaging whiteness and racism from within the tradition of modern tantric Buddhism, which I share below. Their inclusion within this chapter is an attempt to bring awareness of whiteness formally into the tradition so that it might be engaged in a meaningful way. This is a way to start the conversation.

The first text is a *torma* offering, or offering of ritual food in the form of cakes made from barley flour, in which the offering is centered on focusing one's intention upon becoming aware of whiteness and racism, and then working to engage in the liberation from ignorance around race. This torma offering text follows the body of other ritual texts in this vein and contains a section at the end in which one receives the self-empowerment and blessing by Tröma Nagmo a very wrathful black female Buddha who represents the energy of sudden realization of the true awakened nature of our mind. In a sense Tröma is chaotic because often the experience of realization is not easy, nor necessarily convenient. Sometimes it is initially far more comfortable to remain blinded by our ignorance, yet it is not uncommon to find that once one's eyes have been opened, we rarely want to fall back into the slumber of that initial temporary ignorance. The second practice is a short daily meditation text (Sanskrit: *sadhana*) that offers a way to return on a continual basis to the process of familiarizing ourselves with the experiencing of engaging the world free of the bondage of Machik Labdron's Four Devils. Whether these two ritual texts bring benefit is yet to be seen; however, what may be most important is the attempt to engage the tradition by acknowledging whiteness and its shadows and imprints upon the Buddhist tradition.

Bringing the Demons of Race and Oppression to Their Knees: A Tröma Nagmo Torma Offering

In front of me, from a dark midnight blue chojung instantly arises Tröma Nagmo. She is wild, angry and dancing with effortless wrathful passion.

Her red orange hair stands on end wildly,
gnashing her teeth,
grimacing with anger that cuts through intellect,
she provides release from conceptual thought.
She is naked, her black skin, oiled and perfumed,
is warm and supple.
Loosely draped around her, are the freshly flayed skins of an elephant, a tiger and
     a human,
still warm and sticky with blood.
Tröma dances amidst a halo of flames,
the flames of anger, rage, confusion,
and chaotic power.
She wears the customary bone ornaments of the dakinis,
signifying her role as ultimate queen of symbol;
fast, ever darting, her immediate realization annihilates any room for ego-
     clinging.
Her garland of fifty freshly severed human heads,
expose her power to destroy the pain and pleasure of identity,
leaving all within her presence able to recognize mahamudra.
Her body, dabbed with human fat signifies that there is no protection from the
     ultimate realization of expansive non-dual mind.
Her environs, a smoke filled charnel ground,
dark like the night during the new moon invokes fear and anxiety,
it is unsettling and filled with dangerous animals
and unseen beings who support the yogin/i in that they give no comfort,
no level ground upon which to let self-nature settle into assumed habit.
From a dark red syllable Hri a midnight blue light with a reddish tinge radiates
     outwards instantaneously liberating all beings and expanding Tröma's charnel
     ground so that it is endless, with no center or edge. This light then returns,
     blessing me with the full empowerments of body, speech, mind, activity and
     essence and I arise self-generated as Tröma Nagmo fully adorned with her
     attributes; queen of the dakinis bringing sudden mad liberation to every being
     that we encounter.
From myself as Tröma a second light arises from my secret place invoking the
     four principal dakinis as well as an army of millions of wrathful mamos, all
     appearance is overwhelmed by this powerful radiation subduing the kleshas
     of all rendering neurotic self-cherishing into the experience of basic space.

Offerings and Praise

Hum Hum Hum, Tröma Nagmo, mother who cuts through the ignorance of
     difference between self and other, who ransoms the fundamental ignorance of
     racism with wrathful buddha activity allowing myself to release the weapons
     of power and oppression I bow and offer praise.
Ha Ha Ha, Vajra dakini, mother who reveals that all beings who struggle with
     identity-in-appearance in relation to position and status, both high and

low, refined and coarse, coveted and shunned, light-skinned and dark, toil endlessly in samsara not realizing that identity itself is a temporary display of endless appearance, yet illusory in nature, I bow and offer praise.

Ho Ho Ho, Ratna dakini, mother who reveals how the mudras of words and symbols, the constant flow of the illumination of dharmata are sullied and ignorantly forgotten when we use words and symbols to entrap others in an identity that we create for them, allowing us to try to dominate and control those who are by their very nature, our reflections, I bow and offer praise.

Phat Phat Phat, Padma dakini, mother who reveals that the ultimate citadel of mahamudra realization is closed to those who cannot see that the patterned bias of racism and other oppression is a hypocrisy that leaves one to wander like a fool who thinks he is a pandita, or a libertine who thinks she is a siddha, or a bodhisattva who only arises as a demon, I bow and offer praise.

Li Li Li, Karma dakini, mother of activity who reveals that genuine open self-liberated action is not only difficult, it is our samaya-activity, that the unbiased, spontaneous expression of mahamudra is only possible with the heart-of compassion, compassion for self and other, not the habit mind of assumption and projection and other violent conceptions, I bow and offer praise.

Hri Hri Hri, black cloud of tens of millions of mamos, great beings who ride the mind and as a result all phenomena, shatter the shackles that keep us from love, tame our anger and habits of oppressing others based upon appearance and assumption, soften the tightness we feel around difference, expose and remove white supremacy from our dharma centers, and reveal how true dharma cannot be held in a container marred by the fundamental ignorance of racism, to you I bow and offer praise.

Torma Offering

From the basic space of Tröma's mind-essence a kapala arises upon a hearth of three skulls. The syllables RAM, YAM, KHAM arise bringing the qualities of fire, air and water which cause the contents of the kapala to boil so that the blessings of non-dual wisdom, the essence of mahamudra bless the torma, providing it with potency and making it pleasing to Tröma, her retinue as well as local protectors.

Brilliant queen of basic space, Tröma Nagmo, please approach and accept this torma.

Vajra dakini, expansive mind-essence of the dakinis, please approach and accept this torma.

Ratna dakini, she who grants of the qualities of the expression of that which defies expression, please approach and accept this torma.

Padma dakini, heart-essence of the manifestation of the unification of ultimate and bodhicitta, please approach and accept this torma.

Karma dakini, the essence of the tantric activities of pacification, enrichment, magnetizing and destroying, please approach and accept this torma.

Hosts of mamos and worldly dakinis, please approach and accept this torma.

Local protectors and spirits of this place, please approach and accept this torma.

Please accept this pleasing torma and other offerings both real and imagined so that the plague of racism and the oppression and violence associated with it be eradicated from my mind-stream as well as that of others.

May we heal so that authentic relationships are able to arise and appearance is able to be seen for what it is, a magical dance of liberation.

May our dharma centers be inclusive.

May local protectors and spirits commit themselves to the elimination of racism and generalized patterned ignorance.

May the container of the holy dharma be stainless and able to hold the diversity of its practitioners as a sangha united by genuine loving-kindness.

May the demons of spiritual-bypassing be found to be without essence so that we are able to put down our spiritual mania and finally rest our minds in basic space without effort.

May dharma spread and continue to benefit all beings.

From the Hri syllable in my navel, the retinue of Tröma and a multitude of dakinis arise and partake in the torma and other offerings. Pleased, they bless the place of this practice, as well as all beings and return.

Instantly, I receive the full four empowerments of Tröma Nagmo and her retinue, and the visualization dissolves.

Rest in mahamudra.

This tsok was written in the Western pure land of Brooklyn, by Repa Dorje Odzer, unworthy student of the glorious king of tantras, the mahayogi, Gyaltsab Rinpoche, Regent of the Karmapa, and Lama Tsering Wangdu Rinpoche, the very essence of Phadmpa Sangye himself. While this tsok is full of errors and may lead one to ruin, it was written with the genuine aspiration that the demons of racism be brought to their knees and that oppression based upon appearance be eliminated. Gewo.

The Firey Tigle of Tröma Nagmo: A Daily Practice of Instantaneous Severance

Instantly three self-arising ruby colored sindura marks appear on my brow, throat and heart centers respectively.

They pulsate with the blessings of Tröma Nagmo and an endless swarming cloud of dakinis from Uddiyana.

As these three bindus radiate a dark red light, my body and the world around me dissolves into an omniscient midnight blue sphere of dharmata essence with the stillness and vastness of Akshobya.

In this unceasing natural tranquility that is the nature of all things, I rest my mind in no particular manner.

This is nothing other than the roar of the mind of Tröma, the radical sameness, alive and unified, full of everything and yet free of idiotic self-identity, it is everything.

Rest free.

Break the vessel of who you are trying to be.

Allow the mind to remain unborn.

This concise daily Tröma practice was written by the lazy pomous yogi, Repa Dorje Odzer, in the great Western charnel ground of Rikers Island. It cuts deep and unlocks the samaya behavior of the carefree vagabond. May all who meet this sever the ties that cause suffering in samsara, and taste the precious amrita of liberation inherent in daily life.

NOTES

1. Philip Almond, *The British Discovery of Buddhism* (Cambridge: Cambridge University Press, 1988), 13.

2. Christian K. Wedemeyer, *Making Sense of Tantric Buddhism: History, Semiology, and Transgression in the Indian Traditions* (New York: Columbia University Press, 2013). See chapter 4, *The Semiology of Transgression* as it offers a detailed analysis and explanation of issues surrounding reading tantric literature as it relates to ideas around objectivity.

3. bell hooks, *Black Looks: Race and Representation* (Boston: South End Press, 1992), 169.

4. Sarah Harding, *Machik's Complete Explanation: Clarifying the Meaning of Chöd* (Ithaca: Snow Lion, 2003), 117.

5. Ibid., 118.

6. Ibid.

7. Ibid.

8. Ibid., 119.

9. Ibid.

10. Ibid.

11. Ibid., 120.

12. Ibid.

13. Sarah Harding, *Chöd: The Sacred Teachings on Severance* (Boulder: Snow Lion, 2016), 86.

14. Ibid., 250.

15. Geshe Tashi Tsering, *Buddhist Psychology: The Foundation of Buddhist Thought*, vol. 3 (Somerville: Wisdom Publications, 2006), 49.

16. David Molk, trans., *The Chöd Instruction: The Method of Accomplishment on One Seat* (Portland: The Movement Center, year unknown), 21.

Chapter 12

The Interdependence and Emptiness of Whiteness

Bryce Huebner

There is a broad academic consensus that racialized groups are socially constructed, though there is substantial disagreement over precisely what this means. A similar consensus has emerged in the everyday patterns of thought and talk among non-academics in the United States. In many contexts, the acknowledgment that race is socially constructed is thought to be the end of the conversation, and things become much more complicated when the conversation continues.[1] Few academics are willing to defend racial anti-realism and few non-academics are willing to claim that races do not exist—even though many adhere to something like a colorblind ideology. The reasons for this reticence are simple. People who are raised in the United States simply *perceive* others as White, Black, Latinx, and Asian; where they are unsure about someone's race, appeals to ancestry will usually clear up their confusion, and they find that patterns of racial categorization can sustain a wide range of inferences about unobserved traits (including ungrounded assumptions about intelligence, the propensity for aggression, and tolerance for pain). From a psychological perspective, the world appears to be racially organized. Of course, things look different from a biological perspective. The phenotypic differences between racialized groups are skin-deep, and insufficient to ground robust inferences about unobserved traits. Some of these traits are heritable, but this does not make race biologically real, even if it places limits on the kinds of variation that typically emerge in skin-deep differences. So, the scientific consensus is that races are not biologically real kinds.[2]

Against this background, an account of the ontology of whiteness should address three interrelated facts about how people experience race.[3] First, it must explain why people reflexively classify one another on the basis of observable properties including skin color, distinctive phenotypic traits, distinctive displays of fashion, and spoken accent and it must explain why they typically take these forms of classification to ground further inferences about unobserved properties. Second, it must explain why people assume that a person inherits their race from (at least one of) their biological parents—as this is what makes it seem like there is a biological basis for race. And finally, it must acknowledge the fact that race plays an integral role in structuring and organizing ongoing experience, as well as guiding patterns of thought and behavior. More specifically, it must account for the ways in which whiteness shapes the material, social, and inferential practices that are available to those who live in the United States. My primary aim in this chapter is to show that Buddhist nominalism provides a framework for making these claims intelligible.

According to the form of Buddhist nominalism that I develop, whiteness is a conventional strategy for classifying people, which is conjured into existence by the social practices and material realities that organize our experience.[4] Drawing on resources from the work of Dharmakīrti, I argue that we organize our experiences functionally and conceptually, and that we reflexively treat our concepts as if they were tracking essential features of the world; this motivates us to engage in actions that will sustain our ontological illusions, and it fosters patterns of distress and anxiety where our ways of conceptualizing the world are called into question. Through the resulting patterns of action and interaction, "people create the cultures to which they later adapt, and cultures shape people so that they act in ways that perpetuate their cultures."[5] So, in a world where actions are commonly organized around white bodies and white ideologies, many people will internalize whiteness as a lived orientation toward the social world and they will act in ways that perpetuate structures of white supremacy. The internalization of whiteness as a lived orientation toward the world may be most transparent among people who are racialized as white, but the prevalence and stability of white ideology, and white social institutions, can lead to a situation where the "white gaze" is internalized by people who are racialized in other ways as well.[6] Finally, I argue that understanding the factors that give rise to the experience of whiteness can help to motivate ameliorative practices aimed at collective liberation, by focusing our attention on the disconnect between considerations of social justice and our assumed social ontology.[7]

THE EMPTINESS OF SOCIAL CATEGORIES

The author of *Trisvabhāvanirdeśa* (*TSN*), *the Treatise on the three natures*, claims that experience can always be examined from three distinct perspectives.[8] We can ask how things appear to us; we can examine the *process* by which an appearance is fabricated; and we recognize that, contrary to appearances, nothing has a stable or essential nature.[9] Consider the appearance of an illusory elephant, which is conjured into existence by a street magician (*TSN* 27–30). An observer might think that they are experiencing a real elephant. But this experience is produced by a street magician, who applies a mantra to various material items. And as the observer falls prey to the illusion, they assume that what they are seeing is real. Finally, since the elephant does not exist as it is experienced, it will cease to be experienced as *an elephant* once the patterns of interdependence between the magician and the observer are fully understood. Across the *Yogācāra* tradition, philosophers argue that "the objects of our experience, as we experience them, exist only in dependence on our minds."[10] And they often claim that we are easily misled by appearances, treating the things that we perceive and the things that we conceptualize as ultimately real.[11] The model articulated in *TSN* offers a plausible framework for thinking about the ontology of racial kinds, and of whiteness more specifically. Many people "see" whiteness, and they treat it as a property that a person can have or lack; but this experience is fabricated, as habits of attention and action lead to distorted experiences of racialized groups. And we must learn to see through this distortion if we are to engage in the kinds of transformative practice that will rid our world of racial bias.

A similar argument has a long pedigree in Buddhist philosophy.[12] Beginning in the earliest canonical sources, we find arguments against the natural existence of caste, which are grounded on the claim that no observable characteristics could ever "serve as a sign (*liṅga*) that some human individuals belong to a different class or species (*jāti*)."[13] Many Buddhist philosophers have also argued that strategies of social categorization often derive from assumptions about the situations where particular groups of people are likely to be encountered.[14] For example, Dharmakīrti argues that there are no causal factors that would allow a person to perceive the members of the Brahmin class as a distinct cluster from the members of the *śūdra* class, and that differences in categorization "may [very well] come from their practicing particular occupations (*vyāpāraviśeṣa*) [such as muttering prayers and sacrifices] and from [the fact that they are born in a] family (*anvaya*) [traditionally involved in such occupations], as is the case with denominations like 'healer,' 'merchant,' etc. (*vaidyavaṇigvyapadeśa*)."[15] In this respect, he claims that the capacity to distinguish people on the basis of social class is radically different from the capacity to distinguish biological species.[16] You will only "see" someone as a Brahmin if you have been socialized to do so, but you will be able to see that cows and chickens are different kinds of animals without explicit training.[17] From our current perspective, it may seem like racial categories are more natural groupings, as differences in skin color and other phenotypic traits seem like more natural indicators of a person's race. However, the kind of nominalism that Dharmakīrti defends makes it clear that race is also a conceptual fiction—or so I shall argue.

PROCESS NOMINALISM AND *APOHA*

Like many Buddhists, Dharmakīrti draws a distinction between things
that exist ultimately (*paramārthasat*) and things that exist conventionally
(*saṃvṛtisat*). He argues that only causally efficacious things exist ultimately,
and that everything else exists conventionally. But there is a twist: the only
causally efficacious things are momentary particulars. Particulars are "causally related to each other in such a way that one moment in the sequence
acts as the primary cause for the next moment in the sequence."[18] And some
of them interact with the senses, to trigger flows of perceptual experience.[19]
But there are no abstract objects, and there are no persisting entities. Each
particular is unique and distinct, and difference is ontologically primary. Of
course, Dharmakīrti also recognizes that we speak of enduring entities, and
that we treat them as if they belonged to determinate kinds (e.g., pots, cows,
chickens). To accommodate these facts, he develops a version of *apoha*
theory according to which we impose categorical structure on experience to
organize thought and behavior in accordance with our goals; put differently,
we seek out useful patterns of functional classification and project these onto
the dynamic flow of experience as we attempt to engage in goal-directed
action.[20] And through this process, our strategies of categorization impose
conventional structure on the world we encounter.

The details of Dharmakīrti's *apoha* theory are complex. And any interpretation of it will be contentious. My primary goal in this section is not to offer
a substantial intervention into debates over the nature or status of *apoha*.
I simply hope to extract some important insights from a less differentiated
understanding of *apoha* theory.[21] In the next section, I will argue that *apoha*
theory yields a novel framework for thinking about why people perceive
the world as racially structured. But first, I must clarify the view of perception and conceptualization that I take to be at play in Dharmakīrti's *apoha*
framework.

According to Dharmakīrti, sensory contact with causally efficacious things
typically yields perceptual experiences with "nonconceptual" content (*nirvikalpaka*). Since such experiences are the effect of contact with particular
things, they tend to stand in a relatively robust resemblance relation to the
things that have caused them.[22] But we are rarely in a position to see things
as they really are. The world is complicated and noisy, and we always have
limited time to act. So practical activity requires us to focus on particular
aspects of our experience that are likely to be salient to our goals and interests, and acting efficiently requires ignoring those aspects of our experience
that are unlikely to have much bearing on how things go *for us*. This is where
the *apoha* theory begins to take hold. Two things will always differ from
one another in innumerable ways. So our ability to identify things that are

relevant to our interests, to re-identify the things that we learn about, and to see two things as members of the same classificatory kind, requires focusing on the clusters of causal characteristics that are relevant to a particular goal, and ignoring clusters of properties that are irrelevant to seeing these things as similar to one another—and as different from other things.[23] As sentient creatures, we cannot do everything at once; but we can rely upon specific goals and interests to structure our habits of attention, and this allows us to construct conceptual understandings (*savikalpaka*) of the world, which are organized around things that are useful for our purposes. The implication is that experience is always partial, and always structured by our practical needs and interests.[24]

When I think about coffee, a network of interests (e.g., my desire for caffeine, my desire for a particular taste, the pleasure I take in a warm drink) prompts the construction of a coffee-representation, which serves to distinguish coffee from other things that lack these causal properties.[25] And when I see a barista pouring coffee into a mug, this activates karmic imprints (*vāsanās*) of previous experiences, which will recruit this conceptual representation, and if there is some fact about my current experience that has been absent in previous encounters with coffee (e.g., if it comes in an odd colored mug), I will ignore this difference, since it is irrelevant to my goal of drinking coffee. More generally, thoughts about coffee will leave out many of the causal properties that particular cups of coffee have had, as these properties are irrelevant to my goals. This is striking, as any two cups of coffee will differ in innumerable ways that can easily be ignored; but the focus of our attention tends to be on factors that are relevant to the achievement of our goals. And because we ignore numerous differences between coffee experiences, "we can construe both of them as mutually qualified by a negation, namely, their difference from phenomenal forms that do not activate the imprints for the concept [coffee]."[26]

My ability to conceptualize coffee as coffee becomes more precise and more determinate as I exclude more phenomena from the category.[27] To the extent that I become snobbish and exclude "gas station coffee" and coffee from Dunkin' Donuts and Starbucks from the category, the boundaries around my coffee concept will become tighter and to the extent that I happily drink these things, the boundaries around my coffee concept will become fuzzier. But in any case, our ongoing encounters with causal particulars, such as those that constitute cups of coffee, shape our tendencies to attend to some, and to ignore other differences. This ongoing process of attunement, which is shaped by shifting attention away from particular kinds of differences provides the foundation for conceptual cognition.[28] As a result, when we think conceptually, our thoughts are organized by patterns of practical activity. So, while we lose phenomenal clarity as we impose our goals and values on decisions about where to lump and where to split, this loss of clarity is often worth the cost.[29]

THE BIOLOGICAL FRAGILITY OF WHITENESS

Still, not every way of organizing the world will be equally successful. Some ways of lumping and splitting are resilient, as their primary cause lies beyond particular patterns of conceptualizing, others are fragile, showing signs of stability only within a particular conceptual framework. Attempts to milk chickens, like attempts to gather eggs from a cow, are bound to fail no matter where you are. Attempts at milking cows, like attempts to collect chicken eggs, will often succeed, no matter what you happen to call these entities. While cows and chickens differ in innumerable ways, these practical activities can be undertaken without changing the world—and without changing ourselves—in profound ways. So thoughts about milking cows are correct to the extent that they can "serve as a solid basis for successful action."[30] And more generally, where resilient differences emerge, we can rely upon them to develop practically useful strategies for categorizing higher-order entities. But in some cases, differences only persist because of the ways in which we categorize things. I contend that "whiteness" is always a fragile category and that racial categories are "nothing more than superimpositions of divisions, through words and conventions, on a humanity that is ontologically unique and undifferentiated."[31] To see what this fragility amounts to, however, it will help to examine one plausible place to look for a resilient basis for race: Biology.

As Dharmakīrti might predict, things rapidly become complicated when you search for biological nondifferences. Most of the genetic diversity in our species is concentrated within sub-Saharan Africa, and the diversity in the rest of the world is "a subset of the African genetic variation with some newly arisen alleles."[32] But genetic differences emerge both within and between human populations; so two people from the same population are likely to be just as different from one another, genetically speaking, as two people selected from two different populations anywhere in the world.[33] Of course, this is not to deny the existence of traits that can anchor racialized discourse (e.g., skin pigmentation, hair texture, and facial morphology). But these traits also vary within and between populations, and they cross-cut patterns of shared ancestry.[34] For example, most Melanesians look similar to people who are racialized as Black in the United States. They have a "high frequency of dark skin pigmentation, curly black hair (and the ability to grow afros), full lips, round noses, etc."[35] These nondifferences do not reveal a closer relationship to people in sub-Saharan Africa; indeed, like most regularities, these ones seem to derive from environmental similarities (e.g., similarities in temperature, sunlight, and proximity to the equator). Consequently, these nondifferences have had a shallow impact on human biology. But this is not the end of the biological story.

Recent research in population genetics has used clustering algorithms to find evidence of human population structure. These algorithms compare allele frequencies, and attempt to find a unique way of partitioning the data into a specific number of clusters, K, by minimizing differences within a population and maximizing differences between populations.[36] Where K = 5, data from the Human Genome Diversity Cell Line Panel (which includes samples from fifty-two global populations) the population clusters that emerge are anchored to the indigenous peoples of "Sub-Saharan Africa, North Africa and Eurasia west of the Himalayas, Eurasia east of the Himalayas, the Americas, and Oceania."[37] Given the similarities between these clusters and the US census categories, this may seem to reveal a real joint in nature.[38] But we should proceed cautiously. Where K = 6, the Kalash people of northwest Pakistan constitute a sixth cluster; I doubt that we should treat a group of ~4,000 people as a distinct racial category. Where K = 2, we find a population cluster that is anchored in East Asia, Oceania, and the Americas, and a cluster that includes the rest of the world. Finally, a larger dataset—which includes the previous dataset, along with a larger number of geographically distinct African populations, African Americans, Yemenites, Indians, and Native Australians—reveals five sub-Saharan African clusters at K = 7.[39] A racial reading of these data suggests "that there is one Saharan African/European/Middle Eastern/Central Asian/Indian race, one Eastern Asian/Oceanic/American race, and five sub-Saharan African races."[40] This seems far less like a plausible joint in nature. But we cannot settle the question of how many racial groups there are a priori. And if "the race naturalist cannot name and number the so-called races with any specificity or reliability, and on any well-grounded basis, racial naturalism is in trouble."[41]

To be clear, there are causal properties that produce observable differences. And there are even a small number of genetic markers that we can use to distinguish populations; but when we look at larger numbers of genetic markers, we find a huge amount of diversity within any group that we identify.[42] It may be important, for some practical purposes, to categorize people by appeal to genetic nondifferences. But when we do this, we risk mistaking social differences for biological differences;[43] where genetic factors become salient, we are likely to ignore differences rooted in concrete material relations, such as access to medical resources, exposure to higher levels of toxins, and differential levels of racialized stress.[44] And there is reason to think that focusing on biological nondifferences can lead us to ignore important medical differences, while focusing on biological differences can lead us to ignore important medical nondifferences.[45] As I see it, this is a similar problem to the one that worried Dharmakīrti when it came to questions about social caste.[46] Classification on the basis of biological properties is possible. But you have to ignore a lot of conflicting data. You have to ignore many equally real differences in the data that you do take seriously. And you have to decide which properties are relevant to your particular purposes.

> We could classify ripe fruit based on the colour of its skin. Yellow fruits would include bananas and lemons. Red fruits would include strawberries and cherries. This classification system would be stable enough, but it would offer a poor representation of fruit diversity. It follows that classification systems—even reliable classification systems—are not necessarily useful guides to diversity.[47]

As I read the existing data, there are no biological joints in nature. And this is true even though there are patterns that we can reify, in light of assumptions about how people should be lumped together, and how patterns of differences and nondifferences are to be understood.

THE SOCIAL FRAGILITY OF WHITENESS

We also lump people together using normative statuses such as "white" to organize our experience of the world. But here too, boundaries have often expanded and contracted, as light-skinned people have searched for ways to justify their assumption that they were "more developed and more human in comparison with the darker-skinned 'others' (whether African or indigenous) whom they dominated."[48] Maintaining the boundaries around whiteness has required exploiting many different conceptual strategies at many different points in US history, but, in every case, whiteness has been both "the budding product of psychological subjectivity and the structural foundation for dynamic reproduction of racist action."[49] Consider the widely reported fact that Irish immigrants were initially treated as *not-white*. In some respects, this claim might be overblown. But what is clear is that nineteenth-century Americans thought the Irish had distinctive physical characteristics, which marked them off from other light-skinned people. Propagandistic images represented the Irish as dirty, dangerous, and unintelligent. And while their light skin made it easy for Irish people to become white, this nondifference did not guarantee the normative status of whiteness.[50] Only integration into an oppressive identity could do that (and this could only be accomplished by excluding any potential link between Irishness and Blackness).

The sense of superiority that constitutes white identity became even clearer in the early twentieth century, when white people began to fear the collapse of their social supremacy. Virginia's *Racial Integrity Act of 1924*, for example, required each citizen to identify as "white" or "colored" on all legal documents. Whiteness was governed by the infamous "one-drop rule," stating that any evidence of non-white ancestry was sufficient to be classified as "colored." This uniquely American claim about hypodescent would be enough to demonstrate the fragility of this mode of classification—after all, no one else racializes identity in this way, and there is no practical purpose for doing so, aside from grasping at racial purity. But the law also included a curious exception: although a white person needed unambiguous Caucasian ancestry, a person with less than one sixty-fourth "Indian" ancestry would also be considered white. This exception was made to accommodate the large number of high-status Virginians who saw themselves as descendants of Pocahontas and John Rolfe. When a proposal was introduced in 1926 to eliminate this "Pocahontas exemption," it was rejected because it would change the racial status of roughly 20,000 apparently "white" Virginians; so instead, a revision was made that allowed "white" people to have up to one-eighth "Indian" ancestry.[51] In this context, we can see that whiteness is being engineered to preserve power and privilege—high social status was sufficient for whiteness, so long as all future relationships preserved existing levels of racial purity. And if this does not show that whiteness was being conjured into existence,[52] I am not sure what would.

The fragility of whiteness was also on display in the pattern of conceptual engineering that followed in the wake of the *Naturalization Act of 1906*. According to this law, which was a revision of the *Naturalization Act of 1870*, only white people and people of African descent could become US citizens. So, in 1922, a Japanese immigrant, Takao Ozawa, challenged this law by arguing that light-skinned Japanese people were actually white; the Supreme Court held that the color of his skin did not matter, as whiteness *actually* required "Caucasian" ancestry. But things changed three months later, when Bhagat Singh Thind, an immigrant from Northern India, made a case for citizenship on the basis of his status as a high-caste Aryan, and a member of the Caucasian race; here, the court held that there was no consensus regarding the nature of the Caucasian race, and that common sense precluded the possibility of a dark-skinned Caucasian.[53] In both cases, racial difference was specified on the basis of a desire to preserve racial purity. And in this respect, arguments for the existence of whiteness look no less absurd than the arguments that Dharmakīrti was troubled by. But they did not look that way to people in the early twentieth century, and this was largely because of the way that people were socialized to think about the reality of race. Here too, Buddhist nominalism offers resources for thinking about the nature of this socialization. And in the next two sections, I turn to a discussion of the factors that sculpt our default understanding of whiteness.

VĀSANĀS, LEARNING, AND PREPAREDNESS

Like proponents of contemporary learning theory, Dharmakīrti argued that the majority of our goals are organized by two factors: the satisfaction of desires and the avoidance of undesirable outcomes. So, we tend to develop the capacities we need to re-identify aspects of the world that are important to satisfying our goals, and we do so by bringing past experiences to bear on our interpretation of our perceptual states.[54] Where our actions are successful, they tend to be repeated, and where our actions are fruitless, their outcomes tend to be ignored. But in all cases, we think and act with an end in view. In this respect, we are like the rats in a city, who will approach anything that might be food. Every potential food source differs from every other potential food source in innumerable ways—and rats must determine which foods are likely to satisfy their needs. But they quickly learn to avoid locally salient toxins, as they are biologically prepared to learn about connections between food and sickness.[55] If Dharmakīrti's *apoha* theory is roughly correct, then these rats are learning what to eat, by learning which differences they can safely ignore. And they are doing so by relying on karmic imprints (*vāsanās*) that have accumulated over countless generations, as well as vāsanās that are accumulated through learning.

The accumulation of *vāsanās* also plays a critical role in shaping what we experience.[56] Some *vāsanās* are shared by all sentient beings, and provide the basic precondition for all samsaric experience; they function as constraints on the kinds of experiences that sentient creatures have. Other *vāsanās* emerge through learning and attunement to the world as we encounter it. These are the *vāsanās* that anchor our understanding of the world to our habituated needs and interests. They also organize our goals, and shape our conceptual experiences. But importantly, *vāsanās* are not persisting mental particulars. They are accumulated through our thoughts and actions, and they continually develop as we think and act. Our actions leave karmic traces on the world. And there is a dense feedback relation between our actions and our habits of thought.[57] How we conceptualize things shapes the actions we engage in; the world is shaped by our actions, and we attune to the structure of the world. In many cases, our actions also impact the parts of the world that others will encounter. And one of the most significant ways we affect our shared world is through shared habits of labeling and identifying things.

This enactive view of cognition helps to make it clear why Dharmakīrti thinks that the use of linguistic labels is not *just* a pernicious habit: "everything that people can cognize, whether an expression or something else, is an undertaking—a practical action—for the sake of some goal."[58] We use labels that allow us to generalize from successful practices of excluding things from our awareness and to figure out how to behave in novel situations. Of course, this leads us to misunderstand the structure of the world, as real "things are themselves different, but in conceptual cognition they appear as if nondifferent in that they appear in some single form."[59] But as we learn to ignore various differences, patterns of conceptual awareness arise through interaction between perception and the *vāsanās* that shape our tendencies to lump, split, and categorize. In each case, the resulting form of conceptual awareness will appear to be a simple representation of the world, with the imagined (*adhyavasita*) object having the same apparent status as an extra-mental particular.[60] And since many of our patterns of conceptual thought cluster nondifferent things functionally, we are often able to achieve our goals, even though we are positing illusory universals.

THE INTERDEPENDENCE OF SOCIAL CATEGORIES

I recently attended a ballet performance, which helped me to understand how the interaction between attentional biases and patterns of exclusion produce racialized experiences. The performance highlighted six social roles that women tend to play; and it was danced by five light-skinned women of European descent, one light-skinned Japanese woman, and one Black man. The male dancer's skin pigmentation became perceptually salient, because I was ignoring nondifferences between him and the other dancers. But I was also ignoring differences between the female dancers by treating them as a unified class. In both cases, habits of attention to particular kinds of differences shaped my initial impression, and it was only by attending to what I was ignoring that I began to see how the apparent simplicity of my experience concealed the process through which my experience was being constructed. Put bluntly, I was projecting the differences that I perceived as joints in nature, in a way that felt seamless. There was no magician to mislead me. The way that I conceptualized my experience generated this illusion all on its own. This would be surprising, if it were not so banal.

My experience at this performance is an instance of a larger phenomenon, commonly known in psychology as the other-race effect.[61] We are better at recognizing members of our own racial group; we are more likely to remember the faces of racial in-group members (and to forget the faces of racial outgroup members) and we tend to see racial outgroups as relatively homogenous. In more familiar terms, people who live in predominantly white spaces tend to think that all Black people look the same. Over the course of their first year of life, there is an observable shift in the way that infants categorize faces: focal attention begins to privilege the faces of racial groups that are most common in their environment.[62] This all makes sense. For most of human history, we lived in small groups that were part of larger ethnies.

The members of these groups shared stories, assumptions, and phenotypic features. But there were outsiders. And humans learned to perceive group-based differences, and to see members of other groups as different from themselves. So, it is unlikely that evolutionary *vāsanās* have accumulated that would dispose us toward racial thinking; but it is very likely that we have inherited a tribalist psychology.[63] And like the rat who learns what counts as food, we quickly learn what differentiates racialized groups, and we quickly learn which differences to ignore. But we do not do this on our own. Early understandings of race are probably "based on information children acquire by listening to those around them talk about social differences rather than by attending to physical differences that 'cry out to be named.'"[64] One powerful way that adults shape children's racialized understandings of social groups is by using generic language; after hearing a generic term applied to a group, a child becomes more willing to assume that group members will possess similar inherited and stable traits.[65]

But there are other factors at play, including the material structure of different communities, and the ongoing patterns of thought and talk within these communities. Where religious beliefs are more central to social cat-egorization, beliefs about ethno-religious identities will take on a racialized character.[66] While people in the United States rely on facial features and assumptions about racial ancestry in determining a person's racial identity, Brazilians are more sensitive to skin tone.[67] And the attentional biases that emerge in the United States heavily depend on the fact that most white people are primarily exposed to material and social environments that are dominated by white bodies and interests, while excluding the interests and perspectives of people of color.[68]

Beginning in the 1930s, redlining and biased lending drove Black neigh-borhoods into poverty, prevented the establishment of racially mixed neigh-borhoods, and entrenched the racial homogeneity of white neighborhoods.[69] Bias in lending persisted throughout the twentieth century, and the housing crisis disproportionately affected racially mixed neighborhoods, as well as Black and Latinx neighborhoods, contributing to the re-entrenchment of de facto segregation.[70] There are many reasons why these factors are materially, socially, and culturally significant. But they are also psychologically signifi-cant, as people who inhabit shared environments tend to converge on similar psychological and behavioral dispositions, as they learn to devote attention to phenomena that are salient to the stability of their shared material and social environments. This is what allows forms of socialized attention to arise, as behaviors that conform to cultural rules are socially reinforced, while behav-iors that contradict local norms are punished and abandoned.[71]

In a series of recent papers, Shinobu Kitayama and his colleagues have argued that attentional biases arise through a process of cultural attunement. Through active and ongoing participation in culturally scripted patterns of behavior, we gradually develop "attention allocation strategies that are consistent with local cultural assumptions."[72] But just as importantly, we are social niche constructors, and our understanding of what the world affords is dynamically shaped by the social and material structures that we simultaneously create and inhabit. People are rewarded for forms of social engagement that accord with local norms, and they are criticized for acting in ways that are socially "deviant." Consequently, people learn to categorize and ignore aspects of their experience in ways that are culturally sanctioned[73] and since culturally "deviant" forms of categorization are rarely reinforced, many psychological processes will come to reflect the worlds, contexts, and social systems that people are chronically immersed in.[74] To put the point starkly, we accumulate *vāsanās* through our practical engagements in the world, and we accumulate racialized *vāsanās* through forms of practical activity that are shaped by socially entrenched forms of racial exclusion. Our habits of attention are shaped by our learning history and by the goals that are served by prioritizing particular sources of information. Over time, we construct an attentional framework on the basis of everything from statistical regularities to semantic associations, and we adjust our responses in particular situations to fit our motivational and emotional state.[75] And in a constructed social niche that centers whiteness, habits of attention will converge on stimuli that are salient to white goals and white interests, while deflecting attention away from stimuli that conflict with these goals.

To the extent that anyone learns to think racially, this will be the result of living in a world that is thick with structural racism and xenophobia. As those of us who live in the United States watch TV and films, read novels and blogs, and walk through familiar and unfamiliar neighborhoods, we are bombarded with socially structured "evidence" that we are categorizing things correctly. This is no accident! Like the street magician who fabricates an experience of an elephant out of various material items, the ideology of white supremacy fabricates a world that will confirm the ideology of white supremacy. People of color are routinely excluded from positions of social and institutional power, and in this context educational practices typically align with white goals and values.[76] This produces a shared background against which inferences and arguments are often evaluated, while at the same time allowing the pervasiveness of white ideology to fade into the background. This apparent neutrality fosters actions that continue to shape the distribution of social and material power, practices of justification and explanation, as well as legal and normative frameworks that protect white interests.[77] And it allows everyday practices to solidify around "colorblind" ideologies, which promote practices, decisions, and policies that make no reference to race. As a result, white people tend to perceive less racism in their world, and they tend to "indicate less support for anti-racist policy when colorblind ideology is salient."[78] Because white ideology pervasively shapes attentional strategies, white people tend to see whiteness as a background against which to frame their understanding of the world.[79]

The *vāsanās* that accumulate as people in the United States move through social spaces that are shaped by whiteness will impose structure on their practical activities. Of course, there may be other salient factors that push back against this way of perceiving the world. And this kind of effect will be most pronounced in those who inhabit white spaces and encounter predominantly white forms of cultural traditions. But repeated interactions in racialized contexts will lead to the development of attentional strategies and to habituated patterns of ignoring particular kinds of differences between people, and anyone who searches for categorical structures among the remaining differences will end up projecting race onto the world. Consequently, when we experience someone as white, this appearance is thus sustained by three interacting processes: the tendency to ignore differences between "white" people, the tendency to focus on differences between "white" people and "non-white" people, and an *apoha* process that constructs a simple representation, in accordance with the vāsanās that lead us to see "white" people as having a normative status that darker-skinned "others" necessarily lack. But the whiteness that we produce is an illusion, as nothing could have a stable nature that being white requires.[80] Our experience of the world is shaped by our learning history, by aspects of the world we have recently encountered, by the nature of our current situation, and by the current state of our body. And this is because being a successful agent requires adapting to situations that we are chronically immersed within.[81]

Even more importantly, we take part in social and cultural practices—we do not just observe them. These are not just ways of thinking, they are ways of acting in the world and staking out our positions in social space. And as we participate in culturally structured practices, we replicate the forces that impose structure on our social environments, often by imposing additional pressures on one another to conform.[82] The racialized forms of conceptualization that we employ, however, do not carve the world at natural joints, as there are no natural joints to be found; we construct these joints to facilitate particular forms of goal-directed action, and we reify them in ways that lead us to assume that they have a more ultimate reality than they actually have.[83] But no matter how we decide to divide things up, we will not find objective similarities in our social world, aside from those that emerge as "the products of our interactions with the world."[84] And as I see it, these kinds of facts give us very good reason to think that whiteness is conjured into existence.[85]

SHIFTING KARMIC FLOWS

If the arguments I have developed are on the right track, we are now in a position to answer the questions I articulated in the introduction.

1. People classify on the basis of observable properties because they have been socialized to focus on particular differences and to ignore particular nondifferences;
2. The use of racial categories to ground practical inferences derives from commonly observed connections, just as Dharmakīrti would predict; and
3. The assumption that people inherit race derives from observations of generational continuity in skin-deep features and observed correlations between race and social class that are built into the structure of our world (this tendency has also been enhanced by attempts to establish boundaries around whiteness that draw on illicit assumptions about ancestry and white purity).

In each case, the conceptual experience of whiteness depends on feedback from social, economic, and material forces that are organized by attempts to maintain white purity and white supremacy. And the resilience of whiteness depends on continuing efforts to sustain its existence. Put differently, seeing white people as a unified category depends on goals such as white supremacy and racialized oppression. These goals may not be represented consciously, but they are essential to this way of categorizing. This is important, as it means that whiteness is a fragile social category, which only persists through ignorance and through ongoing attempts to manage and sustain that ignorance.[86]

Many white people are afraid to give up their assumed position of supremacy and power. And to preserve the illusion that the world is as it must be, many white people ignore the structural forces that organize and perpetuate racialized oppression. Consequently, they formulate atomistic and individualistic conceptions of racism, which "locate action and experience in isolated individuals abstracted from social context."[87] And as a consequence, worries about enforcing Black-White racial boundaries tend to increase when racialized hierarchies are threatened.[88] Exclusionary attitudes tend to be enhanced when white people consider the possibility of a majority-minority America.[89] And many white people become more likely to see racial differences when they feel economically vulnerable.[90] More generally, racialized anxiety increases attention toward threats, activating *vāsanās* that have been accumulated through previous experiences, and this leads to the construction of more heavily racialized representations.[91]

One of the main tasks of Buddhist epistemology is to undercut biased theories, and to establish a less biased approach to human cognition.[92] If the story

I have told is approximately right, then whiteness retains its causal power because we privilege goals like racial purity, white supremacy, and control over non-white populations. These are ugly goals, which can only survive when they are coupled to a distorted understanding of the causal structure of the world. We ignore the ways in which everyday patterns of thought and behavior are grounded in an exclusionary and oppressive identity; we allow whiteness to persist as a dominant social paradigm, and the feedback relations between our habits of conceptualization and our practical activities perpetuate the samsaric process of racialized world-construction. "As Dharmakīrti might have put it, just as essentialism about one's self perpetuates suffering, essentialism about one's community perpetuates oppression."[93] And I think that there are at least a few significant points where Buddhist resources can be used to decenter these distorted forms of thought and behavior.

First, recall that Dharmakīrti's *apoha* theory suggests that we impose categorical structure on experience in light of our practical goals. Many of us ignore the fact that the practical goals that allow us to see whiteness as a category are oppressive and exploitative. But the cultivation of wisdom requires us to acknowledge the ways in which whiteness depends on racial oppression. And to the extent that we become aware of this, we can direct our attention toward changing the social structures that make us see whiteness as a real joint in nature, or at the very least withdrawing our support for those social structures. This is a way of changing our practical orientation toward the world, which focuses our attention on the structural forces that organize and perpetuate racialized oppression, and to the extent that we are committed to following the bodhisattva path, this awareness will motivate us to eliminate the epistemic distortions inherent in perceiving the world whitely, and to actively work to bring about the well-being of our fellow humans.

Second, there is reason to believe that we can begin to change our understanding of social categories by shifting to a higher level of generality. Seeing yourself as the member of a mixed-race group can shift patterns of attention, and patterns of categorization.[94] And in some cases, seeing others as part of a shared struggle for a shared end can help to minimize patterns of bias and discrimination. For example, shared social identities "can override biases that are built upon years of social exposure and perceptual expertise."[95] Indeed, these forms of collective identification can even affect the kinds of facial memory and processing effects that I addressed above as the other-race effect.

> This thought is given expression in an art motif depicting a crocodile with one stomach and two heads locked in struggle over food. If they could but see that the food was, in any case, destined for the same stomach, the irrationality of the conflict would be manifest to them.[96]

A Buddhist perspective should push us in a similar direction. But committing to practices of mutual aid and mutual support across racial lines probably requires more than simply seeing points of nondifference. A well-known meditative technique known as "exchanging self for other" may be useful in this regard. We usually direct our actions toward the preservation of our own needs and interests, and the minimization of our own suffering. To intervene on this habitual pattern of thought, Tenzin Gyatso proposes the following meditative practice:

> On one side you visualize your own normal self, the self that is totally impervious to others' well-being and an embodiment of self-centeredness . . . on the other side, you visualize a group of beings who are suffering, with no protection and no refuge . . . [then] . . . view yourself as a neutral third person impartial observer, who tries to assess whose interest is more important here. Isolating yourself in the position of neutral observer makes it easier for you to see the limitations of self-centeredness, and realize how much fairer and more rational it is to concern yourself with the welfare of other sentient beings.[97]

By engaging in a practice like this, we can work to change the attitudes we have formed about our "self," and attitudes we have formed about "others." And more importantly, we can see where our self-interested habits are inhibiting our feelings of compassion, because we privilege our own perspectives.[98]

To achieve this, however, we need a final and more fundamental shift in how we relate to the world. Specifically, we need to acknowledge the emptiness of whiteness as a category.[99] This requires seeing the people who we are socialized to treat as white as differing along innumerable dimensions. For if white people are not a "real" group, then there is nothing to work to preserve. This is likely to require a great deal of Buddhist practice, as it requires not just seeing the skin-deep differences between people who are racialized as white, but also acknowledging that there is nothing that makes them all white aside from an oppressive ideology. I think that any chance at successfully internalizing an understanding of these facts will require a great deal of meditative practice, focusing on the emptiness of whiteness, and its interdependence on oppressive practices. The goal of shifting our patterns of thought and conceptualization in this way is not merely a self-directed practice.[100] It is to make a profound change in our motivations, our behavior, and our motivation to change the karmic flows that constitute our world. As Yogācāra philosophers have long noted, the transformation of thought is intimately connected to the transformation of the world, and the transformation of the world is a necessary condition for the transformation of thought.[101]

NOTES

1. Lewis Gordon, "Critical Reflections on Three Popular Tropes in the Study of Whiteness," in *What White Looks Like: African-American Philosophers on the Whiteness Question*, ed. George Yancy (London: Routledge, 2004), 173–194, 183.

2. Though see Quayshawn Spencer, "A Radical Solution to the Race Problem," *Philosophy of Science* 81, no. 5 (2014): 1025–1038.

3. cf. Gordon, "Critical Reflections," 183–184.

4. Clevis Headley, "Deligitimizing the Normativity of "Whiteness": A Critical Africana Philosophical Study of the Metaphoricity of "Whiteness," in *What White Looks Like: African-American Philosophers on the Whiteness Question*, ed. George Yancy (London: Routledge, 2004), 87–106.

5. Hazel Rose Markus and Alana Conner, "The Culture Cycle," 2011, https://www.edge.org/response-detail/11527 (accessed April 1, 2018).

6. George Yancy, *Black Bodies, White Gazes: The Continuing Significance of Race in America,* 2nd ed. (Lanham, MD: Rowman & Littlefield, 2016).

7. John D. Dunne, "On Essences, Goals and Social Justice: An Exercise in Buddhist Theology," *Buddhist Theology: Critical Reflections by Contemporary Buddhist Scholars* (1999): 275–292.

8. *TSN* commonly attributed to Vasubandhu in Tibetan sources, though its authorship is highly contested. See Jonathan C. Gold, *Paving the Great Way: Vasubandhu's Unifying Buddhist Philosophy* (New York: Columbia University Press, 2014), 148–149 for reasons to interpret this work as the culmination of Vasubandhu's Yogācāra philosophy; see Matthew T. Kapstein, "Who Wrote the Trisvabhāvanirdeśa? Reflections on an Enigmatic Text and Its Place in the History of Buddhist Philosophy," *Journal of Indian Philosophy* 46, no. 1 (2018): 1–30 for skepticism about the authorship of *TSN*.

9. Gold, *Paving the Great Way.*

10. Jay L. Garfield, "Vasubandhu's *Trisvabhāvanirdeśa* (*Treatise on the three natures*). Editor's Introduction," in *Buddhist Philosophy: Essential Readings* (Oxford: Oxford University Press, 2009), 35–45, 37.

11. Gold, *Paving the Great Way*, 158.

12. Vincent Eltschinger, *Caste and Buddhist Philosophy: Continuity of Some Buddhist Arguments Against the Realist Interpretation of Social Denominations*, trans. R. Prevereau (Delhi: Motilal Banarsidass, 2012), xvii.

13. Eltschinger, *Caste and Buddhist Philosophy*, 23.

14. Ibid., 11.

15. PVSV 157.16–18, trans. in Eltschinger, *Caste and Buddhist Philosophy*, 113.

16. This type of argument has a long history within Buddhist thought. Its earliest articulation occurs in the Sutta Nipāta, in a discussion with Vāseṭṭha on the question "Who is a Brahmin"; for a further discussion of this sutta, as well as the other early antecedents of this argument in Buddhist philosophy, see Eltschinger, *Caste and Buddhist Philosophy*, 17–24.

17. Ibid., 109.

18. John D. Dunne, *Foundations of Dharmakirti's Philosophy* (New York, NY: Simon and Schuster, 2004), 86.

19. Dunne, *Foundations of Dharmakirti's Philosophy*, 89.

20. *Apoha* theory is a distinctively Buddhist approach to the defense of nominalism, and the term *apoha* designates a process of constructing meaning through exclusion.

21. Amita Chatterjee, "Funes and Categorization in an Abstraction-free World," in *Apoha: Buddhist Nominalism and Human Cognition*, eds. Mark Siderits, Tom Tillemans, and Arindam Chakrabarti (New York: Columbia University Press, 2011), 247–257.

22. Dunne, *Foundations of Dharmakirti's Philosophy*, 87.

23. Ibid., 91.

24. Chatterjee, "Funes and Categorization in an Abstraction-free World."

25. The argument in this paragraph follows Dunne, *Foundations of Dharmakirti's Philosophy*, 93–94.

26. Dunne, *Foundations of Dharmakirti's Philosophy*, 94.

27. Dan Arnold, *Brains, Buddhas, and Believing: The Problem of Intentionality in Classical Buddhist and Cognitive–Scientific Philosophy of Mind* (New York: Columbia University Press, 2014), 10.

28. Jonardon Ganeri, "Apoha, Feature-Placing, and Sensory Content," in *Apoha: Buddhist Nominalism and Human Cognition*, eds. Mark Siderits, Tom Tillemans, and Arindam Chakrabarti (New York: Columbia University Press, 2011), 228–246.

29. Dunne, *Foundations of Dharmakirti's Philosophy*, 87.

30. Brigit Kellner, "Why Infer and Not Just Look?" in *The Role of the Example (Dṛṣṭānta) in Classical Indian Logic*, eds. Ernst Steinkellner and Shoryu Katsura (Wien: Arbeitskreis für tibetische und buddhistische Studien Universität Wien), 1–51, 2, cited in Catherine Prueitt, "Karmic Imprints, Exclusion, and the Creation of the Worlds of Conventional Experience in Dharmakīrti's Thought," *Sophia* 57, no. 2 (2017): 313–335.

31. Eltschinger, *Caste and Buddhist Philosophy*, 163.

32. Koffi N. Maglo, "The Case Against Biological Realism About Race: From Darwin to the Post-genomic Era," *Perspectives on Science* 19, no. 4 (2011): 361–390, 374.

33. Noah A. Rosenberg, "A Population-genetic Perspective on the Similarities and Differences among Worldwide Human Populations," *Human Biology* 83 (2011): 659–684.

34. Adam Hochman, "Replacing Race: Interactive Constructionism About Racialized Groups," *Ergo, an Open Access Journal of Philosophy* (2017): 4.

35. Quayshawn Spencer, "Philosophy of Race Meets Population Genetics," *Studies in History and Philosophy of Science Part C* 52 (2015): 46–55, 50.

36. Noah A. Rosenberg, Jonathan K. Pritchard, James L. Weber, Howard M. Cann, Kenneth Kidd, Lev Zhivotovsky, and Marcus W. Feldman, "Genetic Structure of Human Populations," *Science* 298, no. 5602 (2002): 2381–2385.

37. Spencer, "Philosophy of Race Meets Population Genetics," 48.

38. Spencer, "A Radical Solution to the Race Problem."

39. Sarah A. Tishkoff, Floyd A. Reed, Françoise R. Friedlaender, Christopher Ehret, Alessia Ranciaro, Alain Froment, . . . and Scott M. Williams, "The Genetic Structure and History of Africans and African Americans," *Science* 324, no. 5930 (2009): 1035–1044.

40. Adam Hochman, "Racial Discrimination: How Not To Do It," *Studies in History and Philosophy of Science Part C: Studies in History and Philosophy of Biological and Biomedical Sciences* 44, no. 3 (2013): 278–286, 281.

41. Ibid., 281.

42. Koffi N. Maglo, Tesfaye B. Mersha, and Lisa J. Martin, "Population Genomics and the Statistical Values of Race: An Interdisciplinary Perspective on the Biological Classification of Human Populations and Implications for Clinical Genetic Epidemiological Research," *Frontiers in Genetics* 7, no. 22 (2016): 2.

43. Kahn et al., "Open Letter: How Not to Talk About Race and Genetics," March 30, 2018, https://www.buzzfeednews.com/article/bfopinion/race-genetics -david-reich#.wopAymmJ1 (accessed April 1, 2018).

44. Maglo, "The Case Against Biological Realism About Race."

45. Maglo, Mersha, and Martin, "Population Genomics and the Statistical Values of Race."

46. cf. Maglo, "The Case Against Biological Realism About Race," 21 ff.

47. Hochman, "Racial Discrimination," 280.

48. Phia S. Salter, Glenn Adams, and Michael J. Perez, "Racism in the Structure of Everyday Worlds: A Cultural–Psychological Perspective," *Current Directions in Psychological Science* 27, no. 3 (2018): 150–155.

49. Ibid., 2.

50. cf. Noel Ignatiev, *How the Irish Became White* (London: Routledge, 1995), 70; Steve Garner, *Whiteness: An Introduction* (London: Routledge, 2007).

51. Brendan Wolfe, "Racial Integrity Laws (1924–1930)," in *Encyclopedia Virginia*, 2015, http://www.EncyclopediaVirginia.org/Racial_Integrity_Laws_of_the_ 1920s (accessed April 1, 2018).

52. Headley, "Deligitimizing the Normativity of 'Whiteness.'"

53. As Linda Martín Alcoff demonstrates, the fragility of this category was on full display throughout the late nineteenth and early twentieth centuries. Whether Latinx-Americans or Chinese-Americans were considered white, or Black, varied over time, and varied from state to state. And as she rightly notes, the "clear lesson to be learned from this legal history is that race is a construction that is variable enough to be stretched opportunistically as the need arises to maintain and expand discrimination" (Linda Martín Alcoff, "Latino/as, Asian Americans, and the Black–White Binary," *The Journal of Ethics* 7, no. 1 (2003): 5–27, 12).

54. Laura Guerrero, "Conventional Truth and Intentionality in the Work of Dharmakīrti," in *The Moon Points Back*, eds. Koji Tanaka, Yasuo Deguchi, Jay L. Garfield, and Graham Priest (Oxford: Oxford University Press, 2015), 189–219, 201.

55. John Garcia and Robert A. Koelling, "Relation of Cue to Consequence in Avoidance Learning," *Psychonomic Science* 4 (1966): 123–124.

56. Prueitt, "Karmic Imprints, Exclusion, and the Creation of the Worlds of Conventional Experience in Dharmakīrti's Thought."

57. Ibid., 17.

58. PV i.93, in Dunne, *Foundations of Dharmakirti's Philosophy*, 115.

59. PV i.68, in Dunne, *Foundations of Dharmakirti's Philosophy*, 339.

60. PVSV and PV i.75, in Dunne, *Foundations of Dharmakirti's Philosophy*, 346.

61. For a review, see Joanna K. Malinowska, "Cultural Neuroscience and the Category of Race: The Case of the Other-race Effect," *Synthese* 193, no. 12 (2016): 3865–3887.

62. David J. Kelly, Shaoying Liu, Kang Lee, Paul C. Quinn, Oliver Pascalis, Alan M. Slater, and Liezhong Ge, "Development of the Other-race Effect During Infancy: Evidence Toward Universality?" *Journal of Experimental Child Psychology* 104, no. 1 (2009): 105–114; Julie Markant, Lisa M. Oakes, and Dima Amso, "Visual Selective Attention Biases Contribute to the Other-race Effect Among 9-month-old Infants," *Developmental Psychobiology* 58, no. 3 (2015): 355–365.

63. Edouard Machery, "The Evolution of Tribalism," in *Routledge Handbook of the Philosophy of the Social Mind*, ed. Julian Kiverstein (Routledge, 2017); Jay J. Van Bavel and Andrea Pereira, "The Partisan Brain: An Identity-based Model of Political Belief," *Trends in Cognitive Science* 22, no. 3 (2018): 213–224.

64. Lawrence A. Hirschfeld, "Seven Myths of Race and the Young Child," *Du Bois Review: Social Science Research on Race* 9, no. 1 (2012): 17–39, 24.

65. Marjorie Rhodes and Tara M. Mandalaywala, "The Development and Developmental Consequences of Social Essentialism," *Wiley Interdisciplinary Reviews: Cognitive Science* 8, no. 4 (2017).

66. Ibid., 5–6.

67. Jacqueline M. Chen, Maria Clara P. de Paula Couto, Airi M. Sacco, and Yarrow Dunham, "To Be or Not to Be (Black or Multiracial or White): Cultural Variation in Racial Boundaries," *Social Psychological and Personality Science* (2017).

68. Robin DiAngelo, "White Fragility," *The International Journal of Critical Pedagogy* 3, no. 3 (2011): 54–70, 58; Wendy Leo Moore, *Reproducing Racism: White Space, Elite Law Schools, and Racial Inequality* (Lanham, MD: Rowman & Littlefield, 2008).

69. Ta-Nehisi Coates, "The Case for Reparations," *The Atlantic Monthly*, June 2014, https://www.theatlantic.com/magazine/archive/2014/06/the-case-for-reparations/361631/ (accessed April 1, 2018); Alexis C. Madrigal, "The Racist Housing Policy That Made Your Neighborhood," *The Atlantic Monthly*, May 22, 2014, https://www.theatlantic.com/business/archive/2014/05/the-racist-housing-policy-that-made-your-neighborhood/371439/ (accessed April 9, 2016).

70. Emily Badger, "This Can't Happen by Accident," *Washington Post*, May 2, 2016, https://www.washingtonpost.com/graphics/business/wonk/housing/atlanta/??noredirect=on (accessed April 1, 2018); Matthew Hall, Kyle Crowder, and Amy Spring, "Neighborhood Foreclosures, Racial/Ethnic Transitions, and Residential Segregation," *American Sociological Review* 80, no. 3 (2015): 526.

71. Shinobu Kitayama, Jiyoung Park, and Yay-hyung Cho, "Culture and Neuroplasticity," in *Advances in Culture and Psychology*, eds. Michelle J. Gelfand, Chi-yue Chiu, and Ying-yi Hong, vol. 5 (New York: Oxford University Press, 2015), 38–100, 86.

72. Hyekyung Park and Shinobu Kitayama, "Perceiving through Culture: The Socialized Attention Hypothesis," in *Social Vision*, eds. Reginald B. Adams, Jr., Nalini Ambady, Ken Nakayama, and Shinsuke Shimojo (New York: Oxford University Press, 2011), 75–89, 77.

73. Park and Kitayama, "Perceiving through Culture."

74. cf. Nilanjana Dasgupta, "Implicit Attitudes and Beliefs Adapt to Situations: A Decade of Research on the Malleability of Implicit Prejudice, Stereotypes, and the Selfconcept," *Advances in Experimental Social Psychology* 47 (2013): 233–279.

75. Rebecca M. Todd and Maria G. M. Manaligod, "Implicit Guidance of Attention: The Priority State Space Framework," *Cortex* 30, no. 1 (2017): e1–e8.

76. Olúfẹ́mi Táíwò, "Beware of Schools Bearing Gifts: Miseducation and Trojan Horse Propaganda," *Public Affairs Quarterly* 31, no. 1 (2017): 1–18.

77. Moore, *Reproducing Racism.*

78. Phia S. Salter and Glenn Adams, "Toward a Critical Race Psychology," *Social and Personality Psychology Compass* 7, no. 11 (2013): 781–793, 786.

79. Charles W. Mills, "Racial Exploitation and the Wages of Whiteness," in *What White Looks Like: African-American Philosophers on the Whiteness Question*, ed. George Yancy (London: Routledge, 2004), 25–54.

80. cf. Dunne, "On Essences, Goals and Social Justice."

81. Dasgupta, "Implicit Attitudes and Beliefs Adapt to Situations," 271.

82. Park and Kitayama, "Perceiving through Culture," 77.

83. Guerrero, "Conventional Truth and Intentionality in the Work of Dharmakīrti," 210.

84. G. B. Dreyfus, *Recognizing Reality: Dharmakirti's Philosophy and its Tibetan Interpretations* (New York: Suny Press, 1997), 213.

85. Headley, "Deligitimizing the Normativity of 'Whiteness.'"

86. Charles W. Mills, "White Ignorance," in *Race and Epistemologies of Ignorance*, eds. Shannon Sullivan and Nancy Tuana (New York: SUNY Press, 2007), 11–38; Jennifer C. Mueller, "Producing Colorblindness: Everyday Mechanisms of White Ignorance," *Social Problems* 64, no. 2 (2017): 219–238.

87. Salter and Adams, "Toward a Critical Race Psychology," 785.

88. Chen et al., "To Be or Not to Be."

89. For a review, see Maureen A. Craig, Julian M. Rucker, and Jennifer A. Richeson, "The Pitfalls and Promise of Increasing Racial Diversity: Threat, Contact, and Race Relations in the 21st Century," *Current Directions in Psychological Science* 27, no. 3 (2017): 188–193.

90. Amy R. Krosch and David M. Amodio, "Economic Scarcity Alters the Perception of Race," *Proceedings of the National Academy of Sciences* 111, no. 25 (2014): 9079–9084.

91. cf. Rachel D. Godsil and L. Song Richardson, "Racial Anxiety," *Iowa Law Review* 102, no. 5 (2017): 2235.

92. Vincent Eltschinger, "Dharmakīrti," *Revue internationale de philosophie* 253, no. 3 (2010): 397–440, 405–406.

93. Dunne, "On Essences, Goals and Social Justice," 289.

94. Jay J. Van Bavel and William A. Cunningham, "Self-categorization with a Novel Mixed-race Group Moderates Automatic Social and Racial Biases," *Personality and Social Psychology Bulletin* 35, no. 3 (2009): 321–335.

95. Jay J. Van Bavel and William A. Cunningham, "A Social Identity Approach to Person Memory: Group Membership, Collective Identification, and Social Role

Shape Attention and Memory," *Personality and Social Psychology Bulletin* 38, no. 12 (2012): 1566–1578, 1574.

96. Kwasi Wiredu, "Democracy and Consensus in African Traditional Politics: A Plea for a Non-party Polity," *The Centennial Review* 39, no. 1 (1995): 53–64, 57.

97. cf. Tenzin Gyatso, "Training the Mind: Verse 7," n.d., https://www. dalailama.com/teachings/training-the-mind/training-the-mind-verse-7 (accessed April 1, 2018).

98. In conversation, Emily McRae has suggested that there is another reason why this kind of practice is important in the context of racial bias. This practice was initially developed as a way of counteracting our tendency to privilege our own interests, while ignoring the suffering of others. And it helps to entrench the forms of practical motivation that flow from recognizing that "self" and "other" are empty of inherent existence. Likewise, if the argument that I have been developing in this paper is right, then racial categories are empty of biological reality; but we must still attend to patterns of racial injustice. As McRae puts this point, "the ethical imperative to respond to racism demands that we take seriously the social reality of race at the same time that we see it to be empty." This seems exactly right to me.

99. Dunne, "On Essences, Goals and Social Justice," 287.

100. cf. Evan Thompson, "Looping Effects and the Cognitive Science of Mindfulness Meditation," in *Meditation, Buddhism, and Science*, eds. David McMahan and Erik Braun (Oxford University Press, 2017), 47–61.

101. The arguments in this chapter were developed through numerous helpful conversations and online interactions with Eyal Aviv, John Dunne, Aaron Garrett, Quentin Fisher, Adam Hochman, Shen-yi Liao, Karin Meyers, Thi Nguyen, Cat Prueitt, Olufemi Taiwo, and Evan Thompson. And I am incredibly thankful for the comments that I received from Emily McRae and George Yancy—they definitely made this a better paper. Parts of this chapter were also presented in a different form at the MindsOnline conference in 2016. As always, Ruth Kramer was an enormous source of support in thinking through these issues, and this chapter would never have been finished without her help.

Chapter 13

Taking and Making Refuge in Racial [Whiteness] Awareness and Racial Justice Work

Rhonda V. Magee

INTRODUCTION

As a human being born in the racialized and gendered United States of America, where I was deemed—by others—"Black" and "female" at birth, I have long been aware of the various ways that a culture of social identity–based oppression fueled by the ideologies and practices of White Supremacy lead to suffering. White Supremacy is, in fact, all about justifying the pain inflicted on vast groups of people whose suffering has become essential to the privileged existence of others.

The suffering to which I refer here is beyond that which the Buddha came to see as something that naturally arises as part of the human condition (such as sickness, aging, and death). And yet, it is, indeed, suffering.

In my experience, the average teacher of Buddhism (or mindfulness) in America has little to say about how it is that the mind creates and the embodied mind enacts racism, sexism, and other forms of identity-based oppression. And this may in part explain my reluctance, after many years as a student of the teachings of the Buddha, fully to embrace "Buddhism" as a path, as a home suited for me, too.

As a decades-long student of both Western psychology and Buddhist teachings, I have for many years been curious about how the dynamics of the socially embedded mind contribute to such suffering, and thus might also contribute to our liberation from such dynamics. How do racism, bias, and other forms of identity-based oppression show up in Western Buddhist practices and centers of teaching, learning, and engagement?

In this chapter, I reflect on the concepts of Taking Refuge and Making Refuge as means of deepening our capacity to understand race in our own

lives: *taking refuge* in the Buddha, the Dharma, and the Sangha in support of
deepening the capacity for working with bias and racism in ourselves and in
our practice communities; and through those and other intentional practices
as a way of *making refuge* for a sense of diverse and resilient community.

Specifically, in the following pages, I briefly discuss the ancient teachings
of "right view" and of "interdependent co-arising (or dependent origination)"—concepts often said to be at the heart of the teachings attributed to
the Buddha. I show how these concepts may be at the heart of understanding
both how social identity-based suffering arises *and* how we might end such
suffering and experience liberation. In the words of one Buddhist teacher in
the Insight Meditation tradition, "if we understand how our world is created,
we also then become a conscious participant in that creation."[1] Thus, if we
understand how racism and other forms of systematized bias are created in
our world, we can also act to disrupt them. Doing so may be seen as making
refuge for the traditionally marginalized and creating the capacity to be with
the inherent and systemic vulnerabilities of our human condition.

PART 1: TAKING REFUGE AS A PATHWAY
TO RACIAL AWARENESS

Taking Refuge: The Buddhist Invitation to
Commit to the Path of Liberation

"To seek refuge is to look for a place that is safe, a place we can rely on."[2] To
practice in this tradition, whatever the particular sect or stream, is to embrace
the practice of taking refuge in what have been called the Three Jewels: the
Buddha, the Dharma, and the Sangha:

I take refuge in the Buddha, the one who shows me the way in this life.
I take refuge in the Dharma, the way of understanding and love.
I take refuge in the Sangha, the community that lives in harmony and
    awareness.

To practice meditation and the allied disciplines is to experience refuge,
the sense of being engaged in a reliable way of being with reality, a way of
coming to terms with the true nature of our existence, all in an effort to experience liberation from suffering. Fundamentally, refuge may be found within,
wherever we are.

And yet, importantly, as embodied beings, our experiences of suffering
vary depending on the circumstances and situations in which we live and
experience the world. The Buddha taught us about the suffering experienced

by each of us as a result of the arising of a sense of a permanent self in a world where nothing is permanent, and the "separate self" is fundamentally an illusion. I refer to this as existential suffering because it is a feature of our existence as human beings.[3] Less emphasized in the teachings as they have been translated for Western audiences and practitioners of mindfulness are the ways that the Buddha recognized the suffering that was caused by the trainings of our culture and social structures.

In the culture of contemporary America, pervasive, informal trainings in racism and other forms of socialidentity–based bias are deeply embedded and still powerful. Racism—the belief in essential differences in human beings tied in some way to the defined races through notions of biology and culture, and the ideology of differential human value and worth associated with the notion of racial difference—is taught and practiced (most often in subtle ways, but not always) as a broad and central cultural commitment.

Racism operates on personal, interpersonal, and structural and systemic levels. For those whom racist ideas have cast as subordinate or inferior, racism results in additional or surplus suffering—suffering beyond that which we all feel as a result of the development of the sense of the ego and the separate, fixed self. In our society, Whites have been legally, economically, and culturally privileged as presumptively deserving of inclusion and better-than-fair treatment. Non-Whites have suffered the challenge of establishing their right to be treated with equal respect, dignity, and concern.[4]

Because race and racism are prevalent yet very often un-acknowledged forms of suffering in our midst, Taking Refuge in the path and practices association with mindfulness and meditation implicitly supports us in both *seeing clearly* and *healing from* the particular suffering associated with and caused by the practices of race and racism. The personal path of practice may support us, then, in developing racial awareness and in living in a way that promotes the end of race-based suffering in the world.

Mindfulness and Blindspots

When we reflect on the nature of racism—in its personal, interpersonal, and systemic or structural dimensions—we see that it is a subtle and complex nexus of thought, emotion, and sensation that supports degrees of consciousness and unconsciousness about who we are and how the respect we owe one another creates unnecessary or surplus suffering in the world.

Research confirms that bias—a subtle and often unintentional form of racism—is ubiquitous. And with bias comes what sociologists call "blind spots": the invisibility or unconsciousness to us of the ways in which we discount some groups and may discriminate against them or their members in our everyday lives.[5]

The problem of racism (or bias) presents both a challenge and an opportunity for practitioners of Buddhism with an interest in social justice. While some evidence suggests that practices associated with Buddhism, including mindfulness of breath and lovingkindness, can assist in minimizing bias and discrimination, the research in this area is nascent and certainly not yet definitive.[6] Moreover, both research efforts in this area and anecdotal evidence suggest reason for caution.[7] For these reasons, we need to look to more than our mindfulness practices for assistance in minimizing the operation of bias in our lives and increasing our capacity to make refuge for others in our practice communities.

In short, mindfulness and lovingkindness practices may be helpful, but these practices alone cannot yet be deemed effective in eliminating racism in ourselves and in our communities.

The Allied Disciplines

Buddhist teachers traditionally guide practitioners to engage in mindfulness meditation as part of a commitment to taking refuge in the Buddha, the Dharma, and the Sangha. Contrary to many Western mindfulness meditation programs, such Buddhist teachers offer mindfulness meditation as part of a commitment to Buddhist practice, learning, and perhaps religious engagement through the Eightfold Path. In traditional approaches, mindfulness meditation is offered as one part of Buddhist practice and study. It is worth noting that the attention that mindfulness meditation and related practices have received in the contemporary US context is not representative of how mindfulness is situated in most traditional Buddhist contexts.

Moreover, in addition to engaging in mindfulness meditation, practitioners are asked to study and practice much more. Consistent with language used by at least some traditional teachers, I refer to these other practices and commitments as the allied disciplines.[8]

The allied disciplines traditionally include ethical commitments, the discipline of studying both with a teacher and through the study of texts, and the practice of meditation in a practice community. However, in my years of teaching and learning about race and racism, I came to see that addressing racism would require more. Thus, I began to explore what particular disciplines might be proposed as appropriate "allies" for the work of redressing racism.

Research has shown that in addition to bringing people from different backgrounds together—desegregation and integration—engaging people from diverse backgrounds in meaningful contact minimizes bias. Moreover, evidence indicates that colorblind efforts may do more harm than good. While well-meaning in most cases, such efforts serve as barriers to learning about and talking about race and racism in our lives, leading to the perpetuation of under-examined racially disparate outcomes.[9]

Instead, effective training in multicultural understanding and anti-racism counsels addressing and countering racism effectively. Therefore, in my own work as a teacher of both anti-racist education and mindfulness, I have explored incorporating selected texts, instruction on concepts and practices, all of which aim to make the work of addressing bias through awareness practices more effective. The particular texts may vary. The point is that each of us who are in positions to shape practice and learning communities have an obligation to provide resources—to teachers and participants—that deepen our collective understanding of how the marginalized in our communities may perceive the world. We have an obligation to seek to expand the lenses through which we view the world and thereby increase the level of awareness of the potential for discrimination that is inherent in ourselves, our communities, and institutions.

Exploring Social Identity, Culture, and Cultural
History as Racialized Aspects of Everyday Life

To support the deepening of our understanding of race and racism, exploring the construction of social identity is essential. For the purposes of this chapter, I define identity with reference to two aspects—personal and social—which sometimes overlap completely, but may sometimes overlap only tangentially. Personal identity arises in response to the question of how one defines oneself ("Who am I?"). Social identity arises through the ways that we are defined by the outside world, how our embodiments link to the socially, culturally defined categories by which we have come to make sense of the world. And for our purposes here, I define culture as recurring patterns of behavior and lifeways within a given group of people passed down through implicit and explicit teachings, often over generations and, in particular, geographic space.

Buddhist philosophy of the self *as a mental construct* harmonizes in many ways with Western social psychological notions of the socially constructed self. However, as taught in many Western settings, Buddhism often does not address the social self very much, beyond noting its illusory nature. We tend not to hear much, within contemporary Western Buddhist-convert or mindfulness settings, about cultural patterns of oppression and privilege as aspects of how we construct the self.

One notable departure is the teaching of Tsokyni Rinpoche, whose description of the "Social-I"—that sense of the self that comes into being as a result of our lived experiences in the social realm—partakes of Western social-psychological notions of socially contextualized, socially embedded identity. And Tsokyni Rinpoche's concept of the "Useful-I"—the aspect of the Social-I that can be deployed in service of a more compassionate world—may be particularly helpful in deepening our understanding of why it is important to engage in mindfulness of our racial identities in the world.[10]

In the United States, dominant culture and prevailing notions of race and racial identity are and have been for centuries intimately intertwined. Since the settler-colonial era, US culture has categorized individuals and groups according to "race," and, more specifically, has defined "White" as the dominant racial identity over all others. As such, to be racially defined—or "racialized"—as white is to be identified with the lived experience of significant racial privilege when compared to the experience afforded vis-à-vis all other racialized bodies. White Privilege is often subtle. It is often expressed not in what one experiences but in what one is, by virtue of one's Whiteness, likely not given to experience (such as the presumption of criminality, common in the experience of those racialized Black; or, the presumption of foreignness, common in the experience of those racialized as either Asian or Latino). And because each and all of us are consciously or subconsciously trained in White Supremacy and in the cultural contents and imperatives of Whiteness, each and all of us benefit from practices aimed at raising awareness of race and racism in our construction of the self.

The construction of Whiteness as dominant emerged (and yet emerges) through the interlocking effects of more or less intentional racializing projects within institutions such as law, religion, politics, science, education, and more. The personal-systemic actions of these institutions combined to create, legitimize, and reinforce the master narrative of White Supremacy, originally as a justification of the systems, politics, and practices of conquest, slavery, and colonization, through which Whiteness was imbued with not merely symbolic cultural value, but substantive material value. As a result, Whiteness has operated as the "standard" human experience, the norm against which all other experiences within the dominant institutions of society are compared and measured. And even into the contemporary era, its substantive, material value has been maintained its currency, compounded by the invisibility of its dynamics for most of the post–Civil Rights era.

Because it has been both the dominant experience and the experience of the numerical majority, Whiteness has been the least examined among all experiences of race. It has been, in that sense, *the invisible racial experience*, the one racial experience defined primarily, and perhaps until quite recently, by one's experience of never having to think about race.

Most of us have encountered the laudable essay "White Privilege: Unpacking the Invisible Knapsack," through which scholar Peggy McIntosh described her efforts to come to terms with the privileges afforded her as a result of her white skin.[11] The power of the essay is in its critical and insightful reflection on the fact that she had to work hard to see her white skin privilege, much in the way that she knew that men had to work to see how their gender afforded them often subtle privileges in the world, and the ways in which it made her life easier in relationship to people of color who did not possess such privilege. Less well known outside of critical race theory discourse is the work of Barbara Flagg, whose writings enlarge upon the idea of white Privilege by exploring precisely how it is that the invisible experience of it, and of white racialization generally, tends to render *transparent* the white racial character of what appear to be "neutral" norms and standards in the legal and broader social world.[12] In using the word "transparent," Flagg refers to "Whites' unconsciousness of Whiteness, and derivatively, to Whites' use of White-specific criteria of decision." She describes the "transparency phenomenon" as "the tendency of Whites not to think about Whiteness, or about norms, behaviors, experiences or perspectives that are White-specific."[13]

White transparency contributes to the unintentional categorization, stereotyping, and marginalization of non-white-racialized people in ways that are subtle and thus require more than the usual capacity for awareness to be seen and for its effects to be sufficiently understood to disrupt. Flagg has argued, for example, that "employing transparently white norms is a form of marginalization because it ensures that non-whites will be assessed less positively than whites, and so has the consequence that whites will retain the bulk of social power and privilege."[14]

Because of these attributes of white experience—the invisibility of whiteness as an identity in a white-dominated world, and the white-but-transparent and so-called neutral perspective that emerges from that invisible racial identity—the lived experience of Whiteness to those racialized as white has been compared to the experience of water to those born as fish. From the perspective of the fish immersed in water, water may be mistaken for not existing at all; rather, it is just "the way things are." Only when one is able to gain experience of "Not Water" does the reality of the water in which one has been swimming come to be seen as not only real but pervasive.

"Not Whiteness"—the experience of racially Othered (or "Non-White") people in the United States—is akin to the experience of the fish that has been often enough thrust outside of the ocean of Whiteness that the awareness of both Whiteness and Not Whiteness is very real. And yet because the experiences between whites and the racialized Others are so different, it is hard for us to communicate our experiences in ways that maintain a sense of common ground. It is imperative, then, that those racialized as white find ways of opening their capacity to see Whiteness as Whiteness.

The teachings and practices of the Buddha provide possible pathways for those of us seeking to better understand race, racism, and the suffering they cause. In the next section, I discuss how some of those practices support a way of being with reality that may be particularly useful in helping us understand how race and racism have shaped all of our lives.

The Four Noble (or Ennobling) Truths

According to legend, the first teachings of the Buddha described the insights he had gained through his own practice of what would come to be known as the Middle Way. These four insights are well known to even the most novice student of Buddhism:

There is suffering.
There is a cause of suffering.
There is an end to suffering.
The end of suffering arises from following the eightfold path.

Beginning with acknowledgment of the pervasiveness of what in Pali is known as *dukkha*—suffering, pain, or dissatisfaction in human life, the Buddha's teachings invite inquiry into the causes of this, and commitment to exploring ways of ending it. Suffering, the teachings suggest, is caused by three dominant reactions to the challenges of human existence—our tendencies to cling to that which is impermanent, to reject that which is present, and to remain ignorant about the true nature of reality. Suffering may be brought to an end by practicing the essential tenets of the Eightfold Path to liberation, which is comprised of Right View, Right Intention, Right Speech, Right Conduct, Right Livelihood, Right Effort, Right Mindfulness, and Right Concentration. Thus, the core of the Buddha's teachings presents suffering as inherent in the human condition and yet capable of being overcome by any one of us by taking up the journey of the Eightfold Path, the first step of which is the development of Right View.

Right View

Right View is traditionally known as the first step along the Eightfold Path. It is the view that comprehends, that truly sees, the interconnectedness of all things and, from there, comprehends all things through the lens of compassion. It is the view that arises from seeing with a heart steeped in lovingkindness and empathy, orientations toward other human beings that arise from the practice of meditation and the allied disciplines (studying the Dharma and practicing in community).

Right View, or Right Understanding, is what results from truly understanding what is known as the Four Noble (or Four Ennobling[15]) truths. But it is also a way of being with reality that supports deepening our release from suffering and thus enhances our lived understanding of The Truths.

Right View is, as leading Zen teacher Suzuki Roshi described it, "seeing things as it is."[16] Vietnamese monk and peace activist Thích Nhất Hạnh described Right View as seeing—and understanding from the level of experience—the Four Noble truths.[17] And Chogyam Rinpoche described Right View as seeing things as the Buddha saw them, with insight and unbiased perception, or seeing things as they are and realizing things as they are including their inter-related, ultimately illusory, and inherently impermanent nature.[18]

Ultimately, Right View arises and is reinforced by living in accordance with the teachings and practices of the Eightfold Path and by taking refuge in the example of the Buddha, the teachings of the Dharma, and the community of the Sangha.

Meditation, practiced in conjunction with the allied disciplines of study and community engagement, supports the arising and re-arising of Right View. Developing the capacity to calm, concentrate, and observe the habits and conditions of the mind provides a solid pathway toward developing insight into the true nature of what we call reality. The practice of meditation helps us to discern the difference between our illusions and clear seeing.

We can be tempted to think that our perceptions, our conditioned views, *are* the "Right Views." Such is the nature of the mind's capacity to delude itself in an effort to maintain a sense of the solid ego, and as a consequence of living the unawakenedlife.

Thus, an important part of our Buddhist or Buddhist-inspired philosophy and practice is the commitment to reflect on our perceptions, including the thoughts that arise in response to what we perceive and the concepts we construct and the actions and lifeways we are tempted to pursue as a result.

As a consequence of the trainings of our culture, the process by which we perceive ourselves and others involves the process of categorizing one another in terms of what we call race and of assigning meaning and differential value to those categories.

Do these perceptions, associated concepts, thoughts, and ideologies lead to actions in the world which cause harm? If so, we might reflect more on the difference between the views to which we have become attached; and Right View—a view that perceives the illusory nature of race—sees the inherent interconnection of so-called separate races, and seeks the compassionate alleviation of suffering that results from the creation and maintenance thereof.

Reflecting on my own experience, through the lens of Right View, I see, understand, and embrace race as an aspect of my own personal identity (i.e., in describing myself, I am apt to say "I am a Black woman"; or "I am a Black-racialized woman"); *and at the very same time* I experience myself as a being in a breathing relationship with an environment I did not create and on which I depend for my existence. I am thus aware of the reality of the illusory nature of the notion of myself as a "separate self," including within that awareness of the illusory nature of myself as "raced" or racialized. Aware of *both* the relative reality of race (i.e., its reality and import in the social world) *and* of "Blackness" arising in relationship to other, differently racialized beings and bodies in the world, I hold my identity lightly, deploying it where useful in service of compassionate understanding in the world (e.g., when describing the meaning and import of the Thirteenth Amendment's enactment during the post–Civil War period known as the Reconstruction to a class of contemporary law students) and relaxing the sense of it where it is not (e.g., when I am floating in the Pacific Ocean).

Through a life of practice and dedication to the path, any one of us may transform our perceptions, feelings, thoughts, concepts, and consciousness into a higher level of consciousness grounded in Right View and the allied insights of the Eightfold Path. Right View supports Right Intention, and Right Action, and thus is essential to ethical engagement with race and racism. It is the foundation for rightly examining the ongoing, dynamic construction of race, and rightly addressing the suffering caused by—or dependently originating from—the ideology and practices of racism.

Dependent Origination and the Development of the Racialized Self

Known in Pali as *paticca-samuppada*, the process of dependent origination emerged as a core insight of the Buddhadharma. The notion of dependent origination, which has its origins in Indian philosophy predating the Buddha, is a theory of causality:

When there is this, that is.
With the arising of this, that arises.
When this is not, neither is that.
With the cessation of this, that ceases.[19]
Thus, all phenomena are both interconnected and impermanent.

Dependent origination captures the essence of how it is that Whiteness and Not Whiteness construct one another. Whiteness depends for its existence on the notion of Not Whiteness. The two concepts co-arise. As George Yancy describes it, "At the heart of whiteness is a profound disavowal: I am not that! It other words, Whiteness is secured by marking what it is not."[20]

Moreover, dependent origination captures the essence of how it is that we come to *Right View*, how we come to see through our illusions and to see the nature of reality.

The arising of awareness of Right View occurs as a result of clear seeing into the nature of reality. That reality which does not require the need of a sense of a separate self is grounded in a sense of open self-less-ness.

Thus, Right View can assist us in deconstructing the idea of a separate self in terms of which so much of traditional Western interpersonal psychology turns.[21]

Throughout the experience of our daily lives, we come into contact with stimuli through the senses and otherwise to which we react. When we experience pleasure, we tend to cling or grasp to continue the experience of pleasure. When we experience displeasure, we push away.

This happens at the level of personal experience, and, when engaged in without insight, leads to an arising of a sense of separate self, and of what we call the ego. While we experience the self conventionally as fixed and relatively stable, in Buddhist psychology the self is understood to be, like all phenomena, constructed out of collected experiences, called heaps or aggregates of phenomena. The five heaps—form, feeling, perception, formation, and consciousness—describe different aspects of our never-ending effort to solidify and make constant our sense of reality that is inherently changing and impermanent.

We are born into the world without a sense of ourselves as separate, a world in which countless identity-forming projects immediately impinge upon us. The hospital records keeper identifies us and certifies each of us by racial categories created by the state—as "White" or "Black," or "Native American/Indian," and so on. The smiling stranger on the street looks into the arms of the mother cradling an infant and asks, "Is the baby a boy or a girl?" In the homes of our family members, in more or less hushed tones, the question is asked, "Is he light skinned like his mother, or darker, like his father?" And everywhere in America, through the media, through our public institutions, the ocean of Whiteness washes over us all.

Consistent with the teaching of dependent origination—"where there is this, that is"—our countless experiences with and reactions to the aggregates—clinging, pushing away, remaining foggy and confused, but at the same time busily creating narratives that give us a false but important sense of comfort—give rise to the sense of ourselves as separate beings.

The teachings passed down through various Buddhist traditions suggest that the particular identities that accrue to our sense of separate selves and to which we hold to more or less consciously come to be experienced by each of us as more or less fixed through our (often unconscious) clinging to what we find pleasurable, averting what we find disagreeable, and remaining confused about the true nature of reality. Our racial identities, including the sense of ego that is at their core, arise through the process of reacting to our environment and constructing an illusory sense of "me and mine" and "you and yours" as a result. Buddhist scholar William Waldron put it this way:

What we commonly think of as our essential "identity" is actually a complex construct generated by misunderstanding, forged by emotional attachments, and secured by appropriating activities. But since such identities are constructed and construed within a radically dynamic and interdependent world they are necessarily unstable and insecure, and thus require repeated reinforcement and protection to persist. We are caught, in short, in an unending, unhealthy feedback cycle consisting of repetitive, compulsive behavioral patterns, i.e., saṃsāra . . . . "Self-identity" is thus not only a construct based upon an ultimately untenable dichotomy between "self" and "other," but it almost inevitably leads to attachment to "us" and "ours" at the expense of "them" and "theirs."[22]

Thus, conventional ego-based personal identity reifies a sense of self and, in the words of the Buddha, of "me, my and mine." Because we are given to believe that we must fend for ourselves in a world of unevenly distributed resources (and this is more often literally true for some of us than it is for others), the development of this sense of self is not only understandable but worthwhile.

Moreover, we are born into social settings in which groups have been identified, cultures formed, and through complex, dynamic social processes have been reinforced and linked with patterns of group-linked resource distribution of longstanding. These patterns—and the social suffering that results—fall along characteristics as race, religion, national origin, and the like. Quite frequently our patterns of ingrouping and outgrouping fall along these conventional lines as well.

And whether we consciously think so or not, these conditionings lie deep within us, and persist even when we consciously believe we feel or think otherwise. The Buddhist concept of "store consciousness" helps us understand more fully how this might be so.

The Role of Store Consciousness

The last of the "heaps" or aggregates that make up the sense of self is consciousness. An aspect of consciousness is what is called by some Buddhists "Store Consciousness" (or "Storehouse Consciousness)."

Store consciousness is considered by some schools of Buddhism to be the base consciousness in all of us. It is comprised of the seeds leftover from past actions, both individual and as transmitted to the individual through the shared consciousness of our cultures. At an individual level, if we meet someone who reminds us of a beloved family member, we will be more likely to react warmly than if we meet someone who reminds us of someone who has treated us cruelly. At the level of culture, if we have been taught to view some people as more valuable than others based on the notion of racial identity, when we meet someone of the presumptively more valued racial identity, we are inclined to react more favorably than if we meet someone of the less valued racial identity.

As the base or foundation for consciousness, it is the foundation for the insightful perceptive awareness that we call Right View. With deep insight and practice, we are able to water the seeds of awareness that lead us away from the false perceptions that arise from a sense of difference tied to racialization of our own and others' bodies. Nevertheless, awareness of the differences that racialization makes in our life experiences can be a doorway or a bridge into deepening awareness of our interconnectedness. Indeed, it can be the very path we travel to a true sense of freedom.

Examining our store consciousness and other deep teachings is not easy. We may find it difficult to admit these deep-seated beliefs. We may believe that, in doing so, we are betraying those closest to us. However, to really reflect on what we have learned from them as children, we can choose new ways of seeing and engaging the world. Doing so is essential to seeing clearly and to creating the capacity to help liberate others.

Seeing "Whiteness," "Non-Whiteness," and "De-racialization" as Practice

Unlearning racism is a practice that requires not merely seeing, or having Right View, but taking actions with intention and persistent effort. But if we decide that this is a path we seek to take as a part of our Buddhist practice, we may indeed take refuge in the practices of seeing, being with, and unlearning racism. By taking refuge in these pathways to insight, we deepen our capacity to make refuge for ourselves and for others that we will meet along the way.

PART 2: MAKING REFUGE AS A PATHWAY TO RACIAL JUSTICE

What Is "Making Refuge"?

Zack Walsh, Edwin Ng, and Ronald Purser have introduced the concept of "Making Refuge" as a means of deepening the conversation about, and practices of engaged, Buddhism. Introducing the term "socially engaged mindfulness interventions," these scholar-activists have encouraged discussion and thought aimed at bringing Buddhism into more intentional engagement with socially mediated suffering and oppression, including the suffering and oppression caused by race and racism.

> We propose the idea of making refuge as a conceptual placeholder and an analytical rubric for identifying the multifaceted ways by which the conditions of trust and safety necessary for living and dying well together may be cultivated

across manifold lifeworlds by the co-inhabitants of a precarious planet. The
work of making refuge is something all of us must perform in differing ways,
and with differing degrees of ease or difficulty, because our shared exposure to
vulnerability is at once a fact of existential–material inequality and injustice.
Exposure to vulnerability, and thus the promise of #makingrefuge, is something
we share-in-difference.[23]

In the summer of 2017, I joined these scholar-practitioners and a small
group of others, including Mushim Patricia Ikeda, Beth Berila, Doshin
Nathan Woods, and David Loy in a "Think Tank" to explore the concept of
Making Refuge. In the following section, I share some of the reflections and
practices that I offered as part of my participation in that group, and some
of the ways I have continued to explore the implications of the invocation
to both Take Refuge and Make Refuge as part of our practice of Buddhism
together.

Honoring and Mindfully Implementing the Contact Hypothesis

One of the ways that "the conditions of trust and safety necessary for living and dying well together may be cultivated" is through bringing people
together across lines of real and perceived difference under conditions of
equality and sanctioned collaboration. Referred to as the Contact Hypothesis,
decades of research has shown, in study after study, that one of the best ways
to reduce bias is to increase the degree of contact between so-called different
groups, and to support them in engaging in meaningful, intergroup work to
accomplish common goals together, from positions of relative equal status
in the work situation, and with the support of those in positions of authority,
customs, or laws.[24]

And yet research and everyday experience has also shown that, given the
history of racism, oppression, segregation, and the efforts to redress these
over the years, people often feel anxious when coming together as relative
equals across differently racialized groups. This difficulty leads to a cycle of
avoidance of contact, and, because of their particular position in the racial
hierarchy and capacity to remain disengaged from dealing with race in their
lives, leads whites to a position of heightened difficulty addressing racism.
This is indicative of what is known as "White Fragility."[25]

Making Refuge through Compassionate
Identity-Brave Meditation and Other Practice

Zenju Earthlyn Manuel, a Black-racialized Buddhist priest, who also identifies as a queer woman, teaches us to allow awareness of our identity-based
suffering to be a bridge to developing the tenderness necessary for full

empathy, for the will for compassionate action, and for awakening itself. She writes:

> Identity should not be dismissed in our efforts toward spiritual awakening. On the contrary, identity is to be explored on the path of awakening. Identity is not merely a political nature; it is inclusive of our essential nature when stripped of distortion.[26]

The notion of the epistemological centrality of situated living is one that women of color have long brought to discussions of spirituality, freedom, and liberation. When we create space for one another to explore our lived experience, we learn new ways of being free. For example, Black-racialized lesbian female poet and activist Audre Lorde wrote about the power of embodied feeling—what she referred to as "the erotic"—to give us a sense of our own agency, inherent interconnectedness, and capacity for self-liberation and liberation for a broader oppressed world:

> But when we begin to live from within outward, in touch with the power of [living] within ourselves, and allowing that power to inform and illuminate our actions upon the world around us then we begin to be responsible to ourselves in the deepest sense. For as we begin to recognize our deepest feelings, we begin to give up, of necessity, being satisfied with suffering and self-negation, and with the numbness which so often seems like their only alternative in our society. Our acts against oppression become integral with self, motivated and empowered from within.[27]

More recently, Zenju Earthlyn Manuel has written about the need for an embodied practice of coming home, of making sanctuary wherever we find ourselves.[28] These writers join with a growing number of Black Buddhist teachers who call for teaching and practice communities that are race-aware, and even radically so.[29] An essential aspect of this work in a world built by racism is the creation of communities in which we can regularly practice working together to deconstruct our biases and experience embodied connection. Through myriad practices that might be brought to bear with the goal of Making Refuge, we may, in a real sense, rehumanize ourselves and support the rehumanization of others. What follows is a brief exploration of a few such practices as an indication of how this might be so.

Creating Diverse and Racially Just Practice Communities

The personal practice of addressing mindfulness of bias and racism will be unique for each of us. Each of us enters into this aspect of our lives differently positioned and practiced in noticing and investigating this aspect of our life experience. Nevertheless, we tend to have one thing in common: for most of us, the work of addressing our conditionings around race and racism is not easy. Thus, thought and practice must be intentionally devoted to establishing the capacity to work with these issues in diverse communities. While a full discussion of how we may create such communities is beyond the scope of this chapter, some of the core pillars of the work are:

1. Developing the commitment to seeing race and racism, to practicing safe and courageous ways of examining racial bias as a part of the construction of the ego and the self.
2. Engaging in practices of community-building that permit the experience of a sense of safe and caring community as a support for the work of seeing race and racism.
3. Engaging in practices of racial awareness-raising and bias reduction, and in the allied disciplines of study and community-based learning that support the deconstruction of notions of race, of Whiteness, and of racism at every level.

Once we have grounded ourselves in these and other foundations for the work, we turn to practices specifically aimed at working together to minimize our attachments and other habits around race and racism. What follows are a few such examples of practices that may support us in both Taking and Making Refuge in racial awareness work: (1) sitting in inquiry, (2) mindful storytelling, and (3) mindful study in the allied disciplines of multicultural teaching and learning. All three of these practices will support us in both Taking and Making Refuge in racial awareness work.

"Sitting in Inquiry" Practice

Sitting together, which involves inquiring about our lived experience of race, what I call "Sitting in Inquiry," assists us in opening up what social psychologists call "blindspots": dimensions of experience obscured by the conditionings that arise from habits of ignorance, avoidance, or attachment to a view regarding race in the world.

I offer these practices not to beginning mindfulness practitioners, but among those who have already had some degree of mindfulness practice and have been exposed to Buddhist or related teachings and understandings about the nature of the constructed self and of reality itself.

From a place of basic understanding about how the mind works, I invite reflections aimed at turning toward the particular workings we have each experienced around the notion of race. I encourage mindful reflection—noticing bodily sensations, emotions, thoughts, images, or narratives that arise in response to prompts such as:

Q: How do you react to being asked to examine social identity and bias *in our own life and world*?

Q: What are your blindspots? How have they been shaped, reinforced by places and spaces in your life?

Q: How can you become more aware of these biases and their effects?

And:

Q: When it comes to race, what habits of mind, body, being do you notice in yourself? How have you been conditioned to see, be with, and navigate a world in which you know that racism exists?

Q: What suffering have you been *conditioned* to see? What suffering have you been *willing* to see? What are you experiencing *now*?

Q: What suffering have you *not been willing* to see? What *are you right now not willing to feel*?

In examining what arises, we bring care, tenderness, and self-compassion, creating the capacity for nonjudgmental awareness of aspects of our experience that we have been trained to reject. Doing so invites new ways of being with the reality of race and racism in our lives, and with its manifold effects.

As we share what arises in group settings, we deepen our capacity for empathy, and for re-experiencing communities comprised in part through the ideologies and practices of racialized Othering or difference. For purposes of deepening and maintaining the focus, during this practice, on developing greater spaciousness with interior experience, with the support of others, I have found that certain guidelines are essential as supports. At a minimum, I counsel adherence to the important mindful dialogue practices of:

1. speaking first and foremost from our own embodied experience, identifying our present bodily sensations, thoughts, emotions ("my heart is pounding," "I feel a sinking feeling in my stomach," etc.);
2. refraining, as much as possible, from analyzing Others in the room (in colloquial terms, I agree to "stay on my side of the net");
3. noticing and naming when we are interpreting direct experience (e.g., "I noticed that you chose a seat on the other side of the room. And I felt myself feeling embarrassed and wondered if I was being rejected. My story about this is that . . .");
4. questioning others from a place of genuine curiosity.

We begin sitting together, often with our chairs in a circle, a format which has been shown to reinforce feelings of trust and mutuality. We sit in silence, reflecting on each prompt. As we listen to the words, we notice and silently name the emotions we are feeling in the body, noting bodily sensations and feelings, and then we discuss the thoughts and stories that are arising.

If we speak, we are speaking from the place of our grounded, embodied, and lived experience. We try to remain as objective as possible. "I observed . . ."; "When I heard you say . . . ." In the course of our sharing, we may note the interpretations that we are bringing into the situation, using the first-person: "I found myself thinking that . . ." or "the story we are telling ourselves when we hear this is . . . ." And in this way we see, name, and reflect on the process by which we are constructing racial and other meanings in real time.

Finally, as in invitation to others, we name what *curiosity* arises in us.

Mindful Storytelling

Not infrequently, the practice of mindful "Sitting in Inquiry" gives rise to or elicits the desire to place our experiences in greater context. We want to tell stories. We want to define terms. Relying on the capacity to listen with mindfulness and to speak mindfully, we may practice developing the capacity for sharing and reflecting on the "stories" that reflect our experience with race and racism. These are the component elements of what I call "Mindful Storytelling Practices."

Over the years, I have shared my own stories, and invited the sharing of stories from others in the room. For example, I share stories of my experience as a cisgendered woman, racialized as Black, who is now (though I was not always) a member of the upper-middle class, stories which reveal that this particular combination of identity characteristics tends to be confounding for many people. As just one example, I share how I once opened the door to accept a large vase filled with flowers, sent by the dean of my school to Professor Magee on the occasion of my being granted tenure.

I opened the door of my home one afternoon—an apartment in a nearly all-White neighborhood. There I was as a petite Black woman wearing the sweats which were my typical Saturday-at-home attire.

The deliveryman gazed at me. "Flowers for Professor Magee," he said.

I reached out and towards him, preparing to take the vase. "I am Professor Magee," I said.

Clearly somewhat taken aback, the hidden ground of his preconceptions temporarily shook, the man pulled the vase back just a bit rather than release it to me.

"Are you *sure?*" he asked.

And lest I allow any incorrect assumptions to go uncorrected: the delivery-man was a Black man.

I tell the story of my experience on the other side, too, of being a young woman who grew up in the South at a time when it was black and white and there were few people around who did not speak English, and realizing, on moving to California, that I reacted—not altogether with welcome—when I found myself surrounded by people speaking a variety of "different" languages.

I am not proud of the evidence that I have seen within myself that I carry biases like everyone else. But the truth is that we have all been trained in the pervasive teachings of what sociologist Joe Feagin calls the White Racial Frame—the way of interpreting the world that results from centuries of White Supremacist perception, thought, emotion, and conceptualization.[30] In some sense, this inheritance is central to what it means to be "American." By admitting that I, too, have been deeply influenced by the White Frame, that I, too, see the world through biased perceptual lenses, and sharing "stories" that show the persistence of this, we assist in creating spaces within which others may allow their own truths to well up—as tears in their eyes, which may be revealing the in-the-moment experience of "waking up" through emotional awareness; or, as words of admission that they feel safe in exposing to the light of accountability.

Such recognitions and revelations assist us in coming home together to a place where we can know, from inside and between ourselves, what we who stand for freedom and justice for all are truly "up against." The specific work that any one of us must do to become more aware of the ways that race and Whiteness influence our perceptions in subtle ways will vary. And yet whatever the degree of our conditioning in favor of Whiteness or White framing, we can better recognize, investigate, and deconstruct our racial-izing practices through mindfulness-based practices. I describe some of the practices that assist us in this work in a section to come. For now, suffice it to say that by helping us to wake up to the illusory nature of race, and to the attachments and aversions that fuel racism, mindfulness meditation and the allied disciplines may help us with the aspects of the project of minimizing our reliance on race and racial categorizations that present themselves in our own lives. And from there, we can begin to practice together in ways that reflect the aspirations to justice behind the intention of "never again," and demonstrate the application of mindfulness as a means of dismantling race and racism. Such is the practice of Making Refuge, one commitment at a time, one moment in the practice of undoing our biases after another, together.

Mindful Study in the Allied Disciplines of
Multicultural Teaching and Learning

Aware of the capacity for mindful teaching and learning to advance through and by reference to objective or external sources, we commit to study. We read analyses of those who have studied race relations in our culture. We explore terms that arise that we have not heard before. Seeing and becoming comfortable with what we do not know in this area, we take some time to learn, for example, a bit more about the phenomenology of race (and especially, because it is the least studied, of Whiteness), about White Racial Frame, "Race as a Social Construct," the "Contact Hypothesis," "Microaggressions," "White Fragility," and so on. Understanding the importance of context—of placing our own and others' experiences in a broader field of understanding which includes relevant culture in time and geographic space—we devote time to studying aspects of history and experience that we have not learned, especially histories affecting ourselves and members of our communities of practice and daily life. In this way we may discern how best to interpret, understand, practice, and teach the applications of the Buddha relevant to our particular situation in these times.[31]

Practices such as the foregoing—Sitting in Inquiry, Mindful Storytelling, and Mindful Study—are not easy. They require specific, deep, and ongoing commitments to doing the work of personal consciousness-raising and transformation. They require us to move into vulnerability with intentionality and courage and with the aim of addressing racism and racial bias as an aspect of our lived experience in a world in which the illusions of race are real in their consequences, especially in terms of how race continues to affect our chances in life a great deal.

And because we are each differently situated by virtue of our multifaceted social identities, we will each hear the call to move into this sort of vulnerability differently. We may each, and quite legitimately, require different conditions of support if we are to move toward vulnerability in a given space, community, and moment—whether in carefully curated, identity-based practice groups or learning communities, or in integrated groups.

Thus, the work of Making and Taking Refuge is indeed work. It requires intentional and committed effort to bring awareness to how it is that race is made and remade in our own lives, and how racism is produced by and within even Buddhist institutions. It requires work of the sort not yet commonly required or even expected of those who practice Buddhism. It does not arise naturally as a result of the practice of mindfulness meditation. But working to raise our capacity to be with one another in our vulnerability is, I believe, necessary for the work of moving toward a more deeply integrated and loving community. Indeed, it is being together with one another in our vulnerability that is one of the important drivers of the work of building empathy, care, and trust. I offer the foregoing as a means of opening the door to your own reflections about how the practices and teachings of Buddhism might support us in deconstructing our notions of race and reconstructing the habits and conditionings we have all imbibed in a world dominated by Whiteness. May these reflections be of benefit to each and all in a world in which too many have suffered far too greatly as a result of the myriad delusions born of racism, White Supremacy, and other seductive identity-based states of confusion.

CONCLUSION

Deepening our capacities to see racism clearly in all of its forms and variations, from personal to systemic, and deconstructing largely invisible aspects of our lives like the practices and dynamics of Whiteness cannot happen overnight. But in time, our dedication to meditation and the allied disciplines of study and engaged awareness-raising support us in deepening our practices for living more respectfully and indeed lovingly together. By engaging with race and racism more effectively through Buddhist-inspired practices, we open doorways to meeting the great challenges inherent in the work of deconstructing the delusions, dehumanizing patterns, and practices and teachings of Whiteness and White Supremacy and of reconstructing our communities as refuges, for us all.

NOTES

1. Christina Feldman, "Dependent Origination," *Barre Center for Buddhist Studies*, Spring 1999, available at: https://www.buddhistinquiry.org/article/dependent-origination/.

2. Thích Nhất Hạnh, *The Heart of the Buddha's Teachings: Transforming Suffering into Peace, Joy, and Liberation* (Broadway Books, 1999).

3. Andrew Olendzski, *Unlimiting Mind: The Radically Experiential Psychology of Buddhism* (Wisdom Publications, 2010).

4. Ronald Dworkin, *Taking Rights Seriously* (Harvard University Press, 1978).

5. Mahzarin R. Banaji and Anthony G. Greenwald, *Blindspot: The Hidden Biases of Good People* (Bantam Books, 2016).

6. Adam Lueke and Bryan Gibson, "Mindfulness Meditation Reduces Implicit Age and Race Bias: The Role of Reduced Automaticity in Responding," *Social, Psychological and Personality Science* 6, no. 3 (2014): 284–291. Alexander Stell and Tom Farsides, "Brief Lovingkindness Meditation Reduces Racial Bias Meditated by Positive Other-Regarding Emotions," *Motivation and Emotion* 40, no. 1 (2015): 140–147.

7. Both unpublished studies reviewed by the author and informal interviews conducted by the author indicate that mindfulness meditation, even for long-term practitioners, may not always reduce bias.

8. Eknath Eswaran, *The End of Sorrow: The Bhagavad Gita for Daily Living* (Nilgiri Press, 2010), 5.

9. Philip Mazzocco, "Talking Productively about Race in the Colorblind Era," *Kirwan Institute Research Report*, January 2015, http://kirwaninstitute.osu.edu/docs/ki-race-talk-0115-05.pdf.

10. Tsoknyi Rinpoche, *Open Heart, Open Mind: Awakening the Power of Essence Love* (Harmony, 2012).

11. Peggy McIntosh, *White Privilege: Unpacking the Invisible Knapsack* (Philadelphia, PA: Independent School, 1990).

12. Barbara Flagg, *Was Blind But Now I See: White Transparency* (New York: New York University Press, 1997).

13. Barbara Flagg, "'Was Blind, But Now I See': White Race Consciousness and the Requirement of Discriminating Intent," *Michigan Law Review* 91, no. 5 (1993): 953–1017.

14. Barbara Flagg, "On Selecting Black Women as Paradigms for Race and Discrimination Analyses," *Berkeley Journal of Gender, Law and Justice* 10, no. 1 (1995): Article 6.

15. Stephen Batchelor, *Secular Buddhism: Imagining the Dharma in an Uncertain World* (New Haven, CT: Yale University Press, 2017).

16. Suzuki Roshi, "Transcripts," *San Francisco Zen Center*, September 8, 1967, http://suzukiroshi.sfzc.org/archives/index.cgi/670908BU.html?seemore=y.

17. Hạnh, *Heart of the Buddha's Teachings*, 23.

18. See Dzogchen Ponlop Rinpoche, "Guide to the Three-Yana Journey," *Lion's Roar: Buddhist Wisdom for Our Time*, February 15, 2013, https://www.lionsroar.com/guide-to-the-three-yana-journey/.

19. Bhikku Bhodhi, ed., *The Connected Discourses of the Buddha* (Wisdom Publications, 2003).

20. George Yancy, *Look: A White! Philosophical Essays on Whiteness* (Philadelphia: Temple University Press, 2012), 20.

21. Michael St. Clair, *Object Relations and Self Psychology: An Introduction*, 3rd ed. (Brooks Cole, 1999).

22. William Waldron, "Indian Thought and Social Science on the Travails of Identity." Unpublished paper, on file with author.

23. Z. Walsh, E. Ng, and R. Purser, "Mindfulness is Inherently Political," in *#MakingRefuge*, June 24, 2017, https://www.makingrefuge.net/news/.

24. Gordon Allport, *The Nature of Prejudice,* 25 Anniversary Edition (Basic Books, 1979).

25. Robin DiAngelo, "White Fragility," *The International Journal of Critical Pedagogy* 3, no. 3 (2011): 54–70.

26. Zenju Earthlyn Manuel, *The Way of Tenderness* (Wisdom Publications, 2015).

27. Audre Lorde, *Sister Outsider* (Crossing Press, 2007), 58.

28. Zenju Earthlyn Manuel, *Sanctuary: A Meditation on Home, Homelessness, and Belonging* (Wisdom Publications, 2018).

29. Jasmine Syedullah, Lama Rod Owens, and Angel Kyodo Williams, *Radical Dharma: Talking Race, Love, and Liberation* (North Atlantic Books, 2016); Rhonda Magee, "Teaching Mindfulness with Mindfulness of Race and Other Forms of Diversity," in *Resources for Teaching Mindfulness: International Handbook*, eds. Donald McCown, Diane Reibel, and Marc S. Micozzi (Springer Cham, 2017).

30. Joe Feagin, *The White Racial Frame: Centuries of Racial Framing and Counterframing* (New York: Routledge, 2013).

31. Tsoknyi Rinpoche and Eric Swanson, *Open Heart, Open Mind* (Harmony, 2012).

Chapter 14

A Buddhist Phenomenology of the White Mind

Joy Cecile Brennan

The summer I turned fifteen, I attended a month-long class for high school students at a university in my hometown. To get there each day, I took a bus from my white suburb on the west side of town, transferring downtown to a second bus that carried me through the black populated east side of town, arriving finally at the university in a racially diverse east-side suburb. One day on the second bus, where I was almost always the only white person, a fellow passenger struck up a conversation with me. Here's how my memory shows him to me: a suit coat and pants, ill-fitting and shabby; overly skinny frame, with a head that seemed too big for his body; missing some teeth, others crooked and yellowing. In other words, he was, to me, a "poor black man," a type I had been unwittingly trained to take as a "natural feature" of the world.

As he began to speak with me, I felt uncomfortable, but I had also been trained to be polite. He asked how I was. I politely replied. He asked where I was headed. I politely replied. He asked if I was a religious person. I told him I was "spiritual but not religious." About five to ten minutes of this, and my stop arrived.

When I stood to walk up the aisle, he extended his hand to shake mine. I extended mine back. When my hand met his, the feeling of something strange in my palm prompted me to look down. My hand now held a crumpled one-dollar bill. I looked at him amazed, and stammered in polite protest: "Oh, well, no, that's not necessary . . . thank you but I don't need this." He smiled and waved me on: "No, no, that's for you, you take that, that's for you. God bless you." I thanked him hesitatingly, and turned to walk up the aisle, the red of embarrassment overtaking my face.

Up to that point, I had not been sure if the other fifteen or so people on the bus were paying attention to this. But as I walked up the aisle, I felt eyes on me. The driver pulled the crank to open the door, wishing me a good day. Then, as my feet hit the pavement, I heard peals of laughter suddenly erupt, seemingly from the whole bus. I looked back at the driver, whose head was now down and shaking in restrained laughter, his hand slapping his own thigh in delight. Now on the sidewalk facing the bus, I looked up through the windows. It seemed to me that all the people on the bus were laughing at me. I was astonished, humiliated, and angry. What was going on?

I cannot say for sure what of this did happen and what is embroidered by the doings of memory as shaped by my white consciousness. But I know that as I stood on the pavement the thought dawned that it was I—the middle-class white person—who society expected, and who I expected, to have one-dollar bills to give out, and that he, the poor black man, was the right kind of recipient of those small acts of giving. And each time I remember the event, as I have many times over the intervening few decades, I am again startled by the insight that every day I sat on the bus thinking that I could see and know them—the black people on the bus—but that in some way they could not see or know me. And every time I think of the event, these two thoughts lead me to believe that I know exactly how to interpret what happened: this man had, politely and with good humor, flipped the tables on me, and the whole bus enjoyed the scene. In this interpretive moment, I feel that even I can see the humor in it, and I feel grateful to him for showing me what I did not know, or showing me *that* I did not know.

But then, every time I resolve that this is what happened and every time I allow myself to laugh at myself, a sense of disorientation overtakes me and I find myself swimming in interpretive possibilities: he was mentally disturbed and the other people were laughing at me for being so foolish as to talk to him; he thought it was interesting that this teenaged white girl was on this bus and was acting as an elder, offering me money as a sign of support; he was a religious man and interested in the brief exchange we had on religion and spirituality; and so on. I dismiss each in turn, but then each appears again in my mind as a live possibility. And now I accept that this epistemic disorientation is the point: the tables had indeed been turned, at least insofar as I was knocked from the position of "knower" conferred on me by my whiteness, into the disorientation of extreme unknowing. And that is where I remain. It has been amply demonstrated that whiteness is a construct that is socially, emotionally, psychologically, and somatically reproduced in the group of people who thereby come to be known as—and to know ourselves as—white. My experience on that bus is how I know that by the age of fifteen, I was constructed through and through as white. The general question is then: What can Buddhist thought tell us about how this construct functions? And what therapy can Buddhist traditions of practice recommend as a method of stripping the power from this construct, of exposing it for what it is, of *de*-constructing it?

More specifically, I should like to examine the social epistemology of ignorance that shapes the perceptions and conceptions of whites. Following Charles Mills's work on racialized epistemologies, this chapter examines the epistemic asymmetry between whites and blacks, and the phenomenology of the white mind that manifests the white side of this asymmetry. Mills's work takes up the form of critique that feminist standpoint epistemologists have used to critique the male-gendered subject-formation of the normative knower. In applying this method to race, Mills shows that whites misperceive both Black people and ourselves, taking ourselves as possessors of correct cognition while in fact undergoing, as he has written, "self-deception, bad faith, evasion and misrepresentation."[1] The corollary to this is that black people are racially habituated toward veridical cognition, particularly of us whites, of the history and structure of white supremacy, and, crucially, of how we perceive them. I will call the white subject's side of this epistemic asymmetry a form of "perfect misrecognition": whiteness confers on the white subject a supreme confidence in his/her ability to grasp the world accurately while also causing that white subject to get the world, and his/her white subjectivity's own positioning as a knower of it, exactly backward. Hence, on that bus, I constructed the situation inaccurately. From the perspective of my white mode of cognitive framing I assumed that I "knew" my fellow passengers, all black people. Yet, given my retrospective look at those events on the bus, it appears that I did not know them at all, but they in fact knew me through my construction as white. What is going on here?

This chapter offers a theory of the socially, psychologically, and somatically inscribed epistemology of ignorance that describes how white subjects experience themselves as knowers through appeal to the Mahāyāna Buddhist claim that the world characterized by suffering and delusion is "mind-only." While commonly taken by contemporary interpreters to be a form of idealism consistent with some variation of idealism from within the history of early modern Europe (itself a form of perfect misrecognition that the field of Anglophone Buddhist philosophy, mostly white, has produced), the mind-only claim is not a static assertion about how the world is. Instead, it is a diagnosis. It describes the world of delusion, the world whose overcoming is liberation itself. The mind-only position claims that both a person and her world are essentially historical: that the subject of experience and the object-world toward which she experiences herself to be oriented are entirely caused by, in fact co-created by, and as a consequence saturated with, the past.[2] But the mind-only claim also asserts that one function of this shared historicity of subject and object is to conceal itself. The very forces of the past that manifest the present world also collude to encourage the subject to evade recognition of her shared past with the object-world. Instead of showing forth the temporal-layeredness of person and world—the way that past actions, past emotions, past thoughts, past interactions serve as the causes that produce the present moment's subject and her contemporary object-world—the mind is mistaken for exclusive subjective awareness, which presents itself as transparent and luminous, as a subject and scribe that takes in experience without shaping it, and is thus taken as a reliable source of knowledge.

Therefore, in mind-only thought, mind itself possesses two features key to the analysis of white subjectivity and white ignorance in particular: a cumulative historicity shared by a subject experiencer and her object-world *and* a simultaneous denial of this shared historicity through the felt sense that the mind itself is a translucent and luminous vehicle of knowledge acquisition. These two features, when used to analyze white racialized ignorance, offer a phenomenology of the white mind. The sickness of mind-only is treated, in the early Yogācāra literature that initiates the tradition of mind-only thought, with two liberating practices: the practice of thoroughly knowing (*parijñā*), which refers to recognition of the true features of mind by way of seeing what mind is *not* (that it is *not* transparent, that it is *not* individual, that the affordances of cognition do *not* result in knowledge), and the practice of abandonment, the dropping off of those features. How then can we reach toward the deconstruction of whiteness by leaning back into the kind of non-knowing that abandonment might bring about?

To start seeing how mind-only thought can give an analysis of a racialized subject, and in particular a phenomenology of the subject of a racialized epistemology of ignorance—a willfully blind white person who yet takes herself to be a normative knower—it helps to think through two distinct paradigms of the exemplary Buddhist accomplished figure. The Buddhist tradition, generally speaking, considers the end point of the tradition's practices to be the condition of awakening or enlightenment. Awakening is essentially liberative. It is freedom from cyclic existence (*saṃsāra*) itself, where that existence is characterized by suffering and impermanence. But it is also intrinsically a state of supreme knowledge, since the tradition considers the acquisition of some kind of knowledge that, in turn, garners perfect cognition to be determinative of awakening. It is for this reason that a Buddha, an awakened one, is said to "see reality as it is." So, awakening in Buddhist traditions of thought and practice is the supreme epistemic achievement, and this achievement brings about liberation from suffering.

What kind of being is it that the tradition takes to possess this supreme knowledge? Who is the tradition's ideal epistemological subject? And what structures of power and modes of relationship to others are inscribed in this notion of the exemplary realized figure? Two such paradigmatic figures from within Buddhist traditions are striking in their contrast. The first comes from narrative traditions and philosophical discourses about the historical Buddha himself, largely drawn from the South Asian Buddhist context. Who was he? What features characterized his body and mind? How did he look and act? How did he strike other people and what effect did he have on them? As John Powers has shown, the Indian Buddhist tradition's own expressions of the exemplary figure of the historical Buddha represent him as a "great man" in every sense of the word. His physical beauty and athletic prowess are unparalleled, he possesses superhuman powers like walking on water, levitation, and super-sensory perception, his attractive physique overwhelms women and other men alike. His supreme manliness is even signified by his possession of one of the thirty-two distinguishing marks of any Buddha, a "penis enclosed in a sheath like a royal stallion."[3] He is a bull, a lion, a king.

This vision of a Buddha as the supreme physical subject and the supremely powerful subject inscribes into his body and his social or cosmological station the tradition's view of him as the ideal epistemological subject. It does this by drawing on and normativizing two important features of the historical Buddha's life: that he was born into the ruling caste and that he was a man. Although the historical Buddha himself rejected caste as an organizing system for his religious community and established a women's monastic community alongside that for men, the caste-based system that equated knowledge and purity with the higher castes, and the gender hierarchy that made men the normative subjects of both power and knowledge were preserved through the tradition's depictions of the Buddha's body, powers, and actions. By means of this conjoining of ideal social and cosmological status and ideal physical manliness with ideal epistemological subjecthood, the tradition connects the Buddha's position at the top of existing social and cosmological hierarchies to his possession of supreme knowledge. They seem to serve as signs of one another: we ordinary beings know that he possesses supreme knowledge precisely because of his social and cosmological dominance, and likewise we know that he is rightly dominant in those realms because he is, by definition, the possessor of ultimate knowledge.

As Buddhist ideas, narratives, images, and practices move across space and time, the ideal subject of the tradition transforms. In medieval China, we find a Buddhist image of the ideal knower that stands as a challenge and even rebuke to the Buddha as the bull-man, the king whose lion's roar expresses his ultimate knowledge. The Chan school, which develops beginning in the fifth century in China, breaks the logic of this ideal. In the Chan hagiographical tradition, the ultimate knower is the non-knower, the one who relinquishes any fixed position from which he may confidently pursue knowledge and gain power. Instead, he lives amid a constant reversal: a reversal of understanding, a reversal of power, a reversal of life and death, a reversal of self and other, a reversal of knower and known. The images that capture him are puzzling because they express this reversal: they might mix that which we now call natural with the man-made, or mix the high with the low, the animate with the inanimate.[4] The Chan master as non-knower is socially ambiguous. He is still usually gendered male, but otherwise he has no clear fixed social position. Sometimes he is from a wealthy or educated background, one that he has largely abandoned in pursuit of the Buddha way. But he is equally likely of humble origins. He tends to be described as uninterested in marking himself with the signs of prestige, though he may do so when circumstances call for it. Thus, the stories in which he figures may find him in humble or anonymous stations, or rather appearing before the emperor.[5] We cannot, in other words, read his body and station as evidence of his knowledge, or vice versa, as we could with that idealized image of the historical Buddha as kingly knower. The images and stories of these Chan masters are often called iconoclastic because they shatter the Buddhist norm of what a true inheritor of the awakened understanding of a Buddha should be like. Instead of a person with kingly self-possession of his faculties and the power to make everyone who encounters him recognize his supreme knowledge, the Chan iconoclast is portrayed as limited, bound by time, place and circumstance, appearing sagely to those who understand him but a simple fool to those who do not.

These two distinct representations of the Buddhist tradition's normative epistemological subject function by different logics. The first shares the operative logic of the normative epistemology in what Charles Mills has referred to as the "*racially hierarchical* polity" that instantiates the global white domination of which our contemporary world is heir and sustainer.[6] In both contexts, the signs of who is considered a knower exactly replicate the signs that tell us who possesses material, social, and political power. The kingly Buddha as knower can be read as reinforcing both the class and gender hierarchies of the historical Buddha's time. In the racially hierarchical polity, whiteness is a sign of knowledge and blackness a sign of ignorance, and the epistemic authority of whiteness is usually required to back up any claim to knowledge put forth by a nonwhite person.

The Chan master as non-knower, on the other hand, stymies the logic of reading body, station, and power as signs of knowledge, and vice versa, by turning the ideal epistemological subject into a non-knower. This non-knowing is understood in Chan/Zen thought as linked to the concept of no-mind, which itself arises within Mahāyāna philosophy, and in the mind-only school in particular, as the result of a number of conceptual pressures weighing on Buddhist philosophy. The major tension was between two distinct orientations toward knowledge itself that were present in Buddhist philosophy from its earliest days, and frequently found right alongside one another. These two orientations are moreover reflected in the two distinct images of the ideal Buddhist subject and knower just outlined. The Buddha as supreme physical subject, supremely placed in caste and cosmology, and possessing supreme knowledge reflects an inclination in Buddhist thought toward a certain kind of trust in the affordances of the cognitive faculties. The Chan master as non-knower, who relinquishes not just supremacy of any sort, but also any claim to knowing with certainty and fixity who he is or what the world around him is like, reflects Buddhist thought's hesitancy about the dispensations of cognition, precisely because the world a being encounters through cognition is understood to be already shaped by the karmic inheritance of that being, and is thus precisely *not* to be trusted as a guide to knowledge.

The first tendency, the inclination toward epistemic confidence in the affordances of experience, appears to be engrained in the framework for describing conditioned reality that is employed in non-Mahāyāna Abhidharma. This philosophical tradition analyzes all aspects of what Buddhist thought takes to be constructed reality, including the arising of, causal connectivity between, and cessation of cognitive events, by way of appeal to what is called the analysis of phenomena.[7] Such analysis is an investigative process whereby the individual who has undertaken the path to awakening examines the contents of her life-world, including inner states and external objects, to discern things like its features, the kinds of phenomena that habitually arise, what kinds of phenomena tend to give rise to what other kinds, whether or not the phenomena that arise are wholesome (in the sense of conducive to awakening) or unwholesome, and so on. This process is categorized within the Buddhist Abhidharma traditions as one of the seven limbs of awakening, or one of the seven practices that itself leads to the awakening and liberation from suffering that is the goal of the Buddhist path. For our purposes, the upshot of this practice is that it demonstrates the Buddhist commitment to taking cognition—how the world appears in our experiences—as a guide on the path and thus as conferring knowledge.

But this commitment exists in tension with another major commitment of Buddhist philosophy. The whole arc of Buddhist philosophy tends toward the notion that unless we have experienced the kind of epistemic achievement that the Buddha experienced, our experiences are essentially delusional. For this feature of the tradition, it is not just one's interpretations of one's own experiences that are problematic. Rather, the very objects that are presented in cognition are themselves the results of habit-formations, one's long-nurtured and deep-seated distortions that serve to mold not just experience, but even the inner and outer objects that one encounters, which is to say one's whole life-world. Thus, the path requires my recognition that in some very real sense the things that my mind delivers to me and holds up for me to examine are themselves not vehicles to knowledge, but obstacles preventing knowledge.

Here we join up with the Yogācāra-Vijñānavāda or mind-only school of Mahāyāna Buddhist thought. To understand this tradition's eponymous claim that the constructed world characterized by suffering is "mind-only" requires two things: knowing what is meant here by "mind" and situating the "mind-only" claim within the path context in which it originally appears. We best understand what mind means by understanding what the "only" is meant to eliminate. As Sonam Kachru has shown with regard to the work of one of the greatest early expositors of mind-only, the fourth-century scholar-monk Vasubandhu, the mind-only claim itself takes a position on the tension just described: the tension between trust in what the faculties afford us and suspicion of the same. Kachru shows that the "only" does not eliminate material things from the list of existent things, but rather names as false one entire approach to understanding how experience comes about: the idea that the world is constituted by discrete objects that, when they come into contact with a mental organ, give forth an experience. That is, Vasubandhu's mind-only rejects the idea that knowledge itself consists in what the subject identified with the organ of cognition experiences through cognitive episodes. Instead, Kachru carefully shows how Vasubandhu's mind-only thought provides an alternative causal account, one in which a subject of experience and the world toward which she is oriented arise together as a joint effect in a beginningless sequence of causes.[8] On this account, the experiences a subject takes himself to undergo are caused not by the object-world he encounters (where "object-world" includes things we understand to be inner objects, like thoughts, feelings, memories, and habits), but are rather caused by the same thing that causes the object-world that the subject encounters in experience. This thing is, quite simply, the past.

Accordingly, three features characterize the "mind" of mind-only. First, the mind is historical. It is through and through shaped by and saturated with the actions, experiences, feelings, thoughts, and so on, that occurred in the past. To be a minded being is to be an essentially historical being. Second, despite its essential historicity, the mind tends to "believe" in the phenomenological presentation of experience, wherein a subject-self experiences itself to encounter a world, and experiences its own cognitions to be caused by that encounter. In other words, the mind identifies with the cognitive faculty and then takes that faculty as translucent, as not standing in the way of but instead straightforwardly facilitating the acquisition of knowledge. This, in mind-only thought, is what the Buddha meant when he said that delusion lies at the base of all conditioned (*saṃsāric*) experience. It is also a critique of that other tendency of the Buddhist tradition, the ones that trusts the faculties as vehicles toward knowledge. Third, the mind is collective. Buddhist thought has from its origin sought to account for the fact that the phenomenal quality of subjectivity is shared across groups and that these groups of beings encounter different kinds of object worlds in their experiences. For Buddhist thought, the salient classes are cosmological: humans and animals, hungry ghosts, gods, and the denizens of the hell realms. Taking the cosmos to demarcate different worlds, we can expand this notion of cosmos to the different worlds that groups of human beings experience, here the world of the white person and the world of the black person. To assert "mind-only" is, then, to assert that our subjectivities and our object-worlds are shaped through and through by the past, that despite this there is an ego-identification with the cognitive organ such that we mistake the causes of our experience for our object-world itself, rather than the forces of the past, and that these first two features are shared among a group of beings.

The mind-only claim is, moreover, put forth in early Yogācāra texts as part of a path process. As with other Buddhist path formulations, this one includes distinct steps which, taken together, are thought to constitute the path that moves a person from the condition of delusion to that of correct cognition, or awakening to "reality as it is." In this path process, three stations or conditions are linked by the two liberating practices of thoroughly knowing and abandoning.[9] The starting station on this path is the condition of delusion, characterized here as a condition of accepting that there are "objects." The middle position is where the subject recognizes that there are no "objects," but that everything is "mind-only." That last step is called "no-mind," an achievement brought about by the abandonment of the historically conditioned, apparently transparent, collective "mind." The starting point, the station of accepting that there are "objects" is the condition of delusion within which the subject is identified with the mind as cognitive faculty. This subject takes her experience to be produced by contact with her object-world; the weight of history is thought to have no bearing. The middle position is mind-only, which is identification of that first position *as* delusion. At this step, the subject starts to see and live within the reality of historical and collective embeddedness, the reality that cognition is itself shaped by this history and this collectivity. And the last position is "no-mind," achieved through the dropping of or abandonment of that historical and shared mind, which continues to try to draw the subject back to the perfect misrecognition of the first step.

The first and second positions are linked by the liberating practice called "thoroughly knowing." Thoroughly knowing is generally glossed in terms of seeing that objects are "merely objects," which is to say that they are not reality itself. To see this is to understand that the subject that identifies the mind with the cognitive faculty that perceives objects (whether external or internal, material or mental) is thereby not in contact with reality itself, precisely insofar as it has not understood the historical embeddedness, collectivity, and perfect misrecognition within which any act of cognition takes place. The practice of thoroughly knowing brings one to rest squarely, without bad faith, in the position of mind-only. One now lives within and takes responsibility for the salient features of one's own historically layered and collective "mind." The second and third positions—mind and no-mind—are in turn linked by the liberating practice called abandonment. This is the practice of relinquishing or dropping-off one's moment-by-moment reappropriation of the distorting features of the collective and historically layered mind within which one's personhood and subjectivity have been shaped. This practice leads to the final position of no-mind, which is identified as a condition of liberating insight, where reality is encountered without the distortions of the historically and collectively embedded "mind."

How then can mind-only diagnose whiteness, and how do the path positions and liberating practices of the mind-only school function within and with regard to the construct of whiteness? Mind-only as a theory of how perfect misrecognition works puts the person who thinks about mind-only in the position where the subject's understanding of the mind itself, the supposedly luminescent organ of vision and understanding, becomes not just *an* obstacle but *the* obstacle to awakening, to clear vision of how the production of suffering works—that it is historical, that it is collective—and of how liberation from it is possible. Because whiteness has, in the racially hierarchical polity, become a marker of the normative epistemological subject, because to be white is a sign of being the quintessential knower and vice versa, the white subject as the quintessential knower is the one who identifies her mind as transparent, as luminous, as an organ of knowledge. Thus, in this polity, the mind-only claim provides an accurate diagnosis for the white subject, for it is she who suffers a perfect misrecognition about the nature of mind itself. The white knower is, as Mills shows, perfectly ignorant. White subjects as knowers refuse to recognize that our subjectivities, our perceptions of black people, and our shared object-worlds show everywhere the signs of the historicity of racism. Whites *trust* our own perceptions and cognitions—of ourselves, of black people, of the shared object-world—and this trust is itself an inability, a willful refusal to see the historicity that shapes those perceptions and cognitions. By encountering the objects of his cognitions as though they point to reality itself, instead of recognizing that they are shaped by the distortions of a long history of racism, the white (mis-)knower refuses to step into the fullness of his subjectivity, and the object-world it was co-created with refuses to take responsibility for himself and the world he exists within.

In this way, mind-only thought when applied to the construct called whiteness gives a phenomenology of the white mind that exists in a necessary relationship with the phenomenology of the black body as described by Charles Johnson. As Johnson describes it, the white gaze perceives the black person foremost as body and that black body as a stain. Johnson describes how this white subject's gaze—the gaze of the subject in whose historically layered world the black person has *become* body and stain—submerges the very consciousness of the black person, so that the "stain of the black body seems figuratively to darken consciousness itself, to overshadow [the black man's] existence as a subject."[10] For the white subject, the grotesque achievement of reducing the black person to body and stain is necessary for the full expression of white subjectivity and of white knowing in particular, because it confirms the transparency and luminosity of the white mind. The inner logic is this: if the white subject perceives the black person as body and that body as stain, *then it must be so*. For if it were not so, then it is possible that the white person's perceptions and conceptions represent reality falsely to him. In that case, he is not what he thinks he is: possessed of a mind that is a transparent recorder of reality and vehicle of knowledge. And if he is not that, if he is instead forced to enter into the fullness of the subjectivity that history has made him, then the horrors of that history may overtake him. This inner logic *must* remain out of view of the white subject. This remaining out of view takes the form of his refusal to inhabit, enter into the fullness of, or take responsibility for the historicity and collectivity of his white mind.[11] He chooses instead to focus on his perceptions of objects (including inner objects). Thus, the racially hierarchical polity's representation of the white subject as the normative knower is itself a feature of whiteness and a perfect misrecognition, for this very investment in being a knower is a way for a white person to grant herself permission to continue to ignore the historicity and collectivity of her own mind.

Using mind-only to give a phenomenology of the white mind allows us to see how white ignorance is experienced as knowledge in the white mind. We can then, along with mind-only thought, diagnose the seemingly luminescent or translucent white mind as in fact an *obstacle*. Precisely by taking this mind up as object of reflection, as mirror by which she may know herself, the white person's *actual* mind, the actual mind of "mind only," which for the person shaped by the history of racism into a white person will be a white mind, the mind that is deeply layered, karmically infused and characterized by disposition toward racist action[12] oriented toward a racist world, *that* mind recedes from view. That mind conceals itself behind the false mind of white subjectivity, to which it has given itself over not only willingly, but eagerly, for everything about that layered and karmically shaped historicity of the actual mind tempts it to do so.

If we follow mind-only thought, the inner logic of the white mind as (mis)knower can, it seems, come into view and be thoroughly known for the white subject. But can it be abandoned? Can the historically layered white mind be dropped-off? Can the white knowing subject enter the position of no-mind? I want to say that though the early mind-only tradition delineates the path to no-mind as something that must be undertaken afresh with regard to each moment of experience, for a white subject to aim at the no-mind that has cast off whiteness is to perform a self-contradiction.

In early mind-only thought, the path toward no-mind has two key features: it must be undertaken anew with regard to each new moment of experience, and it must be undertaken endlessly. These two features derive from two commitments of Buddhist thought: the beginninglessness of the delusion that produces any construction, like the construction of whiteness, and the collectivity of any constructed subject-formation. There is in Buddhist thought no point of origination of the causal sequence that gives rise to any given moment of experience. Because past causes are endless, future effects are too. Therefore, one moment of achieving no-mind does not enter one into a permanent state of no-mind. Instead, one moment of no-mind is simply the full abandonment of a given constructed subject-formation *in that moment*. The next moment comes with a freshly constructed subject-formation, which must again be relinquished. The infinity of the task locates it within the Mahāyāna tradition, where the paradigmatic endless task is that of the bodhisattva, a being oriented toward awakening whose path calls her to vow to save all of the limitless suffering beings. But here, the person undertaking no-mind gives himself over to the infinite causes that created his subjective formation and his object-world, causes for which he must take responsibility precisely because his constructed subject-formation and the object-world he encounters are their effects. And because of the collectivity of mind, when a given being with a certain subject-formation undertakes to dispossess himself of it, to abandon it, there is no guarantee that other beings in his group will likewise do so. More likely, they will not. Thus, one being's constant undertaking does not bring the world of that shared subject-formation to an end, any more than one moment of no-mind brings that being's encounter with that subject-formation to an end.

With these characteristics, the mind-only school seems to have put in place a safeguard against the seductions of constructed self-formations. But because of the social situatedness of the white subject as knower, because white knowers are constructed within the racially hierarchical polity, to encourage a white subject to aim at an ultimate epistemic state is to encourage her to collude with her whiteness, to reinscribe herself as supremely knowing, this time under the guise of the non-knower. Here the prescriptions of mind-only thought seem to run afoul of the condition of the white subject as (mis)knower, encouraging her to practice the cultivation of a state—the attainment of no-mind through the abandonment of the historical and collective white mind—which just by aiming at she will fail to reach. Given that a denial of historicity and collectivity are features of whiteness itself, to seek their abandonment is to perpetuate it.

Here then we should stand fast with the distinction between the liberating practices enjoined by the mind-only school and the positions they hold out as possible. The practice of abandonment is distinct from the position of no-mind: the former is one something one undertakes, the latter is an achievement. The position of no-mind is in fact paired with its own liberating practice, "directly realizing" (*sākṣāt-kriyā*). No-mind's status as an ultimate achievement is revealed by the way that the practice of directly realizing differs from those of thoroughly knowing and abandoning; while the latter two lead from one path position to another, directly realizing marks the self-authenticating nature of the ultimate position of no-mind. Because whiteness produces a phenomenology of mind that exists in necessary relationship with the phenomenology of blackness, no white subject can self-authenticate his or her full abandonment of the mind of whiteness. The relationality of racial dynamics throws the white subject back into the endless necessity of practicing thorough knowing and abandoning, aiming at the ultimate state of no-mind only on pain of strengthening the very whiteness one seeks to abandon. Here I recall George Yancy's evocative language of "tarrying in the unfinished present" as a prescription for white subjects, for whom there is no escape hatch from the realities of white racial subject-formation.[13] In the language of mind-only thought, this tarrying is the commitment to the space in between mind-only and no-mind, a commitment to the practice of abandoning white subject-formation while yet thoroughly knowing that because of the *nature* of white subject-formation, and in particular the nature of the white subject as knower, the achievement of no-mind *cannot* be aimed for.

I return now to that event on the bus, or to my memory of that event. The extreme epistemic disorientation I feel whenever I recall the event is itself a marker of whiteness, for it occurs against the backdrop of my implicit position that I should have known exactly what that event was about, that among the people on the bus, all black people except myself, I should have been in epistemic command of the situation, that I could see and know, but could not be seen or known. When in my moments of remembering I aim to come to a satisfying interpretation of the event, an interpretation in which I feel confident, I reach beyond myself, beyond my disorientation, by aiming to know precisely what I cannot know. It is not for me to know what that moment meant to the man who engaged me, or the others who laughed. But the practices of thoroughly knowing and abandoning tell me that I am also not free to step aside from the event, to erase it, to minimize it, or to pretend that I have no idea at all what it was about. The white subject can follow early mind-only thought into the recognition of mind-only through the practice of thorough knowing, but she must then, in the true spirit of mind-only thought, exist endlessly in the space between mind-only and no-mind, working with the practices of thoroughly knowing and abandoning, without seeking certainty in knowledge or self-authentication.

NOTES

1. Charles W. Mills, "White Ignorance," in *Race and Epistemologies of Ignorance*, eds. Shannon Sullivan and Nancy Tuana (Albany: State University of New York Press, 2007), 17.

2. The historicity of the mind is carried within its layered structure by the presence of an unconscious that consists in potentialities that carry the causal power of the past in a latent form through into the future. This unconscious is called the "storehouse consciousness," and it is a key teaching of Yogācāra thought, precisely for its importance to the school's new understanding of how experience is caused. See William S. Waldron's treatment of it in *The Buddhist Unconscious: The ālaya-vijñāna in the Context of Indian Buddhist Thought* (London: RoutledgeCurzon, 2003).

3. John Powers, *A Bull of a Man: Images of Masculinity, Sex, and the Body in Indian Buddhism* (Cambridge, MA: Harvard University Press, 2009), 13. For such general descriptions of a Buddha prevalent in South Asia, see chapter 1 *passim*.

4. Such reversals amid dichotomies are in keeping with the Daoist context that formed the matrix within which the literati of medieval China were receptive to this notion of the non-knower as the ideal epistemological (and liberated) subject. On the relationship between Daoist teachings and the concept of no-mind, which becomes important to Chan/Zen thought and is an expression of this kind of reversal amid dichotomies, see Isabelle Robinet, "De quelques effets du bouddhisme sur la problématique taoïste: aspects de la confrontation du taoïsme au bouddhisme," in *Religion and Chinese Society* (vol. 1), ed. John Lagerwey (Hong Kong: The Chinese University Press, 2004), 411–516.

5. Steven Heine and Dale S. Wright's volume, *Zen Masters* (Oxford: Oxford University Press, 2010) offers recountings of the lives of important Chan teachers that span the history of Chan/Zen from medieval China and Japan to the twentieth century, including stories of encounter dialogues.

6. Charles W. Mills, *The Racial Contract* (Ithaca: Cornell University Press, 1997), 27.

7. Here the phrase "analysis of phenomena" translates the Buddhist concept of dharma analysis (*dharma-vicaya*), itself understood by Buddhist Abhidharma traditions to be one of the seven factors of awakening. The term "phenomena" is not in fact adequate to this technical concept of a dharma as a momentary occurrent event that bears an intrinsic identifying characteristic, simply because not all dharmas are available to awareness. There is within Abhidharma literature a category of dharmas that are separate from awareness, or that can never be objects of cognition (this category is called *citta-viprayukta-dharma*, or literally "dharmas that are separate from the mind"). This ambiguity within the concept of a dharma—whether all things that shape constructed reality are available to cognition or not—is at the heart of the tension I am outlining here. The aspects of the tradition confident in the faculties seem to think they can be, at least insofar as one can make the very idea of a *citta-viprayukta-dharma* an object of reflection, while the less confident aspects of the tradition emphasize that our subjects and our object-worlds are shaped by forces that precisely lie out of view.

8. I here summarize one key argument from Kachru's dissertation, a précis of which can be found in the introduction. See in particular the discussion of Vasubandhu's rejection of empiricism on pages 52–65, particularly Kachru's analysis of Vasubandhu's rejection of what Kachru calls "causal separatism," which he glosses as "the presumed *separability* of that which is cited as cause and that which is cited as effect. How the cause is, taken by itself, is thought to be entirely independent of how the effect taken by itself is." This causal separatism is what mind-only thought rejects when it locates the past as cause of present experience, rather than the object cognized within that experience. Sonam Kachru, "Minds and Worlds: A Philosophical Commentary on the Twenty Verses of Vasubandhu" PhD Thesis, University of Chicago, 2015.

9. On the relationship between, on the one hand, the three path positions of accepting objects, mind-only, and no-mind, and on the other hand the liberating practices of thoroughly knowing and abandoning, see Joy Brennan, "The Three Natures and the Path to Liberation in Yogācāra-Vijñānavāda Thought," *Journal of Indian Philosophy* 46 (2018): 646–647.

10. Charles Johnson, "A Phenomenology of the Black Body," *Michigan Quarterly Review* 32, no. 4 (1993): 595–614, 604.

11. Differently gendered white minds may be differently motivated, but the manifestation of both is still rightly captured by the foregoing phenomenology. The mind of the white woman is dually shaped by whiteness and femaleness. As white, this mind is experienced as the transparent organ of cognition. As woman, this mind is shaped by awareness of the always present possibility—a possibility which takes shape as a feature of being or having a female body—of being made into a body that is abused for the pleasure of a male other. But this fear of abuse is mediated by whiteness and functions therefore as an added lure into complicity with whiteness. On this dynamic, I take the position that Hannah Arendt attributes to Mary McCarthy as consistent with mind-only thought as well as Buddhist thought more broadly. On the question of personal moral responsibility under conditions of pressure, Arendt offers to us McCarthy's judgment that "if somebody points a gun at you and says 'Kill your friend or I will kill you,' he is tempting you, that is all." In Buddhist thought, the consequences of our actions (*karma*) fall on us, even if we were tempted into those actions by a threat to our lives. If the "dictatorship" of the racially hierarchical polity is a white patriarchy, then white women are in a position of constant temptation to whiteness in the face of the threat of rape. The majority give ourselves to the temptation, and the added obscenity is that the threat of rape has been wrongly identified—displaced fully onto the body of the black man—and thus is not resolved. See Hannah Arendt, *Responsibility and Judgment*, ed. and with an introduction by Jerome Kohn (New York: Schoken Books, 2003), 18.

12. Action, or *karma*, is of body, speech, and mind in Buddhist thought.

13. See George Yancy, *Look, a White! Philosophical Essays on Whiteness* (Philadelphia: Temple University Press, 2012), 158–163.

Chapter 15

The White Feminism in Rita Gross's Critique of Gender Identities and Reconstruction of Buddhism

Hsiao-Lan Hu

Identity is a myriad, ever-shifting, ever-changing constellation, not something fixed, rigid, stabile, and enduring.[1]

Well known for her critically acclaimed *Buddhism After Patriarchy: A Feminist History, Analysis, and Reconstruction of Buddhism*, Rita M. Gross (1943–2015) was one of the leading figures in Buddhist feminism. Much of her works sharply critiqued the ways in which binary gender identities are held on to tightly by practitioners of Buddhism, a tradition that is dedicated to the deconstruction of self-identities. Through pointing out the blindspots of patriarchy, she sought to reconstruct Buddhism and bring forth the Buddhist teachings that would sustain a thorough-going deconstruction of identities and support equality and diversity. Her feminist reconstruction of Buddhism, however, contained some blindspots of her own as she did not extend her critique of identity-attachment to race or nationality. As the one and only graduate student she ever had, I feel obligated to carry on her legacies in some way. As a person who happens to be a racial other to her and who has experienced firsthand her blindspots, I feel the best way I can carry on her work is to make her critique more "thorough-going" than it was by applying it to whiteness.

MEETING RITA: THE OBSTACLE OF FEMALE BIRTH

At the 13th Sākyadhitā Conference in Vaishali, India (January 5–12, 2013), Rita gave a talk that was later published in *Tricycle* as "The Man-made Obstacle: Distinguishing Between Problems of Human Birth and Problems of Human Making."[2] In this article, Rita elaborated on the obstacles that she had to work with as a woman, as a feminist scholar, and as a Buddhist practitioner. While acknowledging that, in Buddhist teachings, obstacles can be beneficial because wisdom and compassion can be developed when one works skillfully with obstacles, Rita pointed out a necessary caveat: "This perspective only applies if the obstacle doesn't kill us first."[3] Some obstacles can be so severe that they leave the people facing them immobilized and unable to recover. Rita distinguished the obstacles that necessarily accompany human birth, and the severe obstacles that are "man-made" [*sic*] and so can and should be removed:

> Some obstacles, such as old age, sickness, death, loss, and personal grief go with the territory of having a precious human birth. Other obstacles, such as sexism, racism, poverty, homophobia, religious intolerance, environmental degradation, and nationalism are not attributable to the inevitabilities of being human but are caused by human greed, hatred, and ignoring. Therefore, they can be overcome. It is difficult enough for us to cope with the obstacles inherent in having taken birth. Because some of us manage to cope with socially created obstacles in addition is no excuse or justification for anyone to promote or benefit from them. Buddhists, especially Buddhist teachers, should never suggest that simply because a few people manage to cope well with socially created obstacles, it is permissible for Buddhist leaders and institutions to continue such practices.[4]

Naively telling people that obstacles can be our best allies on the path to awakening is mean, Rita said, especially when the obstacles are the results of systemic injustice and structural violence, such as the obstacle of female birth.

Rita's most salient legacy came from her insistence on addressing the many and severe obstacles placed in front of women that are in fact *man*-made. In her groundbreaking 1993 volume *Buddhism After Patriarchy*, she brought her feminist gaze, and what she called her "prophetic voice,"[5] to Buddhism. Judith Simmer-Brown, Buddhist scholar-practitioner and Rita's close friend for thirty-seven years, said this book "wonderfully applies women's studies methodology in analyzing sources of Indian Buddhism in particular in order to identify promising strands and sources for constructing a feminist paradigm of a patriarchy-free Buddhism."[6] *Buddhism After Patriarchy* has been translated into many languages and earned Rita international fame. While Rita "was shunned by Buddhist scholars, attacked by dharma siblings, and ignored by Buddhist hierarchies for her prophetic voice that advocated the confluence of Buddhism and feminism,"[7] Simmer-Brown writes, "it is especially in Asia that Rita's analysis has been welcomed."[8]

As a matter of fact, *Buddhism After Patriarchy* was my entryway to Buddhist feminism, which I had read a couple of years before I decided that I would write my doctoral dissertation on Buddhist-feminist social ethics.

I remember being struck by the clarity of her arguments and saying to the mentor who introduced it to me that I would like to pursue my degree in a similar field. The mentor, however, warned me that Rita was not exactly acknowledged as a "Buddhist studies scholar" due to methodological issues. As Simmer-Brown puts it, "Gross drew from classical Indian Mahayana texts, isolated and taken out of context in their most accessible English translations, to construct her argument, ignoring the contexts, cultures, practices, and pieties in which they were written."[9] Years later, every time I mentioned to colleagues that I was surprised that I was the only person who ever sought out Rita as an advisor, the response would be a direct or oblique comment about how Rita was not considered a "Buddhist studies scholar" by textual-historians or ethnographers.

In my graduate program at the time, I had abundant resources for feminist theories and religious social ethics—two of my professors and dissertation committee members, Rebecca T. Alpert and Laura S. Levitt, are Jewish feminist scholars, and my main advisor, the late John C. Raines, was a Christian social ethicist and activist[10]—but I lacked guidance from someone who was knowledgeable about Buddhism *and* would support my endeavor in constructing a feminist social ethic from Buddhist teachings. The only Buddhist scholar in residence seemed indifferent, if not dismissive, to both feminism and ethics. Upon the suggestions of my professors, I contacted a few Buddhist scholars in nearby universities to ask if they would be willing to serve on my dissertation committee, and they all replied that what I was planning to do was not within their fields of expertise. Eventually my main advisor John asked me, "If you could have any Buddhist scholar in the world on your committee, who would it be?" I blurted out, "Rita Gross." John proceeded to write an email to Rita on my behalf. Later on Rita loved to tell people that John pretty much *begged* her to be on my committee, often in a tone implying that she would not have considered having me as a student if without that *begging*, even though at the memorial ceremony held during the 2015 AAR right after her passing a few of Rita's long-term friends told me that it had meant a lot to Rita to have me as her one and only graduate student (which she never expressed to me). It seemed to be very important to her to make people know that both an older white man and a younger Asian woman *begged* her on account of her expertise in feminism and Buddhism. From what her friends told me, I gathered that she felt somewhat vindicated as she was finally asked to be on a dissertation committee. She felt people should have asked her to be their dissertation advisors all along and thought that she got slighted in academia because of "the obstacle of female birth"—a sentiment that was front and center in her talk at the 13th Sākyadhitā Conference, though it was somewhat muted in the article published in *Tricycle*.

MAN-MADE OR HUMAN-MADE?:
INTERSECTIONALITY AND BLINDSPOTS

In "Feminism: A Transformational Politic," published in 1989, bell hooks critiqued the tendency for privileged Western white feminists to assume that "racism and class exploitation are merely the offspring of the parent system: patriarchy."[11] Many white feminists of so-called "second-wave feminism" (which I would prefer to call "justice-oriented feminism"[12]), such as Shulamith Firestone, Mary Daly, and Adrienne Rich, certainly held this view.[13] Like many white feminists of her generation, Rita considered androcentrism not just the primal example of systemic injustice, but the root of oppressive social hierarchies. In a book chapter published in 1994, for example, Rita stated regarding her feminist scholarship,

> I had no idea that I had stumbled onto the concern that would occupy much of my scholarly and personal life. Nor did I realize that I had located *the most serious blind spot of contemporary scholarship*, not only in religious studies, but also in all humanistic and social scientific disciplines.[14] (emphasis added)

Mary Keller, citing Franz Fanon, W. E. B. DuBois, Ifi Amadiume, and Amina Wadud, asked, "How did Gross arrive at the evaluation that the most serious blindspot of scholarship was androcentrism?"[15] Keller's question reflects the perspective of the so-called third-wave feminism (which I would prefer to call "diversity-oriented feminism") which, as Randi Warne puts it, is "in favor of a more complex analysis which included race and class, sexualities, age, (dis)ability and ethnic and colonial positionings."[16] For diversity-oriented feminists, intersectionality is a crucial concept in understanding the ways in which each embodied person experiences oppressive social structures. Diversity-oriented feminists' critique of the earlier form of white feminism that considered sexism to be *the* fundamental problem, in the simplest terms, is that women of color "cannot be women first and then Black or Hispanic."[17] To prioritize the obstacles brought about by androcentrism over the obstacles brought about by other forms of institutionalized oppression is to dismiss the lived realities of people who have been more severely affected by white supremacy, imperialist domination, capitalistic exploitation, heterosexism, nativism, and/or Eurocentrism. Indeed, the most common criticism of Rita's feminist scholarship, as Amina Wadud puts it, is that her methodology disallowed concerns of race to be included.[18]

Is that criticism of Rita's feminist scholarship fair? On the one hand, in the roundtable where Amina Wadud issued that criticism, Rita readily dismissed the criticism as a distortion of her work,[19] without taking into serious account Wadud's point about the systemic aspect of racism or other forms of institutionalized social oppression. After all, just as Rita would say that her criticism of sexism and androcentrism is a criticism of a systemic social problem, not a personal attack on any individual man (even though it can easily be argued that sexism, as a systemic social problem, is sustained and perpetuated by individual men acquiescing to and participating in the status quo),[20] so are Amina Wadud's and bell hooks's criticisms of racism and white supremacy (even though the systems depend on individual white persons' acquiescence and participation, too). However, even in "The Man-Made Obstacle," which was published twenty years after the 1994 chapter mentioned above, Rita was still convinced of the primacy of androcentrism as a social problem, "I'm not sure that any other topic that has emerged in Buddhist circles or in academia in the past 40 years is as significant as gender studies" (and she understood "gender studies" to be the inclusion of binary genders only, rather than intersectionality). In fact, the article title itself disclosed where her concerns lied: the *man*-made obstacles (imposed on women), and not necessarily the *human*-made obstacles imposed on the minoritized others, such as the obstacles that are *white*-made, *Western*-made, and *American*-made. For her, the experience of growing up as a poor farm girl under patriarchy put her among the oppressed, and it did not seem to have registered with her that a person could be oppressed in some regards (such as being female and poor) and privileged in others (such as being white and born in the United States). She resisted the suggestion that she might be privileged on account of her white skin and her Americanness. In fact, as related above, she took critiques about her whiteness as personal attacks.

Furthermore, in my personal contacts with her for about nine and a half years, I did experience her repeatedly dismissing my concerns related to ethnicity, nationality, and culture. An anecdote showcased her attitude on the matter: In 2014 I invited Rita for the first time to my Dharma center in Michigan to lead a weekend retreat. After picking her up from the airport, I drove her to my Dharma center called "Amitābha Village Retreat Center." Upon seeing the name, Rita seemed slightly puzzled and, strangely enough, incredulous and withdrawn, "Is this a Pure Land place?" as if asking why I would invite her to teach at a place of devotional Buddhism. I said that the center is non-sectarian and syncretistic, typical of the Chinese Buddhist tradition. Her reaction indicated that she did not know what I was referring to at all, which was surprising to me as I thought that was common knowledge among Buddhist scholars (or at least it is mentioned in every introductory text on world religions nowadays), and so I explained to her that Chinese Buddhists typically would engage in a wide range of practices, such as chanting the Buddha's name, observing precepts, participating in repentance ceremonies, keeping a vegetarian diet (at least on special days), doing volunteer work, donating to charities, going on meditation retreats, reciting and studying various sūtras, listening to Dharma talks, taking Dharma classes, etc.[21] When showing her the facilities and introducing to her the originally mostly Taiwanese immigrant group that had built the retreat center,[22] I used the word "minority" as a self-referent to other Taiwanese and myself. Rita *corrected* me, in her usual tone of correcting my pronunciation of English words, by saying, "Here, by 'minority' we mean blacks; we don't mean you. We have been treating your people rather well, I think." I gathered that, by "we," she meant white Americans, and by "here," she meant the United States, despite the irony that, at the moment of saying "here," she was sitting in a retreat center paid and built by Taiwanese immigrants who had been in the United States for over thirty years, legally "naturalized," and yet still have not been included in the "we" of "Americans."[23] I tried to bring up the various ways in which Taiwanese-Americans, and Asian-Americans in general, are indeed minoritized, such as those discussed in a recent *Lion's Roar* article entitled "Advice for Modern America, From the Painful History of American Buddhism."[24] However, Rita stopped listening as she just could not believe that I would be so "ignorant" as to use the word "minority" as a self-referent.

In "Spiritual Bypassing in the Contemporary Mindfulness Movement," Carla Sherrell and Judith Simmer-Brown write, "White privilege and supremacy afford white people the power to name, define, and interpret the experiences of people of color; this 'right' to dismiss 'the other's' lived experience of oppression, rationalizing it or calling it something else, is a pervasive practice that is older than the U.S. itself."[25] This was the first time I vividly felt Rita's whiteness at work and the way in which she was blind to her Orientalist assumption and condescension—she excluded Asian Americans from the American "we" and simultaneously defined Asian Americans out of "minority," she assumed my ignorance of the correct usage of English words as well as the non-intellectual devotionalism of Taiwanese Buddhists, and she made her contempt clear. I was upset by that experience (I remember emailing another white woman Buddhist teacher who "gets it" to tell her how diminished and infuriated I felt), but I was not exactly shocked (the white teacher I emailed, on the other hand, was) because in many of her writings since *Buddhism After Patriarchy*, as well as in many other emails and conversations, she had advocated for the development of a progressive, post-patriarchal "American Buddhism" and her vision of it never included Asian-American Buddhists.[26] That is, I had known that she considered Asian forms of Buddhism as something stuck in the past and mired in patriarchy, but I did not know that she would dismiss out of hand Asian-American practices and experiences, and of course being frequently made to feel like a "dumb foreigner" unworthy of her attention did not help. I was shocked, however, that in one of her Dharma talks during the retreat, she openly said that she did not care about preserving the Tibetan culture, making a sharp distinction between Vajrayāna Buddhism and Tibetan Buddhism—Tibetan Buddhism is practiced by Tibetans, together with their cultural baggage, and she and other Americans who uphold gender equality supposedly practice the real Vajrayāna Buddhism.

On the other hand, in quite a few other writings, Rita did show that she was aware of intersectionality and the lived experiences of racism, nativism, imperialism, and cultural chauvinism. For example, in *Religious Diversity: What's the Problem? Buddhist Advice for Flourishing with Religious Diversity*, Rita said,

> One may be a member of any given religion, and that identity may be very strong, but it is never one's sole identity. It would be self-deceptive to claim otherwise. One may have a religious identity, but one also has family roles, an occupation, political views, a sexual orientation, a cultural identity, a racial identity, national citizenship, an educational level, membership in an age cohort, sexual identity, gender identity, membership in a denomination within one's larger religion, a relationship with the arts and/or sports . . . and other identities depending on the specifics of one's experience. . . . Even if one is not biracial, bicultural, or a multiple religious belonger, one always has a hyphenated identity.
>
> Furthermore, throughout one's life, these various identities shift and change. Some become more dominant, and others decline in importance or drop away altogether.[27]

Rita was also very aware of diversity-oriented feminists' critiques of the white feminist movement of her generation in North America, even though she did not agree with those critiques:

> By the mid-1980s, the movement had fractured. Many women *complained* that the phrase 'women's experience' did not really include them. *It was claimed* that the movement reflected only white, middle-class, heterosexual women's concerns. Black women, poor women, lesbians, women of other cultures, and many others did not find themselves included in the rhetoric of the feminist-theology movement. . . . Because so many early feminist leaders came from North America, many Asians and Africans *even claimed* that the feminist movement was another colonial project.[28] (emphasis added)

Moreover, in one of the quotes from "The Man-made Obstacle" given above, Rita did recognize the obstacles brought about by "racism, poverty, homophobia, religious intolerance, environmental degradation, and nationalism" in addition to sexism—she was aware that there are other *human*-made obstacles than the *man*-made obstacle of sexism. In her 2009 book, *A Garland of Feminist Reflections: Forty Years of Religious Explorations*, Rita stated, very much in line with diversity-oriented feminists, "A major value of feminist theology is to include the voices that have not been heard, to widen the circle, to learn how to welcome diversity."[29] That is, as a feminist scholar, Rita's writings, and sometimes behaviors, were indicative of inclusivity even though she was not entirely sensitive to people whose minoritized identities she did not personally share.

SEEING INTO THE LIVED REALITIES OF OTHERS AND EVOLVING IDENTITIES

How do we make sense of this contradiction, and where does it leave us regarding Rita's legacies? At this point, I would like to draw from another of her self-identities: a Buddhist practitioner. As a Buddhist practitioner, Rita took the rational, analytical, introspective aspect of Buddhist teachings very seriously, and she frequently challenged people to examine their habitual tendencies and blindspots. In "The Man-Made Obstacle," she acknowledged the blindspots that the socially privileged might have,

> It is well known that, out of self-defense, those on the underside of worldly power and privilege often are double-sighted. *We* can see things from the dominant perspective, the one that is publicly taught and promulgated, but *we* can also see things that those who participate only in the privileged perspective cannot see. This tells us that, *on any topic in which we mainly operate out of privilege, we should be humble. That is why white people are so often so blind to racism or straight people blind to homophobia.* That is also why Buddhists should be much more careful about dismissing issues of social justice as irrelevant to dharma.[30] (emphasis added)

For the dominant and privileged, the system from which they benefit is simply normal. When dissecting the obstacle of female birth, Rita related the story about a male colleague's surprise at the "obviously correct" interpretations contained in *Buddhism After Patriarchy*. The male colleague was surprised because those "obviously correct" interpretations had never occurred to him. Rita's analytical response was, "It hadn't been in his self-interest as a male to notice how male dominant the conventional interpretations are. It is, as realtors say, a matter of 'location, location, location!'"[31] Similar comments can be made about Rita's prioritizing the issue of androcentrism, or her dismissing others' concerns about racism, nativism, neo-colonialism, and cultural chauvinism: it is not exactly in her self-interest to gain an in-depth understanding of the obstacles brought about by skin color or national origin.

The caveat Rita pointed out regarding seeing obstacles as allies is, "This perspective only applies if the obstacle doesn't kill us first." Nowadays, it is a well-known fact that racism and anti-immigration sentiments are obstacles that can and do literally get one killed—American Civil Liberty Unity and Southern Poverty Law Center have both recorded increases of hate killings and hate crimes after the US 2016 election. I know of many immigrants, who are of Asian, Latin-American, and Middle-Eastern descent, have been on alert about their personal safety like I have, particularly when seeing the red MAGA hat. Even when blatant hate crimes are not looming, Sara Lewis points out, "Evidence suggests that stress from repeated and chronic exposure to structural racism is so harmful, it supersedes protective factors like good health care and economic security. In fact, it seems that marginalization, discrimination, and isolation are among the greatest predictors of ill health at the population level."[32] That is to say, the obstacles brought about by skin color or national origin can be even more immobilizing or deadly than the obstacle of female birth, but those are obstacles that Rita did not personally experience and so in these regards she was not exactly "privilege-cognizant."[33] In the quote above, the use of "we" clearly indicated that Rita put herself among those who are "on the underside of worldly power and privilege" as the primary target of her critique was sexism, seemingly unaware that, regarding many other forms of oppressive and deadly social structures, she was not at all on the underside. As Allan G. Johnson puts it, "not being aware of privilege is an aspect of privilege itself."[34] The extent to which she dismissed critiques about white feminism in North America reflects the privilege she enjoyed as a white American woman—the concerns expressed by women of color were non-issues to her because someone of her social location really did not experience them as issues.

The very fact that Rita took the rational, analytical, introspective aspect of Buddhist teachings very seriously—and at the same time was dismissive of Asian Buddhist traditions, especially in their devotional practices, considering them stuck in the past and irredeemably patriarchal—itself says much about her social location and perspective as a Western academic. Joseph Cheah traced and critiqued the colonial history of Western Orientalist scholars' construction of "pure" and "authentic" Buddhism based on texts and their distrust of the traditions preserved by Asian Buddhists themselves.[35] "Remnants of this project or the processes of racialization that embodies whiteness and white supremacy can still be seen in our academy today, in that the study of textual Buddhism by Buddhist scholars is favored to the neglect of lived Buddhism itself," Cheah concluded.[36] In reflecting on a field experience, Paul Crowe wrote, "In the academy, we focus almost exclusively on abstraction and conceptualization. There seemed . . . to be a fundamental disconnect between rationalist, Enlightenment-based European traditions of philosophy and the mode of teaching assumed by compilers of Buddhist texts."[37] Abstracting and extracting "core" Buddhist principles from textual sources is perhaps unavoidable in conceptualizing and constructing Buddhist feminism—I myself am guilty of doing that in my own attempt at constructing Buddhist-feminist social ethics (however, instead of faulting Asian cultures as a whole for corrupting "core" Buddhist principles, I problematize the perspective of the socially privileged, in any society)[38]—but it is problematic when such a text-based, rational, and analytical approach leads one to dismiss the rest of the traditions and to essentialize the Buddhists practicing them. Holly Gayley cautions, "In seeking to deconstruct gender binaries and essentialisms, we need to take care not to essentialize Buddhism as a textually-derived set of doctrines whose application or effects are self-evident in any way. . . . This not only runs counter to current feminist approaches, it risks reproducing a colonial and orientalist legacy of prioritizing textual Buddhism."[39] Simmer-Brown also sees that to essentialize Buddhism is to engage in an Orientalist enterprise and to assert "a privilege from the perspective of white, middle-class, western Buddhism that disrespects and disempowers the Buddhisms of the world."[40]

Despite not being in the social locations that bear the brunt of racism or anti-immigration violence, and despite inheriting the Orientalist construction and privileging the textual and intellectual Buddhism, Rita had a strong commitment to Buddhist practices and believed that a Buddhist practitioner should look deeper into oneself and into the realities around us. Drawing from her painful experience of having the obstacle of female birth overlooked and dismissed, Rita certainly understood the necessity of looking into other *human*-made obstacles and seeking to remove them for others: "We should not excuse overlooking serious obstacles to dharmic practice such as poverty, racism, sexism, homophobia, and so forth by naively reciting that obstacles can be one's best friend on the path. . . . We must not slide into the temptations provided by the three poisons, the most dangerous of which, in this case, is ignoring."[41] As a scholar-practitioner, Rita was committed to removing ignorance in more than one sense. She would certainly agree with Barack Obama when he said in his commencement speech at Rutgers University in 2016, "In politics and in life, ignorance is not a virtue."[42]

Furthermore, as Rita said in the quote that opens this chapter, "identity is a myriad, ever-shifting, ever-changing constellation, not something fixed, rigid, stabile, and enduring." Identities are not only multiple and hyphenated; identities evolve, and they evolve not just on the individual level, but on the sociocultural level as well. Rita's critique of the gender binary based on the understanding of the composite and ever-changing nature of self can be easily applied to other binaries, such as Western/Asian, white/non-white, American-born/immigrant, and intellectual/devotional. The identities that have been labeled as "Western," "American," "Asian," "Asian-American," "Asian Buddhist," and "American Buddhist" are all evolving. The composition of "Westerners" is changing: in "Western Self, Asian Other: Modernity, Authenticity, and Nostalgia for 'Tradition' in Buddhist Studies," Natalie E. Quli points to the fact that "Westerners are complex hybrids, and some Westerners are also Asian American"[43] despite how some Westerners, like Rita, think of them as perpetual foreigners (who have been treated "rather well" and so do not count as "minority"!). Even if Asian Americans can be excluded from "Americans" (they cannot and should not), the composition of "American Buddhists" is changing as well: Melanie L. Harris points out that the composition of "American Buddhists" is no longer just white: "The truth is, over the past ten to twenty years, many African American women, through the models of Alice Walker, Jan Willis, bell hooks, and others, have been flocking to the Dharma doors of Buddhism, in part to deal with racism."[44] The identities and experiences of "Asian-American Buddhists" are also changing: Chenxing Han's work on young adult Asian-American Buddhists reveals the extent to which the identities and practices of Asian-American Buddhists are hybrid and ever-changing, and the same can be said about second-generation white Buddhists.[45] In an online forum held in 2006, Charles S. Prebish acknowledged that "Buddhism in America is incredibly diverse and no longer seems to fit into the neat typologies of previous decades."[46] After all, just as an individual's identities are complex and constantly evolving, so are identity categories and cultural traditions: "As an invention of the present projecting itself onto the past, tradition is always in movement, being contested, forgotten, remembered, reinvented, augmented, abandoned, revived, and above all, lived."[47]

As a Buddhist practitioner, Rita also understood the harm of clinging to identities and the need to work toward non-attachment to self-identities:

Someone committed to a rigid, inflexible, monolithic identity, contrary to some popular ideas, has neither a strong nor a viable ego. It is in fact very brittle and fragile, easily threatened by change and diversity, timid and often overcome by fear. By contrast, those who recognize that identity is always hyphenated and changing are cheerful, flexible, and easily accommodate new information and situations. . . . In the long run, identity is not something to reinforce or to hang on to, but something more like a cane or a stepping-stone. We use it as long as we need it to steady ourselves, but eventually it becomes a prison rather than an aide. Then we let go. We become so confident, so much simply ourselves, that we are no longer attached to stories or labels in communicating to others who we are. . . .

Relaxing and taming our fear and rigidity about identity is most important in regard to those identities most likely to cause harm both to self and others when held too tightly. Those potentially harmful identities certainly can derive from religion, gender, race, nation, culture, class, sexual orientation, and political affiliations. It is easy to develop hostile, oppositional *us/them* styles of identity around such issues, and it is easy to see simply by following the daily news how much suffering such identities can inflict on others, when held too tightly, with too much attachment.[48]

I am sure Rita would agree that her comment here applies to the self-identities she had, both the ones she held dearly, such as Buddhist-feminist scholar-practitioner, and the ones she did not think too much about but nevertheless were present, such as white, Western, and America-born. Her fierce dedication to dismantling binary gender identities can and should be extended to dismantling other forms of binary identities and the unreflective attachments to them, such as Western and Eastern, white and non-white, "American" and "immigrant," and even the oppressed and the oppressor. Rita clearly identified herself as one of the oppressed, and by way of thinking in binaries she resented any suggestion that in certain regards she might be among the privileged and, worse, might be complicit in some oppressive social structures herself.

Ironically, it is through refusing to see the reality of her whiteness, the reality of how her identity as a white American allowed her to presume her experience as a woman to be universal and her understanding of Buddhism to be the real Buddhism, that she participated in systems that diminish people of color who are immigrants but are excluded from the "black-and-white" understanding of race and so not even given the "right" to talk about race. Despite some sweeping acknowledgment of the harm done by various -isms, as quoted above, I do not recall Rita ever specifically reflecting on her whiteness, or any privilege and assumption that came along with it. Over the years I have encountered quite a few American white women who self-identify as Buddhists, who are inspired by Rita's Buddhist deconstruction of the binary gender identities, and who are enthusiastic in following her call of constructing a newer, better "American Buddhism" that is without the patriarchal baggages of Asians. Like Rita, they refuse to acknowledge their whiteness, and when they do talk on race, they talk about it in a very "black-and-white" manner that forecloses Asian immigrants' right to join the conversation. Also like Rita, they self-identify as the oppressed and get "very brittle and fragile, easily threatened by change and diversity, timid and often overcome by fear" when anyone, white or non-white, tries to point out their Orientalist assumptions and behaviors. One of them actually shut down the conversation by asserting that she has "a good heart." The matter is not that they are not good Buddhists or that they do not make effort in looking into realities and attenuating their attachments to binary identities. Rather, the matter is that they do not go far enough in examining "those identities most likely to cause harm both to self and others when held too tightly," as Rita said in the quote above.

CONCLUSION

As a Buddhist-feminist scholar-practitioner, Rita was committed to looking directly into realities, dismantling systems that cause suffering (or at least those systems that she personally experienced to be causing suffering), removing ignorance, attenuating attachment to identities, and liberating women and men from the prison of rigid identities such as gender. There might be lived realities and social structures that she could not see well due to her attachment to certain aspects of her identities that she did not exactly explore, such as her status as a white American who easily assumed her experience and understanding to be the norm, but that is true of each embodied human being with finite existence and limited perspective. I think the best way for the next generation of Buddhist-feminist scholar-practitioners who feel indebted to her groundbreaking scholarship on Buddhist feminism, such as myself, to carry on her legacies is, first of all, to follow her in her dedication to looking directly into realities as they truly are, even if (*or especially when?*) those realities are not experienced in our immediate surroundings. Secondly, we need to strive to attenuate our attachments to our various identities, whatever they might be. At the same time, we need to remind ourselves of the importance of examining our own blindspots and taking seriously the obstacles that we do not personally experience but are still *human*-made and harmful to others, no matter how much we want to see ourselves as among the oppressed or having a good heart and thus not possibly doing any harm to others.

NOTES

1. Rita M. Gross, *Religious Diversity: What's the Problem? Buddhist Advice for Flourishing with Religious Diversity* (Eugene, OR: Cascade Books, 2014), 162.

2. Rita M. Gross, "The Man-Made Obstacle: Distinguishing Between Problems of Human Birth and Problems of Human Making," *Tricycle*, Summer 2014 (https://tricycle.org/magazine/rita-gross-female-birth, accessed March 31, 2018).

3. Gross, "The Man-Made Obstacle."

4. Ibid.

5. Rita M. Gross, *Buddhism After Patriarchy: A Feminist History, Analysis, and Reconstruction of Buddhism* (Albany, NY: State University of New York Press, 1993), 134.

6. Judith Simmer-Brown, "Rita Gross's Contribution to Contemporary Western Tibetan Buddhism," *Buddhist-Christian Studies* 31 (2011): 71.

7. Judith Simmer-Brown, "What Water? Feminism, Shambhala Buddhism, and the Feminine Principle," *The Arrow: A Journal of Wakeful Society, Culture & Politics* 3, no. 1 (September 2016, "Buddhism & Feminism"): 22.

8. Simmer-Brown, "Rita Gross's Contribution to Contemporary Western Tibetan Buddhism," 71.

9. Simmer-Brown, "What Water? Feminism, Shambhala Buddhism, and the Feminine Principle," 23.

10. For some of his activism, see http://www.philly.com/philly/obituaries/john-raines-84-civil-rights-activist-cleric-and-temple-prof-20171113.html, https://www.nytimes.com/2017/11/17/obituaries/john-raines-84-who-evaded-capture-in-an-fbi-break-in-dies.html, and https://www.washingtonpost.com/local/obituaries/john-raines-accomplice-in-1971-burglary-that-revealed-fbi-abuses-dies-at-84/2017/11/15/5aa54d98-ca16-11e7-aa96-54417592cf72_story.html?utm_term=.161918d60bf9.

11. bell hooks, "Feminism: A Transformational Politic," in *Talking Back: Thinking Feminist, Thinking Black* (Boston, MA: South End Press, 1989), 19. See also bell hooks, *Ain't I a Woman* (London: Pinto Press, 1982).

12. In general, I resist the labels of "second-wave feminist" and "third-wave feminism," and I prefer referring to them as "justice-oriented feminism" and "diversity-oriented feminism." The former set of labels implies a generational divide that does not really exist. A feminist who was active during the so-called second-wave feminism may be very concerned about diversity issues, and a feminist who was born after the so-called "third-wave feminism" does not necessarily concern themselves with the experiences of minority "others."

13. See Linda Martín Alcoff, "What Should White People Do?" *Hypatia* 13, no. 3 (1998): 10–11.

14. Rita M. Gross, "Studying Women and Religion: Conclusions Twenty-Five Years Later," in *Today's Woman in World Religions*, ed. Arvind Sharma (Albany, NY: State University of New York Press, 1994), 327.

15. Mary Keller, "Raced and Gendered Perspectives: Towards the Epidermalization of Subjectivity in Religious Studies Theory," in *Gender, Religion and Diversity: Cross-Cultural Perspectives*, eds. Ursula King and Tina Beattie (London and New York: Continuum, 2004), 89.

16. Randi R. Warne, "Gender," in *Guide to the Study of Religion*, eds. Willi Braun and Russell T. McCutcheon (London and New York: Cassell, 2000), 146.

17. Keller, "Raced and Gendered Perspectives," 88.

18. Amina Wadud, "Roundtable: Feminist Theology and Religions Diversity," *Journal of Feminist Studies in Religion* 16, no. 2 (2000): 90–100.

19. Gross, "Response," 129–311.

20. See George Yancy, "#IAmSexisst," *The New York Times*, October 24, 2018 (https://www.nytimes.com/2018/10/24/opinion/men-sexism-me-too.html); bell hooks, *The Will to Change: Man, Masculinity, and Love* (New York: Washington Square Press, 2004); Rosemary Radford Ruether, *Sexism and God-Talk: Toward a Feminist Theology* (Boston, MA: Beacon Press, 1993), 182–188.

21. Paul Crowe's field work offers a good snapshot of the range of practices at a Chinese Buddhist temple. Paul Crowe, "Amitābha's Birthday and Liberation of Life," in *Studying Buddhism in Practice*, ed. John S. Harding (London and New York: Routledge, 2012), 130–141. Regarding Chinese Buddhist syncretism, see my "Syncretism and Exclusivism: Characteristics of Chinese Mahāyāna Buddhism in Relation to the Racial Integration in Lansing Buddhist Association," *Sheng Yen Studies*, no. 9 (2017): 355–356. See also Chenxing Han, "Diverse Practices and Flexible Beliefs among

Young Adult Asian American Buddhists," *Journal of Global Buddhism* 18 (2017): 11–14.

22. The ethnic composition of the group is very different now. See Hsiao-Lan Hu, "Syncretism and Exclusivism: Characteristics of Chinese Mahāyāna Buddhism in Relation to the Racial Integration in Lansing Buddhist Association," *Sheng Yen Studies*, no. 9 (2017): 349–382.

23. For a relevant discussion regarding Asians being seen as perpetual foreigners, see Joseph Cheah, *Race and Religion in American Buddhism: White Supremacy and Immigrant Adaptation* (London and New York: Oxford University Press, 2011), 132–133.

24. Funie Hsu and Hondo Lobley, "Advice for Modern America, From the Painful History of American Buddhism," *Lion's Roar: Buddhist Wisdom for Our Time*, March 14, 2018 (https://www.lionsroar.com/advice-for-modern-america-from-the-painful-history-of-american-buddhism/, accessed on March 31, 2018). See also See Hu, "Syncretism and Exclusivism," 357.

25. Carla Sherrell and Judith Simmer-Brown, "Spiritual Bypassing in the Contemporary Mindfulness Movement," *ICEA (Initiative for Contemplation, Equity, and Action) Journal: Social Justice, Inner Work & Contemplative Practice* 1, no. 1 (July 2017): 81.

26. For an excellent critique of such an "American Buddhism" that excludes Asian-Americans, see Natalie E. Quli, "Western Self, Asian Other: Modernity, Authenticity, and Nostalgia for 'Tradition' in Buddhist Studies," *Journal of Buddhist Ethics* 16 (2009): 15–18.

27. Gross, *Religious Diversity*, 158.

28. Ibid., 164–165.

29. Rita M. Gross, *A Garland of Feminist Reflections: Forty Years of Religious Explorations* (Berkeley: University of California Press, 2009), 216–217.

30. Gross, "The Man-made Obstacle." For a brief account of the feminist standpoint theory, see Alison Bailey, "Locating Traitorous Identities: Toward a View of Privilege-Cognizant White Character," *Hypatia* 13, no. 3 (1998): 28–30.

31. Gross, "The Man-made Obstacle."

32. Sara Lewis, "Relative Inequality, Absolute Equality," *The Arrow: A Journal of Wakeful Society, Culture & Politics* 3, no. 1 (September 2016; "Buddhism & Feminism"): 19–20. The researches she cites are James W. Collins Jr., Richard J. David, Rebecca Symons, Adren Handler, Stephen N. Wall, and Lisa Dwyer, "Low-Income African-American Mothers' Perception of Exposure to Racial Discrimination and Infant Birth Weight," *Epidemiology* 11, no. 3 (2000): 337–339, and M. G. Marmot, S. Stansfield, C. Patel, F. North, J. Head, I. White, E. Brunner, A. Feeney, and G. Davey Smith, "Health Inequalities among British Civil Servants: The Whitehall II Study," *Lancet* 337, no. 8754 (1991): 1387–1393.

33. Ruth Frankenburg, *White Women, Race Matters: The Social Construction of Whiteness*, 5th edition (Minneapolis, MN: University of Minnesota Press, 1993), 123; Bailey, "Locating Traitorous Identities," 27–42.

34. Allan G. Johnson, *Privilege, Power and Difference*, 2nd edition (New York: McGraw Hill, 2006), 119.

35. Cheah, *Race and Religion in American Buddhism*, 19–35.

36. Ibid., 35.

37. Crowe, "Amitābha's Birthday and Liberation of Life," 138.

38. Hsiao-Lan Hu, *This-Worldly Nibbāna: A Buddhist-Feminist Social Ethic for Peacemaking in the Global Community* (Albany, NY: State University of New York Press, 2011).

39. Holly Gayley, "Where Do We Look for Buddhist Feminism?" *The Arrow: A Journal of Wakeful Society, Culture & Politics* 3, no. 1 (September 2016; "Buddhism & Feminism"): 15.

40. Simmer-Brown, "What Water? Feminism, Shambhala Buddhism, and the Feminine Principle," 23.

41. Gross, "The Man-made Obstacle."

42. Allie Malloy, "Obama Knocks Trump at Rutgers: 'Ignorance is not a Virtue,'" *CNN Politics*, May 25, 2016 (http://www.cnn.com/2016/05/15/politics/obama-donald-trump-rutgers-university/, accessed March 31, 2018).

43. Quli, "Western Self, Asian Other," 9.

44. Melanie L. Harris, "Buddhist Resources for Womanist Reflection," *Buddhist-Christian Studies* 34 (2014): 110.

45. Han, "Diverse Practices and Flexible Beliefs among Young Adult Asian American Buddhists," 1–24.

46. Charles S. Prebish, "Forum: Diversity and Divisions in American Buddhism," *Lion's Roar: Buddhist Wisdom for Our Time*, December 1, 2006 (http://www.lionsroar.com/forum-diversity-and-divisions-in-america-buddhism/, accessed March 31, 2018).

47. Quli, "Western Self, Asian Other," 10.

48. Gross, *Religious Diversity*, 172.

Afterword

Charles Johnson

To study the way is to study the self. To study the self is to forget
the self. To forget the self is to be enlightened by all things. To be
enlightened by all things is to remove the barriers between oneself and
others.

—Dogen

During its 2600-year history, Buddhism has widely traversed our planet, and
in every country where it has taken root it assumes to one degree or another
the social and cultural characteristics of that place and time. As it has grown
increasingly in popularity in America from the post-World War II period to
today, the Buddhadharma has taken on features specific to converts who bring
to it a particular form of historical conditioning and suffering. These American converts, perhaps prepared for Buddhism's arrival by the Christian social
gospel a century ago, and the fusion of religion and politics by the wing of
the civil rights movement represented by Martin Luther King Jr., tilt toward
the embrace of Thích Nhất Hạnh's "Engaged Buddhism," and a version of
spiritual practice that, instead of avoiding political questions, enthusiastically
pursues their implications for a religion once mistakenly judged to be passive
and indifferent to the concerns of social activists who demand change and the
realization of the ideals embodied in such "sacred," secular documents as the
Declaration of Independence and the Constitution.

Generally, for those who seek refuge from suffering and desire the happiness that comes from awakening, there is nothing lacking in the Buddhadharma's Theravada, Mahāyāna, and Vajrayana traditions. Everything is there,
as it should be with a philosophy that is coherent, consistent, complete, one
that is the most radical, emancipatory, and revolutionary in my experience,

309

and led Christian theologian Paul Tillich to refer to it as "one of the greatest, strangest, and at the same time most competitive of the religions proper."[1] It is competitive exactly to the degree that it is *non*-competitive and non-dualistic, an orientation toward life that avoids the divisions and divisiveness that are the primary causes of our social problems. And like everything in existence, it too is characterized by impermanence and change, an example being the transition from Theravada to Mahāyāna Buddhism. All this underscores why Dharma practice, begun in the sixth century BC, has proven itself to be universally appealing, why at one time a third of the human species were the Buddha's students or followers, and why some of the greatest artists in the world have been Buddhist priests.

But for those of us who are American converts to Buddhism, and live in a nation historically stained by racism, 244 years of slavery, the oppression of women, the slaughter of Native Americans and theft of their lands, and the systemic practices devoted to maintaining the dominance of WASP males, it is natural and even inevitable that we wonder how the doctrines and disciplines of the Dharma might be applied to alleviating social injustice and inequality. This meditation is all the more urgent when we consider the fact that whites make up only between 17 percent and 30 percent of the world's population while people of color (POC) account for between 70 percent and 83 percent; and we are fast experiencing the "browning" of an America where whites cling fiercely to economic, cultural, and political dominance. For several years now, this question—the relationship of Buddhism to political change—has been fiercely debated in mass-market Buddhist publications such as *Tricycle: The Buddhist Review*, *Lion's Roar*, and *Buddhadharma: The Practitioner's Quarterly*. However, what is new in this discussion, and revealed by the contributors to *Buddhism and Whiteness*, is the effort to find common ground between ancient Buddhist ideas and principles with feminist theory, existential phenomenology, and Critical Race Theory, and Critical Whiteness Studies.

For those of us who have spent our adult lives in the practice of meditation and study of the Tripitaka or "three baskets" of Buddhism (*sūtras*, *ahbidharma* literature, and *vinaya* or rules for monks and nuns), it is obvious that unlike Critical Race Theory, which was conceived in academic settings and then "weaponized" for social activism (for example, such irrefutable facts as the truth of white privilege), the Dharma cannot be so used, for it is nonviolent, non-materialistic, and especially nondualistic. And most important of all, its goal is to make us free, *truly* free. Even free of Buddhism itself. ("I have taught you Dharma, like the parable of the raft, for getting across, for not retaining," said Shākyamuni. "You monks . . . must not cling to right states of mind and, all the more, to wrong states of mind.")

Shākyamuni Buddha taught the doctrine of *anatta* or non-self as one of the three marks of everything existing. This powerful insight means that no self (or ego) exists in the sense of being a permanent, eternal, integral, and independent substance within an individual. Such a truth is very attractive for all of us battling various forms of racial and gender essentialism. But like everything in the Buddhadharma, it is just a tool for our liberation, one that we will leave behind when we reach a later stage of development. This is why the Buddha said if practitioners became *attached* to the idea of non-self, he would instead teach a doctrine *of* self.

For the ultimate goal of Buddhist practice is Nirvana or an individual awakening that leads to our experience of things in their true impermanence, codependency, and emptiness (*shūnyatā*). No two odysseys to awakening are the same for everyone. No one can do this for us. One progresses alone, and what one experiences can no more be transmitted to another than one can explain to a blind man the beauty of an orchid. Therefore, Thích Nhất Hạnh reminds us that "In Buddhism, we never talk about Nirvana, because Nirvana means the extinction of all notions, concepts, and speech." So no, we cannot weaponize Buddhism or bend it toward any social agenda or political party and still call what we are doing the Buddhadharma. All this Thích Nhất Hạnh has made clear in his beautiful and concise statement on the "14 Principles of Engaged Buddhism," where in the first principle he states, "Do not be idolatrous or bound by any doctrine, theory, or ideology, even Buddhist ones. Buddhist systems of thought are guiding means; they are not absolute truth."

However, as the contributors to this volume demonstrate, an understanding of Buddhism, especially its ethical or moral program presented in the Eight-fold Path and *pāramitās* or *brahmaviharas*, leads us to a more civilized and compassionate way of life, one free from what Bhikkhu Bodhi calls the layers of "conceptual paint"—interpretations and illusions based upon our social, racial, and gender conditioning—that distort and obscure our experience of reality. When writing of how Buddhism can in fact make a meaningful con-tribution to our discussion on how to make the world less oppressive, many of the contributors here write with the authority of learned Buddhologists—I am thinking of the excellent articles by Leah Kalmanson and Bryce Huebner. Others draw upon George Yancy's important insights concerning the phe-nomenology of the black body (and my own early work on this subject in the 1970s). And yet others, like Sharon A. Suh, eloquently place *karunā* (com-passion) and all that it implies at the center of a Bodhisattva-inspired practice that has proven itself to be of tremendous value for healing people of color who have suffered for centuries under the "white gaze."

Suh's article recalls for me the wisdom in Buddhist teacher Claude AnShin Thomas's statement that "I cannot think my way into a new way of living,

I have to live my way into a new way of thinking." And he has also said, wisely, that "Peace is not an idea. Peace is not a political movement, not a theory or a dogma. Peace is a way of life: living mindfully in the present moment. . . . It is not a question of politics, but of actions. It is not a matter of improving a political system or even taking care of homeless people alone. These are valuable but will not end war and suffering. We must simply stop the endless wars that rage within. . . . Imagine, if everyone stopped the war in themselves—there would be no seeds from which war could grow."

Thomas, a former soldier in Vietnam and the author of *At Hell's Gate: A Soldier's Journey from War to Peace* became a mendicant monk after participating in one of Thích Nhất Hạnh's retreats for veterans. There, he was exposed I am sure to several principles of "Engaged Buddhism." Among these are

Principle 2: Do not force others, including children, by any means whatsoever, to adopt your views, whether by authority, threat, money, propaganda, or even education. However, through compassionate dialogue, help others renounce fanaticism and narrowness.

Principle 6: Do not maintain anger or hatred. Learn to penetrate and transform them when they are still seeds in the mind.

Principle 7: Be in touch with what is wondrous, refreshing, and healing both inside and around you. Plant seeds of joy, peace, and understanding in yourself in order to facilitate the work of transformation in the depths of your consciousness.

Principle 8: Do not utter words that can create discord and cause the community to break. Make every effort to reconcile and resolve all conflicts, however small.

Principle 9: Do not utter words that cause division and hatred. . . . Do not criticize or condemn things of which you are not sure. Always speak truthfully and constructively. Have the courage to speak out about situations of injustice, even when doing so may threaten your safety.

Principle 10: Do not use the Buddhist community for personal gain or profit, or transform your community into a political party. A religious community, however, should take a clear stand against oppression and injustice and should strive to change the situation without engaging in partisan conflicts.

These principles capture the essence of our daily spiritual practice. And for Suh the Dharma gate that leads to healing people of color, whites, and probably the world is "broken openheartedness." Why? Because, as spiritual teacher Ruth King points out in her book *Mindful of Race: Transforming Racism from the Inside Out*, life in the splintered, relative-phenomenal realm of Samsara where things arise and are unraveled in a fortnight can never be perfect or perfected in accordance with ideas or ideals of perfection. And neither can we. This acceptance of ourselves, and the nature of relative experience (*samvriti satya*) is the beginning of what I call epistemological humility. How does a Dharma follower then move through the world? Our movement is an example of disinterested, deontological ethics, which, like that found in Kantian philosophy, is "interested in the act, never the fruit." In the *Astasahasrika-prajñaparamita* ("The Perfection of Wisdom"), we learn,

> a bodhisattva . . . should behave equally to all sentient beings. He should produce thoughts that are fair to all sentient beings. He should handle others with thoughts that are impartial, that are friendly, that are favorable, that are helpful. He should handle others with thoughts that are nonconfrontational, that avoid harm, that avoid hurt, that avoid distress. He should handle others, all sentient beings, using the understanding of a mother, using the understanding of a father, the understanding of a son and the understanding of a daughter. . . . He should be trained to be the refuge for all sentient beings. In his own behavior he should renounce all evil. He should give gifts, he should guard morality, he should exercise patience, he should exert vigor, he should enter into contemplation, and he should master his wisdom! He should consider dependent origination backwards and forwards, and he should instigate, encourage, and empower that in others.

The beauty and importance then of *Buddhism and Whiteness* lie in the challenge it—and American converts to Buddhism—places before us to grapple with the age-old question of spirituality's relationship to politics and our social and racial lives. My hope is that we shall do so with the proto-empirical approach that the Buddha emphasized during his forty-five years as a teacher:

> Do not go by oral tradition, by lineage of teaching, by hearsay, by a collection of scriptures, by logical reasoning, by inferential reasoning, by reflection on reasons, by acceptance of a view after pondering it, by the seeming competence of a speaker, or because you think "The ascetic is our teacher." But when you know for yourselves, "These things are unwholesome, these things are blamable; these things are censured by the wise; these things, if undertaken and practiced, lead to harm and suffering," then you should abandon them.

NOTE

1. Paul Tillich, *Christianity and the Encounter of the World Religions* (New York: Columbia University Press, 1963), 54.

Bibliography

Adams, Sheridan, Mushim Patricia Ikeda, Jeff Kitzes, Margarita Loinaz, Choyin Rangdrol, Jessica Tan, and Larry Yang, eds. *Making the Invisible Visible: Healing Racism in Our Buddhist Communities*. 3rd ed. Woodacre, CA: Spirit Rock, 2000.

Adiele, Faith. *Meeting Faith: The Forest Journals of a Black Buddhist Nun*. New York: W. W. Norton, 2004.

Ahmed, Sara. "Declarations of Whiteness: The Non-Performativity of Anti-Racism." *Borderlands* 3, no. 2 (2004). http://www.borderlands.net.au/vol3no2_2004/ahmed_declarations.htm.

Ahmed, Sara. *Living a Feminist Life*. Durham, NC: Duke University Press, 2017.

Ahmed, Sara. *On Being Included*. Durham, NC: Duke University Press, 2010.

Ahmed, Sara. "A Phenomenology of Whiteness." *Feminist Theory* 8, no. 2 (2007): 149–168.

Alcoff, Linda Martín. "Epistemologies of Ignorance: Three Types." In *Race and Epistemologies of Ignorance*, edited by Shannon Sullivan and Nancy Tuana, 39–58. Albany: State University of New York Press, 2007.

Alcoff, Linda Martín. "Latino/as, Asian Americans, and the Black–White Binary." *The Journal of Ethics* 7, no. 1 (2003): 5–27.

Allport, Gordon. *The Nature of Prejudice*. Boston, MA: Addison-Wesley, 1954.

Almond, Philip. *The British Discovery of Buddhism*. Cambridge: Cambridge University Press, 1988.

Analayo, Bhikkhu. *Satipatthana: The Direct Path to Realization*. Birmingham: Windhorse Publications, 2004.

Anand, Dibyesh. "Archive and the Poetics of 'Exotica Tibet.'" In *Tibetan Borderlands*, edited by P. Christiaan Klieger, 49–66. Leiden, Netherlands: Brill Publishers, 2006.

Andrade, Dale. "Westmoreland Was Right: Learning The Wrong Lessons From the Vietnam War." *Small Wars and Insurgencies* 19, no. 2 (2008): 145–181.

Applebaum, Barbara. *Being White, Being Good: White Complicity, White Moral Responsibility, and Social Justice Pedagogy*. Lanham, MD: Lexington Books, 2010.

Arendt, Hannah. *Responsibility and Judgment*. Edited and with an introduction by Jerome Kohn. New York: Schoken Books, 2003.

Arnold, Dan. *Brains, Buddhas, and Believing: The Problem of Intentionality in Classical Buddhist and Cognitive–Scientific Philosophy of Mind*. New York: Columbia University Press, 2014.

Arthington, Phil. "Mindfulness: A Critical Perspective." *Community Psychology in Global Perspective* 2, no. 1 (2016): 92.

Badger, Emily. "This Can't Happen by Accident." *Washington Post*, May 2, 2016. https://www.washingtonpost.com/graphics/business/wonk/housing/atlanta/??noredirect=on (accessed April 1, 2018).

Baldwin, James. *The Fire Next Time*. London: Penguin Books, 2007.

Baldwin, James. *The Price of the Ticket: Collected NonFiction, 1948–1985*. New York: St. Martin's Press, 1985.

Banaji, Mahzarin R., and Anthony G. Greenwald. *Blindspot: The Hidden Biases of Good People*. New York: Bantam Books, 2016.

Batchelor, Stephen. *The Awakening of the West: The Encounter of Buddhism and Western Culture*. Berkeley: Parallax Press, 1994.

Batchelor, Stephen. *Secular Buddhism: Imagining the Dharma in an Uncertain World*. New Haven, CT: Yale University Press, 2017.

Berlant, Lauren. *The Queen of America Goes to Washington: Essays on Sex and Citizenship*. Durham, NC: Duke University Press, 1997.

Bernasconi, Robert. "Kant as an Unfamiliar Source of Racism." In *Philosophers on Race: Critical Essays*, edited by Julie K. Ward and Tommy L. Lott, 145–166. Malden, MA: Blackwell, 2002.

Bernasconi, Robert. "Who Invented the Concept of Race? Kant's Role in the Enlightenment Construction of Race." In *Race*, 11–36. Malden, MA: Blackwell, 2001.

Bhodhi, Bhikku, ed. *The Connected Discourses of the Buddha*. Somerville, MA: Wisdom Publications, 2003.

Blair, Irene V., Jennifer E. Ma, and Alison P. Lenton. "Imagining Stereotypes Away: The Moderation of Implicit Stereotypes through Mental Imagery." *Journal of Personality and Social Psychology* 81, no. 5 (2001): 828–841.

Bodhi, Ven Bhikkhu. "What Are the Four Noble Truths?" *Tricycle*. https://tricycle.org/magazine/impermanence-and-four-noble-truths/.

Bond, George. *The Buddhist Revival in Sri Lanka: Religious Tradition, Reinterpretation and Response*. Columbia: University of South Carolina Press, 1988.

Borup, Jørn. "Branding Buddha-Mediatized and Commodified Buddhism as Cultural Narrative." *Journal of Global Buddhism* 17 (2016): 41–55.

Branch, Taylor. *At Canaan's Edge: America in the King Years 1965–68*. New York: Simon and Schuster, 2006.

Braun, Erik. *The Birth of Insight*. Chicago: University of Chicago Press, 2013.

Brennan, Joy. "The Three Natures and the Path to Liberation in Yogācāra-Vijñānavāda Thought." *Journal of Indian Philosophy* 46 (2018): 646–647.

Brons, Lajos. "Facing Death from a Safe Distance: Saṃvega and Moral Psychology." *Journal of Buddhist Ethics* 23 (2016): 83–128.

BuddhaDharma. "Free the Dharma: Race, Power and White Privilege in American Buddhism." *BuddhaDharma: The Practitioner's Quarterly* (Summer 2016).

Burton, David. "Knowledge and Liberation: Philosophical Reflections on a Buddhist Conundrum." *Philosophy East and West* 52, no. 3 (2002): 326–345.

Burtscher, Michael. "Facing 'the West' on Philosophical Grounds: A View from the Pavilion of Subjectivity on Meiji Japan." *Comparative Studies of South Asian, Africa, and the Middle East* 26, no. 3 (2006): 367–376.

Butler, Johnnella E. "African American Literature and Realist Theory: Seeking the 'True True.'" In *Identity Politics Reconsidered*, edited by Linda Martín Alcoff, Michael Hames-García, Satya P. Mohanty, and Paula M. L. Moya, 171–192. New York: Palgrave, 2006.

Campany, Robert Ford. "On the Very Idea of Religions (in the Modern West and in Early Medieval China)." *History of Religions* 42, no. 4 (2003): 287–319.

Carrette, Jeremy. "Grace Jantzen: A Feminist Voice Expanding the Philosophy of Religion." *The Guardian*, May 10, 2006. https://www.theguardian.com/news/2006/may/11/guardianobituaries.gender (accessed March 14, 2018).

Carrette, Jeremy, and Richard King. *Selling Spirituality: The Silent Takeover of Religion.* New York: Routledge, 2005.

Carvalho, Antonio. "Assembling Mindfulness: Technologies of the Self, Neurons and Neoliberal Subjectivities." Paper presented at sixth STS Italia Conference/Sociotechnical Environments, Trento, Italy, November 24–26, 2016. https://www.researchgate.net/publication/320934809_Assembling_Mindfulness_Technologies_of_the_Self_Neurons_and_Neoliberal_Subjectivities (accessed March 30, 2018).

Cesaire, Aime. *Discourse on Colonialism.* Translated by Joan Pinkham. New York and London: Monthly Review Press, 1972. Originally published as *Discours sur le colonialisme* by Editions Presence Africaine, 1955. http://abahlali.org/files/_Discourse_on_Colonialism.pdf.

Chatterjee, Amita. "Funes and Categorization in an Abstraction-free World." In *Apoha: Buddhist Nominalism and Human Cognition*, edited by Mark Siderits, Tom Tillemans, and Arindam Chakrabarti, 247–257. New York: Columbia University Press, 2011.

Cheah, Joseph. *Race and Religion in American Buddhism: White Supremacy and Immigrant Adaptation.* New York: Oxford University Press, 2011.

Che Guevara, Ernesto. *Socialism and Man in Cuba.* 1965. Reprint, Atlanta, GA: Pathfinder Press, 2009.

Chen, Jacqueline M., Maria Clara P. de Paula Couto, Airi M. Sacco, and Yarrow Dunham. "To Be or Not to Be (Black or Multiracial or White): Cultural Variation in Racial Boundaries." *Social Psychological and Personality Science* (2017). doi: 1948550617725149.

Chin, Justin. "Attack of the White Buddhists." In *Mongrel: Essays, Diatribes, and Pranks*, 113–118. New York: St. Martin's Press, 1999.

Cleveland, Christena. "So Much of the Privileged Life is About Transcendence." *On Being,* July 7, 2017. https://onbeing.org/blog/christena-cleveland-so-much-of-the-privileged-life-is-about-transcendence/ (accessed March 12, 2018).

Coates, Ta-Nehisi. "The Case for Reparations." *The Atlantic Monthly*, June 2014. https://www.theatlantic.com/magazine/archive/2014/06/the-case-for-reparations/361631/ (accessed April 1, 2018).

Coates, Ta-Nehisi. *We Were Eight Years in Power*. New York: One World, 2017.

Coleman, James William. *The New Buddhism: The Western Transformation of an Ancient Religion*. New York: Oxford University Press, 2002.

Combahee River Collective Statement. *Women's Studies Quarterly* 42, nos. 3–4 (1981): 210–218.

Copeland, Shawn. "Memory, Emancipation, and Hope: Political Theology in the 'Land of the Free.'" *The Santa Clara Lectures* 4 (November 9, 1997): 6.

Craig, Maureen A., Julian M. Rucker, and Jennifer A. Richeson. "The Pitfalls and Promise of Increasing Racial Diversity: Threat, Contact, and Race Relations in the 21st Century." *Current Directions in Psychological Science* 27, no. 3 (2017): 188–193.

Curley, Melissa Anne-Marie. *Pure Land/Real World: Modern Buddhists, Japanese Leftists, and the Utopian Imagination*. Honolulu: University of Hawai'i Press, 2017.

Dasgupta, Nilanjana. "Implicit Attitudes and Beliefs Adapt to Situations: A Decade of Research on the Malleability of Implicit Prejudice, Stereotypes, and the Self-concept." *Advances in Experimental Social Psychology* 47 (2013): 233–279.

Daugherity, Brian. "Review of Peace and Freedom: The Civil Rights and Antiwar Movements in the 1960s." *H-South*. https://networks.h-net.org/node/512/reviews/798/daugherity-hall-peace-and-freedom-civil-rights-and-antiwar-movements.

Davies, Bret. "Naturalness in Zen and Shin Buddhism: Before and Beyond Self and Other Power." *Contemporary Buddhism* 15, no. 2 (2014): 433–447.

Davies, William. *The Happiness Industry: How the Government and Big Business Sold Us Wellbeing*. London: Verso, 2015.

Dawson, G., and L. Trunbull. "Is Mindfulness the New Opiate of the Masses? Critical Reflections from a Buddhist Perspective." *Psychotherapy in Australia* 12, no. 4 (2006): 60–64.

Devine, Patricia G., and Andrew J. Elliot. "Are Racial Stereotypes Really Fading? The Princeton Trilogy Revisited." *Personality and Social Psychology Bulletin* 21, no. 11 (1995): 1139–1150.

Devine, Patricia G., Patrick S. Forscher, Anthony J. Austin, and William T. L. Cox. "Long-Term Reduction in Implicit Race Bias: A Prejudice Habit-Breaking Intervention." *Journal of Experimental Social Psychology* 48, no. 6 (2012): 1267–1278.

Dharmapala, Anagarika. "The World's Debt to Buddhism." In *Asian Religions in America: A Documentary History*, edited by Thomas A. Tweed and Stephen Prothero, 133–137. Oxford: Oxford University Press, 1998.

DiAngelo, Robin. *What Does it Mean to be White? Developing White Racial Literacy*. New York: Peter Lang, 2016.

DiAngelo, Robin. "White Fragility." *The International Journal of Critical Pedagogy* 3, no. 3 (2011): 54–70.

DiAngelo, Robin. *White Fragility: Why it's so Hard for White People to Talk about Racism*. Boston: Beacon Press, 2018.

Dovidio, John F., and Samuel L. Gaertner. "Aversive Racism and Selection Decisions: 1989 and 1999." *Psychological Science* 11, no. 4 (2000): 315–319.

Dreyfus, Georges. *Recognizing Reality: Dharmakirti's Philosophy and its Tibetan Interpretations*. Albany: State University of New York Press, 1997.

Dunne, John D. *Foundations of Dharmakirti's Philosophy*. Somerville, MA: Wisdom Publications, 2004.

Dunne, John D. "On Essences, Goals and Social Justice: An Exercise in Buddhist Theology." In *Buddhist Theology: Critical Reflections by Contemporary Buddhist Scholars*, edited by Roger R. Jackson and John J. Makransky, 275–292. New York: Routledge, 2000.

Dworkin, Ronald. *Taking Rights Seriously*. Boston, MA: Harvard University Press, 1977.

Eltschinger, Vincent. *Caste and Buddhist Philosophy: Continuity of Some Buddhist Arguments Against the Realist Interpretation of Social Denominations*. Translated by R. Prevereau. Delhi: Motilal Banarsidass, 2012.

Eltschinger, Vincent. "Dharmakīrti." *Revue internationale de philosophie* 253, no. 3 (2010): 397–440.

Emerson, David. *Trauma Sensitive Yoga: Bringing the Body into Treatment*. New York: W. W. Norton, 2015.

Emerson, Michael, and Christian Smith. *Divided by Faith: Evangelical Religion and the Problem of Race in America*. New York: Oxford University Press, 2000.

Eswaran, Eknath. *The End of Sorrow: The Bhagavad Gita for Daily Living*. Nilgiri Press, 2010.

Eze, Emmanuel. "The Color of Reason: The Idea of 'Race' in Kant's Anthropology." In *Postcolonial African Philosophy: A Critical Reader*, 103–104. Cambridge, MA: Blackwell, 1997.

Eze, Emmanuel. *Race and the Enlightenment: A Reader*. Cambridge, MA: Blackwell, 1997.

Feagin, Joe. *The White Racial Frame: Centuries of Racial Framing and Counter-Framing*. New York: Routledge, 2013.

Feldman, Christina. "Dependent Origination." *Barre Center for Buddhist Studies*, Spring 1999. https://www.buddhistinquiry.org/article/dependent-origination/.

Fields, Rick. *How the Swans Came to the Lake*. Boulder, CO: Shambhala Publications, 1992.

Fischer, Kathleen. *Women at the Well: Feminist Perspectives on Spiritual Direction*. New York: Paulist, 1988.

Flagg, Barbara. "On Selecting Black Women as Paradigms for Race and Discrimination Analyses." *Berkeley Journal of Gender, Law and Justice* 10, no. 1 (1995): Article 6.

Flagg, Barbara. "'Was Blind, But Now I See': White Race Consciousness and the Requirement of Discriminating Intent." *Michigan Law Review* 91, no. 5 (1993): 953–1017.

Flagg, Barbara. *Was Blind, But Now I See: White Race Consciousness and the Law*. New York: New York University Press, 1997.

Foucault, Michel. *Discipline and Punishment: The Birth of the Prison*. New York: Penguin, 1977.

Foulk, Griffith T. "Ritual in Japanese Zen Buddhism." In *Zen Ritual*, edited by Steven Heine, 21–82. Oxford: Oxford University Press, 2007.

Frost, Robert. "A Servant of Servants." In *North of Boston*, 24. New York: Henry Holt, 1915.

Gallagher, Brendon. "The Vietnam War and the Civil Rights Movement." AR*Net*, February 20, 2014. http://www.americansc.org.uk/Online/Vietnam_Civil_Rights. htm.

Gallegos, Alicia. "AAMC Report Shows Decline of Black Males in Medicine." *AAMC News*, September 27, 2016. https://news.aamc.org/diversity/article/decline-black-males-medicine/.

Gampopa. *The Jewel Ornament of Liberation: The Wish-fulfilling Gem of the Noble Teachings*. Translated by Khenpo Konchog Gyaltsen Rinpoche. Boston: Snow Lion, 1998.

Ganeri, Jonardon. "Apoha, Feature-Placing, and Sensory Content." In *Apoha: Buddhist Nominalism and Human Cognition*, edited by Mark Siderits, Tom Tillemans, and Arindam Chakrabarti, 228–246. New York: Columbia University Press, 2011.

Garcia, John, and Robert A. Koelling. "Relation of Cue to Consequence in Avoidance Learning." *Psychonomic Science* 4 (1966): 123–124.

Garfield, Jay L. *Engaging Buddhism: Why It Matters to Philosophy*. Oxford: Oxford University Press, 2015.

Garfield, Jay L. "Vasubandhu's *Trisvabhāvanirdeśa* (*Treatise on the three natures*). Editor's Introduction." In *Buddhist Philosophy: Essential Readings*, edited by William Edelglass and Jay Garfield, 35–45. Oxford: Oxford University Press, 2009.

Garfield, Jay L. "What Is It like to Be a Bodhisattva? Moral Phenomenology in Śāntideva's Bodhicaryāvatāra." *Journal of the International Association of Buddhist Studies* 33, nos. 1–2 (2012): 333–357.

Garfield, Jay L., and Bryan W. Van Norden. "If Philosophy Won't Diversify, Let's Call It What It Really Is." *New York Times*, May 11, 2016. https://www.nytimes.com/2016/05/11/opinion/if-philosophy-wont-diversify-lets-call-it-what-it-really-is.html.

Garner, Steve. *Whiteness: An Introduction*. London: Routledge, 2007.

Gay, Roxane. *Bad Feminist: Essays*. New York: HarperCollins, 2014.

Gleig, Ann. *American Dharma: Buddhism Beyond Modernity*. New Haven, CT: Yale University Press, 2019.

Gleig, Ann. "Dharma Diversity and Deep Inclusivity at the East Bay Meditation Center: From Buddhist Modernism to Buddhist Postmodernism?" *Contemporary Buddhism: An Interdisciplinary Journal* 15 (2014): 312–331.

Gleig, Ann. "Queering Buddhism or Buddhist De-Queering? Reflecting on Differences Among Western LGBTQI Buddhists and the Limits of Liberal Convert Buddhism." *Theology & Sexuality* 18, no. 3 (2012): 198–214.

Gleig, Ann. "The Shifting Landscape of Buddhism in America." *BuddhaDharma*. https://www.lionsroar.com/the-shifting-landscape-of-buddhism-in-america/.

Godsil, Rachel D., and L. Song Richardson. "Racial Anxiety." *Iowa Law Review* 2235 102, no. 5 (2017). https://ilr.law.uiowa.edu/print/volume-102-issue-5/racial-anxiety/.

Gold, Jonathan C. *Paving the Great Way: Vasubandhu's Unifying Buddhist Philosophy*. New York: Columbia University Press, 2014.

Goodman, Charles. *Consequences of Compassion: An Interpretation and Defense of Buddhist Ethics*. Oxford: Oxford University Press, 2009.

Gordon, Lewis. "Critical Reflections on Three Popular Tropes in the Study of Whiteness." In *What White Looks Like: African-American Philosophers on the Whiteness Question*, edited by George Yancy, 173–194. London: Routledge, 2004.

Graham, Elaine L., ed. *Grace Jantzen: Redeeming the Present*. Burlington, VT: Ashgate, 2009.

Graham III, Herman. *The Brothers' Vietnam War: Black Power, Manhood, and the Military Experience*. Gainesville: University Press of Florida, 2003.

Grimes, Katie. "*Black Exceptionalism*: Anti Black Supremacy in the Aftermath of Slavery." In *Anti-Blackness and Christian Ethics*, edited by Vincent Lloyd and Andrew Prevot, 41–60. Maryknoll: Orbis Press, 2017.

Gross, Matthias, and Linsey McGoey, eds. *Routledge International Handbook of Ignorance Studies*. New York: Routledge, 2015.

Guerrero, Laura. "Conventional Truth and Intentionality in the Work of Dharmakīrti." In *The Moon Points Back*, edited by Koji Tanaka, Yasuo Deguchi, Jay L. Garfield, and Graham Priest, 189–219. Oxford: Oxford University Press, 2015.

Gutiérrez Baldoquín, Hilda, ed. *Dharma, Color, and Culture: New Voices in Western Buddhism*. Berkeley: Parallax Press, 2004.

Gyatso, Tenzin. "Training the Mind: Verse 7." https://www.dalailama.com/teachings /training-the-mind/training-the-mind-verse-7 (accessed April 1, 2018).

Hall, Simon. *Peace and Freedom: The Civil Rights and Antiwar Movements in the 1960s*. Philadelphia: University of Pennsylvania Press, 2005.

Hall, Simon. "The Response of the Moderate Wing of the Civil Rights Movement to the War in Vietnam." *Historical Journal* 46, no. 3 (2003): 669–701.

Hall, Stuart, ed. *Representation: Cultural Representations and Signifying Practices*. Thousand Oaks, CA: SAGE Publications, 2007.

Hall, Matthew, Kyle Crowder, and Amy Spring. "Neighborhood Foreclosures, Racial/Ethnic Transitions, and Residential Segregation." *American Sociological Review* 80, no. 3 (2015): 526–549.

Hames-García, Michael. *Identity Complex*. Minneapolis, MN: University of Minnesota Press, 2011.

Harding, Sarah. *Chöd: The Sacred Teachings on Severance*. Boulder: Snow Lion, 2016.

Harding, Sarah. *Machik's Complete Explanation: Clarifying the Meaning of Chöd*. Ithaca, NY: Snow Lion Publications, 2003.

Headley, Clevis. "Delegitimizing the Normativity of "Whiteness": A Critical Africana Philosophical Study of the Metaphoricity of "Whiteness." In *What White Looks Like: African-American Philosophers on the Whiteness Question*, edited by George Yancy, 87–106. London: Routledge, 2004.

Hegel, Georg Wilhelm Friedrich. *Lectures on the History of Philosophy.* Vol. 1. Translated by E. S. Haldane. London: Kegan Paul, Trench, Trübner and Co., 1892.

Heine, Steven, and Dale S. Wright. *Zen Masters.* Oxford: Oxford University Press, 2010.

Heisig, James W., Thomas P. Kasulis, and John C. Maraldo, eds. *Japanese Philosophy: A Sourcebook.* Honolulu: University of Hawai'i Press, 2011.

Heschel, Abraham Joshua. *The Sabbath: Its Meaning for Modern Man.* New York: Farrar, Straus and Young, 1951.

Hickey, Wakoh Shannon. "Two Buddhisms, Three Buddhisms, and Racism." In *Buddhism Beyond Borders: New Perspectives on Buddhism in the United States,* edited by Scott A. Mitchell and Natalie E. F. Quli, 44–46. Albany: State University of New York Press, 2015.

Hickman, Christine B. "The Devil and the One Drop Rule: Racial Categories, African Americans, and the U.S. Census." *Michigan Law Review* 95, no. 5 (1997): 1161–1265.

Hicks, John. *An Interpretation of Religion: Human Responses to the Transcendent.* New York: Macmillan, 1989.

Hirschfeld, Lawrence A. "Seven Myths of Race and the Young Child." *Du Bois Review: Social Science Research on Race* 9, no. 1 (2012): 17–39.

Hochman, Adam. "Racial Discrimination: How Not To Do It." *Studies in History and Philosophy of Science Part C: Studies in History and Philosophy of Biological and Biomedical Sciences* 44, no. 3 (2013): 278–286.

Hochman, Adam. "Replacing Race: Interactive Constructionism About Racialized Groups." *Ergo, an Open Access Journal of Philosophy* 4, no. 3 (2017): 61–92.

Hollywood, Amy. *Acute Melancholia and Other Essays: Mysticism, History and the Study of Religion.* New York: Columbia University Press, 2016.

hooks, bell. *Black Looks: Race and Representation.* Boston: South End Press, 1992.

hooks, bell. *Salvation: Black People and Love.* New York: William Morrow, 2001.

hooks, bell. *Talking Back: Thinking Feminist, Thinking Black.* Toronto: Between the Lines, 1989.

hooks, bell. *Teaching to Transgress.* New York: Routledge, 1990.

hooks, bell. *Writing Beyond Race: Living Theory and Practice.* New York: Routledge, 2013.

Horton, Myles, and Paulo Freire. *We Make the Road by Walking: Conversations on Education and Social Change,* edited by Brenda Bell, John Gaventa, and John Peters. Philadelphia, PA: Temple, 1990 reprint ed.

Hughes Seager, Richard. *Buddhism in America.* New York: Columbia University Press, 1999.

Ignatiev, Noel. *How the Irish Became White.* London: Routledge, 1995.

Inoue, Enryō. "Addressing the Divine." Translated by Gerard Clinton Godart. In *Japanese Philosophy: A Sourcebook,* edited by James W. Heisig, Thomas P. Kasulis, and John C. Maraldo, 630. Honolulu: University of Hawai'i Press, 2011.

Inoue, Enryō. "The Temple of Philosophy." Translated by Gerard Clinton Godart. In *Japanese Philosophy: A Sourcebook,* edited by James W. Heisig, Thomas P. Kasulis, and John C. Maraldo, 629–630. Honolulu: University of Hawai'i Press, 2011.

Isaacs, Arnold R. *Vietnam Shadows: The War, Its Ghosts, and Its Legacy*. Baltimore: Johns Hopkins University Press, 2000.

Jackson, Carl T. "D. T. Suzuki, 'Suzuki Zen,' and the American Reception of Zen Buddhism." In *American Buddhism as a Way of Life*, edited by Gary Storhoff and John Whalen-Bridge, 39–56. Albany: State University of New York Press, 2010.

James, William. *The Varieties of Religious Experience: The Gifford Lectures 1901–1902*. Glasgow: Collins, 1960.

Jantzen, Grace M. *Becoming Divine: Toward a Feminist Philosophy of Religion*. Bloomington: University of Indiana, 1999.

Jantzen, Grace M. *Power, Gender, and Christian Mysticism*. New York: Cambridge University Press, 1995.

Jennings, Willie. *The Christian Imagination: Theology and the Origins of Race*. New Haven, CT: Yale University Press, 2011.

Johnson, Charles. "A Phenomenology of the Black Body." *Michigan Quarterly Review* 32, no. 4 (1993): 595–614.

Johnson, Charles. *Taming the Ox: Buddhist Stories and Reflections on Politics, Race, Culture, and Spiritual Practice*. Boulder, CO: Shambhala Publications, 2014.

Johnson, Charles R. "The King We Need: Martin Luther King, Jr., Moral Philosopher." *Lion's Roar*, January 15, 2018. https://www.lionsroar.com/the-king-we-need-charles-r-johnson-on-the-legacy-of-dr-martin-luther-king-jr/.

Josephson, Jason Ānanda. *The Invention of Religion in Japan*. Chicago: University of Chicago Press, 2012.

Josephson, Jason Ānanda. "When Buddhism Became a 'Religion': Religion and Superstition in the Writings of Inoue Enryō." *Japanese Journal of Religious Studies* 33, no. 1 (2006): 143–168.

Josephson-Storm, Jason Ānanda. "The Superstition, Secularism, and Religion Trinary: Or Re-Theorizing Secularism." *Method and Theory in the Study of Religion* 30 (2017): 1–20.

Kachru, Sonam. "Minds and Worlds: A Philosophical Commentary on the Twenty Verses of Vasubandhu." PhD thesis, University of Chicago, 2015.

Kahn, J., et al. "Open Letter: How Not to Talk About Race and Genetics." *BuzzFeed*, March 30, 2018. https://www.buzzfeednews.com/article/bfopinion/race-genetics-david-reich (accessed April 1, 2018).

Kaleem, Jaweed. "Buddhist 'People of Color Sanghas,' Diversity Efforts Address Conflicts About Race Among Meditators." *HuffPost*, November 18, 2012. https://www.huffingtonpost.com/2012/11/18/buddhism-race-mediators-people-of-color-sangha_n_2144559.html.

Kalmanson, Leah. "Decolonizing the Department: Peter K. J. Park and the Profession of Philosophy." *Journal of World Philosophies* (Winter 2017): 60–65.

Kalmanson, Leah. "Pure Land Ecology: Taking the Supernatural Seriously in Environmental Philosophy." In *Japanese Environmental Philosophy*, edited by J. Baird Callicott and James McRae, 29–46. Oxford: Oxford University Press, 2017.

Kapstein, Matthew T. "Who Wrote the Trisvabhāvanirdeśa? Reflections on an Enigmatic Text and Its Place in the History of Buddhist Philosophy." *Journal of Indian Philosophy* 46, no. 1 (2018): 1–30.

Kelly, David J., Shaoying Liu, Kang Lee, Paul C. Quinn, Oliver Pascalis, Alan M. Slater, and Liezhong Ge. "Development of the Other-race Effect During Infancy: Evidence Toward Universality?" *Journal of Experimental Child Psychology* 104, no. 1 (2009): 105–114.

Keown, Damien. *The Nature of Buddhist Ethics*. New York: Palgrave, 2001.

Khandro. *This Precious Life: Tibetan Buddhist Teachings on the Path to Enlightenment*. Rev. ed. Boulder, CO: Shambhala Publications, 2005.

Kifner, John. "Report on Brutal Vietnam Campaign Stirs Memories." *New York Times*, December 28, 2003. http://www.nytimes.com/2003/12/28/us/report-on-brutal-vietnam-campaign-stirs-memories.html.

King Jr., Martin Luther. "Beyond Vietnam: A Time to Break Silence." *American Rhetoric: Online Speech Bank*. http://www.americanrhetoric.com/speeches/mlka timetobreaksilence.htm.

King Jr., Martin Luther. "Nomination of Thích Nhất Hạnh for the Nobel Peace Prize." January 25, 1967. http://www.hartford-hwp.com/archives/45a/025.html.

King Jr., Martin Luther. *A Testament of Hope: The Essential Writings and Speeches of Martin Luther King, Jr.*, edited by James M. Washington. New York: Harper-Collins, 1991.

King Jr., Martin Luther. *Where Do We Go From Here: Chaos or Community?* Boston: Beacon Press, 2010.

King, Richard. *Orientalism and Religion: Postcolonial Theory, India, and "the Mystic East"*. London: Routledge, 1999.

Kitayama, Shinobu, and Hyekyung Park. "Perceiving through Culture: The Socialized Attention Hypothesis." In *The Science of Social Vision*, edited by Reginald B. Adams, Jr., Nalini Ambady, Ken Nakayama, and Shinsuke Shimojo, 75–89. New York: Oxford University Press, 2011.

Kitayama, Shinobu, Hyekyung Park, and Yay-hyung Cho. "Culture and Neuroplasticity." In *Handbook of Advances in Culture and Psychology*, edited by Michelle J. Gelfand, Chi-yue Chiu, and Ying-yi Hong, Vol. 5, 38–99. New York: Oxford University Press, 2015.

Kongtrul, Dzigar. *The Intelligent Heart: A Guide to the Compassionate Life*. Boulder, CO: Shambhala Publications, 2016.

Kongtrul, Dzigar. *Training in Tenderness: Buddhist Teachings on Tsewa, the Radical Openness of Heart that Can Change the World*. Boulder, CO: Shambhala Publications, 2018.

Kornfield, Jack. *The Art of Forgiveness, Lovingkindness, and Peace*. New York: Bantam, 2008.

Krosch, Amy R., and David M. Amodio. "Economic Scarcity Alters the Perception of Race." *Proceedings of the National Academy of Sciences* 111, no. 25 (2014): 9079–9084.

Kyabgon Kyabgon, Traleg. *Karma: What It Is, What It Isn't, Why It Matters*. Boulder, CO: Shambhala Publications, 2015.

Langer, Ellen J. *Mindfulness*. Reading, MA: Addison-Wesley Publishing, 1989.

Lawrence III, Charles R. "The Id, the Ego, and Equal Protection: Reckoning with Unconscious Racism." *Stanford Law Review* 39 (1987): 317–388.

Lears, Jackson. *In These Times*. October 22, 2004. http://inthesetimes.com/article/1421.

Leath, Jennifer. "Canada and Pure Land, a New Field and Buddha-Land: Womanists and Buddhists Reading Together." *Buddhist–Christian Studies* 32 (2012): 57–65.

Leo Moore, Wendy. *Reproducing Racism: White Space, Elite Law Schools, and Racial Inequality*. Lanham, MD: Rowman & Littlefield, 2008.

Lion's Roar. "Hear the Lions Roar." *Lion's Roar*, March 2016, 41.

Lion's Roar. "Tributes Honor Passing of Ven. Suhita Dharma, First African-American Buddhist Monk." *Lion's Roar*, January 1, 2014. https://www.lionsroar.com/tributes-honor-passing-of-ven-suhita-dharma-first-african-american-buddhist-monk/.

Lion's Roar. "Why Is American Buddhism So White?" *Lion's Roar*, November 10, 2011. https://www.lionsroar.com/forum-why-is-american-buddhism-so-white/ (accessed March 29, 2017).

Longchenpa. *Finding Rest in the Nature of the Mind: Trilogy of Rest*. Translated by Padmakara Translation Group. Boulder, CO: Shambhala Publications, 2017.

Lopez Jr., Donald S. *A Modern Buddhist Bible: Essential Readings from East and West*. Boston: Beacon, 2002.

Lopez Jr., Donald S. *The Scientific Buddha: His Short and Happy Life*. New Haven, CT: Yale University Press, 2012.

Lorde, Audre. *Sister Outsider: Essays and Speeches,* New Foreword by Cheryl Clarke. Berkeley, CA: Crossing Press, 1984. Reprinted 2007.

Lorde, Audre. "The Uses of Anger: Women Responding to Racism." In *Sister Outsider*, 124–133. Freedom, CA: Crossing Press, 1984.

Lowe, Lisa. *Intimacies of the Four Continents*. Durham, NC: Duke University Press, 2015.

Lueke, Adam, and Bryan Gibson. "Mindfulness Meditation Reduces Implicit Age and Race Bias: The Role of Reduced Automaticity in Responding." *Social, Psychological and Personality Science* 6, no. 3 (2014): 284–291.

Lugones, Maria. "The Coloniality of Gender." In *Globalization and the Decolonial Option*, edited by Walter D. Mignolo and Arturo Escobar, 367–390. New York: Routledge, 2009.

Machery, Edouard. "The Evolution of Tribalism." In *Routledge Handbook of the Philosophy of the Social Mind*, edited by Julian Kiverstein, 88–101. New York: Routledge, 2017.

Madrigal, Alexis C. "The Racist Housing Policy That Made Your Neighborhood." *The Atlantic Monthly*, May 22, 2014. https://www.theatlantic.com/business/archive/2014/05/the-racist-housing-policy-that-made-your-neighborhood/371439/ (accessed April 9, 2016).

Magee, Rhonda. "Teaching Mindfulness with Mindfulness of Race and Other Forms of Diversity." In *Resources for Teaching Mindfulness: International Handbook*, edited by Donald McCown, Diane Reibel, and Marc S. Micozzi, 225–246. Cham: Springer, 2017.

Maglo, Koffi N. "The Case Against Biological Realism About Race: From Darwin to the Post-genomic Era." *Perspectives on Science* 19, no. 4 (2011): 361–390.

Maglo, Koffi N., Tesfaye B. Mersha, and Lisa J. Martin. "Population Genomics and the Statistical Values of Race: An Interdisciplinary Perspective on the Biological Classification of Human Populations and Implications for Clinical Genetic Epidemiological Research." *Frontiers in Genetics* 7, no. 22 (2016): 2.

Malinowska, Joanna K. "Cultural Neuroscience and the Category of Race: The Case of the Other-race Effect." *Synthese* 193, no. 12 (2016): 3865–3887.

Mandelbaum, Michael. "Vietnam: The Television War." *Daedalus* 111, no. 4 (1982): 157–169.

Mander, Mary S. *Pen and Sword: American War Correspondents, 1898–1975.* Champaign: University of Illinois Press, 2010.

Manuel, Zenju Earthlyn. *Sanctuary: A Meditation on Home, Homelessness, and Belonging.* Somerville, MA: Wisdom Publications, 2018.

Manuel, Zenju Earthlyn. *The Way of Tenderness: Awakening Through Race, Sexuality, and Gender.* Somerville, MA: Wisdom Publications, 2015.

Maraldo, John C. シ ゛ョン・マ ラ ル ト ゛. "Nihon no kindai shoki ni okeru seiyō tetsugaku no sesshu" 日本の近代初期における西洋哲学の摂取 [The Reception of Western Philosophy in Early Modern Japan]. Translated (from the English) by Shirai Masato 白井雅人. *International Inoue Enryo Research* 2 (2014): 200–216.

Markant, Julie, Lisa M. Oakes, and Dima Amso. "Visual Selective Attention Biases Contribute to the Other-race Effect Among 9-month-old Infants." *Developmental Psychobiology* 58, no. 3 (2015): 355–365.

Markus, Hazel Rose, and Alana Conner. "The Culture Cycle." *Edge*, 2011. https://www.edge.org/response-detail/11527 (accessed April 1, 2018).

Masato, Shirai. 白井雅人. "Inoue Enryō 'tetsugaku issekiwa' to Nishida Kitarō" 井上円了『哲学一夕話』と西田幾多郎 [Inoue Enryō's *Evening of Philosophical Conversation* and Nishida Kitarō]. *Kokusai tetsugaku kenkyū* 国際哲学研究 1 (2012): 101–108.

Massingale, Bryan, "The Systemic Erasure of the Black/Dark-Skinned Body in Catholic Ethics." In *Catholic Theological Ethics Past, Present, and Future: The Trento Conference*, edited by James Keenan (Maryknoll, NY: Orbis Books, 2011).

Massingale, Bryan. "*Vox Victimarum Vox Dei*: Malcolm X as Neglected 'Classic' for Catholic Theological Reflection." *Catholic Theological Society of America Proceedings* 65 (2010): 72.

Masuzawa, Tomoko. *The Invention of World Religions: Or How European Universalism Was Preserved in the Language of Pluralism.* Chicago: Chicago University Press, 2005.

Matilal, Bimal. "Ignorance or Misconception? A Note on Avidyā in Buddhism." In *Buddhist Studies in Honor of Walpola Rahula*, edited by Somaratna Balasoorriya, 154–164. London: Roundwood Press, 1980.

Mazzocco, Philip. "Talking Productively about Race in the Colorblind Era." *Kirwan Institute Research Report*, January 2015. http://kirwaninstitute.osu.edu/docs/ki-race-talk-0115-05.pdf.

McIntosh, Peggy. *White Privilege: Unpacking the Invisible Knapsack.* Philadelphia, PA: Independent School, 1990.

McKittrick, Katherine. *Demonic Grounds: Black Women and the Cartographies of Struggle.* Minneapolis: University of Minnesota Press, 2006.

McMahan, David L. *The Making of Buddhist Modernism*. Oxford: Oxford University Press, 2008.

McRae, Emily. "Equanimity in Relationship: Responding to Moral Ugliness." In *A Mirror is for Reflection: Understanding Buddhist Ethics*, edited by Jake Davis, 336–351. New York: Oxford University Press, 2017.

Merleau-Ponty, Maurice. *Husserl at the Limits of Phenomenology*. Translated by Leonard Lawlor. Evanston, IL: Northwestern University Press, 2001.

Mignolo, Walter. "Introduction: Coloniality of Power and De-colonial Thinking." In *Globalization and the Decolonial Option*, edited by Walter D. Mignolo and Arturo Escobar, 1–20. New York: Routledge, 2010.

Mikulich, Alex. "Becoming Authentically Catholic and Truly Black: On the Condition of the Possibility of a Just Peace Approach to Anti-Black Violence." In *Becoming Nonviolent Peacemakers: A Virtue Ethic for Catholic Social Teaching and U.S. Policy*, edited by Eli S. McCarthy. Washington, DC: Georgetown University Press, in press.

Mills, Charles W. *Black Rights/White Wrongs: A Critique of Racial Liberalism*. New York: Oxford University Press, 2017.

Mills, Charles W. "Kant and Race, Redux." *Graduate Faculty Philosophy Journal* 35 (2014): 125–157.

Mills, Charles W. "Race and Global Justice." In *Domination and Global Political Justice: Conceptual, Historical, and Institutional Perspectives*, edited by Barbara Buckinx, Johnathan Trejo-Mathys, and Timothy Waligore, 181–205. New York: Routledge, 2015.

Mills, Charles W. *The Racial Contract*. Ithaca, NY: Cornell University Press, 1997.

Mills, Charles W. "Racial Exploitation and the Wages of Whiteness." In *What White Looks Like: African-American Philosophers on the Whiteness Question*, edited by George Yancy, 25–54. London: Routledge, 2004.

Mills, Charles W. "White Ignorance." In *Race and Epistemologies of Ignorance*, edited by Shannon Sullivan and Nancy Tuana, 11–38. Albany: State University of New York Press, 2007.

Mitchell, Scott. "The Tranquil Meditator: Representing Buddhism and Buddhists in U.S. Popular Media." *Religion Compass* 8, no. 3 (2014): 81–89.

Moeller, Carol J. "Moral Attention: Toward a Liberationist Ethics of Everyday Life." PhD diss., University of Pittsburgh, 1998.

Mohanty, Satya P. *Literary Theory and the Claims of History*. Ithaca, NY: Cornell University Press, 1997.

Mohanty, Chandra, and Linda Carty, eds. *Feminist Freedom Warriors*. Chicago, Illinois: Haymarket Books, 2018.

Molk, David, trans. *The Chöd Instruction: The Method of Accomplishment on One Seat*. Portland, OR: The Movement Center, year unknown.

Moskos Jr., Charles C. "The American Combat Solider in Vietnam." *Journal of Social Issues* 31, no. 4 (1975): 25–37.

Mueller, Jennifer C. "Producing Colorblindness: Everyday Mechanisms of White Ignorance." *Social Problems* 64, no. 2 (2017): 219–238.

Murdoch, Iris. *Sovereignty of Good*. Routledge, 1970.

Nāgapriya, Dharmachāri. "Poisoned Pen Letters? D. T. Suzuki's Communication of Zen to the West." *Western Buddhist Review*. http://www.westernbuddhistreview. com/vol5/suzuki-gentium.html.

New York Times. "Editorial." *New York Times*, April 7, 1967. https://www.walterli ppmann.com/docs1083.html.

Nghiem, An, and Peggy Rowe. "What Happens When Two Giants Meet?" *Mindfulness Bell* 72 (Summer 2016). http://www.mindfulnessbell.org/news-updates/when-giants-meet.

Nhất Hạnh, Thích. "For Warmth." In *Call Me By My True Names: The Collected Poems*, 15. Berkeley, CA: Parallax Press, 1999.

Nhất Hạnh, Thích. *Good Citizens: Creating Enlightened Society*. Berkeley: Parallax Press, 2008.

Nhất Hạnh, Thích. *The Heart of the Buddha's Teachings: Transforming Suffering into Peace, Joy, and Liberation*. New York: Broadway Books, 1999.

Nhất Hạnh, Thích. *The Miracle of Being Awake: A Manual on Meditation for Activists*. Sri Lanka: Buddhist Publication Society/BPS Online, 2006. http://what-bud dha-said.net/library/Wheels/wh234.pdf.

Nhất Hạnh, Thích. *The Miracle of Mindfulness: A Manual on Meditation*. Translated by Mobi Ho. Boston: Beacon Press, 1975.

Nhất Hạnh, Thích. *Old Path White Clouds: Walking in the Footsteps of the Buddha*. Berkeley: Parallax Press, 1991.

Nossiter, Adam. "'Let Them Call You Racists': Bannon's Pep Talk to National Front." *New York Times*, March 10, 2018. https://www.nytimes.com/2018/03/10/world/europe/steve-bannon-france-national-front.html (accessed March 11, 2018).

NPR. "How the Hidden Brain does the Thinking for Us." *Morning Edition Transcript*, National Public Radio, January 25, 2010. http://www.npr.org/templates/s tory/story.php?storyId=122864641 (accessed May 27, 2012).

Olendzski, Andrew. *Unlimiting Mind: The Radically Experiential Psychology of Buddhism*. Somerville, MA: Wisdom Publications, 2010.

Omni, Michael, and Howard Winant. *Racial Formation in the United States: From the 1960s to the 1990s*. 2nd ed. New York: Routledge, 1994.

Park, Peter K. Y. *Africa, Asia, and the History of Philosophy: Racism in the Formation of the Philosophical Canon*. Albany: State University of New York Press, 2013.

Patterson, Orlando. *Slavery and Social Death: A Comparative Analysis*. Cambridge, MA: Harvard University Press, 2018.

Payne, Brian Keith. "Prejudice and Perception: The Role of Automatic and Controlled Processes in Misperceiving a Weapon." *Journal of Personality and Social Psychology* 81, no. 2 (2001): 181–192.

Pearson, Adam, John F. Dovidio, and Samuel L. Gaertner. "The Nature of Contemporary Prejudice: Insights from Aversive Racism." *Social and Personality Psychology Compass* 3, no. 3 (2009): 314–338.

Pema Kunsang, Erik, compiler and trans. *A Tibetan Buddhist Companion*. Boulder, CO: Shambhala Publications, 2003.

Piacenza, Joanna. "*TIME*'s Beautiful, White, Blonde 'Mindfulness Revolution.'" *HuffPost*, January 29, 2014. https://www.huffingtonpost.com/joanna-piacenza/time-mindfulness-revolution_b_4687696.html (accessed March 29, 2014).

Pike, Nelson. *Mystic Union: An Essay in the Phenomenology of Mysticism.* Ithaca, NY: Cornell University Press, 1992.

Pintak, Lawrence. "'Something Has to Change': Blacks in American Buddhism." *Lion's Roar*, September 2001, https://www.lionsroar.com/something-has-to-change-blacks-in-american-buddhism/.

Plaskow, Judith, and Carol Christ, eds. *Weaving the Visions: New Patterns in Feminist Spirituality.* New York: Harper and Row, 1989.

Powers, John. *A Bull of a Man: Images of Masculinity, Sex, and the Body in Indian Buddhism.* Cambridge, MA: Harvard University Press, 2009.

Prebish, Charles S. *Luminous Passage: The Practice and Study of Buddhism in America.* Oakland, CA: University of California Press, 1999.

Prueitt, Catherine. "Karmic Imprints, Exclusion, and the Creation of the Worlds of Conventional Experience in Dharmakīrti's Thought." *Sophia* 57, no. 2 (2017): 313–335.

Purser, Ron, and David Loy. "Beyond McMindfulness." *HuffPost Blog*, July 1, 2013. Updated August 31, 2013. https://www.huffingtonpost.com/ron-purser/beyond-mcmindfulness_b_3519289.html# (accessed May 15, 2018).

Queen, Christopher S. *Engaged Buddhism in the West.* New York: Wisdom Publications, 2000.

Quli, Natalie. "Western Self, Asian Other: Modernity, Authenticity, and Nostalgia for 'Tradition' in Buddhist Studies." *Journal of Buddhist Ethics* 16 (2009): 1–38.

Ray, Reginald, "Tibetan Buddhism in the West." In *In the Presence of Masters*, 235–241. Boulder, CO: Shambhala Publications, 2004.

Rhodes, Marjorie, and Tara M. Mandalaywala. "The Development and Developmental Consequences of Social Essentialism." *Wiley Interdisciplinary Reviews: Cognitive Science* 8, no. 4 (2017).

Ricard, Matthieu. *A Sniper's "Mindfulness"* (blog). http://www.matthieuricard.org/en/blog/posts/a-sniper-s-mindfulness (accessed May 15, 2018).

Rinpoche, Chögyam Trungpa. *Cutting Through Spiritual Materialism.* Boulder, CO: Shambhala Publications, 1973.

Rinpoche, Patrul. *Words of My Perfect Teacher.* Lanham, MD: Altamira Press, 1994.

Rinpoche, Tsoknyi, and Eric Swanson. *Open Heart, Open Mind: Awakening the Power of Essence Love.* New York: Harmony Books, 2012.

Ritschl, Albrect. *Theologie und Metaphysik.* Bonn: Marcus, 1887.

Robinet, Isabelle. "De quelques effets du bouddhisme sur la problématique taoïste: aspects de la confrontation du taoïsme au bouddhisme." In *Religion and Chinese Society*, edited by John Lagerwey, Vol. 1, 411–516. Hong Kong: The Chinese University Press, 2004.

Robles, Frances, and Jose A. Del Real. "Stephon Clark Was Shot 8 Times Primarily in His Back, Family-Ordered Autopsy Finds." *New York Times*, March 30, 2018. https://www.nytimes.com/2018/03/30/us/stephon-clark-independent-autopsy.html (accessed July 16, 2018).

Rohn, Alan. "How Did the Vietnam War Affect America?" *The Vietnam War*, April 7, 2016. http://thevietnamwar.info/how-vietnam-war-affect-america/.

Rose, Nikolas, and Joelle M. Abi-Rached. *Neuro: The New Brain Sciences and the Management of the Mind.* Princeton, NJ: Princeton University Press, 2013.

Rosenberg, Noah A. "A Population-genetic Perspective on the Similarities and Differences among Worldwide Human Populations." *Human Biology* 83 (2011): 659–684.

Rosenberg, Noah A., Jonathan K. Pritchard, James L. Weber, Howard M. Cann, Kenneth Kidd, Lev Zhivotovsky, and Marcus W. Feldman. "Genetic Structure of Human Populations." *Science* 298, no. 5602 (2002): 2381–2385.

Roshi, Suzuki. "Transcripts." San Francisco Zen Center, September 8, 1967. http://suzukiroshi.sfzc.org/archives/index.cgi/670908BU.html?seemore=y.

Ryan, Josiah. "'This Was a Whitelash': Van Jones' Take on the Election Results." *CNN*, November 9, 2016. https://www.cnn.com/2016/11/09/politics/van-jones-results-disappointment-cnntv/index.html.

Salguero, C. Pierce. "Translating Meditation in Popular American Media." *Patheos*, March 2, 2014. http://www.patheos.com/blogs/americanbuddhist/2014/03/translating-meditation-in-popular-american-media.html (accessed March 30, 2018).

Salter, Phia S., and Glenn Adams. "Toward a Critical Race Psychology." *Social and Personality Psychology Compass* 7, no. 11 (2013): 781–793.

Salter, Phia S., Glenn Adams, and Michael J. Perez. "Racism in the Structure of Everyday Worlds: A Cultural–Psychological Perspective." *Current Directions in Psychological Science* 27, no. 3 (2018): 150–155.

Sandoval, Chela. *Theory Out of Bounds: Methodology of the Oppressed.* Minneapolis: University of Minnesota Press, 2000.

Santa Fe New Mexican. "Santa Fe Public Schools Gives Students Option of Skipping Fiesta." *Santa Fe New Mexican*, August 30, 2017. http://www.santafenewmexican.com/news/education/santa-fe-public-schools-gives-students-option-of-skipping-fiesta/article_6d01e403-77bd-5db8-abbf-c48b5ae8a46a.html.

Śāntideva. *The Bodhicaryāvatāra.* Translated by Kate Crosby and Andrew Skilton. New York: Oxford University Press, 1998.

Schopenhauer, Arthur. *The World as Will and Representation.* Vol. 1. New York: Dover Publications, 1969.

Seager, Richard Hughes. *Buddhism in America.* New York: Columbia University Press, 1999.

Sekida, Katsuki. *Zen Training: Methods and Philosophy.* New York: Weatherhill, 1985.

Sgam-po-pa, Khenpo Rinpochay Könchok Gyaltsen, and Trinlay Chödron. *The Jewel Ornament of Liberation: The Wish-Fulfilling Gem of the Noble Teachings.* Ithaca, NY: Snow Lion Publications, 1998.

Sharf, Robert. "Experience." In *Critical Terms for Religious Studies*, edited by Mark C. Taylor, 94–116. Chicago: University of Chicago Press, 1998.

Sharf, Robert. "Losing Our Religion." *Tricycle*, Summer 2007. https://tricycle.org/magazine/losing-our-religion-2/.

Sherrill, Martha. *The Buddha from Brooklyn.* New York: Random House, 2000.

Shields, James Mark. "Zen and the Art of Treason: Radical Buddhism in Meiji Era (1868–1912) Japan." *Politics, Religion, and Ideology* 15, no. 2 (2014): 1–19.

Shotwell, Alexis. *Against Purity: Living Ethically in Compromised Times.* Minneapolis: University of Minnesota Press, 2016.

Simmer-Brown, Judith. "The Crisis of Consumerism." In *Mindfulness in the Market Place: Compassionate Responses to Consumerism*, edited by Allan Hunt Badiner, 3–8. Berkeley: Parallax Press, 2002.

Slater, Alice. "The U. S. Has Military Bases in 80 Countries. All of Them Must Close." *The Nation*, January 24, 2018. https://www.thenation.com/article/the-us -has-military-bases-in-172-countries-all-of-them-must-close/.

Sopa, Geshe Lhundub, Leonard Zwilling, and Michael J. Sweet. *Peacock in the Poison Grove: Two Buddhist Texts on Training the Mind*. Boston: Wisdom Publications, 1996.

Spelman, Elizabeth. "Managing Ignorance." In *Race and Epistemologies of Ignorance*, edited by Shannon Sullivan and Nancy Tuana, 119–134. Albany: State University of New York Press, 2007.

Spencer, Quayshawn. "Philosophy of Race Meets Population Genetics." *Studies in History and Philosophy of Science Part C* 52 (2015): 46–55.

Spencer, Quayshawn. "A Radical Solution to the Race Problem." *Philosophy of Science* 81, no. 5 (2014): 1025–1038.

Spitzer, Fr. Robert J. *The Light Shines on in the Darkness: Transforming Suffering Through Faith*. New York: Ignatius Press, 2017.

Sprentak, Charlene, ed. *The Politics of Women's Spirituality: Essays on the Rise of Spiritual Power within the Feminist Movement*. New York: Doubleday, 1982.

Stanford University. "Martin Luther King, Jr. and the Global Freedom Struggle." In *King Encyclopedia*, Stanford University. http://kingencyclopedia.stanford.edu/ encyclopedia/encyclopedia/enc_kings_trip_to_india/.

St. Clair, Michael. *Object Relations and Self Psychology: An Introduction*. 3rd ed. Belmont, CA: Cengage Learning, 2000.

Steele, Ralph. *Tending the Fire: Through War and the Path of Meditation*. Los Angeles: Sacred Life Publishers, 2014.

Stell, Alexander, and Tom Farsides. "Brief Loving-Kindness Meditation Reduces Racial Bias, Mediated by Positive Other-Regarding Emotions." *Motivation and Emotion* 40, no. 1 (2015): 140–147.

Still Water Mindfulness Practice Center. "Thích Nhất Hạnh, Martin Luther King, Jr. and The Dreams We Hold." http://www.stillwatermpc.org/dharma-topics/thich-nhat-hanh-martin-luther-king-jr-and-the-dreams-we-hold-3/.

Suh, Sharon A. *Silver Screen Buddha: Buddhism in Asia and Western Film*. New York: Bloomsbury, 2015.

Suh, Sharon A. "Women in Asian/Asian North American Religions: Whose Asian/ North America? Whose Religion." *Journal of Feminist Studies in Religion* 31, no. 1 (2015): 137–142.

Sullivan, Shannon. *Good White People: The Problem with Middle-Class White Anti-Racism*. Albany: State University of New York Press, 2014.

Sullivan, Shannon. "White Ignorance and Colonial Oppression: Or, Why I Know So Little about Puerto Rico." In *Race and Epistemologies of Ignorance*, edited by Shannon Sullivan and Nancy Tuana, 153–172. Albany: State University of New York Press, 2007.

Sullivan, Shannon. *Revealing Whiteness: The Unconscious Habits of Racial Privilege.* Bloomington: Indiana University Press, 2006.

Sullivan, Shannon, and Nancy Tuana, eds. "Introduction." In *Race and Epistemologies of Ignorance*, 1–10. Albany: State University of New York Press, 2007.

Swearer, Donald. *The Buddhist World of South-East Asia.* Albany: State University of New York Press, 1995.

Swinburne, Richard. *The Existence of God.* Oxford: Clarendon Press, 1979.

Syedullah, Jasmine, Lama Rod Owens, and Angel Kyodo Williams. *Radical Dharma: Talking Race, Love, and Liberation.* Berkeley, CA: North Atlantic Books, 2016.

Tachikawa, Musashi. "Mandala Contemplation and Pure Land Practice: A Comparative Study." In *Toward a Contemporary Understanding of Pure Land Buddhism: Creating a Shin Buddhist Theology in a Religiously Plural World*, edited by Dennis Hirota, 101–126. Albany: State University of New York Press, 2000.

Táíwò, Olúfẹ́mi. "Beware of Schools Bearing Gifts: Miseducation and Trojan Horse Propaganda." *Public Affairs Quarterly* 31, no. 1 (2017): 1–18.

Takashi, Shimizu. "Aim of the Idea of Pure Experience: William James, Nishida Kitaro and Inoue Enryo." *Annual Report of the Inoue Enryo Center* 24 (2016): 55–71.

Takezawa, Yasuko. "Translating and Transforming 'Race': Early Meiji Period Textbooks." *Japanese Studies* 35, no. 1 (2015): 5–21.

Tanaka, Kenneth. "Dramatic Growth of American Buddhism: An Overview." *Dharma World*, July–September 2011. https://rk-world.org/dharmaworld/dw_2011 julyseptdramaticgrowth.aspx.

Tecumseh Teuton, Sean. "Internationalism and the American Indian Scholar." In *Identity Politics Reconsidered*, edited by Linda Martin Alcoff, Michael Hames Garcia, Satya P. Mohanty, and Paula M. L. Moya, 264–284. New York: Palgrave Macmillan, 2006.

Tenold, Vegas. *Everything You Love Will Burn: Inside the Rebirth of White Nationalism in America.* New York: Nation Books, 2018.

The Vietnam War. "The Buddhist Crisis." *The Vietnam War*, February 15, 2014. https://thevietnamwar.info/buddhist-crisis/.

Thomas, Claude Anshin. *At Hell's Gate: A Soldier's Journey from War to Peace.* Boulder, CO: Shambhala Publications, 2004.

Thompson, Evan. "Looping Effects and the Cognitive Science of Mindfulness Meditation." In *Meditation, Buddhism, and Science*, edited by David McMahan and Erik Braun, 47–61. Oxford University Press, 2017.

TIME. August 4, 2003 (162, no. 5). http://content.time.com/time/covers/0,16641,2 0030804,00.html (accessed March 29, 2018).

TIME. February 3, 2014 (183, no. 4). http://content.time.com/time/covers/0,16641,2 0140203,00.html (accessed March 29, 2018).

Tishkoff, Sarah A., Floyd A. Reed, Françoise R. Friedlaender, Christopher Ehret, Alessia Ranciaro, Alain Froment, . . . and Scott M. Williams. "The Genetic Structure and History of Africans and African Americans." *Science*, 324, no. 5930 (2009): 1035–1044.

Todd, Rebecca M., and Maria G. M. Manaligod. "Implicit Guidance of Attention: The Priority State Space Framework." *Cortex* 30, no. 1 (2017): e1–e8.

Tomoe, Moryia. "Social Ethics of 'New Buddhists' at the Turn of the Twentieth Century: A Comparative Study of Suzuki Daisetsu and Inoue Shūten." *Japanese Journal of Religious Studies* 32, no. 2 (2005): 283–304.

Townes, Emilie. *Womanist Ethics and the Cultural Production of Evil*. New York: Palgrave, 2006.

Tranby, Eric, and Douglas Hartman. "Critical Whiteness Theories and the Evangelical 'Race Problem': Extending Emerson and Smith's *Divided by Faith*." *Journal for the Social Scientific Study of Religion* 47, no. 3 (2008): 341–359.

Tricycle. "Difference and Harmony: An Interview with Zenju Earthlyn Manuel." *Tricycle*, November 8, 2011. https://tricycle.org/trikedaily/difference-and-harmony-interview-zenju-earthlyn-manuel/.

Tsering, Geshe Tashi. *Buddhist Psychology: The Foundation of Buddhist Thought*. Vol. 3. Somerville, MA: Wisdom Publications, 2006.

Tweed, Thomas A. "Night-Stand Buddhists and Other Creatures: Sympathizers, Adherents and the Study of Religion." In *American Buddhism: Methods and Findings in Recent Scholarship*, edited by Duncan Ryuken and Christopher S. Queen, 71–90. New York: Routledge, 1999.

UNM Newsroom. "University Seal Remains the Same." *UNM Newsroom*, November 15, 2016. https://news.unm.edu/news/university-seal-remains-the-same.

Unno, Taitetsu. *Shin Buddhism: Bits of Rubble Turn into Gold*. New York: Doubleday, 2002.

Van Bavel, Jay J., and William A. Cunningham. "Self-categorization with a Novel Mixed-race Group Moderates Automatic Social and Racial Biases." *Personality and Social Psychology Bulletin* 35, no. 3 (2009): 321–335.

Van Bavel, Jay J., and William A. Cunningham. "A Social Identity Approach to Person Memory: Group Membership, Collective Identification, and Social Role Shape Attention and Memory." *Personality and Social Psychology Bulletin* 38, no. 12 (2012): 1566–1578.

Van Bavel, Jay J., and Andrea Pereira. "The Partisan Brain: An Identity-based Model of Political Belief." *Trends in Cognitive Science* 22, no. 3 (2018): 213–224.

Van der Kolk, Bessel. *The Body Keeps the Score: Brain, Mind, and Body in the Healing of Trauma*. New York: Penguin Books, 2014.

Varvaloucas, Emma. "Okay As It Is, Okay As You Are: An Interview with Merle Kodo Boyd." *Tricycle*, Fall 2013. https://tricycle.org/magazine/okay-it-okay-you-are/.

Vasubhandu. *Abhidharmakośabhāṣyam*. Vol. 2. Translated by Louis de La Vallée Poussin (French) and Leo M. Pruden. Fremont, CA: Asian Humanities Press, 1991.

Vedantam, Shankar. *The Hidden Brain: How Our Unconscious Minds Elect Presidents, Control Markets, Wage Wars and Save Our Lives*. New York: Spiegel and Grau, 2010.

Waldron, William. "Indian Thought and Social Science on the Travails of Identity." Unpublished paper, on file with author.

Waldron, William S. *The Buddhist Unconscious: The ālaya-vijñāna in the Context of Indian Buddhist Thought*. London: RoutledgeCurzon, 2003.

Walsh, Z., E. Ng, and R. Purser. "Mindfulness is Inherently Political." In *#MakingRefuge*, June 24, 2017. https://www.makingrefuge.net/news/.

Wayman, Alex. "The Meaning of Unwisdom (Avidyā)." *Philosophy East and West* 7, no. 1 (1957): 21–25.

Wedemeyer, Christian K. *Making Sense of Tantric Buddhism: History, Semiology, and Transgression in the Indian Traditions*. New York: Columbia University Press, 2013.

Weil, Simone. *Oppression and Liberty*. Translated by Arthur Wills and John Petrie. New York and London: Routledge and Kegan Paul, 1958.

Whipps, Judy D. "Touched by Suffering: American Pragmatism and Engaged Buddhism." In *American Buddhism as a Way of Life*, edited by Gary Storhoff and John Whalen-Bridge, 101–124. Albany: State University of New York Press, 2010.

Whitaker, Justin. "Better than Zizek: A Critique of Contemporary Spirituality (and Many Buddhists) Worth Investigating." *Patheos*, February 14, 2013. http://www.patheos.com/blogs/americanbuddhist/2013/02/better-than-zizek-a-critique-of-contemporary-spirituality-and-many-buddhists-worth-investigating.html (accessed March 30, 2018).

Williams, Angel Kyodo. *Being Black: Zen and the Art of Living with Fearlessness and Grace*. New York: Viking Compass, 2000.

Williams, Angel Kyodo. "The World Is Our Field of Practice: An Interview with Krista Tippett." *On Being*, April 18, 2018. https://onbeing.org/programs/the-world-is-our-field-of-practice-apr2018/.

Williams, Angel Kyodo, Lama Rod Owens, and Jasmine Syedullah. *Radical Dharma: Talking Race, Love, and Liberation*. Berkeley: North Atlantic Books, 2016.

Willis, Jan. "Community of 'Neighbors': A Baptist–Buddhist Reflects on the Common Ground of Love." *Buddhist–Christian Studies* 34 (2014): 97–106.

Willis, Jan. *Dreaming Me: An African American Woman's Spiritual Journey*. New York: Riverhead Books, 2001.

Willis, Jan. *Dreaming Me: Black, Baptist and Buddhist: One Woman's Spiritual Journey*. Somerville, MA: Wisdom Publications, 2008.

Winfield, Pamela. "Why So Many Americans Think Buddhism is Just a Philosophy." *The Conversation*, January 22, 2018, 2. http://theconversation.com/why-so-many-americans-think-buddhism-is-just-a-philosophy-89488.

Wiredu, Kwasi. "Democracy and Consensus in African Traditional Politics: A Plea for a Non-party Polity." *The Centennial Review* 39, no. 1 (1995): 53–64.

Wolfe, Brendan. "Racial Integrity Laws (1924–1930)." In *Encyclopedia Virginia*. Article published February 17, 2009. Last modified November 4, 2015. http://www.EncyclopediaVirginia.org/Racial_Integrity_Laws_of_the_1920s (accessed April 1, 2018).

Wolski Conn, Joann. *Women's Spirituality: Resources for Christian Development*. Mahwah, NJ: Paulist Press, 1986.

Yancy, George. *Black Bodies, White Gazes: The Continuing Significance of Race*. Lanham, MD: Rowman & Littlefield, 2008.

Yancy, George. *Black Bodies, White Gazes: The Continuing Significance of Race in America.* 2nd ed. Lanham, MD: Rowman & Littlefield, 2016.

Yancy, George. "Dear White America." *New York Times,* December 24, 2015. https ://opinionator.blogs.nytimes.com/2015/12/24/dear-white-america/.

Yancy, George. "The Elevator Effect." In *Black Bodies, White Gazes: The Continuing Significance of Race,* 1–31. Lanham, MD: Rowman & Littlefield, 2008.

Yancy, George. "Interpretive Profiles on Charles Johnson's Reflections on Trayvon Martin: A Dialogue between George Yancy, E. Ethelbert Miller, and Charles Johnson." *Western Journal of Black Studies* 38, no. 1 (2014): 1–12.

Yancy, George. *Look, A White! Philosophical Essays on Whiteness.* Philadelphia: Temple University Press, 2012.

Yancy, George. "Whiteness and the Return of the Black Body." *The Journal of Speculative Philosophy* 19, no. 4 (2005): 215–241.

Yancy, George. "Whiteness: 'Unseen' Things Seen." In *Black Bodies, White Gazes: The Continuing Significance of Race,* 33–64. Lanham, MD: Rowman & Littlefield, 2008.

Yancy, George, and Charles Mills. "Lost in Rawlsland." *New York Times,* November 16, 2014. https://opinionator.blogs.nytimes.com/2014/11/16/lost-in-rawlsland/ (accessed March 22, 2018).

Yang, Larry. *Awakening Together: The Spiritual Practice of Inclusivity and Community.* Boulder, CO: Shambhala Publications, 2017.

Yang, Larry. "Buddha is Culture." *Huffpost Religion,* September 19, 2012. https://www. huffingtonpost.com/larry-yang/buddha-culture_b_1192398.html.

Yang, Larry. "Dharma is Culture." *Huffpost Religion,* June 27, 2012. https://www.huf fingtonpost.com/larry-yang/Dharma-culture_b_1599969.html.

Yang, Larry. "Sangha is Culture." *Huffpost Religion,* July 10, 2012. https://www.huf fingtonpost.com/larry-yang/sangha-culture_b_1600095.html (accessed September 5, 2015).

Yetunde, Pamela Ayo. "Buddhism in the Age of #BlackLivesMatter." *Lion's Roar,* February 8, 2017. https://www.lionsroar.com/buddhism-age-blacklivesmatter/.

Index

absolute truth (*paramartha-satya*), 33, 34

accountability, 145, 197, 200–201; cross-cultural engagement and, 184; Mohanty and, 194–96; spiritual practice and, 99, 111

activism: Buddha and, ix, x; dharma and, x. *See also specific topics*

Adiele, Faith, 119

afflicting emotions. *See kleshas*

ahimsa (nonviolence), 127, 133

Ahmed, Sara: body for, 12, 13; feminist killjoy of, 2–3, 4, 7, 12, 13, 17–18n10; habitual tendencies and, 198; on killjoy assignment, 8; *Living a Feminist Life* by, 2; on trauma and violence, 13–14

Alcoff, Linda Martín, 103

Alexander, M. Jacqui, 200

allied disciplines: Making Refuge and, 272–73; Taking Refuge and, 256–57

Almond, Philip, 209

American Academy of Religion conference (2017), 1; audience discomfort at, 5–6; Buddhist killjoy survival kit and, 6, 7; co-bearing witness at, 7; hypervisibility and hyperinvisibility at, 6; question and answer period at, 6–7; white male scholars at, 6–7

Amida Buddha, 71–72, 74

Analayo, Bhikkhu, 32–33

Anand, Dibyesh, 193

anatta (non-self): black Buddhists and racism and, 83–84, 85–86, 88, 90–91, 94, 95–96; existence and, 83–84; Manuel and, 34; Owens on, 90; social self and, 90

ancestor practices: Berry and, 88; Buddhist Peace Fellowship workshop (2015) and, 21; familiarity and, 89; Hardy and, 88–90; Steele and, 131

Angelou, Maya, 11

anicca (impermanence), 84

apoha theory, 232–33, 244

appearance: racial identity and, 43; white delusion and, 43–44

attachment: Black Prophetic Tradition and, 147; identities and, 305; to self, 10

attentional biases: Kitayama and, 240–41; racial categories and, 239, 240

avidyā (ignorance): Buddhist philosophy and, 48; craving and, 144; defining, 47–48; delusion and, 50; liberation and, 49; Matilal on, 47–48; remedying, 44; subject-object duality and, 163; suffering and, 48–49, 174;

white ignorance and, xvii, 49–50; whiteness as, 218; willful, 154

awakening: embodied, 33; Manuel on, 33, 266–67; mind-only thought and, 280

awakening mind. *See bodhicitta*

awareness: conceptual, 238–39; dharma and, of whiteness, 208, 211; Sitting in Inquiry and nonjudgmental, 269

Baien, Miura: Josephson-Storm and, 63–64; on religion, 64

Bakhtin, Mikhail, 183

Baldwin, James, 167; on love, xix–xx; on white delusion, 54; on white ignorance, 46–47

Batts, Hasshan, 195

bearing witness, 148; at American Academy of Religion conference (2017), 7; liberation and, 143; racial binary and, 150

beloved community, 32

Bernasconi, Robert, 62

Berry, Devin, 88

Bhante, Suhita Dharma, 131, 140n100

Bilge, Sirma, 197

biological fragility, of whiteness, 234–36

black Buddhists and racism: *anatta* and, 83–84, 85–86, 88, 90–91, 94, 95–96; ancestor practices for, 88–90; body and, 83; choosing blackness for, 92; embodied for, 86, 91, 95; Four Noble Truths, 84, 85; liberation and, 91–94, 95; love and, 93; lovingkindness practices and, 85, 93; Ma'at and, 86–87, 93; meditation and, 85; memoirs of, 79; racialized suffering and, 80, 82–83, 94; *Radical Dharma* on, 80, 82, 150–52; Roshi and, 91–92; self-love and, 84–85, 95–96; silence and, 91; social conditioning and, 91; visibility and, 86–88; Washam and, 91; Williams on, 79–80; Willis on, 80–81; Zenju and, 81. *See also* racialized suffering

Black Lives Matter, 82, 93; Engaged Buddhism and, 133; visibility and, 86

"Black Looks" (hooks), 210

black otherness, 167

Black Prophetic Tradition: attachment and, 147; liberation and, 145

blindspots: Gross and, 293, 300; mindfulness and, 255–56; obstacles and, 305; Sitting in Inquiry and, 268

Bodhi, Bikkhu, 84

bodhicitta (awakening mind): self-cherishing and, 164, 175; Tibetan Buddhist Mind Training and, 165, 166

bodhimanda (seat of enlightenment), 8

body: Ahmed and, 12, 13; black Buddhists and racism and, 83; Buddhist killjoy and, 16; Buddhist killjoy survival kit and, 4; as hypervisible and hyperinvisible, 12; racialized trauma and, 11, 12, 13–14; transcendence and, 10–11

Braun, Erik, 24

broken openheartedness, 10

Brons, Lajos, 174

Brown, Michael, 86, 150

Buddha: activism of, ix, x; castes following, ix–x; Chan school on, 281–83; Eightfold Noble Path and, 85; existence and, 83–84; First Discourse of, ix; five *khandas* and, 84; representations of, 280–83; suffering and, 254–55

Buddha Nature, 200

Buddhism: Chinese Buddhists, 297–98; concepts of, xix; early Western transmission of, 209–11; global, 210; "I-maker" and, viii; Inoue and, 68, 71; key teaching of, viii; in Meiji period, 65, 67, 68; mental self and, 257; Protestant, 23; as religion, 64; representations of, 100–101; second wave, 120; in Victorian era, 209. *See also* convert meditation-based Buddhism; Engaged Buddhism;

non-liberating Buddhism and
mindfulness; Pure Land Buddhism;
tantric Buddhism
Buddhism After Patriarchy (Gross), 293,
294, 300
buddhisms, 211; colonialism and, 210
Buddhist ethics, 164, 173–74,
175, 176n7. *See also* moral
phenomenology
Buddhist feminism, 294; Asian cultures
and, 301–2; Keller and, 296. *See also*
Gross, Rita M.
Buddhist killjoy, xi, 1–2, 18n11; body
and, 16; sangha and, 3; survival kit
of, 4
Buddhist killjoy survival kit, 17;
American Academy of Religion
conference (2017) and, 6, 7; bodies
and, 4; Buddhist lama and, 7; choice
and, 12; other killjoys and, 4; POC
retreat and, 9, 11; time and, 4, 11;
trauma and, 15
Buddhist lama and, 7
Buddhist modernism, in Asia, 22, 31;
Asian Buddhist agency and, 24;
characteristics of, 23; colonialism
and, 23, 38–39; critiques of, 23–24;
in Myanmar, 24; oneness and, 37–
38; racial hierarchies and, 23–24
Buddhist modernism, in North America,
24, 31; Asian American immigrants
and, 25; Buddhist Peace Fellowship
workshop and, 21; cultural
preservation and, 25–26; cultural
rearticulation of, 25; diversity
and, 21–22; *dukkha* and, 35–36,
38; essential, 23; self-indulgent
narcissism and, 128. *See also* convert
meditation-based Buddhism; Manuel,
Zenju Earthlyn; Yancy, George
Buddhist moral psychology, 54
Buddhist nominalism: *apoha* theory
and, 232–33, 244; attentional
strategies and patterns and, 242;
ballet performance and, 239; biased

theories and, 244–45; biological
fragility of whiteness and, 234–36;
classifying with, 230; conceptual
awareness and, 238–39; Dharmakīrti
and, 230–31, 237; emptiness of
social categories and, 230–31;
exchanging self for other and, 245;
karmic flows and, 243–45; social
fragility of whiteness and, 236–37;
TSN and, 23–231; *vāsanās* and,
238–39, 240, 241, 243; white gaze
internalized in, 230. *See also* racial
categories
Buddhist Peace Fellowship, 27;
ancestors and 2015 workshop of, 21
Buddhist philosophy, xvii; avidyā and,
48; epistemologies of ignorance and,
47; Japan and, 61–62; knowledge
and, 51; Longchenpa and, 54–55;
Śāntideva and, 56; Vasubhandu and,
48, 49
Burton, David, 51
bus memory, 277–78, 289
Butler, Johnnella, 183

Campany, Robert Ford, 65
capitalism, x; individualism and, 99;
King, M., on, 127; spiritual practices
commandeered by, 99–100
Carvalho, António, 108
causality: dependent origination and,
262; white delusion and, 50, 51–54
CDL (Community Dharma Leadership),
28
Center for Transformative Change:
lethal anti-black violence and, 156;
mudras at, 157
Chah, Ajahn, 32
Chan hagiographical tradition, 281;
non-knower in, 282–83
Cheah, Joseph, 301; cultural and racial
rearticulation of, 24–25; on racial
hierarchies and Buddhist modernism
in Asia, 23–24; on white supremacy,
154

Che Guevara, Ernesto, 187
Chin, Justin, 106–7
Chinese Buddhists, 297–98
chöd tradition: compassion and, 212–13;
   Dorje, M., and, 222; Dorje, R., and,
   218–19; dynamics of neurosis and,
   212; ego-clinging and, 208, 212,
   216, 217; fear and, 212; *kleshas* in,
   207–8, 219–20, 223; non-duality
   and, 222; self-clinging and, 207;
   Treasury of Precious Instructions
   and, 218; visualizations in, 207. *See
   also* Machik, Labdron
Christian evangelicals: individualism
   and, 22–23; whiteness and, 22
civilization markers: philosophy as, 63,
   65; religion as, 64–65
Civil Rights Movement: fire metaphor
   and, 132–33; Vietnam War and, 120,
   127–28
Clark, Stephon, 109–10
Coates, Ta-Nehisi, 110
collective witness, 157
Collins, Patricia Hill, 197
colonialism: *buddhisms* and, 210;
   Buddhist modernism, in Asia and,
   23, 38–39; cross-cultural engagement
   and, 201; diversity and representation
   and, 153–54; Fiestas de Santa Fe
   and, 46; Kongtrul on de-colonizing
   and, 198; modernity and, 106;
   Theravada meditation in Myanmar
   and, 24; Tibetan genocide and, 192
color-blindness, 22, 229; anti-racist
   policy and, 241–42; harm of, 256–
   57; willful, 53
commodity: Buddhism as, 191, 192–93;
   mindfulness as, 191
Community Dharma Leadership (CDL),
   28
compassion: *chöd* tradition and, 212–13;
   hooks on, 186; King, M., on, 126;
   self-loving, xx
conceptual understandings
   (*savikalpaka*), 238–39; clarity and,
   233–34; coffee and, 233

consciousness: organs and, 96n16; store,
   264, 265; transforming, 167, 175.
   See also critical consciousness
Contact Hypothesis, 266
convert meditation-based Buddhism, 21,
   25, 154; forums and literature for,
   26–27; *Making the Invisible Visible*
   and, 26; POC challenges to, 26–27;
   POC retreats and teachers and, 27;
   power structures in, 26; Protestant
   Buddhism and, 23; whiteness and,
   22; Yang on, 29
counter-stereotyping, 170–72, 178n38
craving: avidyā and, 144; equanimity
   and, 54, 57; suffering and, 143–44
Crenshaw, Kimberlé, 197
critical consciousness, 102, 182;
   education for, 194; mindfulness and,
   197–200; non-liberating, 196–97;
   teacher and, 199; true-true and,
   197–98
Critical Philosophy of Race, xvii
critical whiteness studies, 22
cross-cultural engagement, 200;
   accountability and, 184; colonizing
   tendencies and, 201
Crowe, Paul, 301–2
Cuevas, Bryan, 209
Curley, Melissa Anne-Marie, 72

Damashii, Bushi Yamato, 91
Daugherity, Brian, 128
Davis, Angela, 201
death, xviii; whiteness and, xix
delusion: avidyā and, 50; causation and,
   50, 51–54; cause and effect and,
   51–52. *See also* white delusion
dependent origination, 264; causality
   and, 262; heaps and, 263
Devil of Exaltation: joy and, 215; merit
   and, 216
Devil of Inflation: ego-clinging and,
   216, 217; white supremacy and, 217
devils, 212, 218; Devil of Exaltation
   and, 215–16; Devil of Inflation
   and, 216–17; Dorje, R., on, 219;

Immaterial Devil and, 214–15; *kleshas* and, 219–20; Material Devil, 213–14. *See also chöd* tradition
Devine, Patricia, 170–71
Dewey, John, 201
Dhammapada: house-builder in, viii; verses 153 and 154 of, viii
dharma: activism and, x; analysis, 290n7; awareness of whiteness and, 208, 211; class privilege and, 210–11; Euro-American, 31; Inoue and, 70; Manuel on, 35; in Meiji period, 66, 67; Owens on, 83; pseudo-dharma, 191; racialized suffering and, 82–83; radical, 155; white identity and, 30; Yang on Euro-American, 31
Dharmakīrti, x, xvii; *apoha* theory of, 232–33, 244; Buddhist nominalism and, 230–31, 237; conceptual understandings and, 233; essentialism and, 244; linguistic labels and, 238; nonconceptual content and, 222; on social class, 231, 236; ultimate and conventional existence and, 232
Dharmapala, Anagarika, 25
dharma-philosophy, 73, 74
DiAngelo, Robin, 101
Diem, Ngo Dinh, 119–20
directly realizing (*sākṣāt-kriyā*), 289
diversity and representation: Buddhist modernism in North America and, 21–22; colonial experience and, 153–54; genetic diversity and, 234; Kongtrul on, 184; PWDCs and, 151–52; Seager and, 152; will to whiteness and, 154
Dorje, Mikyö, 222
Dorje, Rangjung, 218; four devils and, 219
duality: avidyā and subject-object, 163; Machik on, 214
DuBois, W. E. B., 183

dukkha (suffering): Buddhist modernism in North America and, 35–36, 38; collective suffering and, 36; existence and, 84; Four Noble Truths and, 84, 260; Manuel on, 35–36
Dunbar-Ortiz, Roxanne, 183
dynamics of neurosis, 212
Dzogchen meditation retreat, xv; racial joke at, xvi

East Bay Meditation Sangha, 38
ego-clinging, 208; Devil of Inflation and, 216, 217; dynamics of neurosis and, 212
Eightfold Noble Path: Four Noble Truths and, 85; Right View, 260–62; suffering and, 260
Emerson, David: on body-centered healing, 16; somatic healing and, 15
Emerson, Michael, 22
emptiness: of social categories, 230–31; of whiteness, 245; whiteness and, 3–4
Engaged Buddhism, 207; Black Lives Matter and, 133; Hạnh and, 120, 129, 185; King, M., and, 126–27; Steele and, 131; Vietnam War and, 128
epistemic asymmetry, 279
epistemologies of ignorance: Buddha representation and, 280–83; Buddhist philosophy and, 47; bus memory and, 277–78, 289; knower and, 278, 286; mind-only thought and, 279–80; non-knower and, 282–83; racially hierarchical polity and, 282; social, 279; spiritual practice and, 103; white ignorance and, 45
equanimity, xv; craving and, 54, 57; cultivating, 55–56; refraining as, 56–57; Yancy on, 57
essentialism, 244; racial, 62, 67
ethical orientation, 190
exchanging self for other meditation, 245

existence: *anatta* and, 83–84; *anicca*
    and, 84; Dharmakīrti and, 232;
    dukkha and, 84
existential joy, xvii–xviii
Eze, Emmanuel, 106

Farsides, Tom, 171–72
Feagin, Joe, 271
fear *(saṃvega): chöd* tradition and, 212;
    moral phenomenology and, 174–75
Fearless warrior practice, 157
feeling tones *(vedana)*, x, 10, 16
feminism: body and, 13;
    intersectionality and, 296. *See also*
    Buddhist feminism
Feminist Freedom Warriors and, 201
feminist killjoy: Ahmed and, 2–3, 4, 7,
    12, 13, 17–18n10; as sensationalist, 2;
    survival kit of, 4, 8, 17–18n10
Fields, Rick, 144
Fiestas de Santa Fe, 46
First Noble Truth: attachment and, 147;
    Black Prophetic Tradition and, 145;
    freedom and, 144–45; knowing and,
    144; suffering and, 143–44
five *khandas*, 84
Flagg, Barbara, 259
forgetting, 181, 183
Foucault, Michel, 100, 108;
    governmentality and, 109
Foulk, T. Griffith, 69, 70
four devils. *See* devils
Four Noble Truths, ix; black Buddhists
    and racism, 84, 85; *dukkha* and, 84,
    260; Eightfold Noble Path and, 85;
    right mindfulness and, 188–89; Right
    View and, 260
Four Reminders teaching, 174
fragility of whiteness, 99, 173, 243, 266;
    biological, 234–36; social, 236–37
freedom: First Noble Truth and, 144–45;
    of religion, 66; suffering and, 158
Freire, Paulo, 182, 187
Fronsdal, Gil, 102
Frost, Robert, 199

García, Michael Hames, 194
Garfield, Jay, 164
Gay, Roxane, 17n7
genetic diversity and, 234
goms (habituate), 166
governmentality, 109
Graham, Herman, III, 121–22
Gross, Rita M.: Asian-American
    Buddhists and, 298–99; binaries
    and, 302–3; blindspots of, 293,
    300; *Buddhism After Patriarchy* by,
    293, 294, 300; Chinese Buddhists
    and, 297–98; criticism of, 296–97;
    on dissertation committee, 295;
    identities and, 303–4; "The
    Man-made Obstacle" by, 293–94,
    297, 299–300; privilege of, 301,
    304; Simmer-Brown on, 294,
    295
Gyatso, Tenzin, 245

habituation: *goms* and, 166; to suffering,
    166
HallSimon, 127–28
Haney, Dawn, 21
Hạnh, Thích Nhất, ix, x, 186; American
    Buddhism and, 128; on child self,
    xx; Engaged Buddhism and, 120,
    129, 185; hooks and, 185; King M.,
    and, 120–21, 123, 124–25, 185; on
    mindfulness, 133, 185; on Right
    View, 261; on self-immolation, 124;
    Vietnam War and, 120, 185
Hardy, JoAnna, 88–90
Harris, Melanie L., 303
Hartman, Douglas, 22–23
heaps, 263, 264
Hegel, G. W. F., 61, 63, 71; on religion,
    64, 73
Heschel, Abraham Joshua, 18n19
Hickey, Wakoh Shannon, 26
hierarchies, 154; Buddhist modernism
    in Asia and, 23–24; oneness and
    cultural, 37–38; Owens on, 151;
    Radical Dharma and dharma of,

150–51. *See also* diversity and
representation
Hobgood, Mary E., xix
Holland, Unique: on liberation, 94; on
visibility, 87–88
hooks, bell, 17, 181, 184, 192,
200; "Black Looks" by, 210; on
compassion, 186; education for
critical consciousness and, 194;
embodying ideas of, 186; Hạnh
and, 185; love and, 187; on white
supremacy, 166–67, 169–70
house-builder, viii
hypervisibility, xi; American Academy
of Religion conference (2017) and,
6; body and, 12

I Am Not Your Negro (movie), ix
identity: appearance and racial, 43;
attachment to, 305; Gross and,
303–4; Manuel on, 34–35, 266–67;
national, 148; Taking Refuge and
social construction of, 257. *See also*
white identity
ignorance. *See* avidyā; white ignorance
"I-maker," viii
Immaterial Devil, 214; white supremacy
and, 215
impermanence *(anicca)*, 84
implicit bias: counter-stereotyping and,
170–72, 178n38; hiring and, 169,
170; intervention program, 170–71;
lovingkindness and, 171–72; racism
and, 168–69
IMS. *See* Insight Meditation Society
individualism: capitalism and, 99;
Christian evangelicals and, 22–23;
IMS and, 31–32; love and, 101;
sanghas and, 31; Yang on, 31
Inoue, Enryō, 64, 65; on absolute,
69, 74; Buddhism and, 68, 71;
dharma and, 70; Eurocentrism and,
69; Josephson-Storm on, 68–69,
71; Nishida and, 70; pared-down
Buddhism of, 69, 70–71; Pure Land

Buddhism and, 73–74; suchness for,
69–70; temple of philosophy of, 74;
tetsugaku and, 67, 68
Insight Meditation Society (IMS), 25,
27, 254; individualism and, 31–32;
mindfulness for, 32; *Satipatthana
sutta* and, 32; Spirit Rock Meditation
Center and, 39
interdependent co-arising, 254
interoception, 15
intersectionality, 194; feminism and,
296; original sources and, 197
Isaacs, Arnold R., 122–23

James, William, 105
Jameson, Fredric, 101
Jantzen, Grace, 100; modernity and,
106; mysticism and, 103, 104–6;
*Power, Gender and Christian
Mysticism* by, 104; on privatizing
spirituality, 103, 104, 106; on
spirituality, 105
Japan: Amida and, 71–72, 74; Buddhist
philosophy and, 61–62; dharma-
philosophy in, 73, 74; Pure Land
Buddhism, 71–72. *See also* Meiji
period
Jim Crow, 22
Johnson, Charles, xv, 5–6, 126–27;
interdependence and, 9; on privilege,
301; on white gaze, 286–87
Josephson-Storm, Jason Ānanda,
61–62, 66; Baien and, 63–64;
on Inoue, 68–69, 71; on religion,
64

Kachru, Sonam, 284, 291n8
Kant, Immanuel, 61, 71; on Greek
philosophy origin, 62–63; history
of philosophy for, 62–63, 68;
mysticism and, 105–6; Park on,
62–63; personhood for, 106; racial
essentialism of, 62, 67; racism and,
62, 103–4; rationality and, 103, 106
karmic flows, 243–45

karmic imprints (vāsanās), 238–39, 240, 241
Keller, Mary, 296
Kerouac, Jack, 128
killjoy. *See* Buddhist killjoy; feminist killjoy
killjoy survival kit, 2; feminist, 4, 8, 17–18n10. *See also* Ahmed, Sara; Buddhist killjoy survival kit
King, Martin Luther, Jr.: beloved community and, 32; "Beyond Vietnam" speech of, 123, 126; on capitalism, 127; Commitment Card of, 133; on compassion, 126; criticisms of, 123–24; Engaged Buddhism and, 126–27; Hanh and, 120–21, 123, 124–25, 185; mutuality and, 9, 32; Nobel Prize for Peace and, 126; nonviolence and, 127; Riverside Church speech of, 120–21; Vietnam War and, 120, 121, 125–26
King, Ruth, 27
Kitayama, Shinobu, 240–41
kleshas (afflicting emotions), 207–8, 223; devils and, 219–20; Machik and, 219
knower, 286; bus memory and, 278; racially hierarchical polity and, 287
Kongtrul, Dzigar: on colonizing and de-colonizing, 198; diversity and, 184; on Tsewa, 184
Kornfield, Jack, 131
Krishnamurti, xviii, xix
Kyabgon, Traleg, 163; on objectifying, 164; potentiality and, 173

Langer, Ellen: on mindfulness, 187–88; on mindlessness, 187–88
leadership positions, 153
learning theory, 238
Leath, Jennifer, 72–73
lethal anti-black violence: Brown and, 86, 150; Center for Transformative Change and, 156; election (2016)

and, 301; Martin and, 57, 86, 110; racism as, 109; Roof and, 133
LGBTQI practitioners, 30, 149; promoting queerness, 95; queer theory and, 197
liberation: avidyā and, 49; bearing witness and, 143; black Buddhists and racism and, 91–94, 95; Black Prophetic Tradition and, 145; Holland on, 94; lovingkindness and, 93–94; Owens on, 93, 94; self-love and, 95; Williams on, 92, 93–94
Lion's Roar, 152–53
Living a Feminist Life (Ahmed), 2
Loncke, Katie, 21
Longchenpa, 54–55
Lopez, Donald S., 23
Lopez, Donald S., Jr., 209
Lorde, Audre, 195; embodied feeling and, 267; market fundamentalist culture and, 183; on self-care, 16
love: Baldwin on, xix–xx; hooks and, 187; individualism and, 101; Ma'at on, 93. *See also* self-love
lovingkindness (*metta*): implicit bias and, 171–72; liberation and, 93–94; racism and, 85, 93, 255–56
Lowe, Lisa, 154
Loy, David, 191

Ma'at, Jylani, 86–87; on love, 93
Machik, Labdron, 207–8; Devil of Exaltation and, 215–16; Devil of Inflation and, 216–17; on duality, 214; Immaterial Devil and, 214–15; *kleshas* and, 219; *Machik Namshe* by, 212, 222; on Material Devil, 213–14
Machik Namshe (Machik's Complete Instructions) (Machik), 212, 222
Magee, Rhonda, 85
Mahāyāna tradition, 288
Making Refuge, 253–54, 265; allied disciplines and, 272–73; compassionate identity-brave

meditation and, 266–67; Contact Hypothesis and, 266; Mindful Storytelling and, 270–71; Mindful Study and, 268, 272–73; practice communities and, 267–68; Sitting in Inquiry and, 268–70; Think Tank on, 266; work of, 272–73

Making the Invisible Visible, 26

Malcolm X, 101–3

Mander, Mary S., 120

"The Man-made Obstacle" (Gross), 293–94, 297, 299–300

Manuel, Zenju Earthlyn, 3, 10, 27; *anatta* and, 34; on awakening, 33, 266–67; background of, 33, 37; on dharma, 35; on *dukkha*, 35–36; embodied awakening of, 33; familiarity and, 89; on identity, 34–35, 266–67; on relative difference, 36–37; sanctuaries of, 11, 267; on Two Truths doctrine, 33–34; *The Way of Tenderness* by, 85

Martin, Trayvon, 57, 86, 110

Mason-John, Valerie, 85

Massingale, Bryan, 106

Material Devil, 213–14

Matilal, Bimal, 47–48, 50

McIntosh, Peggy, 258–59

McKittrick, Katherine, 15

McMahan, David, 23, 24

McMindfulness, 191

meditation: black Buddhists and racism and, 85; exchanging self for other as, 245; Willis and, 81. *See also* convert meditation-based Buddhism; mindfulness; Theravada meditation; Tranquil Meditator

meditation text (*sadhana*), 223

Meeting Faith (Adiele), 119

Meiji period (1868–1912): Buddhism in, 65, 67, 68; China scholarly lineage and, 66; dharma in, 66, 67; freedom of religion in, 66; philosophy in, 61, 63; purity in, 67; racial hierarchies

in, 75n8; *shūkyō* in, 66–67; *tetsugaku* in, 67. *See also* Inoue, Enryō

meishin (superstition), 67

memory, 277–78, 289

mental self, 257

merit, 216

The Method for Accomplishment on One Seat (Dorje, M.), 222

metta. See lovingkindness

Mian, Ali Altaf, 17n2

Middle Way, 260

Mikulich, Alex, 110

Mills, Charles, x, 145; racialized epistemologies of, 278; racially hierarchical polity and, 282; on racism of Kant, 103–4; on white delusion, 57; on white ignorance, 44, 45, 49, 168; white knower and, 286

mindfulness, 258; blindspots and, 255–56; as commodified, 191; critical consciousness and, 197–200; ethical orientation and, 190; Four Noble Truths and right, 188–89; Hạnh on, 133, 185; IMS and, 32; Langer on, 187–88; learning and, 188; McMindfulness and, 191; nonviolence and, 133; qualities of, 188; racism and, 255–56; requirements of, 190; right, 188–90; temporal disruption and, xx; trauma and, 16. *See also* non-liberating Buddhism and mindfulness

Mindful Storytelling, 270–71

Mindful Study, 268, 272–73

mindlessness: consequences of, 188; forms of, 187–88

mind-only thought, 291n11; abandonment and, 286, 289; awakening and, 280; epistemologies of ignorance and, 279–80; Kachru on, 284; no-mind and, 285–90; path process and, 285; thoroughly knowing and, 285; white ignorance and, 287; Yogācāra literature on,

280; Yogācāra-Vijñānavāda and, 283–84

Mitchell, Scott, 100, 107

modernism. *See* Buddhist modernism, in Asia; Buddhist modernism, in North America

Mohanty, Chandra, 181, 200; accountability and, 194–96; collaborative work and, 194–95; Feminist Freedom Warriors and, 201; knowledge and, 195, 196; true-true and, 194–96

Montagnards, 123

Moon, Sun Myung, xix

moral phenomenology: anti-racism and, 167; counter-stereotyping and, 170–72, 178n38; de-centering and, 173; ethical self-transformation and, 164; experience and, 162; fear and, 174–75; habitual structures and, 166; implicit bias and, 168–72, 178n38; naming and, 172–73; potentiality and, 173; subjective structures and, 162–63; suffering and, 174; transforming consciousness and, 167, 175; white experience and, 161–62; white gaze and, 169

Moskos, Charles C., Jr., 121

mudra, 157

Mueller, Jennifer, 52

Muksang, Gangpa, 213, 214, 217

Muste, A. J., 124

mysticism: Jantzen and, 103, 104–6; Kant and, 105–6; power and, 105; privatized spirituality and, 106

Native Americans, 182, 192; racial categories and, 237

Naturalization Act of 1906, 237

Ng, Edwin, 265

nirvikalpaka (nonconceptual content), 222

Nishi, Amane, 67

Nishida, Kitarō, 70

no-mind, 285, 286, 287, 290; abandonment and, 289; features of, 288

nonconceptual content (*nirvikalpaka*), 222

non-duality, 222

non-liberating Buddhism and mindfulness: commodified, 191, 192–93; critical consciousness and, 196–97; McMindfulness, 191; pseudo-dharma, 191; racism and, 193; Ricard on, 190–91; Smith, G., and, 193–94

non-self. *See anatta*

nonviolence (*ahimsa*): King, M., and, 127; mindfulness and, 133

Obama, Barack, 302

Occupy Movement, 156

Omi, Michael, 25

oneness, 10–11; Buddhist modernism in Asia and, 37–38; cultural hierarchies and, 37–38; radical dharma and, 155; Yang on, 30

opacity of whiteness, xix

other-race effect, 239, 244

Owens, Rod: on *anatta*, 90; on being something and nothing, 90–91; on dharma, 83; on hierarchy, 151; on liberation, 93, 94; *Radical Dharma* by, 80, 82, 150–52; on silence, 85

Ozawa, Takao, 237

Pali Canon, 28, 33

paramartha-satya (absolute truth), 33, 34

Park, Peter K. J., 61, 71; on Kant, 62–63

Path to Cessation of Suffering, 189

Peck, Raoul, ix

people of color (POC). *See specific topics*

People of Color (POC) retreats: bodies and, 8, 9, 10–11; broken openheartedness and, 10; Buddhist killjoy survival kit and, 9, 11;

emotional vulnerability at, 10;
Kornfield and, 131; mindfulness
at, 8–9, 10; mutuality and
interdependence at, 9; racialized
trauma and, 8, 10; at Spirit Rock
Meditation Center, 39, 131–32; time
and, 4; *vedana* and, 10; white gaze
and, 4, 9; Zora at, 7–8
perfect misrecognition, 279
phenomenology. *See* moral
phenomenology
philosophy: as civilization marker, 63,
65; Hegel and, 61, 63, 64, 71, 73;
in Meiji period, 61, 63; *tetsugaku*,
67, 68, 74; white identity of, 61.
See also Buddhist philosophy; Kant,
Immanuel
Piacenza, Joanna, 108
POC. *See* people of color; People of
Color retreats
population genetics, 235
post-racial era, vii
power: convert meditation-based
Buddhism and, 26; ethics and, 218;
mysticism and, 105; racial categories
and, 237, 243; spiritual practice and,
100, 101–2
Power, Gender and Christian Mysticism
(Jantzen), 104
Powers, John, 281
practice communities, 267–68
Prebish, Charles S., 303
predominantly white dharma
communities (PWDCs), 150;
diversity shift for, 151–52; patriarchy
and whiteness and, 151
privatized spirituality: Jantzen on, 103,
104, 106; mysticism and, 106
privilege: class, 210–11; Gross and,
301, 304; Johnson on, 301; white,
161, 211, 258
Protestant Buddhism and, 23
pseudo-dharma and, 191
psychological materialism,
110

Pure Land Buddhism: Inoue and,
73–74; Japan and, 71–72; Womanist-
Buddhist discourse and, 72–73
Purser, Ronald, 191, 265
PWDCs. *See* predominantly white
dharma communities
queer theory, 197

Quli, Natalie, 24, 303

racial categories, 229–30; attentional
biases and, 239, 240; attentional
strategies and patterns and, 242;
biological nondifferences and,
235–36; cultural practices and, 242;
emptiness of whiteness as, 245;
environmental similarities and,
234–35; generality and, 244; genetic
diversity and, 234; genetic markers
and, 235; illusion of, 261–62, 271;
Irish immigrants and, 236; learning
theory and, 238; Native Americans
and, 237; *Naturalization Act of 1906*
and, 237; one-drop rule and, 237;
other-race effect and, 239, 244;
population genetics and, 235; power
and, 237, 243; Right View and,
261–62; single, vii; as social
construct, 229; tribalist psychology
and, 240. *See also* Buddhist
nominalism
racial contract, 100
racial essentialism, 62, 67
racialized epistemologies, x; bus
memory and, 277–78, 289; Mills
and, 278
racialized suffering, 94; dharma practice
and, 82–83; social practices and, 80
racialized trauma: body and, 11, 12, 13–
14; dealing with, 13–14; POC retreat
and, 8, 10; trauma-informed yoga
and, 12, 14–15; trauma-sensitive
mindfulness, 16
racially hierarchical polity, 286; knower
and, 287; Mills and, 282

racism: defining, 109; implicit bias
and, 168–69; Kant and, 62, 103–4;
lethal anti-black violence and, 109;
levels of, 255; lovingkindness and,
85, 93, 255–56; mindfulness and,
255–56; neighborhoods and, 240;
owning, 220–21; suffering and, 255;
systemic, vii; unlearning, 265
radical dharma: convergence and, 156;
oneness and, 155
Radical Dharma (Williams, Owens, and
Syedullah), 80, 82, 152; on dharma
of hierarchy, 150–51
radical openheartedness (Tsewa), 182,
194, 199
Rajneesh, Bhagwan Shree, xviii
rationality, 103, 106
redlining, 240
Registered Yoga Teacher (RYT), 12
relative truth (*samvrtti-satya*), 33, 34
religio, 65
religion: Baien on, 64; Buddhism as, 64;
as civilization marker, 64–65; Hegel
on, 64, 73; Josephson-Storm on, 64;
Meiji period and freedom of, 66;
shūkyō as, 66–67
representation of Buddhism, 100–101
Ricard, Matthieu, 189–90
right mindfulness: Four Noble Truths
and, 188–89; Ricard on, 189–90
Right View, 254; Four Noble Truths
and, 260; racial categories and, 261–
62; separate self and, 262–63; store
consciousness and, 265
Rinpoche, Chogyam, 261
Rinpoche, Jetsun Khandro, 174, 175,
199, 200; pseudo-dharma and, 191;
radical openheartedness of, 182
Rinpoche, Tsokyni: Social-I and, 257–
358; Useful-I of, 257–58
Roof, Dylann, 133
Roshi, Suzuki, 261
Roshi, Zenju, 91–92
Royce, Josiah, 32
RYT. *See* Registered Yoga Teacher

*sadhana (*meditation text), 223
sākṣāt-kriyā (directly realizing), 289
Salguero, C. Pierce, 116n65
sanctuaries, 11, 267
sanghas: beloved community and, 32;
Buddhist killjoy and, 3; Dzogchen
meditation retreat, xv, xvi; East Bay
Meditation Sangha, 38; individualism
and, 31; invisible whiteness and, 3;
white supremacist, 1; Williams on
white, 79–80. *See also* American
Academy of Religion conference
(2017); convert meditation-based
Buddhism
Sangye, Padampa, 207
Śāntideva, 56
Satipatthana sutta, 32
savikalpaka. See conceptual
understandings
Sayadaw, Ledi, 24
scapegoating, xix
Schleiermacher, Fredrich, 105
Schopenhauer, Arthur, 146
Seager, Richard Hughes, 152
seat of enlightenment (*bodhimanda*), 8
seeing, ix
Sekida, Katsuki, 144; attachments for,
147; on suffering, 146
self-care, 16
self-cherishing, 176n11; *bodhicitta* and,
164, 175; naming, 172; objectifying
and, 164; self-other binary and,
164–65; Sopa on, 164; subject-object
duality and, 163
self-clinging, 207
self-immolation, 119; Hạnh on, 124;
Steele on, 129
self-love: black Buddhists and, 84–85,
95–96; liberation and, 95
self-loving compassion, xx
sexual abuse, 151
Shambhala Meditation Center of
Atlanta, 150–51
Sharf, Robert, 23
Sharpe, Gina, 27

Sherrell, Carla, 298
Shields, James Mark, 71
Shotwell, Alexis, 181, 185
shūkyō (religion), 66–67
Siddhārtha, ix, 220
Simmer-Brown, Judith, 110, 298; on Gross, 294, 295
Sitting in Inquiry: blindspots and, 268; curiosity and, 269, 270; empathy and, 269; nonjudgmental awareness and, 269
skillful means (*upaya*), 22, 211
Slater, Alice, 132
Smith, Christian, 22
Smith, Gene, 193–94
social class: Dharmakīrti on, 231, 236; generality and, 244; privilege, 210–11
social fragility, of whiteness, 236–37
Social-I, 257–58
Soen, Shaku, 25
soil and earth: environmental degradation and, 221; Siddhārtha and, 220
somatic healing, 15; TSY and, 16
Sopa, Geshe Lhundub, 164; on Tibetan Buddhist Mind Training, 165
Soto Zen lineage, 22
Spelman, Elizabeth, 46
Spirit Rock Meditation Center, 39, 131–32
spiritual materialism, 191, 198
spiritual practice, white American: accountability and, 99, 111; capitalism and, 99–100; Chin on, 106–7; critical consciousness and, 102; epistemologies of ignorance and, 103; individualism and, 101; Malcolm X and, 101–3; mapping and, 101; power and, 100, 101–2; psychological materialism and, 110; white supremacy and, 103. See also Jantzen, Grace; predominantly white dharma communities; Tranquil Meditator

Steele, Ralph, 121; ancestor practices and, 131; Bhante and, 131; Engaged Buddhism of, 131; fire metaphor and, 132–33; People of Color retreats and, 131; on self-immolation, 129; self-medicating, 130; *Tending the Fire: Through War and The Path of Meditation* by, 129; as Vietnam War volunteer, 129–30; Willis and, 130
Stell, Alexander, 171–72
"Still I Rise" (Angelou), 11
store consciousness: heaps and, 264; Right View and, 265
suffering: avidyā and, 48–49, 174; Buddha and, 254–55; craving and, 143–44; Eightfold Path to liberation and, 260; First Noble Truth and, 143–44; freedom and, 158; habituation to, 166; "I" and, viii; impermanence and, 84; internalization of hatred and, 83; moral phenomenology and, 174; Path to Cessation of Suffering, 189; racial divide and, 148–49; racism and, 255; Schopenhauer on, 146; Sekida on, 146; Taking Refuge and, 255; white supremacy and, 253. See also dukkha; racialized suffering
Suh, Sharon, 107–8
Sullivan, Shannon, 111, 170
superstition. See *meishin*
Suzuki, D. T., 128
Suzuki, Shunryu, 30, 120
Swami Bhashyananda, xviii
Syedullah, Jasmine, 80, 82, 150–52

Taking Refuge, 253; allied disciplines and, 256–57; anti-racism counsels and, 257; dependent origination and, 262–64; McIntosh and, 258–59; mental self and, 257; mindfulness and blindspots in, 255–56; Right View and, 254, 260–63; social identity construction and, 257; store consciousness and, 264–65; suffering

and, 255; Three Jewels and, 254;
Useful-I, Social-I and, 257–58; white
transparency and, 259; work of,
272–73
tantric Buddhism, 207, 220–21;
meditation text in, 223; samaya and,
222; torma offering in, 223–24;
Tröma Ngakmo and, 223–27;
Wedemeyer on, 209–10. *See also*
chöd tradition
*Tending the Fire: Through War and The
Path of Meditation* (Steele), 129
tetsugaku (philosophy): Inoue in, 67, 68;
pure, 68, 74
Teuton, Sean Tecumseh, 201
Thaye, Jamgon Kongtrul Lodro, 218
Theravada meditation, 24
Theravadin Buddhism, 25
third-wave feminism, 296
Thomas, Claude Anshin, 122, 129
Three Jewels, 254–55
Thubten, Anam, 155
Tibetan Buddhist communities, US, 192
Tibetan Buddhist Mind Training:
bodhicitta and, 165, 166; habituation
to suffering and, 166
Tibetan Buddhist Resource Center,
193–94
Tibetan genocide: Smith, G., and, 193–
94; US and, 192
TIME magazine: Piacenza on, 108; on
Tranquil Meditator, 107, 108
torma offering, 223–24
Tranby, Eric, 22–23
Tranquil Meditator: governmentality
and, 109; Mitchell on, 100, 107;
racism as murder and, 109; Suh on,
107–8; *TIME* magazine on, 107, 108;
Vedantam on, 111; Žižek on, 109
trauma: Ahmed on, 13–14; Buddhist
killjoy survival kit and, 15; collective
witness to, 157; imprint of, 14, 15;
mindfulness meditation and, 16;
slavery and, 157–58; somatic healing
and, 15; stress hormones and, 14;

van der Kolk on, 13, 14, 15. *See also*
racialized trauma
trauma-informed yoga, 12; benefits of,
14; choice-based language on, 14–15
trauma-sensitive mindfulness, 16
Trauma Sensitive Yoga (TSY), 15;
somatic healing and, 16; *vedana* and,
16
Treasury of Precious Instructions
(Thaye), 218
tribalist psychology, 240
Trisvabhāvanirdeśa (*TSN*), 230; racial
kinds and, 231
Tröma Ngakmo: instantaneous
severance practice of, 226–27;
offerings and praise to, 224–25;
torma offering of, 223–24, 225–26
true-true: Butler and, 183; critical
consciousness and, 197–98; Mohanty
and, 194–96; rememory and, 183–84
Trungpa, Chogyam, 191, 198
Tsewa (radical openheartedness), 182,
199; Kongtrul on, 184
TSN. See Trisvabhāvanirdeśa
TSY. *See* Trauma Sensitive Yoga
Two Truths doctrine, ix, 3, 22; absolute
truth, 33, 34; Manuel on, 33–34;
relative truth, 33, 34; Yang on,
30–31

Unification Church, xix
United States (US). *See specific
topics*
upaya (skillful means), 22, 211
Useful-I, 257–58

Vajrayana. *See* tantric Buddhism
van der Kolk, Bessel, 13, 14, 15
vāsanās (karmic imprints), 238–39, 240,
243; practical activity and, 241
Vasubhandu, 48, 49, 284
vedana (feeling tones), x, 10; TSY and,
16
Vedantam, Shankar, 111
Victorian era, 209

Vietnam War, 134n13; Adiele and, 119; African American presence in, 121–23; African slavery and, 125–26; Buddhist Crisis and, 119–20; Civil Rights Movement and, 120, 127–28; Engaged Buddhism and, 128; fire metaphor and, 132–33; Graham on, 121–22; Hạnh and, 120, 185; Isaacs on, 122–23; King, M., and, 120, 121, 125–26; Mander on, 120; masculinity in, 122; Montagnards in, 123; mutilation in, 122; protests, 120; second wave Buddhism and, 120; Steele volunteering for, 129–30; Thomas in, 122; Willis and, 119

Vimalasara. *See* Mason-John, Valerie

violence: visibility and, 86. *See also* lethal anti-black violence

Vipassana tradition, 86, 120; Berry and, 88

visibility: Hardy and, 88; Holland on, 87–88; Ma'at and, 86–87; violence and, 86

Wadud, Amina, 296–97

Waldron, William, 263–64

Walker, Alice, 72, 131–32

Walsh, Zack, 265

Washam, Spring, 91

The Way of Tenderness (Manuel), 85

Wedemeyer, Christian K., 209–10

Weil, Simone, 200

Wheel of Life, 163

Wheel–Weapon Mind Training, 165–66

white delusion: appearance and, 43–44; Baldwin on, 54; causality and, 50, 51–54; cognitive error and, 53–54; epistemic maneuvers for, 52–53; equanimity and, xv, 50, 54–57; knowledge and, 51; Mills on, 57; Mueller and, 52–54; white ignorance and, 50; Yancy on recognizing, 57

white gaze: hiring and, 169; internalizing, 230; Johnson on, 286–87; moral phenomenology and, 169; POC retreats and, 4, 9

white identity, 23; dharma and, 30; as normative, 22; of philosophy, 61

white ignorance, 177n28; avidyā and, xvii, 49–50; Baldwin on, 46–47; deconstructing, 44–45; epistemologies of ignorance and, 45; individual cognition and, 45; maintaining, 46; Mills on, 44, 45, 49, 168; mind-only thought and, 287; miscognition and, 45–46; psychological forces and, 46–47; racial contract and, 100; white delusion and, 50

whiteness. *See* specific topics

white normalcy, 167

white privilege, 161; skillful means and, 211; as subtle, 258

White Racial Frame, 271

white racial socialization, 112n5

white supremacy, viii; Cheah on, 154; creation of, 258; Devil of Inflation and, 217; hooks on, 166–67, 169–70; Immaterial Devil and, 215; Malcolm X and, 102; preserving, 243; rejection and, 81; representation of Buddhism and, 100–101; sanghas and, 1; spiritual practice and, 103; subtle, 22; suffering and, 253

white transparency, 259

Williams, Angel Kyodo: Center for Transformative Change and, 156; on liberation, 92, 93–94; *Radical Dharma* by, 80, 82, 150–52; on white sanghas, 79–80

Willis, Jan, 80; meditation for, 81; Steele and, 130; Vietnam War and, 119

Wilson, Darren, 86

Winant, Howard, 25

Womanist-Buddhist discourse, 72–73

Yancy, George, 35, 45, 262, 289; aversion narratives and, 55; on equanimity, 57; on whiteness and black otherness, 167–68

Yang, Larry, 22, 26, 27; background of, 28; on beloved community and sangha, 32; on canonical legitimacy, 28–29; on community as practice, 32; on convert culture, 29; critical-constructivist revisioning of, 33; on culture, 29; East Bay Meditation Center and, 28; on Euro-American dharma, 31; on individualism, 31; on oneness, 30; on Pali Canon, 28, 33; *Satipatthana* sutta and, 32; at Spirit Rock Meditation Center POC retreat, 39; on Two Truths doctrine, 30–31

yoga: breath and, 16; RYT, 12. *See also* trauma-informed yoga; Trauma Sensitive Yoga

Yogācāra tradition, x, 231, 245, 290n2

Yogācāra-Vijñānavāda, 283–84

Young, Andrew, 125

Zenju, Roshi, 81

Zimmerman, George, 57, 86

Žižek, Slavoj, 109

Zora (POC silent retreat attendee), 7–8

Contributor Notes

Joy Brennan is assistant professor of Buddhism and East Asian religions at Kenyon College. She specializes in Yogācāra Buddhist thought and its reception in the Chan and Huayan traditions of Chinese Buddhism. She is writing a manuscript on the Yogācāra school's theory of delusion and human transformation. She is also a Sōtō Zen Buddhist priest and leader of the Mount Vernon Zen Sangha in Mount Vernon, OH.

Justin von Bujdoss is an American tantric Buddhist teacher and chaplain. He was ordained as a repa in the Karma Kamstang tradition of Tibetan Buddhism by His Eminence Goshir Gyaltsab Rinpoche in 2011 and given the name Repa Dorje Odzer and has over twenty years of experience with Buddhist practice. Justin was appointed as the first dedicated Staff Chaplain for the New York City Department of Correction where he also serves as Executive Director of Chaplaincy and Staff Wellness for the 13,000 employees who work throughout the New York City corrections system and supervises all spiritual care throughout the agency. He is author of the forthcoming book *Modern Tantric Buddhism: Embodiment and Authenticity in Dharma Practice* to be published by North Atlantic Books in October 2019. Justin is also a cofounding teacher in the experimental tantric Buddhist sangha, Bhumisparsha, along with Lama Rod Owens.

Laurie Cassidy, PhD, is a theologian and spiritual director. Cassidy was associate professor at Marywood University in Scranton, Pennsylvania. Her first book, edited with Alex Mikulich, is entitled *Interrupting White Privilege: Catholic Theologians Break the Silence* (Orbis, 2007). Her latest book, *The Scandal of White Complicity in U.S. Hyper-Incarceration: A Non-Violent Spirituality of White Resistance* (New York: Palgrave, February 2013), is coauthored by Alex Mikulich and Margie Pfeil. With a master's degree in Christian Spirituality from Creighton University she has ministered in the area of spirituality for the past thirty years through spiritual direction and retreats throughout the United States. She is certified as a mindfulness meditation facilitator from UCLA's Semel Institute for Neuroscience and Human Behavior. Her teaching and research explore how Christian mysticism can be a resource for personal and social transformation.

Ann Gleig is assistant professor of religion and cultural studies at the University of Central Florida. She has published a number of articles on North American Buddhism in the *Journal of Global Buddhism* and *Contemporary Buddhism: An Interdisciplinary Journal*; her first monograph, *American Dharma: Buddhism Beyond Modernity*, was published by Yale University Press in 2019.

Hsiao-Lan Hu received hir PhD in Religion from Temple University and is currently associate professor of Religious Studies & Women's and Gender Studies at the University of Detroit Mercy. Ze teaches broadly in Asian religions, women and gender issues in world religions, and comparative religious ethics and contemporary social issues. Hir monograph *This-Worldly Nibbāna: A Buddhist-Feminist Social Ethic for Peacemaking in the Global Community* (SUNY, 2011) is an interdisciplinary study that combines the philosophy and sociology of early Buddhism, engaged Buddhism, poststructuralist feminist theory, liberation theology, socioeconomic studies on globalization, and peace studies.

Bryce Huebner is associate professor at Georgetown University. He completed his PhD at the University of North Carolina, Chapel Hill, before doing postdoctoral research in psychology at Harvard University and in the Center for Cognitive Studies at Tufts University (working with Dan Dennett). He has published both theoretical and empirical research in philosophy and the cognitive sciences. His current research focuses on the role of reinforcement learning in social cognition, the relationships between individual and group agency, and the nature of emotional states; over the past couple of years, he has started writing more about Buddhist philosophy, and he is trying to draw all of these threads together.

Charles Johnson, University of Washington (Seattle) professor emeritus and the author of 23 books, is a novelist, philosopher, essayist, literary scholar, short story writer, cartoonist and illustrator, author of children's literature, and screen-and-teleplay writer. A MacArthur fellow, Johnson has received a 2002 American Academy of Arts and Letters Award for

Literature, a 1990 National Book Award for his novel *Middle Passage*, a 1985 Writers Guild award for his PBS teleplay "Booker," the 2016 W.E.B. Du Bois Award at the National Black Writers Conference, and many other awards. The Charles Johnson Society at the American Literature Association was founded in 2003. In November, 2016, Pegasus Theater in Chicago debuted its play adaptation of *Middle Passage*, titled "Rutherford's Travels." Dr. Johnson's most recent publications are *The Way of the Writer: Reflections on the Art and Craft of Storytelling*, and his fourth short story collection, *Night Hawks*.

Leah Kalmanson is associate professor in the Department of Philosophy and Religion at Drake University (Des Moines, Iowa). She received her PhD in philosophy from the University of Hawai'i at Mānoa in 2010. Her current research interests are in comparative philosophy and postcolonial studies. She has published articles in journals such as *Comparative and Continental Philosophy*, *Continental Philosophy Review*, *Frontiers of Philosophy in China*, *Hypatia*, *Journal of World Philosophies*, *Philosophy East and West*, and *Shofar*, and has coedited volumes including *Levinas and Asian Thought* (with Frank Garrett and Sarah Mattice, Duquesne University Press, 2013), *Buddhist Responses to Globalization* (with James Mark Shields, Lexington Books, 2014), and *Asian and Latin American Philosophies in Dialogue* (with Stephanie Rivera Berruz, Bloomsbury, 2018).

Jessica Locke is assistant professor of Philosophy at Loyola University Maryland in Baltimore. Her research focuses on Buddhist ethics, moral psychology and cross-cultural philosophy.

Rhonda V. Magee, MA, JD, is professor of law at the University of San Francisco. She teaches Mindfulness-Based Interventions, and is a student of awareness and compassion practices from a range of traditions. She is a facilitator of mindful and compassionate communication. She is a fellow of the Mind and Life Institute. Rhonda's teaching and writing support compassionate problem-solving and presence-based leadership in a diverse world, and humanizing approaches to education. She sees awareness practices as keys to personal, interpersonal, and collective transformation in the face of challenge and opportunity. The author of numerous articles on mindfulness in legal education, including *Educating Lawyers to Meditate?* 79 UMKC L. Rev. 535 (2011), and *The Way of ColorInsight: Understanding Race and Law Effectively Using Mindfulness-Based ColorInsight Practices*, 8 Georgetown J. of Mod. Crit. Race Perspectives 251 (2016), Rhonda is a thought and practice leader in the emerging fields of contemplative legal and higher education.

Emily McRae is assistant professor of philosophy at the University of New Mexico. She specializes in Tibetan Buddhist philosophy, ethics, moral psychology, and feminism. She has published articles on issues in comparative moral psychology in both Western and Asian philosophical journals and volumes, including *American Philosophy Quarterly, History of Philosophy Quarterly, Journal of Religious Ethics, Philosophy East and West,* and *The Oxford Handbook of Buddhist Ethics.* Her translation, with Jay Garfield, of the nineteenth century Tibetan master Patrul Rinpoche's *The Essential Jewel of Holy Practice* was published by Wisdom Books.

Carolyn M. Jones Medine is professor of religion and professor in and director of the Institute for African American Studies at the University of Georgia. She is the coauthor of *Ancient and Modern Politics: Negotiating Transitive Spaces and Hybrid Identities* (Palgrave 2012) and the coeditor, with Igbigbolade S. Aderibigbe, of *Contemporary Perspectives on Religions in Africa and the African Diaspora* (Palgrave 2015) as well as numerous articles. She has written articles on African American Buddhists, including Alice Walker, Jan Willis, and others.

Carol J. Moeller received a PhD in philosophy from the University of Pittsburgh in 1998 (as well as doctoral certificates in women's studies and in cultural studies) and a BA from Oberlin College. She was a Greenwall Fellow in Bioethics and Health Policy at Johns Hopkins and Georgetown Universities (01–03). Since 1997 she has been a professor of philosophy at Moravian College in Bethlehem, PA, specializing in social justice. She is a member of the Future of Minority Studies Project and is a longtime Buddhist and anti-racist, queer, disability, and feminist activist.

Sharon A. Suh is professor of theology and religious studies at Seattle University. Suh earned her PhD in Buddhist Studies from Harvard University and is the author of *Being Buddhist in a Christian World: Gender and Community* (University of Washington Press, 2004) and *Silver Screen Buddha: Buddhism in Asian and Western Film* (Bloomsbury Press, 2015). In addition to her academic work, Suh completed "200-hour yoga training certification," trauma-informed yoga training, and Level I certification in Mindful Eating-Conscious Living.

Jasmine Syedullah is assistant professor of Africana studies with a focus in prison studies at Vassar College. She holds a PhD in Politics with a designated emphasis in feminist studies and history of consciousness from University of California Santa Cruz. Her current manuscript-in-progress is a feminist-of-color political theory of domestic violence which conjoins nineteenth and twentieth century abolitionist struggles against slavery and incarceration. Syedullah is also coauthor of an activist book project, *Radical Dharma: Talking Race, Love, and Liberation*, published by North Atlantic Books in June 2016.

Rima Vesely-Flad, PhD, is assistant professor of religion and social justice and director of peace and justice studies at Warren Wilson College. She is the author of *Racial Purity and Dangerous Bodies: Moral Pollution, Black Lives, and the Struggle for Justice* (Fortress Press, 2017). She is currently at work on Black Buddhists and liberation. She holds a doctorate in social ethics from Union Theological Seminary, a master's degree from Columbia University's School of International and Public Affairs, and a BA from the University of Iowa. She teaches on Buddhist social ethics, environmental justice, critical race theory, and social movements.

Jan Willis, BA and MA in Philosophy, Cornell University; PhD in Indic and Buddhist Studies, Columbia University, is professor of religion emerita at Wesleyan University in Middletown, Connecticut and now visiting professor of religion at Agnes Scott College in Decatur, GA. She has studied with Tibetan Buddhists in India, Nepal, Switzerland, and the US for five decades, and has taught courses in Buddhism for over forty-five years. She is the author of five books and numerous articles on various topics in Buddhism—Buddhist meditation, hagiography, women and Buddhism, and Buddhism and race. Her memoir, *Dreaming Me: Black, Baptist, and Buddhist*, received starred reviews in Publishers Weekly and Library Journal. In December of 2000, *TIME* magazine named Willis one of six "spiritual innovators for the new millennium." In 2003, she was a recipient of Wesleyan University's Binswanger Prize for Excellence in Teaching. *Newsweek* magazine included a profile of Willis in 2005 and, in its May 2007 edition, *Ebony* magazine named Willis one of its "Power 150" most influential African Americans.

George Yancy is professor of philosophy at Emory University and Montgomery Fellow at Dartmouth College. He is the author, editor, and coeditor of over twenty books and is known for his influential essays and interviews in the *New York Times* philosophy column "The Stone."